DATE DUE			
JUL 5 '8			

MASTERS, PRINCES, AND MERCHANTS

Volume I - Text

Master Alain of Lille and Master Peter the Chanter.
Manuscript from the Abbey of Ottoburen (1228-1246).
MS London, British Museum, Cod. Addit. 19767.

Masters Princes and Merchants

THE SOCIAL VIEWS OF

PETER THE CHANTER & HIS CIRCLE

Volume I — Text

by John W. Baldwin

PRINCETON UNIVERSITY PRESS, PRINCETON, NEW JERSEY

1970

Publication of this book has been aided by the Whitney Darrow
Publication Reserve Fund of Princeton University Press and by
the John Simon Guggenheim Memorial Foundation.

This book has been composed in Linotype Granjon

PRINTED IN THE UNITED STATES OF AMERICA

BY PRINCETON UNIVERSITY PRESS, PRINCETON, NEW JERSEY

For my son,
PETER

CONTENTS
VOLUME ONE

Part Five: *Reform*

LIST OF ILLUSTRATIONS

Frontispiece: Master Alain of Lille and Master Peter the Chanter. MS London, British Museum, Cod. Addit. 19767, fol. 217r.

Facing p. 18: Peter the Chanter disposes of his house at Gerberoy. MS Arch. dép. de l'Oise, G. 7391.

Facing p. 19: Bishop Maurice and Peter the Chanter as papal judge delegates. MS Paris, AN L 903, n.3.

PREFACE

ALTHOUGH many historical works pose new questions while drawing on old sources, the claim of this book rests on the discovery of new evidence. While gathering materials for a study on the medieval theories of the just price at the Bibliothèque Nationale in Paris in 1953-1955, I came across unpublished theological manuscripts which immediately caught my eye. From my limited experience as a historian I had imagined the great scholastic theologians from Abelard to Thomas Aquinas to be occupied with issues too abstract to be seriously concerned with affairs usually included in history books. But these theological writings originating from Paris at the turn of the twelfth and thirteenth centuries treated a rich variety of subjects affecting the practical existence of medieval men. When I encountered in these parchment folios discussions of the newly built fortifications around Paris, chancery clerics, mercenary soldiers, taxes on movables, and commercial partnerships, I wondered whether I had not happened upon testimony about important events and practices. After this initial acquaintance, I had to rely on inertia, if not strength of character, to resist abandoning the just price and not to pursue this new discovery. Fortunately the demands of an academic career prompted me to finish the original project and the munificence of research foundations provided opportunities to return to the Bibliothèque Nationale to enlarge my familiarity with these medieval theologians.

The salient characteristic which distinguished these theologians from those preceding and following was their intense interest in practical questions. Concerned with moral theology, they not only formulated ethical theorems, but attempted to apply them to the infinite variety of human behavior. Their approach was that of casuistry which stressed case studies and concrete examples. Because of this preoccupation they debated the problems of contemporary society with independence and insight. Setting themselves apart from their theological colleagues by this practical bent, they formed a cluster around one central figure, Peter the Chanter, who provided inspiration for their common interests. For this reason I have been able to place them in orbits revolving about the Chanter, some close to the center of his influence, others farther out on the perimeter. By restricting attention to those writers who knew Peter the Chanter personally at Paris and who reflected his interest in practical ethics, I have been able to distinguish a circle of ten or more members. As active masters of theology, these men regularly lectured on the Scriptures and debated theological issues. Their lectures were recorded in Biblical commentaries and their disputations in a form of scholastic literature known as *questiones*. They popularized their views in ethical treatises, guides to confessors, and sermons. Except for the sermons,* I have investigated their writings systematically for their social views.

As moral theologians, Peter the Chanter and his circle had interests as broad as life itself. With equal ease they explored the sublime mysteries of the eucharist and the dark intimacies of fornication. As teachers and clergymen they assembled their ideas for the classroom and the parish, so that much of their discussion is not readily available to the modern reader. For these reasons I have been obliged to select only those subjects of social importance and to arrange them according to a plan. Whatever organizational scheme may be discerned in this book is my responsibility. To this end I have envisaged Peter the Chanter and his circle in front of Notre-Dame on the east end of the Ile-de-la-Cité looking westward down the Seine. Across the Petit-Pont to the Left Bank was the academic quarter of Paris which reminded them of their activities as masters. Directly in front of them at the western end of the Cité the stone tower of the royal palace arose above the crowded houses. This structure represented the seat of political authority in France. Across the Grand-Pont to the Right Bank was the commercial section of Paris with its bustling wharves and noisy markets. These three directions recalled to the theologians the three groups of people, masters, princes, and merchants, which form the three themes of this book. But their writings encompassed much more than these segments of the Parisian population. Behind them were the towering vaults of the newly reconstructed cathedral of Notre-Dame which proclaimed the authority of the clergy. As clerics themselves, the Chanter's circle devoted greatest attention to ecclesiastical life, as might be expected. The sheer size of their discussion, however, has prevented me from including the clergy as a distinct subject, but, as will be seen, clerical interests constantly colored their views on the rest of society. More surprising to the modern reader is the omission of the peasants who composed the overwhelming majority of the population in the twelfth century. Except when these humble men came into contact with the clergy or the princes, the Parisian theologians paid little attention to their peculiar problems. The fields without the walls of Paris where the peasant toiled were beyond the ken of Peter the Chanter and his circle.

The term "social" when applied to history is, for my purposes, a loosely

---

* Their sermons have yet to be collected, authenticated, and edited. The largest group belongs to Stephen Langton and has been recently studied by Phyllis Barzillay Roberts in *Studies in the Sermons of Stephen Langton* (Studies and Texts, Toronto, Pontifical Institute of Mediaeval Studies, 16, 1968). It is evident that Langton's sermons contain very little of direct relevance to social issues.

defined adjective. By it I simply mean the occupations of teaching, ruling, and trading performed by masters, princes, and merchants. When I speak of the theologians' "social views," therefore, I refer to what they thought about the essential functions, obligations, and misbehavior of these groups. If this can be called social history, it does not represent the most recent use of the term. For the past forty years medieval social historians have been less patient to listen to the recitation of social conditions by contemporaries and more eager to formulate their own questions. Employing charter material susceptible of statistical analysis and enlisting the cooperation of other social scientists such as demographers and sociologists, the new social historian attempts to understand the underlying structure of society, its essential mechanisms and its total mentality. Social class, mobility, hierarchy, and like concepts dominate his interests. My use of the Parisian theologians stands in the older tradition of Achille Luchaire's *La société française au temps de Philippe Auguste* (1909) who collected opinions about French society from contemporary observers then available. To Luchaire's picture drawn from chroniclers, papal letters, lives of saints, and vernacular literature, I have added another perspective from the Parisian masters.

As observers of contemporary society Peter the Chanter and his circle were hindered by defects which should be remembered lest the modern reader be led to expect more than he will receive. Since they were theological masters and members of the clerical order, an obvious ecclesiastical bias pervades their writings. At times their judgments degenerate to conventional and pietistic moralizing which prevents them from seeing contemporary conditions realistically. For example, one prominent member of the group objected to princes exacting revenues from cities because of their implication with usury, although all contemporary rulers taxed cities heavily. In another case the theologians resisted the movement to convert arbitrary *tailles* into fixed, regular payments—despite the important advantages of this reform to the peasants and bourgeoisie—because the *tailles* were originally illicit. More exasperating to the modern reader, they frequently neglect to pose questions which we would like asked or concentrate on issues which to us seem secondary. Exact contemporaries of the emerging university at Paris, for example, they are silent about the formation of the corporation of masters. As members of the clergy they could have told us more about the contributions of their class to political administration. Because of these biases, omissions, and weaknesses their view of society inevitably has an uneven texture which is further accentuated by the nature of their writings. Produced in the disputations of the schools, their discussions are often fragmentary and inconclusive. Questions are raised, for example about the damages by hunting dogs to the fields of peasants, but no answers are provided.

Despite their evident defects, as moral theologians these writers were obliged to analyze and understand the contemporary conditions they proposed to evaluate. To the modern historian their analyses are of more interest than their judgments. More important, they provide the social historian for the first time with the point of view of the university professor and enable him to see the contemporary scene through the eyes of the intellectual class. As moral theologians, moreover, these men were not content to remain passive observers of their surroundings, but their analyses were preparatory to protest and reform. Like the Old Testament prophets whom they studied earnestly, they were pungently critical of the evils of the day. Often their independent stand was unappreciated, but occasionally their reform programs enlisted support and brought results. Modern historians must therefore reckon with Peter the Chanter and his circle not only as observers but as reformers in their society.

My task has been not only to recount the social views of the Parisian masters but also to render them comprehensible in their historical context. The Chanter's circle were not isolated and unique observers, but often expressed commonplace opinions closely comparable to those voiced by others. Whenever relevant I have compared them with better known writers such as the chroniclers, Alexander Neckham, Peter of Blois, Stephen of Tournai, and others. More important, the Parisian theologians treated many problems in common with their academic colleagues, the canon lawyers. Since many of their discussions presupposed canonist debates, I have found it necessary to include a minimum of canonist discussion to understand the essential issues. For these purposes I have relied chiefly on the Bolognese canonists Gratian, Rufinus, Simon of Bisignano, and especially Huguccio. The use of Huguccio, however, presents a problem. An active teacher before 1190 at Bologna, the canonist was an exact contemporary of Peter the Chanter at Paris, but I have found no evidence that either knew the other's work directly. Although the mutual influence between the Bolognese canonist and the Parisian theologian must remain conjectural, I have nonetheless employed Huguccio as a representative of contemporary canonist opinion because of the comprehensive character of his writing, and his acknowledged authority. The theologian's views should be situated in the context of contemporary practice as well, in order to assess their significance; otherwise, one is at a loss to separate the real from the academic issues. Here I have relied on modern studies wherever possible, although at times I have been obliged to reconstruct the practical context myself with less than satisfying results. Even within the scope of masters, princes, and merchants, the theologians treated such a breadth of subjects—ranging from Scriptural lectures to jongleurs, to instruments of foreign exchange—that I cannot expect to exhaust each subject in itself. My hope has rather been to supply enough historical context to illuminate the masters' opinions. In the end it should be remembered that this study cannot claim to depict medieval society as it actually was but merely gives an assessment of the clerical views of that society which may some day contribute to the larger goal.

To succeed, a work of scholarship requires a balance between what is and what is not already known. To be sure, one hopes to discover something new, but preparation is necessary. Now that my book is finished, I am more fully convinced than before that this is an exploratory study. Following the Parisian masters afar into many fields, I became aware of the scarcity of any familiar landmarks established by scholarship. While trusting that sufficient preparations were available to make possible a start, I realize that it would be presumptuous to regard my conclusions as definitive. I shall be content if I have shown a new way which will entice others to follow and improve. When I first became acquainted with the writings of Peter the Chanter and his circle in 1953, only one, the Chanter's *Verbum abbreviatum*, was available in print. Consequently, my chief work has been among manuscripts. Since then, however, important editions have appeared which have immeasurably relieved my labors. From 1954 Monsieur Jean-Albert Dugauguier has been engaged in the monumental task of editing the *Summa de sacramentis et animae consiliis* of Peter the Chanter. Although the work is not yet complete, he most generously allowed me access to transcriptions of the *questiones* which he will publish in one final volume. The Reverend Dr. F. Broomfield has recently brought out an edition of Thomas of Chobham's *Summa confessorum*. It appeared too late for the writing of this book, but Dr. Broomfield has kindly allowed me to consult the typescript and the page proofs for purpose of citation. The Reverend Mother Marie-Pascal Dickson has been at work on the *Summa* of Robert of Courson and shared with me her knowledge of Courson's manuscripts. Without their prodigious achievements in editing the manuscripts, my own efforts would now be far from completion. While composing various drafts of the book, I took occasion to profit from the expertise of numerous friends. Marie-Thérèse d'Alverny, John F. Benton, Giles Constable, Grace Frank, Peter Herde, Frederic C. Lane, and Walter Ullmann all kindly read sections of the manuscript in early draft, and my colleagues at the Johns Hopkins University listened patiently to a section in the historical seminar. They can judge my susceptibility to wise counsel. Marthe Dulong helpfully reviewed some of my transcriptions from the medieval manuscripts. Finally, I wish gratefully to acknowledge material support from the Horace H. Rackham School of Graduate Studies at the University of Michigan, the George A. and Eliza Gardner Howard Foundation at Brown University, the John Simon Guggenheim Memorial Foundation, and the Behavioral

Science Fund of the Ford Foundation, which enabled me to work on the manuscripts in Paris. The Guggenheim Foundation has generously provided a subsidy for publishing this work.

Because this study is largely based on manuscript documentation, I have included the hitherto unpublished Latin texts in the references. The result has been to charge the already laden scholarly apparatus almost to the point of floundering. For this reason I have been obliged to eliminate all Latin quotations derived from printed versions and to include only the citation. Those who wish to compare my discussions with the texts must refer to the published versions of Peter the Chanter's *Verbum abbreviatum* and *Summa de sacramentis et animae consiliis* and Thomas of Chobham's *Summa confessorum*.

PART

ONE

PETER

THE CHANTER AND
HIS CIRCLE

❧ CHAPTER I ❧

Peter the Chanter

IT IS TYPICAL of medieval documentation that the date of Peter the Chanter's death—which occurred in 1197—should be known, but that the date of his birth should not. If he lived a normal life span of fifty to seventy years, he was born between 1127 and 1147, but such figures are conjectural.[1] In his writings Peter made two oblique allusions to his relatives which suggest that his family were knights within the ranks of feudal society.[2] This social station is further supported by other evidence which specify both the name and the location of the Chanter's family. A fourteenth-century manuscript of one of Peter's writings designates him as *Petrus de Hosdens cantor Parisiensis*.[3] More precisely, several charters dealing with the donations of tithes and the disposal of a house identify Master Peter, Chanter of Paris, with the family which took its name from Hodenc-en-Bray in the Beauvaisis.[4] In 1183 Philip of Dreux, Bishop of Beauvais, attested that Master Peter of Hodenc gave the small tithes of Hodenc to the Hôtel-Dieu of Beauvais.[5] In another charter referring to the same donation, four years later, Bishop Philip identified Master Peter of Hodenc as the Chanter of Paris.[6] Two further charters indicate that Master Peter also made donations from the tithes of Hodenc to the Cistercian Abbey of Beaupré in the diocese of Beauvais.[7] All of these transactions were made with the consent of the Chanter's brother, Walter of Hodenc, a knight, and his two sons Peter and Ralph, also knights.[8] The charters from the Beauvaisis contain numerous names derived from Hodenc, which cannot be directly connected with the lineage of the Chanter,[9] but the evidence is clear that Peter originated from the family of Hodenc, one of the petty nobility of the Beauvaisis.

It is also known that Peter the Chanter held a house in the town of Gerberoy because in 1185 Peter turned over the possession of this house to Haimericus, canon of Gerberoy, until six pounds of Beauvais money had been paid to Haimericus. The canon had paid out this sum to redeem the house from a certain woman named Aia.[10] Owing Aia six pounds on the house for some unexplained reason, Peter apparently borrowed the money from Haimericus, pledging the house as security.[11] Located eight kilometers to the north of Hodenc-en-Bray, Gerberoy was the seat of an important feudal family in the Beauvaisis.[12] From the end of the tenth

3

century the lords of Gerberoy had been the vidames of the Bishops of Beauvais until the family became extinct in 1193. Since the Hodencs often subscribed to the acts of the vidames of Gerberoy throughout the second half of the twelfth century, they were in all likelihood connected by lord-vassal relations.[13] Crowning a small hill, twelfth-century Gerberoy possessed encircling walls, a castle, and a church of secular canons dedicated to Saint Peter. Even today the town retains its medieval features and proportions. Gerberoy and Hodenc-en-Bray lay at the frontier between the Ile-de-France and Normandy. On an east-west axis between Beauvais and Rouen they were twenty kilometers from the episcopal city of Beauvais. Twelve kilometers to the west was Gournay-en-Bray, whose powerful lords usually followed the dukes of Normandy. No more than thirty kilometers to the south was the great castle of Gisors, the traditional rendezvous of the kings of France and the dukes of Normandy. In this position the nobility of Gerberoy and Hodenc were exposed to the hostilities between the Capetian kings of France and the Plantagenet dukes of Normandy, which increased in violence throughout the second half of the twelfth century. As early as 1079 Gerberoy was besieged during a rebellion of Robert Curthose against his father, William the Conqueror. Since the bishops of Beauvais were related to and champions of the Capetians, the vidames of Gerberoy often bore the brunt of Plantagenet vengeance. In 1160 King Henry II in a campaign against Robert, Count of Dreux, and Henry, Bishop of Beauvais, both brothers of King Louis VII, set fire to the town and pulled down the walls. At the end of the century the Capetian-Plantagenet rivalry reached a crescendo when Bishop Philip of Beauvais, cousin of King Philip Augustus, used his diocese as a base of operations against Normandy during King Richard's absence on the Third Crusade and his subsequent captivity in Germany. After his release from prison, Richard employed Gournay in 1197 to counterattack against the diocese of Beauvais and succeeded in taking the Bishop captive. During the campaign of this year Gerberoy was once more besieged by the Normans under the leadership of John, Richard's younger brother. These three sieges of Gerberoy were only highpoints in the general story of warfare in the region. Like the Vexin lying to the south, the western frontiers of the Beauvaisis were drenched with blood and charred with fire of the Capetian-Plantagenet conflict. These were the conditions of Peter the Chanter's early years, and even before his death in September 1197 he could have heard news of the latest siege of Gerberoy. The peace afforded to the Beauvaisis by the French conquest of Normandy in 1204 was enjoyed by his nephews Peter and Ralph and their heirs, but was never part of Peter the Chanter's world.

A number of manuscript copies of his works and several chroniclers designate the Chanter as Peter of Reims.[14] Although this name could have been derived from his election to the deanship of Reims in 1196 shortly before his death, such cognomens often indicate the place of birth. Peter's family undoubtedly stemmed from Hodenc-en-Bray in the Beauvaisis, but it is not impossible that he was born in Reims one hundred fifty-five kilometers to the east, and indeed this is particularly likely because of the unsettled conditions of his ancestral home. In all events, when Archbishop William of Reims invited Peter to accept the position of Dean of Reims in 1196 he reminded the Chanter of his earlier schooling in the city and how the church of Reims was his first nurse to impart the milk of sound doctrine.[15] Since the date of the Chanter's birth is uncertain, it is difficult to know when he studied at Reims and who his teachers were. Although Peter knew the famous Master Alberic by reputation, he probably arrived too late to have heard him lecture.[16] A more likely candidate for the Chanter's teacher was Master Robert *de Camera* whose presence in the city is attested from 1149 to 1165, when he became Bishop of Amiens.[17] Although little is known of Robert's career and no writings can yet be attributed to him, he is the one former master who is mentioned at all frequently by Peter the Chanter. Not only did Peter cite his theological opinions, but he recounted numerous stories about his life and activities, as will be seen. Despite this uncertainty about the Chanter's teachers, it is known that Peter held a prebend in the church of Reims. Robert of Courson, the Chanter's closest and most trusted student, recorded that when Peter left Reims, the chapter compelled him to retain his prebend there because of his salutary influence and exceptional utility for the church.[18] Perusal of the Chanter's subsequent writings yields ample evidence of his general familiarity with the city.[19] When he searched for a concrete example of church practices, more often than not he chose one from Reims.[20] On at least two occasions he also depicted the relations between the Jewish and Christian communities of Reims.[21]

The date and circumstances of Peter of Hodenc's arrival at Paris cannot be determined with assurance. The sole information on this matter comes from Caesar of Heisterbach's *Dialogus miraculorum*, which is rich in anecdotes about Paris at the turn of the century, although it was not composed until 1219-1223. Caesar relates that in the years following Thomas Becket's death a controversy arose over whether the archbishop was a traitor to his country or a martyr for the liberties of the church.[22] This issue was debated at Paris between a certain Master Roger, who accused Becket of the former charges, and Master Peter the Chanter, who defended his reputation as a saint. Since there is evidence that the debate actually took place, one may conjecture that it occurred during the short interval between Becket's death on 29 December 1170 and his canonization by Pope Alexander III on 21 February 1173, because after Becket's sainthood was officially recognized little point for controversy remained.

5

Writing long after the event, Caesar of Heisterbach identified Master Peter as the Chanter of Paris, although he did not actually hold that position for another decade. The designation of Peter as master is nonetheless plausible because the account of the debate indicates an academic disputation of the kind normally conducted by accredited teachers. On the tenuous evidence presented by Caesar of Heisterbach, therefore, the conclusion may be hazarded that Peter of Hodenc appeared in Paris as a master by 1173 at the latest. When Peter does appear in the charter records after 1183, he is occasionally identified by his academic title of Master,[23] but little charter evidence survives of his teaching activities. The main sources for his life as a teacher are the written records of his lectures and disputations.

Whatever his previous career at Paris, Peter was elevated to the dignity of Chanter of Notre-Dame sometime during the year 1183. His immediate predecessor was Walter, whose last surviving act occurred in 1180.[24] In 1183, when Peter gave the tithes of Hodenc to the Hôtel-Dieu of Beauvais, he was not yet designated by the ecclesiastical office,[25] but on 4 January 1184 when Pope Lucius III at Rome wrote a letter to Paris he was already aware that Peter was Chanter of Notre-Dame.[26] Peter's bequest of his Hodenc tithes to the Hôtel-Dieu of Beauvais in 1183, on the eve of his election (renewed in 1187), and his disposal of his house at Gerberoy in 1185 probably indicate that he was settling his affairs at home in view of assuming a permanent position at Paris. Holding this office until 1197, the year of his death,[27] he was so well known that the term "Chanter" or "Chanter of Paris" was deemed sufficient to identify him.[28] As *Cantor* or *Precentor* of the cathedral Peter's main responsibilities concerned the activities of the choir. Although he was nominally responsible for supervising the offices or liturgical services, correcting and maintaining the song books, and instructing the choir boys, in practice he delegated these tasks to the Subchanter (*Succentor*) and others. To indicate his rank and authority the Chanter carried a staff (*baculus*) and occupied the first seat on the left or Epistle side of the choir opposite to the Dean on the right. An illustration of the Chanter's jurisdiction over the deportment of the choir may be found in one manuscript of Peter's *Summa de sacramentis* which recounts the details of a disturbance between two clerics of Notre-Dame who came to blows in the choir and whose altercation was finally adjudicated by the Chanter himself.[29] Although Peter's writings display ample familiarity with the offices, he did not often write about liturgy as such.[30] Since his chief interests were teaching moral theology and participating in church government, the specifically liturgical activities of the choir were in all probability left to the Subchanter. Peter never exceeded the rank of deacon,[31] but within the hierarchy of Notre-Dame he was the second ranking dignitary of the cathedral chapter. His name generally followed the Dean's in charters issued by the chapter. Since the office of Chanter provided the holder with a prebend or church living, Peter the Chanter—who retained his prebend from Reims—became technically a pluralist when he accepted it.[32] The extant charters of Notre-Dame show Peter the Chanter's frequent involvement in the work of the church and the chapter under its Bishop, Maurice of Sully (1160-1196) and its deans, Hervé (1184-1191), Michael (1192-1195) and Hugh Clement (1195-1216).[33] Peter's position at the cathedral is also indicated by King Philip Augustus' charter, issued before his departure on the Third Crusade in June 1190, when the King assigned to Hervé, Dean, and Peter, Chanter, the responsibility for the construction of Notre-Dame if the episcopal see should fall vacant during his absence.[34] The Chanter's contribution to the work of his church, however, was not always harmonious. It will be seen that he vociferously objected to the new building program of Bishop Maurice of Sully and contested the acceptance of alms from dubious sources for this purpose.* Peter's scrupulous conscience rendered him an independent and often difficult member of the chapter even in more ordinary affairs. For example, Robert of Courson reported that during the time of Dean H. (Hervé or Hugh?) someone wished to endow a prebend at Notre-Dame for himself or his son.[35] Although the entire chapter consented to the arrangement, the Chanter refused to accept this simoniacal form of buying entrance to the cathedral chapter.

Not only involved in the immediate concerns of his own church, Peter the Chanter was also engaged in broader ecclesiastical affairs of northern France. The charters of the Ile-de-France indicate that he often served as an arbitrator chosen by contending parties, or as a judge delegate appointed by ecclesiastical superiors to decide litigation.[36] In these duties he was frequently associated with other dignitaries of Notre-Dame as well as with other prelates of the region.[37] While many of these cases involved relatively local matters, others touched on affairs as far off as Troyes, Cambrai, Meaux, and Châlons-sur-Marne.[38] To be selected as a judge in so many and such significant cases implies expertise in canon law as well as a reputation for moral rectitude and impartiality. In one case, Peter the Chanter and Stephen, Abbot of Sainte-Geneviève, judged with the advice of men prudent and skilled in the law.[39] In another, Peter and Michael, Dean of Notre-Dame, availed themselves of the legal counsel of both clerics and laity and even of councillors (*sapientes*) of the royal palace.[40] The Chanter's growing reputation as a judge delegate is reflected in the frequency with which he was employed by the papacy. It is possible that Pope Alexander III made use of him even before he was named

* See below, pp. 66ff. and 308ff.

7

Chanter at Paris,[41] but in all events Lucius III appointed him at least once.[42] With succeeding popes his number of calls to judge increased, until Celestine III appointed him at least six times.[43] Peter's most important case as a papal judge delegate occurred in 1196 during the famous divorce proceedings between King Philip Augustus and the Danish princess, Ingeborg.[44] No sooner had the King married the princess, in 1193, than he repudiated her on the obviously specious grounds of consanguinity. Not taking cognizance of the divorce until 1195, the aged and failing Pope Celestine III condemned it and sent two legates to seek a reconciliation between the royal couple.[45] By the following year the affair was still pending and, according to the report of Anders Sunesen, the Danish royal chancellor who observed events from Paris, on 7 April 1196 Michael, Archbishop of Sens, Peter, Bishop of Arras, Guy, Abbot of Cîteaux, Guy, Abbot of Clairvaux, and Master Peter the Chanter were commissioned as papal judge delegates to investigate by what means the King might be induced to take back his estranged wife.[46] If, after a month, their efforts were without result, the two papal legates were instructed to convene an assembly of the Archbishops of Reims, Sens, Tours, and Bourges and their suffragans to force the King to make amends. Since the King was determined to eliminate all doubt about his divorce from Ingeborg, he proceeded with his plans to marry Agnès of Méran, and the maneuvers of the churchmen were fruitless. As the chronicler Rigord remarked, when the prelates assembled on 7 May 1196 they were cowed like dogs fearing to bark for the sake of their hides.[47] Although in this case Peter the Chanter found himself on a losing side, the esteem which he enjoyed is nonetheless measured by the high position of his fellow judges and by the importance of the issue. It is also of interest to note that his co-judge, the Archbishop of Sens, was Michael of Meaux, a former colleague on the theological faculty at Paris and previously Dean of the Chapter of Notre-Dame.[48] Peter's service in the courts of the church introduced him into larger and more influential circles. For example, he was associated in at least three cases with Maurice of Sully, Bishop of Paris, although his writings indicate that he was severely critical of some of the bishop's most cherished projects.[49] If another passage of Caesar of Heisterbach can be trusted, he offered advice to a certain Thibaut, one of the leading bourgeoisie of Paris.[50] King Philip Augustus named him as judge on at least one occasion and instructed him, as has been seen, to supervise the construction of Notre-Dame in the event of Bishop Maurice's death.[51] Yet from a surviving account of a conversation between the Chanter and his sovereign, Peter was sharply critical of Philip's appointments to the episcopacy,[52] and without doubt he risked royal wrath by serving as a papal judge in the delicate affair between the King and Ingeborg. Peter's horizons expanded not only in personal contacts but also in geographical scope throughout his career. Although most of his life was centered on the Beauvaisis, Reims, and the Ile-de-France, several passages in his writings suggest that he also visited Rome.[53] His *Verbum abbreviatum* contains vivid and detailed accounts of the Lateran Council of 1179, which he could have attended before his appointment to Chanter of Paris, although positive evidence is lacking.[54] An early letter of Pope Innocent III, however, furnishes certain proof that Peter did journey to Rome in 1196 or 1197 during the pontificate of Celestine III.[55]

It soon became evident that someone as active in church affairs as Peter the Chanter would eventually be considered for promotion to the prelacy. Peter's first opportunity appeared with the death of Evrard d'Avegnes, Bishop of Tournai, on 28 September 1190, at a time when King Philip Augustus had just departed on the Third Crusade.[56] Tournai was of special concern to the King because of his design to extend the royal domain and involvement in the area of Flanders. It was the death of the heiress to the neighboring Vermandois, for example, which provided Philip with an excuse to return from the crusade late in 1191. Who was to succeed to the see of Tournai, therefore, was a matter of particular concern to the King. Before his departure on the crusade Philip had left specific instructions for filling any bishoprics which fell vacant during his absence.[57] The Queen Mother Adèle and the King's uncle, William, Archbishop of Reims, were appointed regents in his place to grant cathedral chapters permission to elect candidates and to bestow the regalia after consecration. In the forthcoming election of Tournai Archbishop William was empowered not only to safeguard royal interests, but as metropolitan he also had ecclesiastical jurisdiction over the election of the new bishop of Tournai. Most of our information about the election of Tournai comes from a letter written in 1191-1192 by Stephen, Abbot of Sainte-Geneviève in Paris, to Archbishop William which reported that Peter the Chanter had been elected by the chapter to the see of Tournai with the expressed approval of the King.[58] Stephen also mentioned some unspecified irregularity in the election of which the Chanter was ignorant and innocent, and which he urged the Archbishop to rectify. In ornate and rhetorical language the whole letter was designed to promote the candidacy of Peter the Chanter. The next fact which comes to light is that it was not Peter but *Stephen*, who was made Bishop of Tournai, and was consecrated by Archbishop William on Easter Day, 12 April 1192. To judge from Stephen's subsequent letters, this sudden reversal of positions caused the new bishop of Tournai considerable embarrassment. In particular he incurred the displeasure of Pope Celestine III, who exacted such high fees for papal confirmation that Stephen was forced into exile to raise money by extraordinary measures. There can be no

9

doubt as to the original choice, because the obituary of Tournai, expressing the point of view of the chapter, records Peter's election but then adds that he humbly declined the honor.[59] Because of the paucity of evidence, however, one can only speculate as to why the Chanter's candidacy failed. Perhaps he himself refused the promotion, as the obituary of Tournai maintained. On the other hand, since both royal and ecclesiastical authority was concentrated in Archbishop William's hands, it was certainly he who had the power to nullify Peter's election and promote Stephen, although any reasons he had to do so are not at all clear. One guess is that if the irregularity to which Stephen referred was the failure of the chapter to receive prior permission from the regents, William was defending the royal interests on procedural grounds.[60] Apparently, infringements against royal and metropolitan rights had occurred in past elections at Tournai which provoked protests even from the papacy.[61] In any event there is no evidence of rivalry or friction between the two candidates. Before the election Stephen had collaborated with Peter as judge delegate more than with anyone else outside of the chapter of Notre-Dame.[62] It is true, however, that after Stephen's consecration Pope Celestine III instructed Hugh Clement, Dean of Notre-Dame, and the Chanter to enforce his judgment against the Bishop over a disputed prebend, but this action expressed the Pope's ill will and not necessarily Peter's.[63]

Although there is no doubt as to the Chanter's candidacy for Tournai, the next election to which his name has been linked is less well authenticated. The English chronicler Ralph of Coggeshall maintained that after the death of Maurice of Sully, Bishop of Paris, on 11 September 1196 the clergy and people of Paris with the assent of the King elected Peter the Chanter to the episcopal dignity, but he declined the honor because of its heavy burdens.[64] Once more Peter was to lose the chance of a bishopric, for Odo of Sully, and not he, in fact became the next bishop of Paris. Although the English chronicler's report is not contradicted by other known facts, no corroborating evidence has been found for this single detail.[65] Not long after this alleged election to Paris, Peter the Chanter was called to one final ecclesiastical dignity, this time the deanship of Reims.[66] After the death of Ralph, Dean of Reims, on 20 August (probably in 1196),[67] the chapter elected their fellow canon, Peter the Chanter, who still possessed his prebend from Reims. Archbishop William of Reims ratified their choice in writing[68] and dispatched an elaborate letter to Peter inviting him to accept.[69] Perhaps alluding to his negative role in the Chanter's election to Tournai, the Archbishop assured him of his support in this election and hoped that Peter would not cast his eyes about for richer promotions. In an eloquent effort to persuade the candidate, William reminded him of his former childhood and student ties with the mother church and called him home as a son. Finally it was necessary that the Chanter be ordained to the priesthood in fulfillment of the requirements of his new office. Ralph of Coggeshall reports that Peter was not easily persuaded by the Archbishop but that after delegation of burghers from Reims prostrated themselves at his feet, he consented, though only on condition that the chapter of Paris grant him leave.[70] This election was surely genuine because the obituary of Reims accorded to him the title of "our dean."[71]

Elected to the deanship of Reims, Peter the Chanter was prevented by death from assuming his new duties.[72] According to Ralph of Coggeshall, who again provides the fullest account, it was while negotiations for his transfer were being conducted with the chapter of Paris that Peter travelled to the Cistercian abbey of Longpont and commended himself to the prayers of the monks, undoubtedly feeling that his days were few.[73] He had brought with him several books from his library, but when his infirmities increased he drew up his testament and put on the habit of a monk, in which state he terminated his laudable life on 25 September 1197.[74] The Abbey of Longpont was located about eighty kilometers to the northeast of Paris, not far from Soissons, in a wild and beautiful setting characteristic of Cistercian houses. Peter was probably familiar with the place because he had already mentioned it in his *Verbum abbreviatum*.[75] The obituary of Notre-Dame noted that he bequeathed a legacy of forty pounds, with which the chapter bought properties at Vitry-sur-Seine. In the Parisian synodical statutes of the early thirteenth century the Chanter's name was among those designated for prayer,[76] and the conduit *Ecclipsim passus totiens* commemorating his death was collected in the repertory of hymns of Notre-Dame.[77] The remains of Peter the Chanter were prized by the monks of Longpont along with the body of John of Montmirail, who had saved the life of King Philip Augustus at the battle of Bouvines and who had later entered the Cistercian Order. According to the Cistercian Caesar of Heisterbach, Peter was originally buried in the chapter house, but when his place of burial was moved because of new construction his grave emitted an "odor of sanctity" indicative of his blameless life.[78] His feast day was celebrated on 19 May, probably in honor of the event which Caesar described.[79] In the seventeenth century the monks of Longpont and the Bishop of Soissons were the last to witness the remains of the Chanter of Paris.[80] The eighteenth-century erudites Martène and Durand could still read his epitaph,[81] but the desecrations of the Revolution obliterated his grave[82] and the bombardments of 1918 and 1940 reduced the Abbey of Longpont to ruins.

Although the Chanter's ecclesiastical activities left their mark on the charters and chronicles of the Ile-de-France at the end of the twelfth century, these historical sources are nearly mute on his academic career, except for an occasional recording of his title, *Magister*. Since a cathedral chanter was in charge of the choir boys, he was in some chapters also responsible for the rudiments of their education.[83] If Peter supervised elementary schooling at Notre-Dame, it is unlikely that written evidence of these activities would have survived; indeed, the abundant documentation of his academic life concerns exclusively the advanced study of theology. In all probability he delegated whatever instruction the choir boys received to the Subchanter or others. Peter described the activities of the theological master at Paris as threefold: lecturing, disputing, and preaching.[84] From his writings it is clear that Peter participated directly in the first two, and most likely contributed indirectly to the third. In accordance with his suggestion his written works may be divided into these three categories.

Since the chief task of a twelfth-century theologian was to lecture on the Bible, Scriptural commentaries are the written evidence of these classroom activities. The Biblical commentaries of Peter the Chanter constitute the greater part of his written work. While preceding theologians directed their attention primarily to the Psalms and the Pauline Epistles, Peter was the first master at Paris to produce a systematic commentary on all of the books of the Old and New Testaments.[85] Alberic of Trois-Fontaines mentioned his works on the Gospels and the Psalms, and Ralph of Coggeshall praised especially his glosses on the Psalms and the Epistles for expressing briefly and clearly in his own words the contents of Scripture.[86] In addition to these works mentioned by the chroniclers, manuscript commentaries for all the remaining books of the Bible have survived.[87] There can be little doubt that these writings were products of Peter's public lectures because they bear the markings of medieval *reportationes*.[88] From the early twelfth century, a master was accustomed to engage a student, known as a *reportator*, to take down a full account of his lecture or disputation which could later be corrected and revised before it was turned over to the copyist for "publication." Composed in the lecture room as a result of cooperation between teacher and student, these *reportationes* constituted a literary form which stood between the full account of a stenographer and the informal notes of a student. On the whole the Chanter's Scriptural writings are straightforward, simple commentary, but occasionally a mixture of the first and third persons may be found, and such phrases as "he says" or "the master says," or "the master thus distinguishes," also indicate the *reportatio*.[89]

No specific dates have yet been successfully assigned to Peter's individual commentaries, although certain ones are known to have been written before others because of cross references.[90] Since the commentaries are extensive, they could not have been composed in a short time but probably were produced throughout his academic career from the 1170's to his death in 1197. Scattered throughout this great body of Biblical lecturing are ethical opinions relevant to the contemporary scene, a number of which may also be found in Peter's other writings and expecially in his popular manual of ethics, the *Verbum abbreviatum* (1191-1192).[91] Sometimes certain rubrics and chapter titles of the *Verbum abbreviatum* are found in the margins of commentaries to appropriate Scriptural passages where the themes of the *Verbum abbreviatum* are elaborated in the text. Since neither the individual commentaries nor their manuscripts can be precisely dated, it is impossible to determine with assurance whether the commentaries preceded the other writings. For example, it would not be inconceivable for a scribe to have added the rubrics or discussion of the *Verbum abbreviatum* to the margin of the commentary manuscripts. Nonetheless, it seems more likely that while Peter was engaged in his routine lectures on the Bible, he made occasional observations of ethical and contemporary relevance which were noted in his commentaries. At a later date he probably collected and assembled these scattered remarks and appropriate Biblical quotations in his other works, particularly in the *Verbum abbreviatum*. Viewed from this perspective, Peter the Chanter may well have been preparing the ideas and protests of his *Verbum abbreviatum* in the course of his Scriptural lectures.[92]

If lecturing produced the commentary, the written expression of disputation was known as the *questio*, which consisted simply of a systematic investigation of an intellectual proposition by formulating a question, marshalling opposing arguments, and arriving at a solution.[93] Applied to theology, this procedure attempted to resolve conflicting statements of the Bible and the Church Fathers by employing the techniques of Aristotelian logic. *Questiones* may be readily identified by a set of characteristic terminology: *queritur* (it is asked), *quod videtur* (it is seen), *contra* (against this), *obicitur* (it is objected), *sed dicimus* (but we say), *ad hoc respondemus* (to this we reply), and like phrases. It will be seen that the written form of *questio* resulted from the academic exercise of debating intellectual problems in the classroom of the twelfth and thirteenth centuries.

Peter the Chanter's *questiones* were collected in a work generally known as a *Summa*. Because the collection was left unfinished, there is a diversity among the extant manuscripts which presents problems to the modern editor.[94] In the beginning the *questiones* were arranged according to a plan based on the sacraments of the church: baptism, confirmation, extreme unction, consecration of churches, eucharist and penance. When the compiler arrived at the sacrament of penance his efforts at organization broke down and there is little agreement thereafter among the major manuscripts. The remaining material, which pertains to casuistical problems arising from the application of penance, was gathered together without any controlling plan. In other words, the consideration of penance led to posing a great number of specific moral cases which defied logical organization. This breakdown of overall plan caused contemporaries difficulty in ascribing a name to the collection. Some chroniclers and copyists—impressed with the large last section on casuistry—termed it a "*Summa* of counsel," but one manuscript offered its most complete and accurate title: "*Summa* of the sacraments and counsel for the soul." The section on penance exhibited not only an organizational breakdown, but also a disintegration of the internal method. The material throughout the sacramental sections is presented either in the impersonal form or in the first person, indicating a single author. But with penance and casuistry appear the third person, anonymous masters, and even designated masters, suggesting the debates of the schools recorded in the form of *reportationes*. It therefore appears as if the *Summa* of Peter the Chanter was produced in his school with the help of his students and colleagues. While a compiler, who was most likely the Chanter himself, was able to edit the first part of the work, the remaining sections, on penance and casuistry, were left in a primitive form. Because of the size of the *Summa,* the Chanter probably debated these *questiones* throughout his academic career, but the compilation and editing was begun after 1191/92 and was most likely interrupted by his death in 1197.

According to the Chanter, the third and crowning function of the theologian was to preach to others what he had learned from his lectures and disputations. Later in the thirteenth century Peter enjoyed a reputation as a great preacher,[95] but only one sermon can be attributed to him.[96] Whether he preached many sermons or not, the Chanter undoubtedly contributed to the art of homiletics and propagated his own opinions for a wider audience.[97] His *Verbum abbreviatum* was a popular presentation of his own views which stood apart from the more scholarly character of his other writings. Indeed, this work might well have been composed with preaching in mind because some of its chapters were later regarded as sermons.[98] In the opinion of the thirteenth-century bibliographer Henry of Brussels the *Verbum abbreviatum* was the Chanter's most noteworthy writing.[99] Today it is known to have existed in at least ninety manuscripts—an indication of its popularity in the Middle Ages. When, however, the manuscripts of the *Verbum abbreviatum* are investigated closely, they show that, like the *Summa de sacramentis,* this was not a simple work written in one form and at one time, but rather a treatise which evolved through a number of versions.[100] Three principal versions emerge from the manuscripts: a long version consisting of a loosely compiled and leisurely narrated text containing considerable anecdotal and illustrative material, a short version which is more concise and polished, often omitting or shortening the anecdotal material, and finally occasional marginal additions to the short version which echo the long version. To envisage the creation of the *Verbum abbreviatum* two alternatives are possible: it was the product either of expansion or of abbreviation. While the process of expansion and interpolation must remain a possibility, it is more likely that Peter the Chanter first composed the book in the loose and rambling long version and that this was subsequently condensed by the Chanter himself or a student to a more concise and polished edition, which became the popular or vulgate version. Some of the omitted material was restored in the marginal notations. After all, the title of the *Verbum abbreviatum* provided a perfect excuse for condensation. If the work was produced by abbreviation, the long version may be dated 1191/92, and the short version appeared certainly by 1199, most likely by 1197.

The long and short versions follow a common arrangement of subject matter which exhibits a minimum of logical progression.[101] The long version divides the *Verbum abbreviatum* into two parts, one devoted to vices and the other to virtues, and subdivides the material accordingly into chapters.[102] After preliminary chapters on the threefold activities of the theologian (lecturing, disputing, and preaching), the first part deals with sins, such as pride, avarice, ambition, simony, sloth, gluttony and their related manifestations. But within these chapters it also includes those who practice as entertainers, usurers, and prelates, and specific activities such as ordeals, and the superfluous construction of buildings. The second part deals with the theological virtues (faith, hope, and love), the cardinal virtues (prudence, bravery, temperance, and justice), and other good works such as obedience, prayer, and various forms of charity. It concludes with a treatment of the steps of penance (contrition, confession, and satisfaction) and the final punishments and rewards of the future life. Yet within this second part, devoted ostensibly to virtues, one finds the fullest discussion of the prevalent sins of the flesh. Peter the Chanter obviously had little concern for planning his work on a comprehensive scale. In effect he produced a series of loosely related chapters each of which was suggested by the one preceding. The interest of the book lies not in its organization, but rather in its wealth of detail and illustrative material.

In the preface of the *Verbum abbreviatum* Peter the Chanter stated his purpose for writing. Quoting both the philosopher Seneca and the Church Father Augustine, he declared that whatever is well-spoken is at the disposal of the theologian for combating individual vices and commending virtue in individual and ecclesiastical affairs.[103] In the long version he concluded his preface by announcing that he wrote a brief treatise (*fasciculus*) arranged in diverse chapters which employed authorities to rebuke vices and to encourage virtues.[104] Each chapter does in fact contain a large collection of authoritative statements derived from Scripture, the Church Fathers, and Classical writers, and a good number of *exempla* or illustrative stories, interlaced with interpretative comments from the author. Especially in the short version, where these elements are reduced to a concise form, the chapters at first give the appearance of great patchworks of material assembled around the subjects of the chapters. The profusion of authoritative texts, especially from Classical authors, serve to dress up the *Verbum abbreviatum* with literary pretensions not often found in the Scriptural commentaries or the *Summa*.[105] While these latter works were produced for the schools, the *Verbum abbreviatum* points to a broader audience susceptible to ornate and more elegant quotations, yet the marks of the school are not totally absent. It has been seen that the Biblical commentaries, products of the Chanter's lectures at Paris, have numerous passages and rubrics in common with the *Verbum abbreviatum*.* While the relationship is not certain, in all likelihood Peter collected material during his lectures which he later used in the more popular *Verbum abbreviatum*. Moreover, short *questiones* with their corresponding *solutiones* or *determinationes* occasionally appear in the text.[106] Although these do not include the full authorities and arguments, at least the initial question and the final solution are presented. Occurrences of the term *Magister* in the text and the designation of *Verba magistri* in the margins suggest *reportationes*.[107] Equally noteworthy is the fact that one scribe protested that the text of the short version had been corrupted by additions from the Chanter's students.[108] The significance of these comments is not entirely clear, because it is difficult to conceive of chapters of the *Verbum abbreviatum* delivered in the schools as lectures or debates; nonetheless, these notations indicate that the *Verbum abbreviatum*, like the other writings of the Chanter, was produced, to some extent at least, with the aid of the classroom.

* See above, p. 13.

@ CHAPTER II @

The Chanter's Circle at Paris

URING the last decade of his life and throughout most of the
thirteenth century Peter the Chanter enjoyed a reputation as a
prominent master of Paris. One indication of the extent of his
influence is the widespread dispersal of manuscripts containing his works.
His *Verbum abbreviatum* was not only recopied in northwest Europe
but also in the eastern and southern corners of Latin Christendom. Lieb-
hard of Prüfening made an edition of his *Distinctiones Abel* to be used
in Germany.[1] It is nonetheless true that Peter's greatest impact was at
Paris, where as a master he had direct contact with colleagues and students. At Paris the Chanter exerted influence on a number of different
levels. His colorful personality—expressed in vigorous actions and outspoken words—generated a wealth of stories and *exempla* until long after
his death.[2] His wisdom and independence were so respected that he was
consulted not only by students on academic questions but even by the
cardinals at Rome, the Roman lawyers at Bologna, a bishop, a prominent
citizen of Paris, and an accused thief.[3] Although his opinions on technical theological matters were often cited in learned treatises,[4] the characteristic which distinguished Peter the Chanter from other theologians
was a passionate interest in practical morality which was expressed not
only in relation to individual behavior but also in relation to broader
social issues. On the level of social thought and reform the influence of
Peter the Chanter assumes considerable importance.

Although Peter may well have had influence throughout Latin Christendom through the media of his reputation and writings, attention will
be limited to those who knew him personally. The Chanter's influence
among the conflux of men residing at Paris at the turn of the twelfth and
thirteenth centuries spread like the ring of ripples produced by a pebble
cast into a pond, diminishing as they proceed from the center of the circle.
Since colleagues and students were susceptible to Peter's moral and social
ideas in varying degrees, they may be arranged in a series of concentric
circles around the Chanter. Closest to the Chanter were those direct
students who followed their master into the academic profession. The
clearest representative of this inner circle was Robert of Courson, who
studied under Peter, later became a teaching master of theology, and

finally accepted an appointment as cardinal legate in the church to put into effect the theories and reforms of his master. Also within this inner group, but whose position cannot be determined as clearly, was Stephen Langton. It is possible but not certain that Stephen was a student of the Chanter before he became a theological master at Paris, and later Archbishop of Canterbury. His theological interests ranged wider than Peter's, touching speculative matters, but in Bible study and certain doctrines he followed the Chanter closely. On occasion Stephen treated issues of practical and social morality which constituted debates with the Chanter. For these reasons he should be placed closer to the center of Peter's circle than other prominent colleagues of Paris who held aloof from practical morality. Moreover, Stephen's direct student, Geoffrey of Poitiers, had also studied under Robert of Courson, thereby forging another link with the Chanter's group. Also close to the center were those who attempted to apply the Chanter's theories to everyday living in writings known as penitentials, or guides to confessors. Several of these penitentialists, such as Robert of Flamborough, Peter of Poitiers of Saint-Victor, and other anonymous writers, were located in the Abbey of Saint-Victor in Paris. Another group, which came from England, had Thomas of Chobham as its most distinctive member. In all likelihood the Chanter's student at Paris, Thomas attempted to apply the moral principles of his master to the conditions of his native England. Preaching served as another means for spreading ideas. A circle of preachers formed around the Chanter and, represented by Foulques de Neuilly and Jacques de Vitry, their teacher's message was carried into the countryside of France. Yet others, such as Raoul Ardent, Gerald of Wales, and Gilles de Corbeil, were either students or teachers at Paris contemporary with Peter, and acknowledged his influence by quoting and excerpting from his books.[5]

Although most of the Chanter's theological colleagues at Paris did not share his enthusiasm for practical morality but devoted their energies to speculative and metaphysical questions, occasionally they were drawn into discussions on topics of common concern to both themselves and the Chanter. These theologians, therefore, form an outer circle or context in which Peter operated. Although each held individual opinions on specific subjects, they may be classified in at least two schools: the followers of Gilbert de la Porrée, who included Alain of Lille, Simon of Tournai, Master Martin, and in some cases the Chanter himself, and the followers of Peter the Lombard, who generally consisted of Peter of Poitiers, Peter of Capua, Prepositinus and Stephen Langton. Beyond these were the shadowy figures of Michael of Meaux, who is known only through one treatise, and Peter of Corbeil, whose academic writings have not yet been found.

At Beauvais in 1185 Peter, Chanter of Paris, disposes of his house at Gerberoy to Haimericus, Canon of Gerberoy.
(See Append. II, no. 6.) MS Arch. dép. de l'Oise, G. 7391. (PHOTOGRAPH COURTESY OF THE ARCHIVES DÉPARTEMENTALES DE L'OISE.)

At the episcopal palace in Paris in 1192 Bishop Maurice and Peter the Chanter, as papal judge delegates, decided a case between the Abbey of Saint-Victor and William, cleric of Montfort. (See Append. II, no. 38.) The Bishop's and the Chanter's seals are appended. MS Paris, AN L 903, no. 3. (PHOTOGRAPH COURTESY OF THE ARCHIVES NATIONALES.)

ROBERT OF COURSON[6]

Other than the fact of his English birth, very little is known about the family and early life of Robert of Courson.[7] Evidence for his studies is limited to his *Summa* which, although demonstrating familiarity with both Roman and canon law,[8] clearly indicates that theology was his chief subject and Peter the Chanter his chief teacher. More than fifty times during the course of his *Summa* Robert cites the opinion of Peter with approval,[9] often designating him as "our master,"[10] and sometimes with enthusiasm as "our master, the Chanter, of immortal remembrance."[11] Not only do most of these citations indicate that Robert agreed with the opinions of the Chanter, but it will also be seen that he adopted numerous passages from his master so that his *Summa* may be considered a perfected version of the *questiones* of Peter the Chanter.* Since one passage refers to the last year of his master's life (1197), it may be assumed that Courson was a later student of the old Chanter, and this would place his years of study at Paris in the 1190's, although the exact dates cannot be specified.[12]

When Robert's name first appears in the charters in 1200 he bears the title of *Magister*.[13] Later writers such as Caesar of Heisterbach specify that he taught theology at Paris,[14] for which the best evidence is again his *Summa*—obviously a product of his teaching. One book from his personal library has also survived.[15] His teaching career began sometime before 1200 and was undoubtedly terminated with his elevation to the rank of cardinal in 1212.[16] By 1204 Master Robert was also canon of Noyon.[17] Although from 1204 to 1208 he constantly bore this title,[18] it is clear from papal letters and local charters that he resided at Paris.[19] Apparently Robert was granted the customary leave of absence from his chapter to teach at Paris,[20] because he has left no record of participating in the chapter of Noyon.[21] From January 1209 until December 1211 Robert was designated in papal letters and local charters[22] as a canon of Paris. Since he was no longer entitled canon of Noyon, it may be assumed that he relinquished this prebend in exchange for another at Paris, in order to eliminate the inconvenience of absenteeism. It is highly improbable that Robert, who so consistently opposed the practices of pluralism, would have dared to retain two benefices for himself.[23]

Like his teacher Peter the Chanter, Robert of Courson was employed as a judge delegate in numerous cases while a master of theology at Paris.[24] The cases ranged in importance from investigating the elections of major churches such as Reims, Amiens, Troyes, and Thérouanne, to enforcing the grants of prebends to certain masters. Among these affairs we find Robert judging a controversy between the Count of Nevers and the

* See below, pp. 24, 25.

Abbot of Vézelay, reforming the Abbey of Corbie, investigating the tithes of Saint-Martin-des-Champs, judging the rights of crusaders, examining the complaint of consanguinity between the Count of Nevers and his wife, and settling many other such cases. According to Caesar of Heisterbach, Robert also participated—along with Master Richard Poore, Dean of Salisbury—in the famous heresy hunt for the followers of Amaury of Bène at Paris in 1209 and 1210.[25] In most of these cases Pope Innocent III associated Robert with important Parisian ecclesiastical figures,[26] but occasionally some of his associate judge delegates were fellow masters and former colleagues at Paris.[27] A few, such as Master Stephen Langton,[28] and Master Robert of Flamborough,[29] were within the Chanter's circle at Paris.

Robert's activities as judge delegate at Paris prepared him for a new role envisaged by Pope Innocent III. In the spring of 1212 the Pope removed the Parisian professor from his academic career by elevating him to the curia with the title of cardinal priest of Saint Stephen in Mount Celius.[30] One year later, on 19 April 1213, Pope Innocent announced to all Christendom his decision to convene a great council at Rome in 1215. To prepare for the council and preach the crusade he commissioned papal legates throughout the Latin West. Master Robert of Courson, newly created cardinal, was his choice for France. Dispatched to France in April 1213 with letters of accreditation to the clergy and royalty,[31] the cardinal legate travelled back and forth across the realm in discharge of his new duties until the opening of the Lateran Council of 1215 in Rome.[32]

In preparation for the great council, Robert convoked a number of local councils, which were held at Paris in June 1213, at Rouen in February-March 1214, at Bordeaux in June 1214, at Clermont in July 1214, at Montpellier in January 1215, and at Bourges in May 1215.[33] The legislation of his first council at Paris provided Courson with opportunity to enact many reforms which he and his colleagues had originally proposed as professors at Paris.[34] The council at Rouen merely repeated verbatim most of the measures of Paris,[35] as did also the council at Montpellier, though to a lesser degree.[36] In these local councils Robert tested and publicized the reforms of the Chanter's circle before presenting them to the great council of Rome.[37] In addition, Robert found occasion to expose his moral theories by means of public preaching. It is possible that as early as his student days in the 1190's Robert was associated with Master Peter of Roissy and Eustace of Flay in the preaching campaigns of the famous disciple of the Chanter, Foulques de Neuilly.[38] Later in the thirteenth century Jacques de Vitry designated Courson as one of the celebrated preachers of the Chanter's circle,[39] and there is indication that he and Stephen Langton may have conducted a preaching campaign in

Flanders, against usury, especially around Arras and Saint-Omer.[40] If this campaign took place, it must have occurred in the late spring and early summer of 1213, just before Robert convened the Council of Paris which, it will be seen, paid special attention to the problem of usury. Unfortunately, however, none of his sermons have survived intact.[41] As a preacher, Courson's principal commission was to enlist men for a new crusade to rescue the Holy Land. According to the chronicler Peter des Vaux de Cernay, Robert also occupied himself with the more immediate crusade against the Albigensians and made an excursion into the heresy-infected south of France during the summer of 1214.[42] The policies declared against the Albigensians by the Council of Montpellier, held in January 1215, cannot, however, be attributed to Robert. Although convoking the council and contributing to the reform legislation, he returned to the north of France when the council was held. The program against the heretics of the Council of Montpellier was the responsibility of another papal legate, Peter of Beneventano, who actually presided over the assembly.

As the cardinal legate crisscrossed the French countryside, he became involved in petty ecclesiastical affairs as well as more important matters. He judged, for example, the fitness of the Abbot of Saint-Martial of Limoges, divided the town of Saint-Quentin into nine parishes, and confirmed the donation of tithes to the Abbey of Cambron. Some of his activities, however, were more relevant to the problems which he considered as a professor at Paris. In educational affairs he instituted elementary schools at Dijon in December 1213 and regulated the faculties of Paris in August 1215.[43] On behalf of the pope he investigated the charges of consanguinity in the proposed marriage between Erard of Brienne and Philippine of Champagne, and, like the Chanter, he was commissioned to take part in the now tedious matrimonial quarrel between Philip Augustus and Ingeborg.[44] Since Robert was English by origin, his usefulness to his country was not overlooked by King John of England. Robert's term as legate (1213-1215) coincided with the period when the English king made a last but unsuccessful effort to regain those continental possessions taken by King Philip Augustus. Throughout this last stage of Anglo-French conflict Pope Innocent III attempted to distract the two kings by enlisting their common cooperation in a crusade against the infidel. Dispatching envoys to King John and corresponding with Archbishop Stephen Langton, Robert attempted to fix a meeting between the French and English in September 1213.[45] Although John responded courteously to the legate, he was not willing to be deterred from his plan of reconquest. Again in June 1214, when Robert held a council at Bordeaux deep in English territory, he carefully expressed deference to the rights of the English king, but also announced his intention to negotiate a truce between the two kings at the request of Pope Innocent.[46] Not until he was resoundingly defeated by the French at Roche-au-Moine and Bouvines during the following month was John interested in the legate's services. At the end of August John wrote Robert of his decision to suspend hostilities for a period of two weeks,[47] and by September a peace was concluded which was more favorable to John than might have been expected from his desperate position. While Rigord and other French chroniclers attributed the terms to the magnanimity of Philip Augustus, the English chroniclers gave credit to the intercessions of Robert of Courson.

Not all of Robert's efforts as papal legate met with success and approval. For example, in 1214 the Abbot of Moissac complained that the cardinal had sent two delegates to render a canonical inspection after the abbey had already paid the required fees for such inspection. When the Abbot refused to receive the envoys, his abbey was placed under interdict.[48] Later in the same year Robert became involved in a controversy with the abbey at Saint-Martial of Limoges over the fitness of the abbot, in which affair he was accused by the chronicler Bernard Itier, a monk of the abbey, of exacting simoniacal money and promoting the cause of favorites.[49] When Courson attempted to resolve a dispute between the monks of Grandmont and their prior in January 1214, even Pope Innocent III blamed him for judging precipitously and disregarding the decisions of the Holy See.[50] In the spring of 1214 King Philip Augustus and his barons complained to the Pope of Robert's actions against usurers, declaring that he exceeded his legatine commission to preach the crusade. Although defending the legate this time, Pope Innocent promised to counsel Robert to greater moderation in the future.[51]

Resentment towards Courson's legation in France reached a climax in May 1215.[52] When the legate convoked another council, to be held at Bourges, the French prelacy refused to attend. In response Robert apparently declared the delinquents to be excommunicated and suspended from office.[53] Such radical action would undoubtedly require review at the forthcoming Lateran Council of 1215, in Rome. Although the papal decision between the legate and the French prelacy has been lost,[54] Peter of Corbeil, Archbishop of Sens, reported to the chapter of Laon from Rome that the Pope annulled the excommunications and suspensions pronounced by Robert at Bourges.[55] Neither are the chroniclers clear as to the nature of the quarrel between the legate and the French prelates. Although William the Breton cited his lack of discretion in enlisting crusaders[56] and Robert of Auxerre noted the violence and severity of his actions[57]—perhaps recalling the campaign against usury—both suggested that Robert had abused the clergy. The chronicler of Laon specified that he attacked the dignity of prelates and the customs of important churches.[58] It is difficult to assess the justice of the complaints. The cartulary of Laon indicates that the legate suspended at least ten canons of that church for having acquired their prebends by simony.[59] Although the details of this dispute are not specified, Courson undoubtedly accumulated the disaffection of many parties who lost their cases in the countless litigations which he judged as papal legate. Moreover, his social and moral program as expressed in the councils, especially the campaign against usurers, was not calculated to be popular. Whether rightly opposed or not, Robert was soon drawn from France by the opening of the Lateran Council in November 1215.

Although the chronicler of Auxerre maintained that through the insistence of the French bishops Pope Innocent III rescinded many of Courson's acts at the Lateran Council, this statement probably referred to the legate's individual decisions and judgments.[60] But the Council of 1215 marked the end of the effective career of Robert of Courson, and his remaining years formed a disappointing epilogue.[61] Retained at Rome, Robert soon lost his patron with the death of Pope Innocent in 1216. Although the new pope, Honorius III, acceded to the personal wishes of the Cardinal to provide for his nephews, he continued his predecessor's policy of annulling Robert's legatine decisions in France. Finally, in July 1218, Courson was commissioned by the pope as preacher for the Fifth Crusade under the leadership of the Cardinal Pelagius. Before the besieged city of Damietta, he took sick, and died on 6 February 1219. Jacques de Vitry, who was present at the time, reported the death to the Pope in simple terms,[62] and is probably responsible for another story, reminiscent of Peter the Chanter.[63] While at the point of death, Robert reminded those around him of the mortal sin of churchmen who held more than one benefice when one was sufficient. It was claimed too, that when Courson's body was transferred to Jerusalem for burial it was discovered, like the Chanter's, to be dry, intact, and without putrefaction over a year after death.[64]

An active theological master at Paris during the first decade of the thirteenth century, Robert of Courson could normally be expected to have participated in lectures, disputations, and preaching. Although some indication survives of his preaching, there is no evidence of his lectures. Only the activity of disputation[65] is represented by his sole remaining work, a *Summa* which begins: *Tota celestis philosophia . . . ,*[66] and which may be dated 1208-1212/1213.[67]

The character of Robert's *Summa* may be best discerned by comparing it with the *Summa de sacramentis* of Peter the Chanter. Robert prefaced his work by stating that celestial philosophy (that is, theology) consists of good morals and faith, a formula directly inspired by the Chanter.[68] For the youthful knocking at the gate of theology he proposed to offer solid food by treating doubtful questions concerning these two subjects, but first he would begin with morals, and especially penance, because John the Baptist and Christ Himself opened their ministries with a call to repentance. When the organization of Robert's work is examined more closely, it is discovered that the major part is devoted to the subject of penance and moral issues.[69] Robert began with a discussion of penance and the related problems of absolution, the doctrine of the keys, and excommunication, and then passed to moral questions such as simony, the hiring of services, usury, tithes, theft, testaments, plurality of prebends, vows, scandal, oaths, and judicial procedure. After this preoccupation with penance and morality, Robert concluded his work with a brief treatment of the other sacraments of baptism, marriage, eucharist, confirmation, extreme unction, and the consecration of churches. The *Summa* conveys the impression that Robert hurried to finish the work but never actually brought it to completion. Several questions announced in the prologue do not appear,[70] and the whole section on faith, originally promised, is omitted.[71] Despite his original intention to discuss speculative theology, Robert in fact composed a *Summa de sacramentis* like his master the Chanter. Rather than beginning with baptism and the other sacraments before turning to penance, as Peter had done, Robert reversed the plan and placed penance at the beginning because, recognizing its central importance, he wished to treat it at length. While Peter arranged the subject matter in haphazard fashion, Robert attempted to order it logically.

Both Peter's and Robert's *Summae* are literary expressions of the academic activity of disputation. Like Peter, Robert quoted the phrase of Pope Gregory the Great that nothing can be fully understood unless it is first chewed with the teeth of disputation.[72] Within each *questio* Peter had arrayed his authorities and arguments in an informal fashion; after stating the question he followed no regular procedure in arriving at a solution, which in some instances was even omitted. On the other hand, Robert attempted to introduce method into the individual *questiones* by first posing the question, then distinguishing the authorities and arguments for and against the proposition, and finally arriving at some kind of conclusion.[73] While the Chanter's *questiones* stand closer to the disputations of the schools, Robert's work indicates an attempt to present the discussion in a more literate fashion. Finally, when the texts of the two *Summae* are compared, it will be seen that most of the questions posed by Robert were first suggested by Peter.[74] Robert not only entertained questions suggested by Peter, but he often incorporated whole passages from the Chanter's work into his own.[75] In point of fact, most of Robert's passages follow one particular version of the Chanter's *Summa* (manuscript W).[76] It appears as if Robert had this version in hand when he composed his *Summa.* Peter the Chanter's *Summa de sacramentis* was a collection of *questiones* never fully organized or completed. Using one version of the work, Robert of Courson revised the general organizational plan to emphasize penance and morality, arranged the individual *questiones* to follow a more logical progression, and within each *questio* reconstructed the material according to a methodical procedure. To be sure, Robert was the author of a new *Summa* but in another sense his book constituted another draft of work begun by the Chanter. In the last analysis, the *Summa* of Robert of Courson was a final product of the school of Peter the Chanter.

STEPHEN LANGTON[77]

The early career of Stephen Langton, before his election to the archbishopric of Canterbury in 1207, resembles that of his countryman, Robert of Courson. Originating from Langton near Wragby in Lincolnshire, Stephen's family were small, free landholders of Anglo-Danish stock.[78] The eldest of the three sons, Stephen was probably born within the decade 1155-1165.[79] It is impossible to say whether he received his elementary education at the nearby cathedral town of Lincoln or elsewhere.

After Lincolnshire the next scene of Langton's life was Paris. Pope Innocent III, who knew him well, asserted that he had studied there for a long time.[80] The major evidence for his studies is found in the writings he produced during his subsequent teaching career, but these writings do not clearly indicate who were his teachers at Paris. Langton appears to have been influenced by several schools current at Paris without aligning himself exclusively with anyone. In speculative theology such as Christology he followed the lead of Peter the Lombard and his school.[81] When discussing the sacraments and penance he was particularly influenced by Peter the Chanter.[82] When he turned to Biblical exegesis, both he and the Chanter followed the school of Saint-Victor as represented by Andrew of Saint-Victor and Peter Comestor.[83] Stephen made frequent use of the Scriptural commentaries both of Andrew and of Peter the Chanter. When referring to the Chanter from hearsay[84] or when in disagreement,[85] Stephen cited him by name, but often he merely quoted him without acknowledgement.[86] In fact, Stephen's Biblical commentaries were largely built upon the work of Peter. Most important, along with his abstract theology, he discussed practical problems, which were also the Chanter's specialty.[87] Since Langton's writings have not clearly revealed the name of his teacher,[88] it is probable that he had several teachers, one of whom was Peter the Chanter.[89] Because of their difference in age it is likely that Peter was already teaching when Langton came to Paris, but the English student himself became a master in the 1180's, as Peter approached the height of his career. Although their relation as student and teacher is not entirely clear, they were undoubtedly colleagues on the theological faculty. Because of common interests, Stephen Langton may be placed within the circle of Peter the Chanter.

According to the contemporary chroniclers, Stephen Langton was a renowned master of theology at Paris.[90] In a letter of 1207 Pope Innocent specified that he had earned the master's title both in the liberal arts and in theology.[91] While no written evidence has survived of his arts teaching, his theological career is amply demonstrated by a great number of manuscripts produced in his classes. More than the works of any other theologian at the turn of the century his writings illustrate the full program of lecturing, disputing, and preaching proposed by Peter the Chanter.[92] His lecturing is represented by a great volume of Biblical commentaries, several manuscripts of which disclose their classroom origins.[93] Even his inaugural lecture or *inceptio*, delivered at the start of his theological professorship at Paris, has survived.[94] His *questiones,* or the disputations of his school, were gathered in several collections, and, unlike those of the Chanter or Courson, well over a hundred of his sermons have survived. Measured by the amount of written work produced in his classroom, Stephen towered above all other contemporary academic colleagues in any faculty at Paris. This impressive body of writings, moreover, is thoroughly saturated with allusions to the schools at Paris.[95] Although it can only be conjectured when Stephen arrived at the French capital, his writings help to date his career as a theological master.[96] One commentary suggests a date before 1187, but the other writings containing any chronological evidence must be dated after 1187, most likely in the 1190's. Since the first secure date for any of his writings is 1193, one can be certain that he was teaching by then, but only surmise that his theological career had already begun during the 1180's. According to Innocent III Stephen's teaching at Paris was supported by prebends from Notre-Dame and the chapter of York.[97]

Unlike the Chanter and Courson, Langton was not involved in ecclesiastical affairs until the very end of his academic career. Probably in 1205 or early 1206, Master Stephen, canon of Paris, was asked to serve with William, Archdeacon of Paris, and Robert of Courson, to arbitrate in a dispute between the Abbey of Corbie and the Priory of Lihons.[98] Before the judgment was rendered on 9 August 1206, Stephen excused himself from his duties, but promised to ratify their decision. Undoubtedly he had received a call from Rome, early in 1206. In February 1206, he was appointed by Pope Innocent III as judge delegate in the controversy between the Abbot of Saint-Denis and the Abbess of Footel over the Priory of Argenteuil.[99] Again Stephen was absent when the decision was rendered (in September 1207), and Robert of Courson had taken his place.[100]

Since Stephen's service in ecclesiastical justice was relatively light while he was a master of theology, his activities at Paris were largely academic, as the great volume of his writings testifies.

Stephen Langton was recruited from the schools into church administration with less preparation than Robert of Courson. Some time between February and June 1206 Pope Innocent III called Stephen to Rome and created him a cardinal priest with the title of Saint Chrysogonus.[101] At that time King John of England was in conflict with the monks of Canterbury over the election of a new archbishop and both parties had appealed to Rome.[102] Innocent refused the candidates of both sides and induced the monks to elect Stephen in his presence as Archbishop of Canterbury. The election took place in December 1206 and the consecration by the Pope on 17 June 1207, at Viterbo. Protesting that his rights in the election had been violated, King John refused to accept the papal action and denied Stephen entry into England. Pope Innocent maintained that the election had been free and legitimate, and attempted to coerce the king first by placing England under interdict in March 1208, and later by personally excommunicating him in October 1209. Since Stephen's public service in the church began with a storm of controversy, his subsequent career alternated between periods of exile and inactivity, during which he often drops from sight in the historical records, and periods of activity during which every step can be traced. For the first six years as Archbishop (until 9 July 1213) Stephen was on the Continent in exile from his see. Very little is known about his movements except that he visited Rome and Paris at least once each,[103] but he seems to have passed most of the time in seclusion at the Cistercian monastery of Pontigny where, according to one chronicler, he continued his writing.[104]

Coerced by ecclesiastical sanctions and threatened by invasion from the French, King John finally came to terms with the church and surrendered his kingdom as a fief to the pope, during the spring of 1213. Stephen had been in Rome the preceding winter and arrived in France in January 1213 as negotiations proceeded for his return to England. On the eve and morrow of his return the tempo of his activities quickened. It is possible that during the spring he cooperated with Robert of Courson to preach in Flanders against usurers, prior to his crossing to England on 9 July 1213.[105] Upon arrival at London he delivered a sermon to a large crowd at Saint Paul's on 25 August 1213 in which he justified the church's policy during the preceding years of conflict.[106] The next two years were exceptionally busy for Stephen as he resumed duties as Archbishop and attempted to restore normalcy to the English church. With the cardinal legate, Nicholas, he negotiated with the King for the final removal of the interdict, attempted to insure restitution to the clergy for damages suffered during the interdict, and supervised the elections of vacant bishoprics. Sometime between July 1213 and July 1214 he held a council for the Canterbury diocese and enacted statutes regulating the conduct of the clergy.[107] In effect he performed for his diocese what Robert of Courson did for France, and a number of his individual canons were borrowed directly from Courson's legislation. But the Archbishop's activities were not limited to church affairs, but also involved the relations between King John and his barons.[108] The conflict between the King and his magnates worsened after John's defeat at Bouvines, and Stephen increasingly took sides with the barons and helped them to coordinate their grievances in Magna Carta. By this independent position the Archbishop antagonized not only the King but also Pope Innocent who, in the interests of peace, placed his support behind his newly created royal vassal. When Stephen was commanded by the Pope to excommunicate the barons who defended Magna Carta, he refused and was suspended from office. Since Langton undoubtedly had long laid plans for attending the Lateran Council announced for 1 November 1215, he left England in October to appeal his case at Rome.

Once again controversy kept Langton in exile and for the period October 1215 to May 1218 little is known about him. On 4 November Pope Innocent confirmed the sentence of suspension in Rome. Although he was reinstated shortly thereafter, he did not set foot in England for almost three years. With eight suffragan bishops and other English representatives he attended to affairs pertinent to the English church and was present for the discussions of the Lateran Council.[109] There is no way to determine his role in these discussions,[110] but many of the issues had attracted his attention in his own diocesan statutes at Canterbury. His movements after the Lateran Council remain a mystery.[111]

Finally, in May 1218 he returned to England to resume his episcopal duties for the last decade of his life.[112] Although forced to follow the leadership of the papal legate Pandulf for the first three years, he soon assumed direction of both ecclesiastical and royal affairs during the minority of the young King Henry III, renewing for example, statutes for the instruction of the diocesan clergy between 1222 and 1228,[113] and reissuing Magna Carta in 1225. From 1224 to 1226 he and the English prelates granted revenues to the king for the siege of Bedford and the wars in Poitou. Amidst these pressing affairs he found occasion, in 1221 and again in 1223, to revisit Paris, the scene of earlier and perhaps happier years. While returning from Rome in 1221, he was commissioned by Pope Honorius III to settle disputes between the masters and the bishop and chancellor of Paris who were adverse to the growing independence of the university.[114] In 1227 and 1228 he once again disappears from the historical record, but this time it was not controversy but old age and sickness which took their toll.[115] At least sixty-five years of age—of which the last twenty were filled with harassment and disappointment—the Archbishop died at his manor of Slindon on 9 July 1228. Among his many bequests Stephen remembered to include the chapter of Notre-Dame of Paris, which had supported him with a prebend while he was a theological master. Through his brother Master Simon Langton he bestowed a legacy of two hundred pounds in Paris money on his fellow canons.[116]

Peter the Chanter's threefold classification, of lecturing, disputing, and preaching, can be more appropriately applied to Stephen Langton than to any other Parisian theologian at the turn of the century, including Peter himself. Stephen's Biblical lectures attracted special notice from contemporary chroniclers. Observing that Langton's writings were numerous, Otto of Saint-Blaise specified his commentaries to the Psalms, Epistles of the Apostle Paul, Isaiah and the twelve minor prophets.[117] At the end of the thirteenth century Henry of Brussels claimed that Stephen expounded the whole Scriptures in their full and moral sense.[118] When modern scholars began to investigate the Langton manuscripts they discovered that the medieval chroniclers only hinted at the extent of his writing. With the exception of the Psalms, commentaries have been uncovered for every book of the Bible and often in two to four different versions.[119] As a Biblical lecturer Stephen's output far exceeded that of the Chanter, his closest competitor. These Scriptural expositions exist in hundreds of medieval manuscripts which modern scholars have barely begun to classify.[120]

Certain manuscripts explicitly state that these commentaries were delivered as lectures in Paris.[121] This fact is confirmed by other manuscripts, which exhibit characteristics of *reportationes*—the use of the third person, the tag "Master says," the incomplete and unpolished style—all suggestive of teaching techniques.[122] As Langton expounded the Scripture he used not only the Bible but also other glosses and Biblical aids. For example, his commentary on the Epistles of the Apostle is based on the *Magna glosatura* of Peter the Lombard[123] and one of his expositions of Isaiah proceeds from the *Glossa ordinaria*, both marginal and interlineary.[124] In fact, Langton's work often consists of a gloss upon a gloss.[125] He also produced commentaries to the *Historia scholastica* of Peter Comestor, which by Langton's day had become the standard textbook of Biblical history.[126] Many of the commentaries have come down in two or more versions.[127] In some cases, since one version contains both literal and moral interpretations, it appears as if an editor has later dissected the full rendition into two parts.[128] In other cases, differing versions indicate that they were products of different lectures, thus suggesting that Langton commented on certain books two or more times.[129] The great volume of Langton's commentaries would suggest that they were produced over a long academic career. From internal evidence the earliest secure dates which can be assigned to his lectures are between 1187 and 1193.[130] Normally one would expect Stephen to have ceased writing by 1206, the year he left the schools, but it should be remembered that he was forced into retirement at Pontigny from 1207 to 1213, and from 1216 to 1218 at some unknown place on the Continent, where he was free to write. There is no guarantee, therefore, that he did not continue to revise works begun at Paris.

As the Chanter advocated, Stephen practised the rule that lecturing laid the foundation for disputing and preaching. In many commentaries he inserted small *questiones* which anticipate the fuller *questiones* of his disputations.[131] In the commentary to the Apostle Paul, for example, he elaborated questions which were identical to those of his collected *questiones*, and in the margins he inserted rubrics announcing topics which he developed in disputation.[132] Lecturing and disputing therefore went hand in hand in Langton's classroom. In another commentary, sermon themes were also indicated at appropriate passages of Scripture.[133] In addition to the Biblical commentaries, therefore, Stephen Langton produced a large number of *questiones* which have survived in a number of manuscript collections.[134] All that is known about these *questiones* suggests that they originated from the disputations of Langton's school at Paris. Langton's lectures on the Apostle referred to *questiones* and occasionally announced their topics. On the other hand, numerous *questiones* in the manuscript collections refer back to and are textually identical with *questiones* incorporated in the Pauline commentary.[135] One particular collection specifically states that they were actually "determined" or decided by Stephen himself,[136] and the *questiones*, like the commentaries, exhibit the characteristics of *reportationes*.[137] Since the lectures and the *questiones* make mutual references to each other, it is evident that both were produced simultaneously during the course of Langton's teaching.[138] One might expect that they were completed by 1206, when Langton left his academic career, yet it should not be forgotten that he had subsequent opportunities to revise his work.[139] Whatever these revisions, in all likelihood the great bulk of Langton's *questiones* was originally produced in the schools.[140]

Stephen Langton was not only reputed to be a great preacher, like the Chanter and Courson, but over a hundred of his sermons have survived.[141] Among those ascribed to him, a number were preached at important events of his life, such as when he assumed his chair of theology at Paris,[142] when he returned to London after the interdict,[143] and when he translated the relics of Thomas Becket.[144] While they illustrate the homiletic fashions of the early thirteenth century, very few are concerned with the practical issues of social morality.[145]

At least five of Langton's students at Paris can be identified with certainty.[146] According to the chronicler of Evesham they included Master Thomas of Marlborough and Master Richard Poore, who both advanced to important prelacies in England.[147] Thomas taught law at Exeter and Oxford before becoming Abbot of Evesham. After his studies under Langton, Richard Poore became successively Dean of Salisbury (1197), Bishop of Chichester (1215), Salisbury (1217), and Durham (1228),[148] but he also retained connections with the Parisian theologians. During the Great Interdict (1209-1213), while still Dean of Salisbury, Richard returned to Paris to teach theology,[149] where he also served as papal judge delegate on at least six occasions[150] and assisted Robert of Courson—in 1210 —in prosecuting the heretical followers of Amaury of Bène.[151] It was during this period that Robert of Flamborough, writing at the Abbey of Saint-Victor, dedicated his penitential (1208-1213) to his friend, the Dean of Salisbury.[152] Later, as Bishop of Salisbury, Richard issued synodical statutes (1217-1219) which drew heavily on previous legislation of Courson, Langton and the Lateran Council of 1215.[153] If Caesar of Heisterbach's narrative can be trusted, the band of heretics exposed by Courson and Richard Poore contained another of Langton's students, a certain Master Guérin, priest of Corbeil, who had come to Paris to study the arts and had attended Stephen's theological lectures.[154] The one student of Langton, however, who made a career of teaching theology at Paris and produced a treatise which is still extant, was Master Geoffrey of Poitiers.

GEOFFREY OF POITIERS

Almost nothing is known about Geoffrey of Poitiers' biography except his place of origin and his profession. That he came from Poitiers is indicated not only by his name but also by numerous references to the Poitou region in his writings.[155] At the papal court with William of Auxrerre, he represented the masters of Paris in their dispute with the French royalty which resulted from the great strike of 1229. He must have returned to Paris by 1231 because in May of that year Pope Gregory IX wrote to the French king commending the two masters to royal protection against detraction and reprisals for their part in the conflict.[156]

Geoffrey composed a *Summa* consisting of a collection of *questiones* organized in four books according to the scheme of the *Sentences* of Peter the Lombard.[157] Although he occasionally mentioned other contemporaries in passing[158] he most often referred to one or more anonymous teachers whom he designated as "our masters." Frequently he uses this term to distinguish them from the masters whom he names. When his *questiones* are compared with Stephen Langton's it becomes immediately apparent that Langton was himself one of Geoffrey's anonymous masters.[159] A great number of the *questiones* simply rework Stephen's material. On occasion Geoffrey also cites a certain "cardinal" and when other *questiones* are compared with Robert of Courson's, it can be seen that Courson was another of his masters.[160] In fact, all the material in Book IV of the *Summa* devoted to the sacraments is an adaptation of Robert's own *Summa*.[161] At times Geoffrey mentions the Chanter's name, but he does not appear to know him directly and quotes him only through Courson or Langton.[162] Although Prepositinus' influence is also evident,[163] Geoffrey's *Summa* is in the main derived from the work of Stephen Langton and Robert of Courson. A common student of these two masters, Geoffrey of Poitiers united two streams of influence issuing from Peter the Chanter.

It is possible that Geoffrey gained his intimate knowledge of Langton's and Courson's work because of his position as a *reportator* in the classes of his masters,[164] but it is also possible that he merely worked with written copies of his masters' *questiones*. In one instance he wrote separate *questiones* based on Langton's discussion and which were later incorporated into his *Summa*.[165] In all events, when he came to composing his own *Summa* he frequently excerpted, abbreviated and summarized the work of his masters. In some respects the *Summa* of Geoffrey of Poitiers reorganized the confused *questiones* of Stephen Langton in the same way that Robert of Courson improved the *Summa de sacramentis* of the Chanter.[166] The work was compiled concurrent to the Lateran Council of 1215.[167]

The Victorines: Robert of Flamborough, Peter of Poitiers of Saint-Victor, and Anonymous Writers

As his name indicates, Robert of Flamborough originated from a place near Scarborough in Yorkshire, England.[168] His recorded life, however, was spent within the cloister of Saint-Victor in Paris where he was a canon and penitentiary (*penitenciarius*) of the church.[169] From 1205 to 1207 he was a papal judge delegate associated with his countryman Robert of Courson in litigation over the excommunication of the Bishop of Tull and the tithes of Saint-Martin-des-Champs.[170] In September 1209, with his fellow canon Master Peter of Poitiers, he witnessed a charter of the Abbot and Prior of Saint-Victor dealing with a defamed priest.[171] In all of these charters he was designated by the academic title of Master. As confessor at Saint-Victor, Robert composed a *Penitentiale* or a "guide to confessors" which can be dated between 1208 and 1213.[172] At the request of another countryman, Richard Poore, then Dean of Salisbury, Robert composed his *Penitentiale* to serve as a practical manual for priests hearing confessions and administering penance.[173] The work is organized in five books: the first provides general instructions, the second treats marriage, the third treats simony, the fourth discusses sin according to the classification of the seven vices, and the fifth presents a long list of penitential canons. Within the first four books Robert's discussion assumes the form of dialogues between a priest and a penitent. One would expect Robert's work to be inspired chiefly by canon law, and indeed, he employed papal decretals from Alexander III and Innocent III in the manner of a canonist.[174] Huguccio, the foremost canonist of the twelfth century, is also cited and followed throughout the work, and the penitential canons of Book v were largely drawn from the collections of Bartholomew of Exeter and Ivo of Chartres. Yet the discussion of the seven deadly sins is more closely related to the theologians than to the canonists.[175] Although Robert was acquainted with Courson and Richard Poore, both contemporary theologians at Paris, no reference has been found in his work pointing directly to Peter the Chanter.[176] Yet it will be seen that in many respects, Robert of Flamborough's *Penitentiale* fulfills the Chanter's program of casuistry.[177]* In all events, Robert's fellow canons at Saint-Victor who also composed guides to confessors were directly inspired by Peter the Chanter.

All that is known about Peter of Poitiers of Saint-Victor, like his confrère Robert of Flamborough, is his place of origin and the fact of his membership in the chapter of Saint-Victor. Originating from Poitiers, he is distinguishable from his more famous contemporary, Master Peter of Poitiers, theologian and Chancellor of Notre-Dame, by the fact that he was a canon of Saint-Victor.[178] In September 1209, with Robert of Flamborough, he witnessed a charter dealing with a defamed priest, in which he was designated as Master.[179] As far as the records reveal he led a secluded life within the cloister of Saint-Victor, except for possible visits to nearby monasteries.[180] A man of considerable wealth when he died, he bequeathed to Saint-Victor some twenty volumes, to the Abbey of Jard one volume containing the books of Joshua, Judges and Daniel, and to the Priory of Saint-Guénaud two volumes of the Gospels.[181]

Among three works ascribed to him is a penitential.[182] Like the manual of Robert of Flamborough, Peter's *Penitentiale* consists of practical instructions for guiding priests in administering penance. Covering a broad range of human activity, its contents are organized rather loosely.[183] Among the authorities cited by Peter are papal decretals from Eugenius III to Innocent III, the synodical statutes of Paris, canons of the Lateran Council of 1215, and opinions of John Beleth, Maurice of Sully, and Prepositinus,[184] but the name occurring most frequently is that of Peter the Chanter. Not only did Peter of Poitiers quote his opinions, but he also had a good knowledge of the Chanter's *Summa de sacramentis*, which he

* See below, p. 53.

cited by its title.[185] This material drawn directly from the Chanter un-doubtedly places Peter of Poitiers within his circle. Like Flamborough, Peter of Poitiers composed his work shortly after the Lateran Council of 1215.[186]

Early in the thirteenth century the Abbey of Saint-Victor acquired re-sponsibility for hearing confessions and administering penance to the ever growing numbers of students at Paris.[187] To perform these tasks not only did Robert of Flamborough and Peter of Poitiers compose their peni-tentials, but anonymous penitentials were also produced in the abbey church.[188] One example found in the Victorine manuscript (MS Paris BN 14859), which was composed during the pontificate of Pope In-nocent III (1198-1216), combines the works of Robert and Peter.[189] In this penitential the influence of Peter the Chanter is at times conveyed through the intermediary Peter of Poitiers,[190] but it also derives directly from the Chanter's works.[191] Another Victorine manuscript (MS Paris BN 14899) contains penitential instructions organized by general topics.[192] Certain sections, concerning usury, were excerpted directly from the work of Thomas of Chobham, who, it will be seen, was an influential English penitential writer of the Chanter's circle.[193]

THOMAS OF CHOBHAM[194]

Among the band of Englishmen who came to the schools of Paris and as a result of their studies later wrote guides to confessors, the most note-worthy was Thomas of Chobham.[195] His birth at Chobham[196] (a village in Surrey), which may be dated conjecturally between 1158 and 1168,[197] is known to have been illegitimate.[198] In all probability he was the son of the local priest of Chobham, to whose charge he later succeeded. He first appears as a master and a cleric in the court of Richard Fitz-Nigel, Bishop of London (1189-1198).[199] Soon after the death of Bishop Richard in 1198, he transferred his services to Herbert Poore, Bishop of Salis-bury.[200] From August 1199 to the end of his life Thomas' ecclesiastical career was centered upon Salisbury, first as a cleric of the bishop (1201-1204), then promoted to the dignity of subdean (October 1206-ca. 1208), a member of the chapter in 1214, and finally acting as *officialis* for the bishop (1214-ca. 1217).[201] In 1228 he was present at the chapter meeting for the election of a new bishop, apparently with ambitions for the office himself since he came prepared with a papal dispensation excusing his illegitimate birth.[202] He was well provided for in the Salisbury church, holding a prebend from Sturminster in 1205 or 1206, the "golden prebend" of Charminster in Dorset after 1214, as well as being rector of his native village sometime before 1217.[203] His success may have been due to royal favor, because in 1213 King John employed him on an overseas mission for which he gave him twenty marks and later granted him rights to clear land at Chobham.[204] Thomas died sometime between the years 1233 and 1236.[205]

The academic career of Thomas of Chobham is known chiefly from inferences based on meager data. When he appeared in the entourage of the Bishop of London around 1189/1192, he already was designated by the title of Master. His chief work, the *Summa confessorum*, which was composed around 1215, contains references to Paris which suggest first-hand knowledge.[206] Since Peter the Chanter is the only contemporary theologian whom Thomas mentions, one may suspect that he was Thomas' teacher. When Thomas' *Summa* is compared with the Chanter's work this suspicion is confirmed, because it depends heavily on the Parisian professor.[207] Moreover, three of a collection of sermons now located at Canterbury are attributed specifically to Master Thomas of Chobham,[208] and one of these is his inaugural lecture when he began to teach theology at Paris.[209] Again, this is a sermon directly inspired by the Chanter's *Verbum abbreviatum*. In addition, the collection contains fourteen sermons attributed to the "subdean of Salisbury" which were preached in major Parisian churches, including Saint-Germain-des-Prés, Saint-Victor, and Saint-Jacques.[210] Although not certain, it is possible that these sermons also belong to Master Thomas of Chobham. Finally, in a poem written at Toulouse (1229-1232) by the Englishman John of Garland, there is an allusion to a certain Thomas who taught at Paris, to which a gloss in another hand has specified that this is in fact Thomas of Chobham.[211] If the glossator can be trusted, there is further indication that Thomas was at Paris in the thirteenth century. In the charters there are two major undocumented gaps in Thomas' ecclesiastical career in England: (1) before his appearance at the episcopal court of London in 1189/1192, and (2) during the Great Interdict of 1208-1213.[212] From 1217 to 1228 he appeared sporadically at Salisbury but he was definitely absent from chapter meetings in 1222, 1224, and 1225. From this scattered data it is reasonably certain that since Thomas had studied under Peter the Chanter, he had been in Paris before he appeared at London with his master's title in 1189/1192.[213] During the Interdict he perhaps left the realm like his Bishop, Herbert, or even went to Paris like his Dean, Richard Poore.[214] Similarly, he could have returned between 1217 and 1228, when he could have been noticed by John of Garland. As to his inaugural theological lecture at Paris, it was delivered after 1191/1192 for it draws material from the *Verbum abbreviatum* of the Chanter.[215]

Thomas of Chobham's major work was a *Summa confessorum* which, judged by its numerous copies, enjoyed considerable success in the Middle Ages.[216] Announcing in his preface that he wished to skip over theoretical and speculative questions, Thomas intended to treat practical procedures for priests who heard confessions and administered penance.[217] He therefore divided his treatise into seven books dealing with the following questions: (1) What is penance? (2) What are its kinds? (3) What are the sins for which penance is enjoined? (4) Who administers penance and how? (5) By whom and for whom should penance be enjoined? (6) How should the priest receive various kinds of penitents? (7) What satisfaction should be imposed for what sin?[218] The last two books are the longest of the work, Book VI treating in great detail the various professions of penitents, and Book VII discussing the whole range of immoral behavior under the classification of the seven mortal sins. As a practical handbook, Thomas' treatise lacks an academic style and apparatus, yet it probes the varieties of human conduct more deeply and broadly than any previous penitential.[219]

While the *Summa confessorum* indicates familiarity with both Roman and canon law,[220] there is little doubt that Thomas' major source of inspiration was Peter the Chanter.[221] Not only does he cite, borrow *exempla* from, and quote him, but his whole *Summa* is based on the work of Peter. Thomas continued the discussion of numerous subjects originally presented by the Chanter.[222] The English disciple does not always agree with the Parisian master and occasionally he proceeds beyond his teacher by treating conditions peculiar to England; nonetheless, the richness of Thomas' manual benefited directly from the academic discussions of the Chanter and his circle. Although inspired in Paris, Thomas' treatise can be regarded as probably composed in England because of the predominance of English cases cited and its author's concern for the needs of the English clergy.[223] Like the work of Geoffrey of Poitiers and Peter of Poitiers of Saint-Victor it was probably written about the same time as the Lateran Council of 1215.[224]

The Preachers: Foulques de Neuilly and Jacques de Vitry

At the turn of the twelfth century the attention of chroniclers was drawn to a remarkable preaching campaign in the countryside of northern France, conducted by Master Foulques, formerly the priest of Neuilly.[225] During his early years in the parish of Neuilly, lying to the east of Paris, Foulques, like many of his fellow pastors, was hindered by immoral habits and poor training. Touched by divine grace, however, the curé attempted to reform his ways, but when he discovered that his deficient preparation remained an obstacle to his ministry, Foulques resolved to pursue a theological education at Paris and eventually to win the coveted title of Master. According to Jacques de Vitry, his chief inspiration came from Master Peter the Chanter, whose lectures Foulques transcribed on wax tablets.[226] What Foulques learned at Paris on the week days he preached to his parish on Sundays, and soon his fame as a preacher spread to neighboring parishes. To encourage his talents and to improve his style, the Chanter compelled him to preach before a learned audience of students at the church of Saint-Séverin on the Left Bank of Paris. For about two or three years his preaching had little outward effect,[227] but suddenly his words caught fire and his evangelistic career was launched. From 1195, when the chroniclers first took notice, until his death in 1202 Foulques was reputed to be a moving preacher whose sermons wrought wonders and miracles. By and large his preaching dealt with moral issues. Most contemporary accounts agreed that he was particularly effective in converting usurers, prostitutes, and incontinent clergy from their evil ways.[228]

Later Foulques added a fourth dimension to his campaigns, the preaching of the crusade. In a letter of November 1198 commending the evangelist for his efforts, Pope Innocent III gave him permission to enlist the Benedictine and Cistercian monks and regular canons under the supervision of the cardinal legate Peter Capuano to cooperate in the cause of the Holy Land.[229] Foulques' endeavors for the crusade were not as successful as his moral preaching because complaints arose over irregularities and mismanagement of funds.[230] According to Gerald of Wales the evangelist also attempted to negotiate a peace between King Richard of England and King Philip Augustus of France.[231] One of Foulques' first and most successful sermons was delivered at the market square of Champeaux on the Right Bank of Paris where his listeners were so moved by his call for repentance that they tore their clothes and cast themselves at his feet.[232] After Paris the preacher carried his message into the Ile-de-France, Champagne, Burgundy, and the populous regions of Picardy and Brabant, with similar success. Roger of Hoveden's chronicle[233] suggests that Foulques chose Master Peter of Roissy,[234] Robert of Courson, and Eustace the Cistercian abbot of Flay[235] to aid him in his early campaigns. Later, with papal support, he engaged the Cistercian abbots of Columba, Perseigne and Vaux-de-Cernay to preach the crusade.[236] In May 1202, however, a fatal fever ended the evangelist's meteoric career, and he was buried at his parish church in Neuilly where his tomb attracted pilgrims from surrounding regions.

Despite his fame as a brilliant preacher, Foulques de Neuilly left no sermons by which the substance of his message can be known. In all probability most of his preaching was performed in the vernacular tongue,[237] with the exception of his sermon to the scholars at Saint-Séverin, which was probably delivered in Latin. In a revealing comment, Jacques de Vitry noted that when the Parisian masters and students wrote down Foulques' words in their notebooks, and later returned to them, they remarked that his sermons lost their original force.[238] The evangelist's effectiveness obviously lay more in his personality than in his intellect. Although Foulques was evidently not an academic preacher, he remained, nonetheless, a hero of the Chanter's circle. Originally inspired by the Chanter himself, he was remembered after his death in the lectures and disputations of Stephen Langton,[239] in the writings of Gerald of Wales,[240] and especially in the history of Jacques de Vitry.[241]

The chief source for the life and preaching of Foulques de Neuilly is the *Historia occidentalis* of Master Jacques de Vitry.[242] Inspired by his forerunner, Jacques likewise assumed the preacher's mantle and became equally famous for his sermons. Although a number of French places bear the name of Vitry, it now appears that Jacques originated from Vitry-en-Perthois in the Reims region.[243] Since he held urban property and his family cannot be traced to the Champagne nobility, he probably came from wealthy bourgeois circles. According to one account he was a student at Paris when Jerusalem fell to the Saracens in 1187,[244] and earned his master's title by 1193.[245] In his sermons he was fond of recalling events which happened during his Parisian days, which he introduced with phrases such as "I remember when I was at Paris. . . ."[246] His *Historia occidentalis* contains a vivid description of the royal city and its schools on the eve of Foulques de Neuilly's arrival to study under Peter the Chanter.[247] As for Jacques' own teachers, the only contemporary master whom he explicitly cites in his sermons is the Chanter,[248] from whom he also borrowed a number of *exempla*.[249] His *Historia occidentalis* includes a eulogy of the Chanter in unusually extravagant metaphors.[250] Since Jacques was a student in Paris at the height of the Chanter's career, and because of Peter's prominence in Jacques' writings, one may assume that, with Foulques de Neuilly, the future preacher was a product of the Chanter's school. Like the Chanter, Jacques also disposed of his inherited property before embarking on an ecclesiastical career.[251]

Although Jacques perhaps served for a brief time as a priest in Argenteuil, a short distance down river from Paris, the next major stage of his life was situated at Oignies near Cambrai.[252] In all probability he was brought there by friendship with Marie of Oignies, one of the founding saints of the Beguines movement. From at least 1211 to 1216 he was a regular canon of the church of Saint-Nicholas of Oignies where he also engaged in preaching. It was his talents as a preacher, however, that determined his future career. Under the prompting of Foulques, Bishop of Toulouse, who had been expelled from his see and drawn to Oignies by the fame of Marie, Jacques began in 1213 to preach against the Albigensian heretics. His effectiveness in inciting popular enthusiasm for this cause led him to preach the crusade for the rescue of the Holy Land as well. Undoubtedly recognizing his contributions, the canons of Acre elected him in 1216 to their bishopric, one of the major crusading bastions in the Holy Land. In addition to his preaching and episcopal responsibilities in Palestine, Jacques participated in the Fifth Crusade, against Egypt from 1218 to 1221. He was present before the walls of Damietta when Robert of Courson, the papal legate and fellow student of Parisian days, died, in 1219.[253] As crusading affairs in the East worsened Jacques returned to Europe on at least two journeys, by 1228 resigning his bishopric at Acre. Made Cardinal Bishop of Tusculum in 1229, he was occupied with the duties of the papal court until his death, 1 May 1240. A year later his remains were returned to his beloved Oignies.

Since fifty years separate his student days from his death, Jacques de Vitry was a young man when he came under the influence of Peter the Chanter in Paris. He represents, therefore, the last generation of the Chanter's circle who could have known Peter personally. For general purposes Master Jacques de Vitry's writings may be divided into three general categories: letters, history and sermons. His letters mainly concern eastern affairs while he was Bishop of Acre.[254] Among the historical works, his *Historia occidentalis* (1218-1221) paints a florid picture of the Parisian milieu of the Chanter and his circle.[255] His sermons have been assembled in four manuals for preachers: *Sermones dominicales* devoted to the ecclesiastical calendar of Sundays and feast days, *Sermones de sanctis* devoted to the celebrations of the saints, *Sermones vulgares*[256] addressed to various classes and professions of society, and *Sermones communes sive cotidiani*[257] for general or daily use. The last two collections contain a large number of *exempla* or illustrative stories which enliven the text of the sermon, and which attracted the interest not only of the listeners but of scribes who placed them in separate collections.[258] In these sermons and stories Jacques popularized the morality taught by the masters of Paris.

After eulogizing Peter the Chanter and recounting the life of Foulques de Neuilly, Jacques de Vitry enumerated seven famous preachers who followed in their path:[259] "Master Stephen Langton, Archbishop of Canterbury, Master Walter of London, Master Robert of Courson, who was later made a cardinal, the Cistercian Abbot of Perseigne, Master Albericus of Laon, who afterwards became Archbishop of Reims,[260] Master John of Liro and his companion Master John of Nivelles." Langton's and Courson's adherence to the Chanter's circle is well attested in their writings. Among the rest, only one, Adam of Perseigne, is survived by writings, in this case letters, but these reveal little influence of the Chanter.[261]

RAOUL ARDENT, GILLES DE CORBEIL, AND GERALD OF WALES

A short notice of Raoul Ardent's death found in a near-contemporary manuscript of his ethical treatise relates that he was a Master and that he died on 12 September (sometime between 1191/1192 and 1215).[262]

Although his name (in Latin, *Radulphus Ardens*) might suggest the prominent Anglo-Norman family which took its name from the Abbey of Ardenne near Caen,[263] a fifteenth-century manuscript containing another obituary (probably derived from the earlier notice) describes Master Raoul as coming from Beaulieu near Bressuire in the diocese of Poitiers.[264] Allusions to southwest France in his extant writings seem to confirm his Poitevin origins.[265] There is little doubt that as a theologian Raoul belonged to the followers of Gilbert de la Porrée, Bishop of Poitiers. If not a direct student, he nonetheless quoted Gilbert frequently and adopted the characteristic positions of his school.[266] Because of his connections with the *Porretani* and of his knowledge of Peter the Chanter, one may surmise that Raoul had been at Paris, but no clear evidence confirms it.

Raoul Ardent's writings include a collection of sermons,[267] and a major treatise on ethics entitled the *Speculum universale*.[268] Although it treats an encyclopedic range of topics, such as the classification of knowledge, Christology, and the sacraments, by and large the *Speculum* concentrates on moral themes so that in some manuscripts it was designated as a treatise on virtues and vices. The work is carefully divided into fourteen principal books with hundreds of chapters furnished with rubrics.[269] Since Raoul devoted serious effort to organizing his treatise, several manuscripts contain elaborate schematic diagrams to illustrate the author's intention. Essentially an encyclopedia, its material is presented in the most general terms, including little that is specific or anecdotal. The more the *Speculum universale* has been studied by modern students, the more it has been discovered that Raoul depended heavily on the works of others. Not only did he quote extensively from the Scriptures, the Church Fathers, saints' lives, and *Vitae patrum* which he acknowledged, but he also made use of more recent masters such as Gilbert de la Porrée[270] and the *Moralium dogma philosophorum*.[271] His whole scheme of classification of knowledge, for example, is based on that of Hugh of Saint-Victor's *Didascalicon*.[272] Peter the Chanter appears to be Raoul's most nearly contemporary source. Adopting particular stories from the short version of the *Verbum abbreviatum*, Raoul drew his anecdotal and contemporary material from the Chanter.[273] The *Speculum* was probably written towards the end of his life because Book VI, which is lacking in all manuscripts, is preceded by a rubric explaining that death prevented the master from completing this section.[274] Since the Chanter's *Verbum* seems to be Raoul's most recent source, the *Speculum* may be dated after 1191/1192,[275] and it was probably completed before 1215.[276]

Although Raoul Ardent's membership among the *Porretani* is fairly certain because of the tenor of his theological opinions, he may have come under the influence of Peter the Chanter as well. The Chanter himself was often aligned with the followers of Gilbert de la Porrée in the theological controversies of the day. Raoul lived at a time contemporary to the Chanter, and it may be assumed, until evidence is produced to the contrary, that Paris was the scene of his studies and teaching. Since the Chanter was the most recent theologian quoted in the *Speculum universale*, Raoul Ardent may be assigned a place, although nebulous and unsure, in the circle of Peter the Chanter.

Not limited to theological colleagues alone, the Chanter's influence extended to the Paris medical faculty. At the turn of the twelfth century the foremost medical professor at Paris was undoubtedly Master Gilles de Corbeil.[277] Gilles came of a humble family in Corbeil not far up the Seine from Paris, studied medicine at Salerno and Montpellier, and returned to Paris a strong partisan of the techniques of Salerno, with a corresponding antipathy for the theories of Montpellier. Exactly when he appeared in Paris is not clear,[278] but he was already flourishing as a medical master by 1193, when the poet-historian Gilles of Paris took notice of him in his *Carolinus*.[279] His writings dealing with uroscopy, pulse measurement, pharmacy, diagnosis, and symptomatology according to the Salerno doctrines became standard medical texts by the first decade of the thirteenth century.[280] Later tradition founded on veiled allusions in his writings saw him the personal physician to King Philip Augustus and a canon of Notre-Dame.[281] Gilles de Corbeil was dead by 1224, when the chronicler William the Breton mentioned his work.[282]

Between 1219 and 1223,[283] perhaps while canon at Notre-Dame, Gilles de Corbeil wrote a long poem entitled *Hierapigra ad purgandos prelatos*.[284] Since *hierapigra* was a popular laxative (composed mainly of aloes and known since ancient times), the title of Gilles' poem could be accurately rendered as "pills to purge prelates."[285] It consisted of satirical verse which exposed and chastised numerous foibles of the contemporary prelacy. For example, Gilles protested against the papal legate Galon's immoderate enforcement of clerical celibacy at Paris[286] and rebuked the bishops' complacency in the marriage of Philip Augustus and Agnès of Méran,[287] both favorite themes of Peter the Chanter. Not only was Gilles contemporary with Peter at Paris, but his *Hierapigra* turns out to contain verse renditions of the *Verbum abbreviatum*.[288] The Chanter's work provided an excellent model for satirizing the clergy, and by using it Gilles de Corbeil stands within the circle of the Chanter's influence.

Most of Gerald of Wales' active life lies beyond the scope of this study.[289] Descended from distinguished Norman and Welsh lineage, he was a familiar of the prelates and royalty of his day. In the service of the king and church he travelled widely in Ireland, Wales, England, and on the Continent, often making Rome his final destination. As a young man he was appointed Archdeacon to the Welsh see of Saint David's, whose affairs occupied much of his subsequent career. Although inordinately ambitious, he never succeeded in advancing beyond this position. According to his own account he was offered at various times several bishoprics both in Ireland and in Wales, but his heart was always faithful to his own see. A candidate for the bishopric of Saint David's on at least two occasions, he was never elected, and the later part of his life was wearied by four frustrating journeys to Rome in which he pleaded his own case and the cause of the metropolitan dignity of Saint-David's. In his voluminous writings Gerald was seldom reticent but not always accurate about his doings.[290] According to one account he was in Paris at three different times for the sake of learning.[291] In the fall of 1165 he was residing there as a young student of the liberal arts when the future King Philip Augustus was born.[292] Later, from 1176 to the summer of 1179, he studied law and theology at the French capital and there was acclaimed for a particular lecture on canon law.[293] Finally, he relates in another work that in addition to his Parisian studies in arts and theology, the latter for three years, he spent another five years in further theological study.[294] By this statement it cannot be determined whether he meant the third but unspecified sojourn at Paris or whether, as is more probable, he referred to his theological studies at Lincoln after 1194, under Master William *de Montibus*.[295]

Although Gerald characteristically tells less about his Parisian teachers than about his own academic achievements, he does mention certain theological opinions of Peter Comestor, Maurice of Sully, and Peter the Chanter.[296] In particular he acknowledges that he heard Peter Comestor voice a bold stand on the question of clerical celibacy in the presence of his entire school.[297] Furthermore, Gerald studied theology in Paris certainly between 1176 and 1179, and perhaps afterwards, at a time when Maurice of Sully's teaching was terminated, when Peter Comestor (d. ca. 1179) was at least at the end of his career, perhaps even dead, but when Peter the Chanter was emerging as a leading theologian at Paris. The relationship between Gerald of Wales and Peter the Chanter, however, is even closer. Some time before 1199, probably while Gerald was studying theology at Lincoln, he composed a work entitled the *Gemma ecclesiastica*, designed to instruct the Welsh clergy in the sacraments and clerical morality.[298] When he arrived in Rome in 1199 to defend his claims to the see of Saint David's, he presented a copy to Pope Innocent III.[299] The Pope, Gerald proudly relates, kept it in his chamber and would not be separated from it. Compiled from numerous sources, as the author admits in his preface,[300] the book is a treasure of practical instruction and entertaining anecdote. What Gerald does not explain is that much of the material of the book, about one-eighth of the text according to one count, is directly excerpted from the short version of the *Verbum abbreviatum*.[301] Obviously Gerald had a copy of the *Verbum* close at hand when he composed this treatise. The *Gemma ecclesiastica*, then, possessed many ties with the Parisian milieu of Peter the Chanter. Gerald himself studied there at least twice before writing it. If the work was composed at Lincoln, it was while Gerald was a student of William *de Montibus,* who in turn was trained at Paris. And the book won the praise of Pope Innocent III, himself a product of the theological schools of Paris, as will be seen.*

THE SPECULATIVE THEOLOGIANS

Few of the theologians actively teaching in Paris at the turn of the twelfth century shared Peter the Chanter's concern for practical morality. More interested in speculative and abstract issues, most masters rarely participated in discussions relevant to the Chanter and his circle. For this reason these speculative theologians may be placed at the far perimeter of the Chanter's milieu. In his entry for the year 1194 the chronicler Otto of Saint-Blaise noticed that Peter, Chanter of Paris, Alain, and Prepositinus flourished as masters.[302] In effect, these three represented three schools dominating the Parisian theological scene at the turn of the century. Alain of Lille, Simon of Tournai, and Master Martin were followers of Gilbert de la Porrée, and generally known as *Porretani*.[303] (When treating more speculative questions, the Chanter himself was often influenced by this school.) Prepositinus, with Peter of Poitiers, Peter of Capua, and sometimes Stephen Langton generally represented the followers of Peter the Lombard, who dominated the cathedral school of Notre-Dame.[304] Beyond them were other theological masters such as Michael of Meaux and Peter of Corbeil, whose writings are slight or have been lost, so that it is difficult to assess their theological position.

Although it is known that Master Alain originated from the city of Lille, taught theology at Paris for some time, moved south to the vicinity of Montpellier, and died in 1203 as a Cistercian monk at the Abbey of Cîteaux, the chronology of these major stages of his career is not clear.[305] After his death Alain was revered as the *Doctor Universalis* of the church because of the broad range of his writings, which include philosophical poetry, speculative theology, polemical writings, and pastoral theology. Peter the Chanter seems to have borrowed from Alain's speculative treatises produced in the 1170's when, in all likelihood, Alain was a master at Paris,[306] but his more practical works such as the penitential[307] and the manual for preachers[308] are only occasionally relevant to matters which concerned the Chanter.[309]

Master Simon of Tournai taught theology at Paris during the last third

* See below, p. 343.

of the twelfth century, supported by a prebend from the cathedral of his native city.[310] His writings reveal him to have had a blunt, self-assertive personality, a characteristic which was reflected in his subsequent reputation. At the end of the twelfth and throughout the thirteenth century stories circulated which attributed to him arrogance, blasphemy, and the possession of a concubine.[311] It is likely that Simon was afflicted with a stroke because three stories report that he suffered loss of speech and memory. His death may be placed about 1201.[312] His major theological writings include a collection of disputations[313] and a *Summa*.[314] Although part of his *Summa* is very close to the *Sentences* of Peter of Poitiers,[315] by and large Simon of Tournai was most closely associated with the *Porretani*.[316] Primarily interested in speculative questions, he made increased use of Aristotle's writings.[317]

Closely connected with the work of Simon of Tournai is the *Summa* of Master Martin, about whom nothing more is known than can be found in the pages of this work.[318] This *Summa* consists of a large collection of theological *questiones* based not only on Simon of Tournai,[319] but also on Peter of Poitiers,[320] a certain Master Udo, Odo of Ourscamp, and various canonists. Despite these diverse sources, Martin most often adopted the position of the *Porretani*. From the sources it appears as if the *Summa* was composed after about 1195.[321]

Master Peter of Poitiers studied theology under Peter the Lombard, before the latter became Bishop of Paris in 1159.[322] Peter of Poitiers began to teach by 1167, acceded to the theological chair left vacant by Peter Comestor in 1169, was made chancellor of Notre-Dame in 1193, and died 3 September 1205. As cathedral Chancellor, responsible for the records of the church, Peter's name figures prominently in the charters of Paris during the last decade of his life.[323] An important dignitary, his anniversary was recorded in the major churches of Paris,[324] and his theological reputation attracted the notice of chroniclers.[325] His major theological work, the *Sententiarum libri quinque*, was composed early in his career (1168-1170). Although it followed the inspiration of the Lombard, it was not merely a commentary to the Lombard's own *Sentences,* but rather a treatment of open questions which could be resolved by dialectics.[326] As a follower of the Lombard's school, Peter avoided practical matters and questions pertinent to the canonists. Although Peter of Poitiers was a close colleague of the Chanter in the chapter of Notre-Dame (on at least one occasion they served together as papal judge delegates[327]), there is little interchange between their writings.

Peter of Poitiers was succeeded by Prepositinus as Chancellor of Notre-Dame.[328] Like Peter the Lombard, his forerunner and source of inspiration, Prepositinus originated from Lombardy but pursued his studies at Paris. Although there is virtually no information about his early career, it is possible that he was a student of the Lombard himself.[329] He achieved the degree of master by 1185[330] and was teaching theology in Paris by 1193.[331] In 1194 he appeared as *écolâtre* of the cathedral schools of Mainz, endowed with a rich prebend, and was involved in a schism of the see for which he was reprimanded by Pope Innocent III. In 1206 he became Chancellor of Notre-Dame at Paris and like his theological colleagues was busy both as a judge delegate and as a preacher in the Parisian churches.[332] He died on 25 February as attested by two obituary notices, probably in the year 1210, since his last act as chancellor occurred in 1209.[333] His academic writings include a *Summa contra hereticos*,[334] two collections of *distinctiones*[335] similar to those of Peter the Chanter and Peter of Poitiers, and a large *Summa* of theological questions, probably composed between 1190 and 1194.[336] Although Prepositinus occasionally followed Simon of Tournai, his chief source was his countryman, Peter the Lombard, whom he cited frequently throughout his *Summa*.[337] Prepositinus' opinions were noted in the various versions of the Chanter's *Summa*[338] and by other members of the Chanter's circle such as Peter of Poitiers of Saint-Victor[339] and Thomas of Chobham.[340] Stephen Langton drew directly on parts of Prepositinus' work,[341] but these connections involved speculative theology only.

Also within the orbit of the Lombard, Peter of Poitiers, and Prepositinus, was Master Peter of Capua, who wrote a *Summa* of theological questions in 1201/1202 dedicated to Walter, Archbishop of Palermo.[342] This Master Peter should not be confused with another Master Peter Capuano, cardinal deacon and papal legate for France at the turn of the century, who was a nephew of the theologian.[343] Master Peter the theologian was teaching at Paris in 1218 when Pope Honorius III wrote to him concerning the inception of another master.[344]

Great confusion exists over the family origins and early life of a certain Master Michael, who may be called Michael of Meaux.[345] All that can be regarded as certain about his family is that he was the uncle of Adam of Courlandon, who later succeeded him as Dean of Laon.[346] According to the contemporary chronicler Rigord, Michael taught in the schools of Paris[347] before he embarked upon an ecclesiastical career of successive deanships,[348] first of the chapter of Meaux (ca. 1169-ca. 1185),[349] of Laon (ca. 1185-1191),[350] and finally of Paris (1191-1194).[351] In 1194 he received word that he had been chosen Patriarch of Jerusalem, but two weeks later he was elected Archbishop of Sens, where he remained until his death in 1199.[352] Again according to Rigord, he was distinguished by the generosity of his alms.[353] Throughout his career Michael was in frequent contact with Peter the Chanter. As Dean of Meaux before 1185 he was chosen as an arbitrator with Peter,[354] and as Dean of Paris, he and Peter were the two ranking dignitaries of the chapter.[355] When he was

Archbishop of Sens, he was designated as co-judge with the Chanter over the divorce of the king in April 1196.[356] While Michael was Dean of Meaux he compiled a collection of *distinctiones* based on the Psalms.[357] The authenticity of this work is assured because a manuscript originally owned by his nephew, Adam of Courlandon, attributes it to him.[358] Partly based on the treatises of Richard of Saint-Victor,[359] these *distinctiones* belong to the genre of literature produced by Peter the Chanter, Peter of Poitiers, and Prepositinus.[360] Since it chiefly consists of enumerating the figurative interpretations of the Psalms, the work has little practical or ethical content.

Similar confusion reigns over the family origins of Michael's successor to the archbishopric of Sens, Master Peter of Corbeil.[361] Although there is little doubt that Master Peter came from Corbeil, it is most likely that he belonged to a family of low extraction.[362] To contemporary chroniclers he was renowned as a theological master, particularly because he was the teacher of the future Pope Innocent III.[363] In 1198 and 1199 when Master Peter of Corbeil appeared in the charters and papal letters he was designated as canon of Notre-Dame of Paris.[364] After Innocent became pope in 1198 he openly acknowledged his debt to his former teacher at Paris. In 1198 Archbishop Geoffrey of York designated the archdeacon's prebend for Peter. When the dean and chapter resisted this appointment, Pope Innocent promptly took measures to support Peter's candidacy.[365] Less than a year later Master Peter was elected Bishop of Cambrai, but he had barely obtained this dignity when opportunity for higher preferment appeared with the death of Michael, Archbishop of Sens, in 1199. The chapter of the cathedral proceeded to elect Hugh of Noyers, Bishop of Auxerre, but Innocent immediately quashed the election because Hugh had supported Philip Augustus by refusing to publish the interdict against his divorce of Queen Ingeborg.[366] The Pope then promoted the candidacy of his friend and teacher Peter of Corbeil to the see of Sens in 1200, where he remained until his death in 1222. According to the chronicler Geoffrey of Courlon, King Philip, however, found the choice not unpleasing because the new archbishop was a loyal defender of royal causes at Rome and a jovial companion whose conversation the king especially relished.[367] Although Peter of Corbeil's theological opinions were cited by contemporary masters, including the Chanter and Stephen Langton,[368] none of his academic writings have been successfully identified.[369]

❧ CHAPTER III ❧

Theological Doctrine

AS PROFESSIONAL theologians Peter the Chanter and his colleagues naturally occupied themselves with the pertinent issues of their subject, such as the divine nature, the Trinity, Christ, man, sin, grace, redemption, and the sacraments.[1] Their preeminent business was to study and disseminate sacred doctrine. Active at the turn of the twelfth century, they stood midway in a French theological movement which began early in the twelfth century and culminated with the great scholastics of the mid-thirteenth century. The chief pioneers of this theological movement were Anselm of Laon, Peter Abelard, Gilbert de la Porrée, Peter the Lombard, and Hugh of Saint-Victor. The earliest were Anselm of Laon and his brother Ralph, whose school accomplished the prodigious task of collecting, sifting, and organizing the mass of Patristic opinion to render it serviceable for succeeding theologians. Although personally antagonistic to Anselm, Peter Abelard availed himself of these collections and applied to them the techniques of logic and grammar. Attempting to penetrate the divine mysteries with the tools of language and reason, Abelard provoked controversy within theological circles. Similarly, his contemporary Gilbert de la Porrée employed grammar and logic to solve theological problems, but arrived at rival solutions to Abelard's. Although not equal to the genius of these two predecessors, Peter the Lombard popularized many of their theories in his influential book of *Sentences*. Simultaneous to these efforts of theological speculation, Hugh of Saint-Victor established a school at the Abbey of Saint-Victor in Paris which approached theology through exegesis of the Bible.

In contrast to the first half of the century, no single theologian or handful of masters dominated the Parisian scene for its remainder. The study of theology was characterized rather by a small number of schools descended from the earlier masters and which carried on their traditions. These schools existed in no rigid or exclusive sense. In lectures, debates, and writings the masters exchanged ideas with each other, one master adopting the solution of one school to one problem and that of another to another. In the interaction of intellectual discussion they were constantly prone to accommodate, modify, and combine alternative solutions. To determine the existence of these schools with any precision one must compare the solutions of particular theologians to individual problems.[2] Despite these complexities modern historians have distinguished at least three main schools of doctrine surviving from the beginning of the century.[3] The traditions of Peter the Lombard were most prominently perpetuated by Peter of Poitiers, Prepositinus, and Peter of Capua. Although by the end of the century direct theological descendants of Peter Abelard cannot be identified with certainty, the major doctrines of Gilbert de la Porrée were represented by Alain of Lille, Simon of Tournai, Raoul Ardent, and Master Martin. To illustrate the complexity of the situation, Master Martin borrowed liberally from Peter of Poitiers of the Lombard school as well as from Simon of Tournai of Gilbert's tradition. Indeed, these *Porretani,* as they were known, were more influential at the turn of the century than was Gilbert in his own day. Finally, the Biblical approach of the school of Saint-Victor was perpetuated by Richard of Saint-Victor, Andrew of Saint-Victor, and Peter Comestor.

Although Peter the Chanter was not immune to the attractions and controversies of contemporary theologians, it is difficult to place him within the existing doctrinal schools.[4] Like all medieval theologians he relied on the standard textbooks of his day and the available arsenal of Scriptural, Patristic and Classical quotations.[5] When he lectured on the Scriptures, he employed the *Glossa ordinaria* and the *Magna glosatura* of Peter the Lombard, and followed the exegetes of the school of Saint-Victor.[6] In particular he drew extensively on the *Historia scholastica* of Peter Comestor and the commentaries of Andrew of Saint-Victor. When he turned to theological doctrine, he was prone to adopt the solutions of the *Porretani,*[7] particularly those of Alain of Lille.[8] When, however, Peter turned to his particular specialty, practical morality, his antecedents are not at all clear. It is true that he made extensive use of Gratian's *Decretum* and was familiar with the opinions of contemporary canonists to resolve ethical questions, but it is difficult to find predecessors who inspired his casuistic approach. In all likelihood Peter the Chanter was alone responsible for prompting discussion of practical ethics at Paris. Once his presence is acknowledged on the Parisian scene, the rest of his circle can be accounted for. His direct student, Robert of Courson, followed the Chanter closely throughout his *Summa.*[9] The penitential writers, such as Robert of Flamborough, Peter of Poitiers of Saint-Victor, and Thomas of Chobham, drew their inspiration directly from the Chanter's work.[10] Stephen Langton, however, exhibited more independence. In commenting on the Bible he worked within the Victorine framework, and often incorporated passages verbatim from the Chanter.[11] His theological *questiones* raised practical issues in common with the Chanter. Similarly, when discussing sacramental problems he followed Peter's solutions,[12] but when treating questions such as Christology, he frequently adopted the position of the Lombard school.[13] Geoffrey of Poitiers, in turn, borrowed heavily from both Langton and Robert of Courson.[14]

In their *questiones* and commentaries to the Pauline Epistles the theological masters approached doctrinal controversies according to individual inclination. The disputes over the nature of Christ, for example, attracted the more speculatively inclined, such as Peter of Poitiers, Simon of Tournai and Stephen Langton.[15] Peter the Chanter contributed only one *questio* to the discussion,[16] and through his commentary to Romans he earned the dubious distinction of espousing the unorthodox view of "Adoptianism."[17] Robert of Courson's extant writings take no notice of Christological problems, and such dogmatic subjects fell naturally beyond the boundaries of the penitential writers. Other questions, involving the doctrines of grace and redemption, the Chanter and Langton discussed in varying degrees.[18]

Robert of Courson opened his *Summa* by declaring that "All celestial philosophy consists of two things, good morals and faith,"[19] a formula obviously inspired by Peter the Chanter. The term "celestial philosophy" was frequently employed by Peter, and approximates to Bernard of Clairvaux's term, "Christian philosophy."[20] Perhaps it is ultimately derived from the apparition of Lady Philosophy in Boethius' *Consolation of Philosophy*.[21] The separation of theology into faith and morality was expressed by the Chanter throughout his works[22] and reflected a division which had been current at least since the time of Ivo, Bishop of Chartres, in the late eleventh century.[23] Elaborating upon this division in the *Distinctiones Abel*, the Chanter divided each part into two additional sections.[24] Theology consisted of a celestial part, which promised divine knowledge by treating the articles of faith and by combating heresy, and of a subcelestial part which instructed morality by distinguishing between virtues and vices. At the turn of the twelfth and thirteenth centuries most Parisian theologians were discussing the more abstract moral questions, such as the nature of original sin, the influence of sensual appetites, the definition and classification of virtues, and the role of intention in the moral act.[25] Again the theologians participated in these discussions in varying degrees: Stephen Langton and the speculative theologians with regularity, the Chanter on occasion, and Courson and the penitential writers only rarely. The great *forte* of the Chanter and those closest to him was not so much the abstract as the practical side of moral theology.

Of all areas of theology, Peter the Chanter and his circle made their most important contributions to the doctrine of the sacraments.[26] This special emphasis is indicated by the title of the Chanter's *Summa de sacramentis et animae consiliis*, which stood in a tradition reaching back to Hugh of Saint-Victor, a certain Master Simon, and Peter Comestor.[27]

Robert of Courson organized his *Summa* similarly around the principal sacraments,[28] and Stephen of Langton paid particular attention to the subject, often following the Chanter's lead.[29] The sacrament of penance, however, attracted the most attention from the Chanter and his followers. Discussing it at a greater length than all the others, Peter provided those who administered penance with "counsel for the soul" in the second part of his *Summa*.[30] Robert of Courson's preoccupation is illustrated by the fact that penance occupies well over half of his *Summa*.[31] The "Guides to Confessors" of Thomas of Chobham and Peter of Poitiers of Saint-Victor were simply instruction manuals for the priest to apply penance.

Private penance as practiced under Celtic influence by the western church since the early Middle Ages received little doctrinal systematization until the twelfth century. Not until the revival of canon law and theological study were the sacramental characteristics of penance formulated and its constituent elements discussed.[32] Penance was the divine remedy for cleansing sin committed subsequent to baptism. At the end of the twelfth century Peter the Chanter expressed the universal view of western theologians by distinguishing four elements in penance: infusion of grace, contrition of heart, confession of mouth, and satisfaction of deeds.[33] The first two were by nature interior; the last two, external in expression. One of the principal problems occupying the theologians from the beginning of the century was the relative importance of the interior and external elements. Peter Abelard formulated and Peter the Lombard popularized the prevailing view that interior contrition of the heart was the primary act of penance which prompted divine remission of sin.[34] Despite this primacy of contrition, the Lombard also maintained the utility of the external aspects, particularly of confession. Confession provoked shame in the sinner and enlisted the advice and aid of the church in rendering satisfaction. Peter the Chanter and his associates adopted, by and large, the Lombard's general propositions.[35] While Robert of Courson, for example, insisted that in extreme necessity contrition was sufficient to receive divine pardon, he nonetheless upheld the obligation of confession for all to whom the occasion was normally available.[36] Resulting from a century of discussion, the Lateran Council of 1215 imposed on all Christians the minimum requirement of one annual confession.[37]

Confession and satisfaction, the external acts of penance, required the regular participation of the priest, who heard the confession, advised means of satisfaction, and pronounced absolution from sin. To explain the priesthood's role in penance was in fact another major problem facing the theologians of the twelfth century. Closely connected with this problem was the theological doctrine of the keys, according to which Christ transmitted to Peter and subsequently to all priests the authority to "bind and loosen" sins on earth.[38] In what fashion were priests empowered to retain or remit sins? In general the theologians of the turn of the century followed Peter the Lombard, who proposed that the priestly authority of the keys consisted of three functions: (1) the declaration of divine remission of sins, (2) the imposition of penance or the form of satisfaction, and (3) the excommunication of recalcitrant sinners or reconciliation of the truly penitent.[39] The theologians discussed these functions at length and their relationships to the interior aspects of penance. For example, if God alone remits sin, in what sense does the priest cooperate with Him in declaring forgiveness of sin? To this and other questions of external penance the masters proposed varied answers.

Most theologians, however, agreed that the priest's principal function was to advise the sinner about satisfaction required to expiate his sin, chief among which was restitution.[40] During the twelfth century the Roman and canon lawyers, and theologians developed a comprehensive doctrine of restitution which was particularly applicable to penance.[41] As the Church Father Augustine had warned, and as was repeated by Gratian, Peter the Lombard, and the church councils,[42] whatever was gained through dishonest practices must be fully restored before remission of sin could be accorded. To advise about restitution, therefore, was one of the practical duties of the priest who imposed satisfaction on the penitent. The priest could declare that truly repentant sinners who expressed contrition by appropriate confession and satisfaction were reconciled with God and the church. If, however, the sinner refused to be contrite or to express contrition through confession and satisfaction, the priest was authorized to excommunicate him.[43] In general excommunication excluded the sinner from the sacraments, thereby denying him the normal means of salvation afforded by the church. This authority to reconcile and to excommunicate was an interpretation of the priestly keys originating from the Church Fathers. Following this view, the canon lawyers throughout the twelfth century understood the priestly keys primarily as the authority to excommunicate and reconcile. The theologians differed from the canonists by maintaining, as has been seen, that the power of the keys chiefly involved imposing penance and satisfaction. At the turn of the century, the theologians began to divide matters pertaining directly to God from those involving the church.[44] This twofold distinction was parallel to their fundamental division between interior and exterior penance. Peter the Chanter was one of the first to distinguish between penalties imposed by the priest in the name of God and those of an ecclesiastical judge for damages against the church.[45] Although the terminology was not clear by the opening years of the thirteenth century,[46] this distinction eventually resulted in the twofold *fora:* the internal *forum* in which the priest secretly heard confessions and administered penance, and the external *forum*, or the ecclesiastical court which openly heard, tried, and punished crimes. In practice the confessor's internal *forum* was the normal means for imposing penance, but the external *forum* handled notorious and serious crimes against the church.

Since most theologians at the turn of the century agreed that the imposing of penance constituted the chief "key" of the priesthood, they were thereby required to consider the qualifications necessary for a confessor. Pertinent to this problem was the Venerable Bede's opinion, collected by the school of Anselm of Laon, which enumerated two keys: the authority of bind and loosen, and the knowledge to discern.[47] Through his ordination, therefore, every priest received not only the power to administer penance but also knowledge to perform his duties intelligently. While few theologians disputed the first, the definition of the second key presented difficulties immediately apparent from practical experience. Many clerics before their ordination to the priesthood, and even laymen, possessed discerning knowledge, while many ordained priests were obviously deficient in wisdom and skill. Throughout the twelfth century, therefore, most theologians discussed the nature of the sacerdotal keys and how many there were.[48]

To these questions at least two major answers arose. Peter the Lombard declared the predominant opinion that knowledge was one of the sacerdotal keys, although he admitted that not all priests possessed this knowledge.[49] His followers Peter of Poitiers and Prepositinus argued that no priest was so incompetent as not to possess at least a minimum of knowledge.[50] In a similar manner Stephen Langton declared that the priest received at least a "little key" (*clavicula*) of necessary knowledge.[51] Opposing this viewpoint, Peter Abelard and his school denied that knowledge was essentially a sacerdotal key but declared it rather to be an aid to the key of binding and loosening.[52] By eliminating the key of knowledge they, in effect, reduced the priestly keys to one. Although Peter the Chanter occasionally spoke of two keys in the traditional sense, his treatment of the question accorded more nearly with Abelard's.[53] One *questio* produced by his school enumerated three answers without indicating a preference,[54] but another version, which more certainly was the Chanter's, cited the opinion of Master Robert Pullen, a follower of Abelard, who compared knowledge to the handle of a knife.[55] Just as the handle facilitates the use of the blade, so knowledge enables the safe use of the authority to bind and loosen. Peter concluded that knowledge was a key only in the sense of an obligation (*obnoxietas*) to exercise discernment in the process of binding and loosening. Correctly quoting his master's position, Robert of Courson proceeded to the logical conclusion by insisting that the priest received only one key.[56] Following Abelard, Peter the Chanter and Robert of Courson minimized the sacramental character of knowledge required by a priest to administer penance. Ordination did not impart to the priest a body of knowledge but the obligation to acquire it.[57] If such knowledge was not received sacramentally, it was imparted by learning. Not only arguing from common experience, the Chanter and Courson thereby justified their own writings, which provided practical instruction for the priest who had authority to bind and loosen in penance.

By the time of Pope Gregory the Great's *Book of Pastoral Care* the priestly functions of the confessor were commonly envisaged in medical terms.[58] Just as the physician's skills were devoted to curing the ailing body, so the priest's craft pertained to the health of the sinner's soul. In the *Verbum abbreviatum* Peter the Chanter pictured the confessor in the Biblical image (Luke 10 : 34) of the good Samaritan who applied oil and wine to the wounds of the traveller assaulted by brigands.[59] Describing the priestly functions in the confessional, Pope Innocent III employed the same Biblical imagery in the Lateran Council of 1215,[60] and the medical analogy became a standard expression in contemporary "Guides to Confessors."[61] According to the Chanter, however, the spiritual physician encountered serious difficulties in exercising his craft.[62] In particular, the ordinary priest was faced with a bewildering array of questions to be solved. In the *Summa de sacramentis* Peter admitted that certain questions involving marriage, usury, and simony stirred up such controversy among the most skilled theologians that even the lord pope was at a loss to supply answers.[63]

When Peter, therefore, prefaced the penitential section of his *Summa,* he declared that he would not pay as much attention to theoretical matters already solved in the Lombard's *Sentences* as to other questions heretofore untreated.[64] To be sure, Peter in fact entertained theoretical problems posed by the *Sentences*, but the significant novelty of his *Summa* was that it considered practical questions. Commenting on Psalm 107 : 23 ("They that go down to the sea in ships, that do business in great waters, these see the works of the Lord and his wonders in the deep") the Chanter likened his tasks to those of the sailor.[65] Just as the seaman engulfs himself in the raging sea, so the theological master descends into the confusion of life by debating doubtful questions and resolving specific cases. The discussion of specific cases for the guidance of the confessor was the Chanter's and Courson's important contribution to the medieval development of penance.[66] By concentrating on individual and concrete moral questions Peter and Robert inspired the literature of the "Guides to Confessors."[67] Both their general approach and many of their specific solutions were adopted by Robert of Flamborough, Thomas of Chobham, Peter of Poitiers of Saint-Victor, and other anonymous penitentialists.

Echoing his master, Thomas of Chobham declared his intention to omit the subtle and theoretical issues and to dwell on practical matters directly relevant to the priest administering penance in the confessional.[68]

To train priests for their duties in the confessional these penitential guides were closely related to another device, the synodical statutes.[69] The bishop's diocesan synod was an ancient institution for periodically regulating and instructing the local clergy. At Paris, where this practice was well established by the end of the twelfth century, Bishop Maurice of Sully was accustomed to exhort the assembled clergy with a synodical sermon especially designed for the occasion.[70] The bishop and his aides undoubtedly imparted to the synod more practical instruction which took the form of written synodical statutes in later times. The earliest complete set of these statutes appeared at Paris during the episcopate of Maurice's successor, Odo of Sully (1196-1208).[71] The two earliest for England appeared at Canterbury (1213-1214) under Archbishop Stephen Langton and at Salisbury (1217-1219) under Bishop Richard Poore.[72] Dealing with a broad range of clerical activities, these statutes placed special emphasis on liturgy and administering sacraments, among which certain instructions pertained to penance. Thomas of Chobham and Peter of Poitiers of Saint-Victor, who composed their guides after the first synodical statutes had appeared, often referred to them, particularly about sacramental matters.[73] Moreover, the synodical statutes acknowledged the work of the Chanter's circle by providing practical instructions to the confessor. Odo of Sully at Paris, followed by Richard Poore at Salisbury, urged confessors faced with doubtful questions to seek the advice of their bishop and certain wise men (*sapientes viros*) so that they might administer penance with greater confidence.[74] Undoubtedly they referred to the work performed by the Chanter's circle at Paris who devised solutions to these doubtful questions, later to be inserted in the guides to confessors.

Since the early Middle Ages priests administering penance had at their disposal aids known as "penitential canons," which assigned specific spiritual penalties for specific sins.[75] For example, one who committed intentional murder was enjoined penance for seven years, but if he accidentally killed another, his penalty was three years. Penitential canons covering the whole range of immoral conduct were compiled in long lists which served as penitential tariffs for those assigning penance. Such lists, however, presented the priest with several important disadvantages. Not only rigid, mechanical, and reflecting the severe conditions of the early Middle Ages, they often lacked uniformity so that collections differed over the penalties for the same crime. At the turn of the century the ecclesiastical authorities at Paris occasionally accepted these penitential canons. For example, among the list of books Maurice of Sully recommended for his diocesan priests was a collection of penitential canons,[76] and the synodical statutes of Odo of Sully encouraged the clergy to acquire such compilations along with their sacramental and liturgical handbooks.[77] Even Alain of Lille's and Robert of Flamborough's guides to confessors included lists of penitential canons with their other instructions.[78] Eventually, however, the writers of the new "Guides to Confessors" began to react against the defects to the older penitential canons. Peter of Poitiers of Saint-Victor likened the canons to the harsh medicine of a former day which the modern physician of the soul must temper with more flexible and humane remedies,[79] and criticized Robert of Flamborough for including them in his *Penitentiale*.[80] Although Thomas of Chobham referred in passing to the penitential canons, he declared that his treatise would elaborate the subject of penance more fully.[81] The guides of both Thomas and Peter, therefore, omitted the older penitential canons, because the modern physician of the soul could no longer be guided by the rigid and severe remedies of a former day, but must be free and flexible to apply subtle skills for curing the sinner. These skills were the primary subject of the new "Guides to Confessors."

As the Chanter's circle depreciated the older penitential canons in favor of the more subtle craft of the priest, they naturally focused attention on the factor of circumstances. Just as a physician must know the symptoms and conditions of an illness, so a confessor must investigate the circumstances of a particular sin in order to apply correct penitential medicine. For a priest to administer penance to an adulterer, to select a favorite contemporary example, he must know the time, place, and duration of the act, the age, conditions, knowledge, and motivation of the parties, and many other circumstances.[82] Throughout the twelfth and into the thirteenth centuries the Parisian theologians discussed the problem of circumstances from an abstract and a practical point of view.[83] As a problem of moral theology they considered whether circumstances affected the goodness or badness of a moral act, to which question the schools of Abelard, Gilbert de la Porrée, and Peter the Lombard formulated different solutions. Besides considering theoretical issues, certain theologians also considered how circumstances affect morality in a practical way. Influenced by the *Porretani*, who emphasized the concrete and variegated character of moral acts, Peter the Chanter was among those who assigned special importance to circumstances in evaluating the moral act.[84] In his *Verbum abbreviatum* he exhorted the confessor to take care lest he overlook any pertinent circumstance,[85] and in his *Summa* he considered a broad range of circumstances for resolving cases of conscience,[86] assigning their solutions to a "religious and prudent man" (*vir quidam religiosus et prudens*) who was the confessor for whom the Chanter wrote.[87] Although the Chanter, Courson, and the penitentialists made few contributions to the theoretical discussion, they provided the individual priest with a rich store of advice on how to judge specific human acts under a variety of conditions.[88] In the Lateran Council of 1215 Pope Innocent III confirmed their efforts when he urged the discreet priest to inquire diligently into the circumstances of the sinner and his sin.[89]

What were the specific circumstances to guide the confessor in imposing penance? While the more speculatively inclined Prepositinus and Stephen Langton ignored this problem,[90] the more practical-minded masters devised lists for classifying circumstances. Following Gratian's division of cause, person, place, time, quality, quantity, and effect, the canonists Rufinus and Huguccio attempted to group circumstances under several broad categories.[91] Peter the Chanter adopted the popular system of who, what, where, by what means, why, how, and when, which was formulated in hexameter verse in Cicero's *In rhetoricam*,[92] and Courson repeated eight questions closely resembling those in Aristotle's *Nichomachean Ethics*.[93] One of the most extensive and original classifications was provided by Raoul Ardent, who enumerated fourteen circumstances which aggravated an immoral act and thirteen conditions which pertained to the person of the sinner.[94] Although such classifications were especially useful to the writer for compiling a "guide,"[95] it was Thomas of Chobham who made fullest and most practical use of these lists.[96] In a long chapter he demonstrated how many of these categories could be applied directly to penance. Within these lists the masters occasionally employed terms which attributed a social dimension to the factor of circumstance. Although Gratian's category of "person" and the Chanter's and Courson's factor of "who" comprised but did not differentiate social distinctions, their followers began to express the social dimension more explicitly. For example, when Huguccio, Raoul Ardent, and Peter of Poitiers of Saint-Victor employed the term *ordo* (holy orders) they designated the secular clergy. By *religio* and *votum* (holy vows) Huguccio and Raoul identified the monastic clergy. Other categories served to distinguish social groups among the laity. For example, the term *conditio* of Raoul and Peter of Poitiers of Saint-Victor indicated the presence of personal freedom or servitude. Other categories such as *status, dignitas,* and *honor* of Huguccio, *gradus* of Raoul, and *status persone* of Peter of Poitiers of Saint-Victor implied social rank or prestige. Although Huguccio employed the term *officium* (occupation), Thomas of Chobham most fully applied this condition to the laity.[97] Considering the way of life of a lay penitent, Thomas advised the confessor to inquire carefully into his business, income, and craft. Was he engaged in trade, warfare, or farming? Was he parasitically supported as an actor? Did he practise the liberal arts as a grammarian, orator, or rhetorician, or the mechanical arts as a cobbler, pelterer, or carpenter? Since Thomas believed that an occupation was an important circumstance to be considered by the confessor in evaluating the penitent's sin, he made a detailed examination of the major occupations of his day, as will be seen.

The Parisian theologians became interested in occupations or vocations because of the practical requirements of penance. Their approach was similar to that of preachers who realized that their sermons would be more effective if they were directed towards specific social groups. Not only did preachers distinguish between the prelates, priests, monks, and nuns of the clergy, but from the early twelfth century they began to address vocational groups among the laity, such as merchants, knights, and farmers.[98] The first and obvious task of the masters who concerned themselves with penance was to designate those lay occupations whose exercise was patently sinful. Following the canons of the Lateran Council of 1179, Peter the Chanter recalled that manifest usurers, public prostitutes, champions in tournaments, and crossbowmen fell automatically under the ban of excommunication.[99] In addition he repeated the well-circulated opinion of Pope Gregory the Great that the professions of warfare and commerce could scarcely be conducted without sin.[100] Although Peter dealt with the pitfalls and moral problems involved in other occupations, it was his student Robert of Courson who called attention to them as a group.[101] Discussing the administration of penance, Robert designated surgeons, physicians, lawyers, procurers, mimes, courtiers, mongers, cooks, and merchants of dubious wares as morally hazardous vocations requiring special comment.[102] According to Peter and Robert if the priest was to deal effectively with sin, he must be well informed as to dubious lay occupations.

A layman practised his vocation primarily to sustain himself and his family. Since the Lord commanded Adam to eat bread in the sweat of his face (Gen. 3: 19) and the Apostle warned that if a man did not work neither should he eat (1 Thess. 3 : 10), the relationship between labor and vocations became a primary problem for the Parisian masters and suggested another approach to lay occupations. Although the obvious correspondence between labor and manual vocations such as farming, building, and crafts required no comment, what about those professions in which the factor of labor was not immediately apparent? Citing lawyers, physicians, and teachers, Peter the Chanter declared that their earnings must be commensurate with their labor.[103] Elsewhere he discussed those in other occupations such as notaries, judges, and merchants, paying particular attention to their contributions of labor.[104] Again, it was Robert of Courson who gathered the Chanter's scattered notions and coordinated them in a single book—that one of his *Summa* devoted to the "hiring of services." Maintaining that it was difficult to determine whether works could be legitimately hired or sold, especially when some professions seemed to perform no labor and yet demanded exorbitant remuneration,[105] Robert devoted discussion to lawyers, doctors, theologians, masters of arts, and notaries. After these comparatively respectable professions he turned to the more dubious occupations of entertainers, such as prostitutes, mimes, jongleurs, and actors, of manufacturers of doubtful wares, such as dice, chess, poisons, cosmetics, and weapons, of retail merchants, and of tailors who made luxury garments. He concluded with random discussion of masters, mercenary soldiers, notaries, and merchants, which finally served to introduce two subsequent books devoted to usury. By investigating the relations between labor and vocation Robert of Courson provided another detailed treatment of human occupations for eventual use in the confessional.

Since Peter's and Robert's vocational investigations were voluminous, their student and colleague Thomas of Chobham undertook the task of reducing their academic writings to a form serviceable to the ordinary priest. In a section of the *Summa confessorum* instructing the confessor how to receive the penitent, Thomas treated the penitent's occupation (*officium*). As a preliminary, the priest was to distinguish four classes of professions: those which were completely sinful, such as prostitutes and actors, those which could hardly be conducted without sin, such as merchants and mongers, those which were useless, such as the makers of floral wreathes, dice, and other games, and those necessary occupations which were seldom exercised faithfully, such as hirelings and teachers.[106] After this introduction Thomas enumerated eleven occupations, treating each at length.[107] They consisted of actors, champions in duels, hired agents, prostitutes, beggars, teachers, priests, merchants, clerics involved in business, judges, and manufacturers of superfluous articles. Although noting that each vocation was morally dangerous for particular reasons, Thomas was clear neither as to the basis of his selection, nor as to why he omitted other important professions such as the military, medical, and the legal, which also risked moral pitfalls. In his manual Thomas nonetheless made available to his fellow English priests the fruits of the moral teaching at Paris. This interest in occupations among the Parisian theologians found further echo in Jacques de Vitry. He not only addressed his *Sermones vulgares* to specific occupational groups, but when depicting the corruption of western Christendom in his *Historia occidentalis,* Jacques enumerated the professions of merchants, farmers, serfs, physicians, and lawyers and to them he attributed characteristic failings.[108]

Because of the practical demands of the confessional, the Parisian theologians discussed each occupation as a separate entity, making little effort to unify their ideas in coherent social theory. Since their chief task was to evaluate the concrete moral act, not to speculate about the nature of society, they produced little social theory which resembled the hierarchical systems of the scholastic theologians of the mid-thirteenth century under the influence of Aristotelian notions of justice. What their theories lacked in consistency and unity, was compensated by richness of detail. Although their particular views of society were fragmentary and unconnected, their writings provide a brilliant mosaic for the social life of their times.

PART
TWO

MASTERS

❧ CHAPTER IV ❧

Paris and its Schools

PARIS

BORN in the Beauvaisis and schooled at Reims, Peter the Chanter made his mark at Paris, where he was an ecclesiastical dignitary and a master. Except for a trip or two to Rome, an occasional return to Gerberoy, and his last journey along the road to Soissons, there is little evidence that he was absent from the city for any length of time. The Parisian basin within the valley of the Seine formed the geographical context of his mature life.

The Paris of Peter's day was the subject of contemporary letters, occasional verse, and histories composed either to celebrate the city's glories or to warn of its iniquities. In typical medieval fashion, it rarely occurred to their writers to provide a physical description of the city. One important exception, however, is provided by Gui of Bazoches, the well-born, urbane canon and chanter of Châlons. Just as Gui could provide his mother with a charming account of his house overlooking the Marne, so he addressed a letter to a friend describing Paris in lyrical terms.[1] Composed early in the reign of Philip Augustus, and therefore contemporary to the Chanter, his picture is justly well known. In exuberant language he depicted a royal city surrounded by a crown of hills and lying in the lap of a luscious valley which provided it with the delights of Ceres and Bacchus. The lordly river Seine flowing from the east thrust its two arms around an island which formed the heart and marrow of the city. Two suburbs extended from the right and left banks, the meaner of which would have excited the envy of many a city. Two stone bridges connected the island with its suburbs and were designated by their size. The Grand-Pont faced north towards the English Channel, and its opposite, the Petit-Pont, indicated the way towards the Loire. In Gui's view these two banks and the island represented three aspects, the commerce, the schools, and the royalty, for which Paris was renowned.

Since this jubilant recital of Gui of Bazoches fails to offer a complete picture of the Paris of his day, archaeology must supply the details.[2] As Gui indicated, the Grand-Pont led to the commercial quarter of Paris on the Right Bank. The bridge itself, later designated as the Pont-au-Change, was covered with stalls and boutiques of goldsmiths, silversmiths, and especially money changers. Two major markets were situated on this side of the river, one called Champeaux near the cemetery of the Saints-Innocents, the other centered on the Place de Grève. Between and surrounding them were business districts whose streets bore the names of crafts and trades. In the vicinity of Saint-Gervais was the Temple, the Parisian branch of the order of the Templars who by the late twelfth century had become international bankers. Except for the market of Champeaux all of the business and financial area was enclosed and protected by a wall which encircled the Right Bank to the north. This side of the river also contained churches such as the parish church of Saint-Merry located just within the walls, and outside were the Cluniac priory of Saint-Martin-des-Champs and a monastery crowning the butte of Montmartre. In the distance to the north was the royal abbey of Saint-Denis recently rebuilt in the new Gothic style. On the other side of the island the Petit-Pont opened towards the Left Bank dominated by three imposing collegiate churches or abbeys. To the east lay the conglomeration of buildings of the Abbey of Saint-Victor set apart by meadows and vineyards. Leading southerly from the Petit-Pont a road mounted a summit to the Abbey of Sainte-Geneviève. To the west rose the stone tower of the Abbey of Saint-Germain-des-Prés, likewise set apart by meadows and fields. The churches of Saint-Victor and Sainte-Geneviève boasted of flourishing schools within their cloisters, and in the second half of the twelfth century masters and students were increasingly attracted to the Left Bank. As Gui of Bazoches pointed out, some masters even held classes in houses on the Petit-Pont. Yet in contrast to the island and the Right Bank this side of the river still offered a rural aspect, with cultivated vineyards and spacious meadows and fields close at hand.

The island in the Seine known as the Ile-de-la-Cité was the oldest section of Paris and, in the words of Gui of Bazoches, its nucleus. Small and elongated, its two extremities provided two main points of interest. At its western end was situated the royal palace, one of the preferred residences of the Capetian rulers of France, which Gui described as rising head and shoulders above the city.[3] At the eastern end of the Cité and balancing this display of royal authority was the cathedral of the bishop of Paris. Surprisingly enough, in his exuberance Gui neglected to mention the presence of Notre-Dame, which at the time of his writing was being rebuilt in the new Gothic style. From its foundation in 1163 the new Notre-Dame was designed to dominate the Cité and all of Paris by its grandeur and magnificence, but evidently in Gui's day construction had not progressed sufficiently to make a strong impression. Between the new church and the royal palace was the most densely populated quarter of Paris, burgeoning with houses, narrow passages, numerous churches, and even a synagogue.

This sketch suggested by Gui of Bazoches essentially depicts the Paris of King Louis VII when Peter the Chanter first arrived in the late 1160's —or the early 1170's. During the reign of King Philip Augustus (1180-1223) radical transformations took place in the Capetian capital. Although the first stone of Notre-Dame was laid in 1163, almost two decades before the accession of King Philip, the major phases of the cathedral were not achieved until his reign.[4] In 1182 the choir was finished and the high altar was consecrated by a papal legate. By 1196 the nave was completed except for the roof, and four years later work was begun on the west facade, which was not terminated until 1220. The rose window and the great western towers did not appear until the opening decades of the reign of Louis IX. In the twelfth century the realization of Notre-Dame of Paris was primarily the dream of one man, Maurice of Sully, Bishop of Paris.[5] From his election in 1160 to his death in 1196 Maurice was consumed by a single-minded passion for his church. To the south of Notre-Dame and along the Seine, the energetic bishop also rebuilt a spacious episcopal palace with a chapel, a tower, and a connecting gallery.[6]

The construction program of Maurice of Sully was rivaled by that of Philip Augustus. In 1183 the king favored the commercial population of Paris by building the Halles on the site of the market of Champeaux, which consisted of two large sheds surrounded by a wall to protect the merchants' wares from weather and thievery.[7] Conduits brought water down from the springs of Belleville and Prés-Saint-Gervais to supply fountains around the Halles. In 1185, according to the historian Rigord, when the foul smell of unpaved roads became intolerable even in the royal palace, the king took the decision with the bourgeoisie of Paris to pave at least the principal streets and squares of the city.[8] Of all the king's works, however, none was as influential for the development of Paris as the encirclement of the city with walls. On the eve of his departure for the crusade in 1190 Philip commanded the Parisian burghers to enclose the Right Bank with walls strengthened with towers and pierced with gates.[9] Completed within the next decade, these fortifications inscribed a wider circumference than the former wall and included the newly constructed Halles. At the western juncture of the wall with the Seine Philip raised a fortified tower, later known as the Louvre. In 1200 the king continued the fortifications around the Left Bank to enclose the Abbey of Sainte-Geneviève though not the more distant Abbeys of Saint-Victor and Saint-Germain-des-Prés.[10] By 1210 King Philip Augustus had transformed Paris into a walled city comprising a vigorous community of merchants, a growing university of scholars, an imposing cathedral, and the seat of royal administration. While Philip was remaking Paris he was engaged in the more important tasks of driving the English from the continent, greatly increasing the size of the royal domain, and significantly improving royal administration. In effect Paris was rapidly becoming a capital worthy of the Capetians' political achievements.

Unlike the letter of Gui of Bazoches the academic treatises of the Parisian masters were not intended to describe Paris to strangers unfamiliar with the city. As products of teaching these writings were addressed to student audiences who took their surroundings for granted. It is true that when the masters discussed ecclesiastical problems involving exchange of prebends or conflicts of parochial jurisdiction they often referred to specific Parisian examples which were well-known to their listeners.[11] Similarly, the masters were tempted to employ familiar landmarks to illustrate their lessons. For example, in discussing the Biblical episode (Gen. 19 : 17) of Lot's flight to the mountain to escape the destruction of Sodom, Stephen Langton added: "Make yourself a canon in Mont-Saint-Geneviève so that you will be saved," and Master Martin was one among innumerable masters who used the Seine as a concrete example to discuss logical and theological questions.[12] In this way the Paris milieu may be obliquely detected in their writings.

Of all the contemporary theologians at Paris Peter the Chanter appears to have been the most sensitive to his physical surroundings. The major transformations of Paris impressed him deeply and elicited from him sharp reactions. Although he had no intention of commenting on these changes as an observer or a historian, they nonetheless unconsciously conditioned the background of problems which occupied his immediate attention. Without doubt the construction of the new cathedral and episcopal palace was the foremost fact of his physical environment. Chanter of Notre-Dame since at least 1184, he was the second ranking dignitary of the cathedral chapter which shared the new church with the bishop. Since it was the chapter's duty to offer Bishop Maurice their advice and support in this project, Peter undoubtedly attended sessions of the chapter on innumerable occasions to consider plans, execution, and, most important, financing. As Chanter of the cathedral, Peter's official functions were to supervise the services of the choir and to maintain the liturgy of the church, duties which were not made easier by the shouts of the workmen and the hammers of the stonemasons. Since the noise and confusion of the newly emerging Notre-Dame constituted the everyday life of Peter the Chanter, close attention should be paid to passages in his writings which contain sharp protests against what he called "the curiosity and superfluity of building."

The criticism of superfluous building was nothing new. The ancient moralists attacked the Roman passion for grandiose buildings and this Classical moralistic theme was transmitted to the Middle Ages by the Church Father Jerome.[13] Early in the twelfth century the mighty Bernard, Abbot of Clairvaux, whose voice the Chanter's circle heard attentively, thundered against the magnificent edifices of his monastic rivals, the Cluniacs.[14] As a monk speaking to monks he objected to the immense height of Cluny, its immoderate depth, its overly spacious breadth, and its sumptuous ornamentation, which contradicted true monastic humility. The richness of such structures excited the vain admiration of the people, and by inviting their increased donations, defeated true monastic poverty. In a rhetorical burst Bernard exclaimed, "Thus the church clothes its stones in gold but lets its children run naked." Some of the abbot's criticisms of contemporary art and architecture involved aesthetic considerations and were influential in the development of the new Gothic style, but most of his protests proceeded from moral grounds. He nonetheless confined his strongest attacks to monasteries and conceded that bishops and the secular clergy might usefully employ artistic means for instructing the laity. Towards the middle of the century (ca. 1153) Hugh of Fouilloi, a regular canon of Saint Augustine, wrote in a similar spirit.[15] Directing his protests against the richness of episcopal palaces and the battlements of monasteries, he recommended simplicity and moderation for the houses of his own order. At the end of the century expense and ostentation in general and the rage for adding towers to religious edifices in particular drew the criticism of Alexander Neckham, an English cleric and contemporary of the Chanter.[16] Peter the Chanter, neither monk nor regular canon, but like Neckham a member of the secular clergy, assembled similar arguments against the builders of his day.

The problem of extravagant building must have occupied the Chanter for some time. Perhaps he was first provoked at Reims, where Archbishop Sanson had recently remodelled the choir and facade of his cathedral and furnished it with new towers.[17] Numerous references to this theme occur throughout his Biblical commentaries in the form of terse comments or marginal notations to pertinent Scriptural passages.[18] Like scattered lightning and distant rumblings of thunder these doubts occurred to the master while he lectured on the Scripture. The full force of Peter's storm of protest broke in a chapter of the *Verbum abbreviatum* where he assembled not only his lecture material but also a miscellany of other examples and arguments.[19] In wild disarray he cited examples of ancient simplicity ranging from the Old Testament patriarchs who walked with God but lived in tents, to the Gospel account of the Saviour "who had not where to lay His head . . . ."[20] To these Peter added anecdotes of ascetics who disdained glorious abodes, drawn from the lives of the Desert Fathers, the writings of Jerome, and the more recent champion of monastic austerity, Bernard of Clairvaux.[21] In his battle against luxurious edifices the Chanter even enlisted Classical verses from Juvenal, Ovid, Lucan, Vergil, and Horace.

Within the confusion of this rhetorical storm certain objects of Peter's

attack may be discerned. Occasionally he mentioned the palaces and fortifications of princes which were built from the plundering of the poor,[22]
but it is quite clear that his principal targets were churches. Like Bernard
of Clairvaux and Hugh of Fouilloi he protested the transformation of
monastic dormitories, refectories, even barns (*grangie*), into edifices
resembling palaces and castles rather than the habitation of humble
monks.[23] Peter the Chanter outstripped Bernard, however, to press his
attack against the great churches (*maiores ecclesie*) of the secular clergy.[24]
Although he did not specify names, there can be little doubt as to his
final quarry when the circumstances of his life are considered. Less than
a decade after the choir of Notre-Dame had been completed and its principal altar consecrated, Peter wrote that "just as Christ who is the Head
of the body of the church was humble and lowly, so should the apses
(*capita*) of our churches be lower than the edifices."[25] As constructed by
Bishop Maurice of Sully, the apse of Notre-Dame rose a record 105 feet
from the floor when Laon and Sens, its nearest competitors, attained
only 79 feet. Moreover, at a time when Maurice was occupied with his
episcopal palace with accompanying tower, Peter devised a conversation in which a holy prelate prodded a building prelate with these jibes:
"Why do you want your houses so tall? What is the use of your towers
and ramparts? Do you believe that the devil cannot scale them? Nay,
I say that thereby you will become the neighbor and companion of
demons."[26] It requires little imagination to picture Bishop Maurice red-
dening as he scanned these words of the Chanter.[27]

Certain lines of argument may be disentangled from the disarray of
citations which Peter employed against the excesses of church building in
general and of Notre-Dame in particular. Ignoring the aesthetic judgments of Bernard of Clairvaux, he drew upon ascetic and moral criticism.
Like most medieval moralists Peter stressed the standard ascetic themes
of the brevity of life, the vanity of earthly works, and the dangers of
avarice.[28] Decrying with Alexander Neckham the great height of buildings because of their association with ostentatious pride, he took care to
single out the towers, turrets, and castle-like appearance of churches.[29]
Most likely he had in mind the fortress elements of earlier Romanesque
churches, since his comments were less appropriate to Notre-Dame, whose
western towers were not begun until long after the Chanter's death. More
important, however, he agreed with Bernard of Clairvaux that the rage
for building sumptuous churches distracted churchmen from the true
goals of religion. With the great abbot he noted the decline of spiritual
righteousness and the diversion of money destined for the poor.[30]
Finally, in the Chanter's opinion these churches were often constructed
from ill-gotten sources.[31] Through the chicanery of hireling preachers,
money derived from usury and plunder was contributed to these proj-

ects. Because of unsound moral foundations they were in danger of collapse. It will be seen that on these matters the reputation of Maurice of Sully was none too clear, and that in later years Peter the Chanter's stand was contrasted with that of the bishop over accepting donations from usurers for the construction of Notre-Dame.* Both the Chanter and his student Robert of Courson carefully considered the problem of churchmen who accepted contributions from usurers and other dubious sources.[32] The scruples of the Parisian theologians may have had effect on later practice. After enjoining the restitution of ill-gotten gains, the synodical constitutions of William, Bishop of Paris, in the first decade of the thirteenth century, turned to donations for the construction of Notre-Dame.[33] In somewhat ambiguous terms priests were instructed to warn their parishioners about gifts and bequests, to make diligent inquiry into them, and to record faithfully the names of the donors. Although the avowed purpose was to distinguish the generous from the negligent, such practices could also serve to discourage acceptance of alms from ill-gotten gains.

From all appearances Peter the Chanter made little effort to appreciate the great work of Maurice of Sully, yet history provided a strange sequel to the relationship between the Chanter and the new church. In June 1190, on the eve of his departure for the crusade, King Philip Augustus was busy making arrangements for the kingdom during his absence. Among these he decreed that in event of a vacancy of the see of Paris the responsibility for the construction of Notre-Dame should be assigned to Hervé, Dean of the chapter, and to Peter, Chanter of the cathedral, under the general supervision of William, Archbishop of Reims.[34] Undoubtedly Peter was chosen with the dean because of his rank in the chapter. In making this choice the king protested his great love for Notre-Dame and mentioned the eminent suitability of the two men, but Bishop Maurice might well have questioned the soundness of the king's judgment in regard to the Chanter. Fortunately for the future of Notre-Dame Maurice was still alive when the king returned in 1192.

The construction of Notre-Dame bore an indirect consequence for the ecclesiastical life of the Ile-de-la-Cité during the second half of the twelfth century.[35] This densely inhabited island contained many small churches and chapels, some of which assumed parochial functions by the middle of the century. The episcopal cathedral remained nonetheless the major parish church for the Cité and performed the essential services of baptism and burial. When Bishop Maurice of Sully, however, began work on his new edifice, its functions were undoubtedly curtailed by the inconveniences of construction. He undertook, therefore, to reorganize the parish structure of the island on the basis of the existing churches and chapels.

* See below, pp. 135, 136, and 309.

By 1182 he had divided the tiny island into fourteen parishes, some of which consisted of no more than a handful of houses on the single side of a street. When one reads in the *Verbum abbreviatum* a vigorous protest against the proliferation of churches in a certain city, he may strongly suspect that Peter the Chanter had found another item of contention with his bishop. In a chapter entitled "Against the multiplication of churches and altars" Peter contrasted the Scriptural example of Israel which possessed only one tabernacle and later one temple for an entire nation with the modern tendency to "raise altars against altars."[36] In principle each town should possess a single church. Peter conceded that churches should be combined or divided according to the distribution of population, but in populous cities only a few churches should be permitted and always under the jurisdiction of the major church. Although he did not specify contemporary cases, the Chanter evidently judged the parochial reorganization of Maurice of Sully to exceed the limits of reason.

By discouraging the erection of new altars and chapels within established parish limits, Peter hoped to reduce the litigation over ecclesiastical jurisdictions which consumed so much of the clergy's time. In a later chapter of the *Verbum abbreviatum* he devoted attention to the general problem of ecclesiastical exemption.[37] From the early Middle Ages numerous churches, particularly monasteries, obtained from the episcopacy and papacy special privileges which rendered them immune to the normal ecclesiastical authority of the bishop.[38] As a member of the secular clergy the Chanter vigorously disputed these special monastic privileges, citing among many authorities the more recent opinions of Bernard, Abbot of Clairvaux, and Master Gilbert, Bishop of Poitiers. Two conspicuous examples of monastic exemption lay close at hand in the abbeys of Saint-Denis and Saint-Germain-des-Prés, which enjoyed freedom from episcopal supervision before the twelfth century.[39] Why, Peter contested, should they be immune from the authority of their mother church when they have not been able to escape even the jurisdiction of the king?[40] He recalled an anecdote about Suger, Abbot of Saint-Denis, who not only rebuilt his monastery but also secured its high position in the political and ecclesiastical world of the twelfth century.[41] While the abbot was on his deathbed, so Peter's account went, he called Thibaut, Bishop of Paris (1143-1157), to his side and confessed his obedience to the bishop. Repenting of the special privileges of his church, Suger asserted that it was the devil himself who had obtained the exemption from episcopal authority. The Chanter's story, which was also repeated by Gerald of Wales,[42] need not be taken as history, but it represents the point of view of the clergy of the cathedral church. Supporting the episcopal position on exemptions, Peter the Chanter would have approved of the efforts of the bishops of Paris in the early thirteenth century to reduce the privileges of

Saint-Germain-des-Prés and other churches in and around Paris.[43] In 1215 the Lateran Council attempted to restrain monastic incursions on episcopal rights by forbidding certain privileges usurped by monasteries.[44]

The reconstruction of Notre-Dame, the division of the Cité into parishes, and the exemption of monasteries constituted local events of special interest to the clergy. The royal project of encircling Paris with walls, however, was everyone's concern, but the writings of the Chanter also afford a momentary glimpse of this transformation.[45] Discussing the problems of restitution, Peter enumerated in his *Summa de sacramentis* three cases in which the poor suffer loss for the sake of the general welfare of the group. For example, on board ship in a storm at sea the goods of the poor might be jettisoned first to protect the more precious cargo of others, or in a widespread conflagration of a city, the houses of the poor might be razed in order to contain the path of the blaze. Similarly, the dwellings of the poor might be torn down to make place for a wall erected by public necessity. In all three cases, Peter decided, divine law required that those who benefited from the sacrifices of others should contribute to their indemnification.[46] Again, Peter did not indicate any particular city when he debated this academic *questio*, but its relevance to Paris could scarcely have been missed by students when the great fortifications were in progress.

His solution, moreover, seems to have been precisely the one practiced by the Capetians before and after this question was debated. The kings of France were reputed to be willing to respect the rights of those damaged by royal building projects. Writing in England about the same period, Walter Map, for example, tells of King Louis VII tearing down walls, buildings, and other improvements at Fontainebleau which he had unwittingly constructed on the lands of a peasant.[47] More sober testimony of this royal benevolence comes from the year 1186 in a charter of King Philip Augustus, who recompensed a certain butcher for the loss of his stalls at Etampes when the king built new ones.[48] But testimony even exists that the Capetians applied this principle to the construction of their walls at Paris. After the fortifications were completed, the chronicler William the Breton marvelled not so much at their extent and strength, which were matched in other towns, but at the royal sense of equity in constructing them.[49] While written law allowed the construction of walls and moats on the lands of others for public utility, King Philip preferred equity to law and compensated from his own treasury those who suffered loss. The chronicler's account could be exaggerated, but perhaps it contained an element of truth. In 1210 the King gave to the Bishop of Paris a rent on a certain house in exchange for that which the bishop lost on houses near the church of Saint-Thomas-du-Louvre, which were included in the walls of the new fortifications.[50] There is therefore good reason for believing that the Chanter's solution for restoring damages caused by the construction of city walls accorded with the general practice of the Capetians.

THE SCHOOLS

To Gui of Bazoches, Alexander Neckham, and other observers, Paris was preeminently a city of studies.[51] During the course of the twelfth century the Parisian schools gradually surpassed those of Laon, Reims, Orléans, Chartres, and other towns to place the royal city by the end of the century at the fore of learning in northern Europe. Undoubtedly the royal presence on the Ile and the commercial activities on the Right Bank contributed to attracting masters and students, but in the minds of contemporaries it was the fame of teachers such as William of Champeaux, Peter Abelard, Gilbert de la Porrée, Hugh of Saint-Victor, and Peter the Lombard who constituted the preeminence of Paris. At first the schools were located at the cathedral and the Left Bank abbeys of Saint-Victor and Sainte-Geneviève, but soon these cloisters were not sufficient to contain the stream of scholars drawn to Paris. By mid-century masters and students crowded into the Ile-de-la-Cité, eventually penetrated the houses of the narrow Petit-Pont and from thence on to the Left Bank. Although medieval population figures are highly debatable and educational statistics are pure conjecture, modern demographers estimate that the academic community comprised at least ten percent of Paris' total population, which ranged between 25,000 and 50,000 during the reign of Philip Augustus.[52]

Paris' educational leadership was sufficiently acknowledged by the second half of the twelfth century that the masters began to look for a tradition which accounted for its origins and hallowed its existence. From the beginning the church possessed an undisputed doctrine of divine foundation and perpetuation through Apostolic succession. In an effort to compete with these claims of the church, the German empire devised a rival tradition of *translatio imperii*, which envisaged the transmission of imperial authority from the Roman emperors to the German kings. Consciously imitating this latter theory, the scholars of France fashioned their own tradition of *translatio studii*.[53] Expressed in a variety of forms, their theory goes back at least to the Carolingian epoch. In the most comprehensive version learning was envisaged as a divine gift to the Jews which was successively transmitted to the Egyptians, Greeks, and Romans. According to different accounts, it was carried from Rome to France either by Dionysius the Areopagite, who was identified with Saint Denis, the patron saint of France, or by Alcuin, the preceptor of Charlemagne, and was presently flourishing at Paris. Well established by the end of the twelfth century, the tradition of *translatio studii* was restated by Alexander Neckham in considerable detail to explain the seven liberal arts.[54] In his version the patriarch Abraham taught the four liberal arts or the quadrivium in Egypt, whence Plato later brought them to Greece, where, in turn, they were cultivated by Socrates, Plato, Aristotle, Zeno and others. Later Romans such as Cicero, Seneca, Lucan, and Vergil made Italy as renowned for its studies as for its arms. In his own day Alexander celebrated Salerno and Montpellier for medicine, Italy for civil law, but to Paris belonged the honors in sacred scripture and the liberal arts. The Biblical commentaries of Peter the Chanter contain another faint but unmistakable echo of this tradition.[55] Discussing the prophet Isaiah's lament over the succession of the Assyrian and Chaldean empires, Peter was reminded of the succession of letters from the Greeks at Athens to the Latins at Rome and now to the French of Paris. In this passing comment Peter the Chanter obliquely acknowledged the theory of *translatio studii* which endowed the scholar's work with tradition.

In contrast to Italy and the south, academic status in northwest Europe was closely associated with the church.[56] With rare exceptions most Parisian students and masters were members of the clergy. Their place in the church ranged widely from the holy orders of priests, deacons, and subdeacons, to whom vows of celibacy were obligatory, down through the minor orders of acolytes, readers, and porters, to whom marriage was permitted, finally to the simple cleric distinguished only by his tonsure. By this liturgical sign of shaving the crown of the head students and masters were numbered among the clergy and subject to ecclesiastical jurisdiction. Similarly their economic support was derived from their clerical status and varied from the rich prebends of a canon of a collegiate church to the total poverty of a simple cleric, who had only the right to beg alms from men of good will. Teachers were generally called "masters" (*magistri*) or doctors (*doctores*) and students, "scholars" (*scolares*) or "disciples" (*discipuli*), but often the more comprehensive term "clerics" (*clerici*) indiscriminately designated the academic profession. Yet this imprecise terminology required further refinement by the end of the twelfth century. For example, in discussing the clerical order, Peter the Chanter found it necessary to distinguish between ecclesiastical and scholastic clerics.[57] Since the Parisian schools originated in the churches of the Cité and the Left Bank, students and masters were thereafter subject to ecclesiastical authority. Although membership in the clergy implied certain restrictions, it also provided the academic classes with important and tangible privileges. Clerical status affected the essential conditions of academic life such as curriculum, the economic maintenance, and discipline, as will be seen.

Clerical predominance characterized the schools of northwest Europe in general and those of Paris in particular. Since elsewhere, in southern

France and Italy, laymen were more numerous among the academic population, students were in need of more protection than in the northern areas where they benefited from clerical privileges. Particularly at Bologna, towards the end of the twelfth century, students attempted to secure rights essential to their profession by forming corporations or universities organized according to the pattern of the medieval guilds. At Paris, however, where students already enjoyed substantial rights from their clerical status no such "student universities" emerged.[58] Students either entered the school of a particular church or more commonly associated themselves with a particular master. By and large their status depended upon a relationship with an authorized teacher. Described in terms of a guild, they were the apprentices of the masters. Stephen Langton offers a succinct picture of the position of the Parisian student in one of his commentaries.[59] Discussing the Gospel account of Christ calling His disciples, Stephen distinguishes three levels of discipleship, those of knowledge, of familiarity, and of full discipleship or apostleship, an analysis which reflects the experience of clerics newly arriving at Paris. First they seek a master whose school they wish to attend and hear his lessons for a time or two. If they are pleased, they enter his "family," and finally by being assigned a place in his school, they become the master's disciples. About twenty years later, when Robert of Courson promulgated the first university statutes, it was decreed that no one should be considered a student at Paris who did not possess a specified master.[60] In Paris the nucleus of the university was not the student, but the master.

Since teaching was the masters' essential function, he who received the right to teach (*licentia docendi*) could assume the title of master or doctor.[61] In northwest Europe the granting of licenses to teach had become an ecclesiastical monopoly by the twelfth century. In general a specific church granted licenses to the extent of its parochial territory. This educational jurisdiction was supervised by an ecclesiastical official whose role varied with individual churches. Licenses were granted by bishops, abbots, archdeacons, chancellors, and often by an officer known as the *écolâtre* (*scholasticus, magister scholarum*), whose principal function was to oversee the church schools. In Paris during the first half of the twelfth century, for example, the teaching license was issued by the cathedral chancellor for the Ile-de-la-Cité and by the Abbot of Sainte-Geneviève for the Left Bank. At the turn of the century only the chancellor of Notre-Dame appears to perform this function, although it cannot be necessarily assumed that the Abbot of Sainte-Geneviève had relinquished his rights on his side of the river.[62] The whole system was approved by Pope Alexander III (1159-1181), who, desiring to curb abuses, confirmed to the chancellor, *écolâtre*, or other official control over the license and the final responsibility of judging the fitness of candidates.[63]

Although statistics are not available, there is reason to presume that the licensing of masters accelerated at Paris during the second half of the twelfth century. Evidence of teachers' associations can be detected by the beginning of the next century.[64] Although masters possessed privileges by reason of their ecclesiastical status, as a profession distinct from other clerics they had other common interests and goals. To promote these ends they began to organize themselves into corporations or universities after the pattern of medieval guilds. Unlike Bologna, the university of Paris consisted of societies not of students but of masters. There is evidence that during the first decade and a half of the thirteenth century the Paris masters assumed the essential functions of a corporate body by asserting a common purpose, electing officers, enforcing statutes, and commissioning procurators to represent them in law.[65]

Of the greatest importance to their corporate existence was the masters' right to determine their membership through the admission procedure known as inception (*inceptio*). After judging the qualifications of a candidate, the masters "incepted" him into their society by a ceremony in which the candidate delivered an inaugural lecture or performed an inaugural disputation. The two earliest extant inaugural lectures were pronounced by Stephen Langton and Thomas of Chobham when they were incepted into the faculty of theology at Paris.[66] In accordance with guild principles the master was admitted into the society of his craft by the actual performance of his duties. Since this control over admission directly contested the educational jurisdiction of the chancellor of Notre-Dame, a struggle resulted. By 1213 Pope Innocent III secured a compromise through the mediation of the bishop, dean, and archdeacon of Troyes.[67] Although the chancellor was free to grant licenses to teach any one of the subjects, he was forbidden to refuse a license to any candidate supported by a majority of masters teaching either theology, canon law, Roman law, or medicine. As to the license in arts, he could not refuse anyone who was presented by a majority of a committee of six masters of arts composed of three members nominated by the masters and three chosen by the chancellor. It is not clear whether the corporation of masters was free to refuse to incept anyone licensed by the chancellor, but it could compel the chancellor to accept its own candidates. By this step the university secured a precious right towards the control of membership. When in August 1215 Robert of Courson returned as papal legate to Paris, he announced to his former colleagues that he carried a special mandate to reform the academic regime.[68] The regulations which he promulgated constituted statutes for the newly emerging university of Paris. Although many of the provisions merely confirmed previously existing practices, they nonetheless provide a first glimpse of the overall organization of the masters of Paris. Among his numerous regulations

Robert reconfirmed the settlement of 1213 between the university and the chancellor which strengthened the masters' control over admission to their corporation.

The Parisian masters have left no evidence of corporate organization before the year 1200, but the silence of the documents does not preclude the probability of previous developments already in progress for some time.[69] Peter the Chanter and his circle were exact contemporaries with this corporate emergence of the university of Paris. Peter himself, it is true, had been dead since 1197, but Stephen Langton did not leave Paris until 1206, and Robert of Courson did not become papal legate until 1212 and later, in 1215, played an active role in the formation of the university. Lecturing in Paris during the crucial decade, these theologians had little to say about the rights and organization of masters who taught in their day. They were concerned with the license to teach but limited their discussion to the practice of charging fees.[70] As to the formation of masters' societies at Paris their silence is complete. Apparently finding nothing with which to take exception, they had no occasion to mention these academic affairs.

When the Parisian theologians turned to the general functions of the teaching profession, they were content to utter moral exhortations. Peter the Chanter, for example, remonstrated against the pride of teachers, their unworthiness, and manifold forms of culpable silence.[71] Of all the Chanter's circle, Thomas of Chobham offered fullest treatment of the general duties of the master.[72] Writing his *Summa confessorum* in England, however, he had in mind not the Parisian professor in particular but all teachers of boys in general. His discussion best fits the *écolâtre* and the subordinate masters of the local church school who were responsible for the rudiments of education. The profession of teaching, Thomas maintained, contains dangers, because masters are responsible not only for the boys' intellectual but also for their moral formation. Since teachers accept wages from the parents, they are worse than robbers if through neglect their pupils are deficient in knowledge and good conduct. Because of poor instruction, students are often insufficiently trained to make an honorable living, and since they know no other profession, they succumb to thievery and other misdeeds. Thomas therefore exhorted all teachers to perform their duties faithfully since they will be accountable to God for their students' sins and ignorance.

According to Gui of Bazoches and Alexander Neckham four general subjects, liberal arts, medicine, law (both Roman and canon), and theology were taught at Paris towards the end of the twelfth century.[73] Gerald of Wales, who was seldom reticent about his own experiences, claimed that he had studied all of these subjects except medicine during two periods of residence in the city.[74] Writing to the Paris masters in

1208-1209, Pope Innocent III distinguished between professors of arts, of canon law and of theology.[75] In the settlement of August 1213 between the chancellor of Notre-Dame and the university, those who taught theology (*theologia*), canon law (*decreta*), Roman law (*leges*), medicine (*phisica*), and arts (*artes*) were permitted to act separately in judging the qualifications of their candidates.[76] At the turn of the twelfth and thirteenth centuries, therefore, some curricular organization appeared within the masters' corporation at Paris. During the succeeding century the university was divided among the lower faculty of arts and the three higher faculties of medicine, law, and theology,[77] each of which possessed a list of textbooks prescribing its basic subject matter. Alexander Neckham compiled a catalogue of these textbooks early in the thirteenth century which probably reflects his studies at Paris in the late twelfth century.[78] In this list are cited the basic texts for the seven liberal arts, medicine, canon law, Roman law, and theology.

With theology as their profession Peter the Chanter and his colleagues naturally have more to say about this discipline than about any other of the four faculties. Moreover, as theologians intensely concerned with moral problems, they also shared interests with the canon lawyers. Their discussions often consisted of dialogues and debates with the canonists which accepted, modified, or rejected the conclusions of their legal colleagues. Although the liberal arts were regarded as necessary preparation for theology, the theologians felt little need to discuss them in detail, since these basic studies were widely known. Finally, as might be expected, the technical knowledge of medicine was of least concern to the theological masters.[79] Although the Chanter and his circle felt no need to discuss the arts and medicine at length, they nonetheless offered observations which illuminate the teaching of these subjects at Paris, as well as law and theology.

THE LIBERAL ARTS

From the early Middle Ages the liberal arts numbered seven and were divided into the *trivium*, consisting of grammar, rhetoric and logic, and the *quadrivium*, composed of arithmetic, geometry, astronomy, and music.[80] Elementary education began in one form or another with the liberal arts. The numerous schools of cathedrals and other churches provided arts training throughout northwestern Europe which amounted to little more than the rudiments of Latin grammar, but specialized and advanced study in the liberal arts was offered in Paris during the twelfth century. By mid-century the schools of the cathedral, Mont-Sainte-Geneviève, and Saint-Victor and numerous masters on the Cité and Left Bank began to draw students to Paris from all parts of western Europe to study the arts in general and logic in particular. Several accounts surviving from the last quarter of the century offer a general view of the arts at Paris. Sometime after 1176, Godefroy, canon of Saint-Victor and closely associated with the abbey school, composed a verse description of the *trivium*.[81] Similarly, Alexander Neckham included a florid account of the seven liberal arts in his long poem *De laudibus divinae sapientiae*,[82] but most important, he compiled a catalogue of the basic arts textbooks used in Paris at the turn of the twelfth and thirteenth centuries.[83] Grammar was taught from the manuals of Donatus and Priscian and from a wide selection of Classical authors such as Cicero, Ovid, Seneca, Juvenal, and others. Logic was founded on the logical writings of Aristotle, known as the *Organon*, and supplemented by treatises of Porphyry, Boethius, and Cicero. Works of Cicero and Quintilian served as texts for rhetoric, and each subject of the *quadrivium* possessed its standard authorities.

The liberal arts curriculum was the channel by which medieval students were exposed to the literary and intellectual legacy of pagan Antiquity. For example, in the study of grammar they read Vergil and Ovid, and the study of logic introduced them to the dialectic techniques of Aristotle. Grappling with the dangers of pagan learning to the faith and theology of the Christian believer, the Fathers of the early church formulated the conditions under which a Christian could avail himself of the knowledge of pagan Antiquity. From Origen to Augustine the doctors of the Greek and Latin church employed two principal Scriptural images for expressing the relation between pagan letters and Christian faith. As the Jews had despoiled the Egyptians of gold, silver, and raiment on the eve of their exodus to the promised land (Exod. 12 : 35, 36), so Christians were permitted to utilize some of the treasures of pagan wisdom.[84] But, to change the image, human pagan letters being always inferior to divine knowledge they were always to serve theology as handmaidens. Like the captive Canaanite women of the Scriptures (Deut. 21 : 10-13) they could be shaved and cleansed of their filth to be made fit for serving the children of God.[85] Since these justifications for Classical letters had become commonplace by the twelfth century, the Parisian masters referred to them only in passing. Peter the Chanter, like many others before and after, cited the despoiling of the Egyptians and pointed out that even the Apostle Paul had used quotations of the pagan poets Menander and Aratus.[86]

If pagan knowledge could be tolerated in subordination to theology, it followed that the liberal arts, the vehicle of profane culture, could be justified on the same grounds. In a section of the *Decretum* where ancient ecclesiastical authorities were marshalled for and against the question whether ordained clerics should become learned in secular letters, Gratian concluded that this learning was valuable for the understanding of Scripture.[87] Rufinus and Huguccio, who commented on this section, applied Gratian's solution to clerics studying the liberal arts.[88] As long as clerics pursued these disciplines for instruction and not merely for self-satisfaction, they were not to be prohibited. Like the canonists, the Parisian theologians followed the Church Fathers in justifying the study of the liberal arts. As professors in the higher faculty of theology they naturally envisaged the liberal arts as handmaidens to their own discipline.[89] Because this principle was well founded in Patristic opinion, they did not elaborate it, but Peter the Chanter and Stephen Langton referred to it occasionally in their Scriptural lectures. For example, discussing the phrase "the acknowledging of the truth" (Tit. 1 : 1), Peter contrasted the truth of faith with another truth, found in the liberal arts and which does not pertain to the Christian religion.[90] Although the arts do not concern the substance of Scripture, they nonetheless pertain to externals whereby Scripture may be better understood and more subtly investigated. They are therefore the footmen (*pedisece*) of theology.

Stephen interpreted the verse, "they shall beat their swords into plowshares" (Micah 4 : 3), to an end similar to Peter's.[91] The swords are subtle dialectic, rhetoric, and the *quadrivium*, which were converted by the Apostle Paul, Dionysius, Augustine, and others to the rude plows of theology fit for cultivating the fields of the conscience and for producing a harvest of good works. Treating elsewhere the Apostle's statement, "bringing into captivity every thought to the obedience of Christ" (II Cor. 10 : 5), Stephen naturally recalled the Old Testament example of the captured Canaanite women and its appropriate application to the liberal arts.[92] The Israelite represents the theologian and the captive women are the teachers of other faculties. If the theologian, therefore, perceives a comely opinion among the other disciplines, he may adopt it provided that he first shaves off the superfluities and pares away the excess subtleties. By cleansing what is impure and reexpressing in his own words what is valuable, the theologian may finally possess the "captive" wisdom of secular arts. If, however, the theologian neglects to shave his captive but rather nourishes it, the handmaiden becomes the unlawful mistress of theology. A sermon of Jacques de Vitry addressed to students illustrates the currency of these themes by the beginning of the thirteenth century.[93] Here the preacher employed at elaborate length both the images outlined above to demonstrate how each one of the liberal arts contributes to theology. Service to divine knowledge was, then, the fundamental justification for the secular arts.[94]

Since lecturing and disputing provided the masters of theology with little opportunity to demonstrate familiarity with the Classical authors acquired from the liberal arts, Classical quotations and allusions appear rarely in their Scriptural commentaries, theological *questiones*, and guides to confessors. The Chanter's *Verbum abbreviatum* and Gerald of Wales' *Gemma ecclesiastica*, which were composed for a wider audience, however, constitute an important exception. In the *Verbum abbreviatum*, for example, over three-fifths of the chapters contain identifiable quotations and allusions from Classical literature.[95] Many chapters consist simply of large extracts from Classical authors intermingled with Biblical and Patristic passages and more recent *exempla*.[96] Since Seneca's *Epistulae morales* served the theme of the *Verbum abbreviatum* most appropriately, this author was preferred by Peter the Chanter above all other ancient writers.[97] The *Ars amatoria, De remedio amoris,* and *Metamorphoses* of Ovid ranked second, and Horace, Juvenal, Lucan, Vergil, and a few others were drawn upon less frequently.[98] Peter's citations of Seneca and Cicero indicate that he probably did not rely on prepared collections of Classical quotations (*florilegia*) but consulted the works directly.[99] For example, he was unique among his Parisian contemporaries to be familiar with the second part of the collection of Seneca's letters.[100] The Chanter's *Verbum abbreviatum* clearly illustrates how a training in the liberal arts provided a theologian of the late twelfth century with a knowledge of Classical authors to serve as handmaidens to moral theology.

The increased attention devoted to the arts at Paris during the twelfth century was accompanied by a change in the character of liberal studies. Stressing the study of grammar and Classical letters as well as the more scientific subjects of the *quadrivium*, the earlier masters had cultivated the arts both as humanists and as scientists. Later interest, however, was concentrated on logic to the relative neglect of the other arts.[101] Emphasis on logic appeared early in the twelfth century with Abelard and Gilbert de la Porrée, who were first renowned as logicians and later applied their dialectical principles to theology. At this time the study of logic was largely based on the *Categoriae* and *De interpretatione* of Aristotle and the *Isagoge* of Porphyry, all of which were later designated as the *logica vetus*.[102] According to the testimony of Otto of Freising and John of Salisbury, the remainder of Aristotle's logical texts, comprising the *Topica,* the *Analytica priora et posteriora,* and the *De sophisticis elenchis,* became available at Paris by mid-century and were subsequently known as the *logica nova*. The completed canon of Aristotle's logical writings inspired the Parisian masters of arts to renewed study of dialectics throughout the remainder of the century. When in August 1215 Robert of Courson arrived at Paris to reform the university, this preoccupation with logic was well established in the faculty of arts. Among his statutes the basic texts were fully prescribed for the arts curriculum.[103] The regular lectures (*ordinarie*) were limited to logic based on the *Organon*, and to grammar based on both parts of Priscian, but no mention was made of Classical literature either in prose or poetry. Rhetoric, which was to be taught from the *Barbarismus* of Donatus and the *Topics*, the *quadrivium*, whose texts were not mentioned, and philosophy, which was based on Aristotle's *Ethics*, were excluded from the regular sessions and reserved for special classes on feast days. As established by the statutes of Robert of Courson, the main diet of the thirteenth-century arts student consisted of logic and technical grammar seasoned only occasionally with the other arts and philosophy. Furthermore, Courson decreed that no one was allowed to lecture at Paris as a master of arts before he had completed six years of study and was twenty-one years of age. Both his moral and intellectual qualifications were to be judged by the chancellor of Notre-Dame and the masters of the university according to the procedures of the agreement of 1213. After admission to the rank of master of arts, the candidate promised to offer lectures for at least two years, unless he was prevented by reasonable cause.

The rage for logical studies at Paris during the second half of the twelfth century provoked criticism not only from the theologians, as will be seen,* but even from certain masters of arts. Representing the older humanistic attitudes which emphasized Classical literature, these masters recognized the utility of logic, but deplored its emphasis to the exclusion of other liberal disciplines. Although John of Salisbury wrote his *Metalogicon* in 1159 in defense of logic, he severely attacked a group of dialecticians called Cornificians who attempted to apply their skills to all subjects with little foundation in Classical literature.[104] Shortly after, Peter of Blois, writing from Paris, objected to students plunging directly into logic without adequate preparation in the humane letters.[105] During the last quarter of the century Stephen of Tournai complained to the pope of abusive practices in the schools of Paris, among which he noted that the liberal arts had lost their literary character in the hands of immature artists.[106] Also in this humanist vein of criticism, Gerald of Wales reported the opinion of Master Ralph of Beauvais of a previous generation who divided students into three categories: the ragged scholars who wear their learning only for appearance' sake, the superficial scholars who skip from the elementary Donatus and Cato to the study of human and divine law, neglecting the literature of the poets and authors, and finally the true scholars who were solidly grounded in literature and arts and only gradually advanced to logic.[107] Similarly, in his *inceptio* Thomas of Chobham decried those who investigated natural questions before they mastered the fundamentals of the arts.[108]

The masters who criticized the abuse of logic from the humanist point of view found a case in point in the so-called "logical subtleties" (*sophismata logicalia*), a series of school exercises in which the logicians practised their dialectical rules.[109] By the mid-thirteenth century arts students

* See below, pp. 97ff.

were required to spend two years in classroom disputations of *sophis-mata*.[110] Manuscripts originating from the second half of the twelfth century contain lists and illustrations of the problem entertained in these academic exercises, most of which were of a frivolous nature so that the student could more readily perceive the fallacies and apply the logical principles. To take one example, students would be asked to investigate the following proposition: "What you have not lost, you possess. You have not lost horns; therefore, you must have horns."[111] The art of dealing with such sophistic propositions was founded on Aristotle's *De sophisticis elenchis* which John of Salisbury claimed was useful for expos-ing dialectical pitfalls.[112] According to John, if the student sought after truth and not mere verbosity, he could profitably learn from these exercises.

Since it was apparent that the dialecticians might take their sophistic games too seriously, the *sophismata logicalia* drew widespread criticism. Rufinus and Huguccio, while maintaining that dialectics were legitimate, charged that logical sophistry was reprehensible,[113] and Stephen of Tour-nai entered a protest against the *sophismata* practised at Paris in his letter to the pope.[114] Recounting a number of logical exercises discussed at Paris, Alexander Neckham maintained that their effects were often harmful.[115] The Chanter's circle added their voices to these criticisms at the turn of the century. Although Peter approved in principle of the study of logic as preparation for theology, he was against dialectical sophistry. In a chapter of the *Verbum abbreviatum* devoted to decrying foolish and use-less questions in theology he singled out the horn argument for special ridicule.[116] After one has entertained such a logical proposition, he de-clared, he is not so foolish as to touch his forehead to see whether the horns have grown. As a corrective Peter reemphasized Seneca's formula that philosophy should deal not with words but with realities (*res*).[117] In a similar mood, Gerald of Wales, remembering his early days in Paris as an overly enthusiastic student of logic, spread himself entertainingly in nar-rating the frivolities of the dialecticians.[118] His account, which bor-rowed much from Peter the Chanter, recounted the well-known story of the young student fresh from his Paris studies who tried to prove to his father that six eggs could be dialectically multiplied to twelve eggs and who for his breakfast had to be content with the six inferential eggs. To Gerald these dialectical subtleties were spider webs, spun from the en-trails of logicians, which strained for mere gnats.[119] Jacques de Vitry ac-cused the logicians of practising similar *sophistice subtilitates* in his de-scription of Paris prior to the arrival of Foulques de Neuilly.[120] In his sermon to the students of Paris Jacques told the vivid story of a certain Master Sella who taught logic at Paris.[121] One day while promenading in the meadow of Saint-Germain the master was confronted by the apparition of a deceased disciple who was wearing a parchment cloak containing all of the *sophismata* and *curiosites* the master had taught and weighing more than the stone tower of Saint-Germain-de-Prés. The master perceived the point of the vision and immediately renounced his frivolous studies to become a monk. In the Chanter's circle it was felt that the logicians' excesses were open to criticism in and of themselves, but it will be seen that they were subject to more severe criticism when dialectics were applied to theology.*

Medicine and Law

Instruction offered at Paris at the turn of the twelfth and thirteenth centuries included medicine and law. Since these subjects never attained the same importance as the liberal arts and theology, evidence of their instruction is meagre and indirect. Two men, however, who were linked with the Chanter's circle taught these disciplines at Paris. The earliest instruction of medicine in the royal capital, it will be remembered, was associated with the name of Master Gilles de Corbeil.† Passing his formative years at the medical center of Salerno, Gilles became thoroughly indoctrinated with the theories of that school. On his return to France he spent some unhappy days at the rival school of Montpellier before he arrived in Paris by 1193 or earlier. Gilles composed verse treatises on uroscopy, pulse measurement, pharmacy, diagnosis, and symptomatology, in which he expounded faithfully the doctrines of Salerno. In several of his works he intimated that he was the first to teach medicine in the royal city. Although not enough is known about medical instruction in Paris during the second half of the twelfth century to evaluate this claim, it is fairly certain that he provided a new impetus to medical studies there. During the first decade of the thirteenth century commentaries were written to his treatises which indicate that along with the Salerno texts they were regarded as authoritative.[122] The first full and extant records of the curriculum of the faculty of medicine date from 1270, but it is clear from these that the verses of Gilles were still the standard texts of medical instruction at that time.[123]

One of the earliest accounts of legal instruction at Paris originates from the autobiography of Gerald of Wales.[124] As a boy Gerald studied the liberal arts in Paris around the year 1165. From the end of 1176 to the summer of 1179 he was again in the city, as he put it, "to erect the walls of Roman and canon law from the foundations of art and letters" before crowning his learning with the roof of theology.[125] Gerald retained glowing memories of those days in Paris. Apparently his legal training was sufficiently advanced to qualify him to deliver Sunday lectures on the decretals which were so well attended that his hall could scarcely contain

* See below, pp. 97ff.   † See above, p. 41.

the audience. Gerald felt that one lecture was particularly noteworthy and recorded its preamble and subject: whether a judge should found his decision on the allegations of witnesses or on his conscience.[126] Although he does not reveal his resolution of the question, modesty did not prevent him from relating the acclaim with which the lecture was received. Master Roger the Norman, later Dean of Rouen, who had studied law at Bologna but then taught arts at Paris, publicly praised Gerald's legal learning,[127] and Hervé of Montmorency, canon, and later Dean of Paris, marveled that Gerald had acquired such expertise not at the renowned schools of Bologna, but during a short three years of study in Paris.[128] Gerald's own teacher Master Matthew of Angers likewise agreed with this praise. When as Cardinal he was called to the Lateran Council of 1179 by Pope Alexander III, he entrusted his teaching to his prize disciple. Thereafter Gerald offered in his own hostel two daily lectures on Gratian's *Decretum*, one on distinctions, the other on causes. Despite Gerald's obvious immodesty his narrative nonetheless indicates that the teaching of canon law was well established in Paris by 1177. Although the names of many masters are not known, numerous anonymous commentaries to the *Decretum* originating from Paris present indisputable evidence of a flourishing school of canon law at the turn of the twelfth and thirteenth centuries.[129]

Despite these masters of medicine and law, Paris' chief fame lay in the arts and theology. When Alexander Neckham traced the succession of learning from ancient times, he celebrated Paris for the study of the liberal arts and the divine Scriptures. When he considered medicine, it was Salerno and Montpellier that came to mind, and for Roman law he thought of Italy.[130] The statutes of Robert of Courson in 1215 confirm Alexander's judgment. Devoted exclusively to the masters of arts and theology, they make no mention of a curriculum for medicine or law. By the turn of the century the concentration of arts, medicine, and law, in different centers became proverbial.[131] For the arts and theology one studied in Paris, for medicine, Salerno or Montpellier, and for law, Bologna. Since these subjects were of secondary importance at Paris, Peter the Chanter and his circle paid comparatively little attention to their instruction.

Because the liberal arts provided essential preparation for theology, the theologians condescended to view the masters of arts as ancillary to their discipline. Since the professors of the higher faculties of medicine and law provided direct competition for students, however, the theologians were disposed to regard them more critically. The practical use of theology was, for the most part, limited to teaching and preaching, while medicine and law were obviously more suitable for practice. In the Middle Ages as in modern times medical experts often combined the teaching and practicing of their craft. Similarly, it was difficult to distinguish between lawyers who taught and studied their subject matter and those who pleaded in the courts. Occasionally canonists such as Huguccio and theologians such as Robert of Courson attempted to separate by terminology those learned in the law (*iurisperiti*) who sold their legal counsel (*consilium*) from the pleaders in the court (*advocati* or *causidici*) who sold their legal assistance (*patrocinium*).[132] While the advocates ordinarily were not expected to teach, the jurisprudents were not prevented from practicing. More important, the legal profession was regarded as the broadest gateway to public advancement. While a training in theology might qualify one for a prelacy, as the careers of Stephen Langton and Peter of Corbeil demonstrated,[133] Roman and canon law provided more frequent opportunities for high service to princes and churchmen.[134] It was obvious that students of medicine and law possessed more tangible enticements than those of theology. In the rivalry of self-esteem and the competition for good students the theologians naturally tended to depreciate their medical and legal colleagues by calling theirs the "lucrative sciences" (*lucrative scientie*).

Throughout the writings of Peter the Chanter and his circle, repeated protests occur against the competitive superiority of these lucrative sciences, a theme which was neither new nor limited to the theologians. For example, the humanist Peter of Blois, who at one time vaunted his training at Bologna,[135] later (ca. 1160) announced in a letter to a friend that he was abandoning the law of Bologna for the theology of Paris.[136] Among his reasons was the cupidity of the legal profession and the superiority of divine over human law. In subsequent letters he urged two of his correspondents to follow his example.[137] Peter of Blois expressed the point of view of a student, but the Parisian theologians wrote as teachers pressed by rivalry from the lucrative sciences. Gerald of Wales affirmed that he heard the famous Master Mainerius complain in a large company of students that the Sibyl's prophecy had been fulfilled that law would come to obliterate the knowledge of letters.[138] In the same vein, Peter the Chanter accused those who read law for mundane profit of causing neglect in the liberal arts and theology.[139] Elsewhere he noted that students who rush to Salerno to consult the doctors or who pursue knowledge of human but not divine laws are like those who slight the soul for the sake of the body.[140] In his lectures on the Minor Prophets Stephen Langton found occasion to warn students against abandoning theology for the lucrative sciences.[141] For example, commenting on the verse (Hosea 9 : 1) "Rejoice not, O Israel, for joy, as other people; for thou has gone a whoring from thy God, thou hast loved a reward upon every cornfloor," Stephen added: "You love the reward of medicine, Roman law, canon law and other profitable sciences which offer recompense in the present more than the true harvest of holy Scripture."[142] Robert of Courson's protests were against those who pursued the lucrative studies at Bologna, Salerno, or even at Paris for worldly promotion.[143] Through vigils and tears they obtain positions in the courts of worldly satraps, and like contemptible pimps entice prebends from the pseudo-prelates of the church. In Robert's austere judgment such activities were a kind of simony because they sought temporal gain from the spiritual benefits of knowledge.[144] Even the theologian who studied with the intent of advancing to the prelacy was guilty of this sin. Like the money changers whom Christ chased from the temple, all who seek lucrative knowledge should be expelled from the house of learning. By the time that Gerald of Wales' career drew to a close this theme had become a literary convention. In a letter of 1214 dedicating the third edition of his *Itinerarium Kambrie* to Archbishop Stephen Langton Gerald lamented the popularity of medicine, law, and logic with the resultant decline of the liberal arts and literature.[145]

At the time of the Council of Reims in 1131 all monks and other regular clergy in France had been specifically forbidden to pursue the study of medicine and law.[146] These professions which were directly involved in worldly affairs were not only obviously dangerous to monastic seclusion, but profits from lucrative knowledge were hardly consistent with monastic poverty. At the councils of Paris in 1213 and of Rouen in 1214 Robert of Courson renewed these prohibitions against the regular clergy who left their cloisters for the purpose of studying or practicing law and medicine.[147] Unless they returned to their houses within two months they were to be excommunicated and avoided by all, the permission of their abbots notwithstanding. At the council of Paris Robert extended these restrictions to the parish clergy, declaring all clergy having parochial responsibilities forbidden to seek instruction in the "secular sciences," that is, medicine and law, which were of no value to their parishioners' salvation.[148] If parish priests obtained permission to go to school, they must limit their studies to the Scriptures profitable to the spiritual instruction of their charges. Robert thus attempted to implement the former protests of the theological faculty, which he himself shared. By extending the restrictions against the study of medicine and law to the parish clergy and encouraging them to study Scripture, he reduced the numbers of students for the lucrative sciences and recruited for the classes of his theological colleagues.

Courson's program received support from Pope Honorius III's famous bull *Super speculam*, of 1219, which proposed measures for promoting theological learning in general and at Paris in particular.[149] Among them the Pope renewed the prohibition of law and medicine to monks and confirmed Robert's extension of this restriction to clerics with ecclesiastical responsibilities, or more specifically, to archdeacons, deans, provosts, arch priests (*plebani*), chanters, and other clerics having prebends, as well as to priests, who were forbidden to pursue an education in medicine and law and were directed towards theology. Finally, Honorius banned the teaching of Roman law in Paris and its vicinity under penalty of excommunication for both teachers and students. The underlying motivation of this last provision has provoked controversy since the early nineteenth century.[150] Although the principal theme of the papal bull was the promotion of theological studies, the Pope connected the local prohibition with the fact that the laity of the Ile-de-France and elsewhere were not served by Roman law. Many scholars, therefore, have seen the unexpressed motive behind the ban as papal support for the independence of the French king against the imperial pretensions of the German emperor founded on Roman law.[151] Others have taken the explicit motive seriously and interpreted the provision merely as papal support for the theological faculty at Paris.[152] Whatever the principal motives, it is significant that *Super speculam* in fact confirmed and advanced an already existent program for encouraging theological study at Paris. In language florid with metaphors the Pope asserted the superiority of theology over other disciplines and lamented the lack of interested students. Practical ways were devised for providing economic support for theological studies. Competition from the lucrative sciences was reduced by confirming previous restrictions against monks and clerics with ecclesiastical responsibilities. Paris' preeminence in theology was reaffirmed. All of these provisions amounted to fulfilling a program proposed by the theologians for at least three decades. *Super speculam*'s subsequent effect was not only to eliminate Roman law at Paris, but also to reduce the teaching of canon law, and thereby in fact to reduce the competitors to theology. Throughout the thirteenth century Bologna remained the champion of legal studies but Paris was queen of theology.

❧ CHAPTER V ❧

Theologians

AS ACTIVE masters of theology Peter the Chanter and his associates may be expected to provide a detailed picture of the instruction of their own subject at Paris. Among the allusions to theological study which thoroughly saturate their writings an example which might serve as introduction may be found in the Chanter's lectures on the Old Testament book of Ruth. Expanding a suggestion of the *Glossa ordinaria*,[1] Peter interpreted one episode of this endearing Scriptural story to represent the study of theology. After the death of her Israelite husband, Ruth the Moabitess, it may be recalled, decided to forsake her country and to follow Naomi, her mother-in-law.[2] In order to support the impoverished Naomi, Ruth went into the barley fields to glean after the reapers. By chance, the particular field in which she labored belonged to Boaz, a kinsman of Naomi. When the youth who oversaw the reapers identified the new woman working in the fields, Boaz rewarded Ruth's faithfulness to Naomi by allowing her to eat bread and partake of vinegar at the table of the reapers and to gather grain whenever she wished. So Ruth remained with Boaz' workers to glean until the end of harvest.

In his lectures Peter the Chanter produced a moral interpretation (*moraliter*) of this story.[3] Ruth stood for the faithful who wished to learn about the law of God, or in other words, for the student of theology. Naomi was the church, chapter, or prelate who gave the student permission to pursue his education. The barley field represented Holy Scripture which was planted in the prophets, ingrafted in the apostles and evangelists, nourished in the expositors, and in bloom in the doctors of theology. The reapers in the field were the masters or doctors of theology; the youth who oversaw them stood for the archdeacons, archpriests, and provosts who looked after priests and masters and their parishioners and disciples; and finally, Boaz was the prelate of the church. To the Chanter each episode of the story corresponded to an aspect of theological study. Ruth's following the reapers and gleaning what remained represented the novice students who are not yet mature enough to understand weighty problems, but only the lighter opinions which masters leave to beginners. As Boaz visited his reapers with a word of salutation, so the prelate should visit priests and teachers. The overseer of the reapers or the arch-deacons, archpriests, and provosts is called young, not in age, but in courage endowed by grace. As the supervisor reported Ruth to Boaz, so the masters should give account of the devotion of the students they know. Ruth's request to Boaz that she might follow the reapers among the sheaves indicated that the student should not deviate from his teach-er's doctrine. Boaz' kindly invitation to Ruth to remain in his field was the prelate's invitation to the field of learning. The water which he gave Ruth to drink was the water of Shiloah which flows silently without heretical subterfuge. By leaving her family and country Ruth repre-sented the theological student who adheres to God and His doctrine and rejects the philosophers' teaching which, however, is profitable for finite time just as the Hebrews enriched themselves for a time from the spoils of Egypt.[4] More literally, Ruth's forsaking of her home also stood for students who leave their countries and relatives for the sake of study.[5] Boaz' sharing the table of his reapers with Ruth was the invitation to students to attend lectures where the bread of Scripture is broken. That the bread was also dipped in vinegar indicated that theologians should be familiar not only with the benign promises but also with the sharp ad-monitions of the Bible. Ruth's remaining in the field until the harvest was over signified that students should continue their studies until they had acquired the necessary glosses and elements of their learning. Neither should they transfer from one master to another but remain faithful to their teachers until they themselves were qualified to teach.

This figurative interpretation of Ruth which linked the Biblical story with the schools of theology was popular among the theological masters of Paris at the turn of the century. Among three versions of Stephen Langton's commentary on Ruth, two followed this line of interpretation.[6] Although Stephen was not directly dependent on Peter at this section,[7] he nonetheless used the story of Ruth to make observations on the study of theology. For example, when Ruth said to Boaz, "I pray you, let me glean," Langton remarked that lectures should always begin with prayer,[8] and when Boaz told Ruth not to glean in another field, Langton interpreted this to mean not to go to another faculty to hear theology.[9] Similarly, Jacques de Vitry introduced his collection of *Sermones com-munes* with a figurative interpretation of Ruth.[10] As with the Chanter and Langton the fertile field was Holy Scripture and the reapers, the theological masters, but those who followed the gleaners were the preach-ers who explained matters neglected by the theologians.[11]

In contrast to the numbers of masters of arts the theological faculty at Paris was restricted to a few. No more than a score of actively teach-ing masters of theology can be identified with any certainty for the period 1170-1215.[12] In a letter of 1207 addressed to the Bishop of Paris which congratulated the royal city for its celebrity in theology, Pope Innocent III decreed that the number of active professors of theology should not exceed eight except in unusual circumstances in order that the quality of instruction should not be diluted by too many competing masters.[13]

Little evidence has survived as to how the papal restriction corresponded to the actual numbers at Paris, nor as to its enforcement in the years immediately following.[14] Although the compromise of 1213 between the Chancellor of Notre-Dame and the university provided means for limiting the number of theological masters, an exact figure was not mentioned.[15] By 1218 Pope Honorius III had declared that Innocent's limitation was no longer observed and ordered the Chancellor to license a certain candidate who had been refused.[16] Nonetheless the number of teaching theologians probably never exceeded fifteen by the mid-thirteenth century.[17] When Robert of Courson turned to the masters of theology in his statutes for the university in 1215, he dealt exclusively with the age of the candidates and length of the course.[18] No one could lecture publicly as a full master before his thirty-fifth year and without at least eight years of study of the texts. As an intermediate stage, however, those who had studied theology for five years were permitted to deliver semi-public lectures[19] provided that they were not held before the third hour on days when the regular masters taught. No one could be admitted to the formal lecturing and preaching at Paris until he was approved both in character and knowledge. Robert undoubtedly understood this final approval to the rank of master of theology, like that to master of arts, to be determined by the Chancellor of Notre-Dame and the faculty of theology according to the procedures of 1213.[20]

Unlike his account of the regulations for the masters of arts, Robert of Courson's description made no mention of the basic textbooks for theology, since it was normally assumed that the fundamental authority for this subject was simply the Scriptures with their auxiliary glosses.[21] Throughout the twelfth century the theologians were entitled masters of the sacred page (*magistri sacre pagine*), and theological learning began with the Bible. Other treatises, such as the *Summae*, were not designed for the basic curriculum of public instruction, but were composed for the personal use of masters and students. Only the renowned *Book of Sentences* of Peter the Lombard was considered comparable with the Bible in the theological education at Paris. In a well-known passage Peter the Chanter described the functions of the theologian as follows:[22]

> The training of Holy Scripture consists of three exercises: reading (*lectio*), disputing (*disputatio*) and preaching (*predicatio*) against which prolixity is the enemy, the mother of oblivion, and the step-mother of memory. First, reading is laid down like the basement and

foundation for what follows, so that from this source all support is derived by the other two exercises. Secondly, the structure or walls of disputation are put in place for, as Gregory says, nothing is fully understood or faithfully preached unless first chewed or ground by the tooth of disputation. Thirdly the roof of preaching is erected so that he who hears says, "I came" and thus the crowd draws the crowd.[23] One should preach after, not before, the reading of Holy Scripture and the investigation of doubtful matters. The Christian religion truly consists of faith and of good conduct of which reading and disputation pertain to faith and preaching to conduct. After the roof of preaching has been put in place so that we and our neighbors are protected from the heat, rain, hail and wind of vice, the consistory of the palace of the High King will be completed in which He distinguishes laws and right.

The first two functions of *lectio* and *disputatio*, which formed the common educational method of the schools, were practiced by other masters as well as by those of theology, while the last duty of *predicatio* was reserved for the theologians. Peter the Chanter not only explicitly discussed these three techniques, but he and his colleagues also practiced them during their careers at Paris, thus producing written evidence of these forms of teaching activity.

LECTIO

At its root the term *lectio* simply means "reading," but in the practice of the Parisian schools reading acquired a more restricted and academic connotation. To read (*legere*) a text could mean to expound a basic text before an audience, or, in other words, to lecture.[24] When a master lectured on an authority he both read it publicly and explained it to his students. In the *Verbum abbreviatum* Peter the Chanter distinguished two kinds of *lectio*: the admonishing type (*ammonitoria*) in which passages read privately became self-evident and the expository (*expositoria*) in which difficult passages were explained in the schools.[25] The literary result of *lectio* was a genre of writing known as the commentary or the gloss. As the masters studied privately or lectured publicly they produced numerous commentaries and glosses to the fundamental texts of different disciplines, but it is often difficult to distinguish between the two forms in the written record.

From earliest Christian times Bible reading produced a voluminous literature of Scriptural commentaries.[26] Origen of Alexandria among the Greek Church Fathers and Jerome and Augustine among the Latins developed exegetical methods and authoritative explanations in their Biblical commentaries. Throughout the early Middle Ages churchmen in the West excerpted and collected what they considered to be the best of Patristic material. The compilation and assimilation of Patristic comments on the Bible was perfected at the beginning of the twelfth century by a group of theologians at Laon. Under the leadership of Anselm of Laon, his brother Ralph, and Gilbert the Universal, they compiled the *Gloss*, an authoritative Scriptural commentary composed of opinions of the Church Fathers. (By the thirteenth century it was called the *Glossa ordinaria*.) Its shorter portions, inserted between the lines of the Scriptural text, were designated the *Interlineary Gloss,* while the longer sections, written along the margins of the text, were known as the *Marginal Gloss*. By the middle of the twelfth century the *Gloss* to the Psalms and the Epistles of Paul, books of particular theological interest, had been further expanded by Gilbert de la Porrée in the *Media glosatura* and still further by Peter the Lombard in the *Magna glosatura*. With the older *Gloss* these became the standard tools of Biblical exegesis for masters teaching theology.

At Paris, the foremost center of Scriptural study during the middle decades of the twelfth century, was the abbey school of Saint-Victor. One of its priors, Hugh of Saint-Victor, outlined a program of exegesis both in his commentaries and in a short pedagogical manual entitled the *Didascalicon*. According to Hugh the Bible should first be interpreted literally in an attempt to understand the grammatical sense and the historical meaning of the text as the sacred authors wrote it. After the literal sense was firmly grasped, the exegete could pass to the spiritual interpretations of allegory, which understood the Scriptural narratives as symbolizing theological doctrines in general and conceptions of Christ in particular, and tropology, which saw Biblical history as Christian morality and conduct. In addition to these three levels of interpretation other scholars of Saint-Victor revived a fourth, the anagogical, which viewed the Scriptural accounts as eschatological. This fourfold program was originally derived from the Church Fathers, but Hugh and the Victorines provided Biblical scholarship at Paris with new impetus and inspiration. Hugh's leading disciples emphasized two different characteristics of their master. Richard of Saint-Victor applied himself to the figurative interpretations by selecting passages which demanded skill in allegorical and moral explanation. For example, his specialty was to construct elaborate spiritual lessons based on the Song of Solomon, the vision of Ezekiel, Noah's ark, and the Mosaic tabernacle. Andrew of Saint-Victor, on the other hand, followed Hugh's emphasis on the literal interpretation as the foundation for Bible study. Turning his attention towards the Old Testament, Andrew became acquainted with contemporary Jewish exegesis and even learned Hebrew to master the literal and historical sense of the Biblical narrative. It was this approach which chiefly inspired the theological masters who lectured publicly at Paris at the turn of the century. Peter Comestor, Chancellor of Notre-Dame, who died about 1179, composed a compendium of Biblical history, later entitled the *Historia scholastica,* which became a current textbook for theological education. These *Histories* were based on the literal commentaries of Andrew of Saint-Victor for the sections devoted to patriarchal narrative. Likewise, both Peter the Chanter and Stephen Langton freely used Andrew's work in their lectures on the Old Testament. Although they did not ignore the spiritual senses of Scripture, they agreed with Hugh and Andrew that the edifice of Biblical interpretation must be firmly founded on literal and historical study.

In the *Verbum abbreviatum* Peter the Chanter prefaced his discussion of *lectio* with a protest against verbosity in Scriptural studies. The title of the book itself was derived from the Apostle Paul (Rom. 9 : 28): "An abbreviated word the Lord will make upon the earth . . . ." Developing this theme, Peter declared that if Christ the Word, the unencompassable Son of God, Whom the whole world cannot contain, consented to be circumscribed in the virgin's womb, how much more the word of the sacred page which He bequeathed to us as an earnest and pledge of His love should be shortened.[27] This word is our road leading directly and quickly to eternal blessedness. Since not only sacred Scripture, but even ancient philosophy repudiated prolixity, Peter excerpted appropriate passages from the *Epistolae morales* of Seneca.[28] After this prologue and a brief description of the threefold interpretation of Holy Scripture, the Chanter applied this theme more specifically to superfluous Biblical glosses. This critical note against the glosses was not entirely new. Early in the century Robert of Melun had questioned their whole utility, charging that they distracted attention from the Bible itself,[29] but the Chanter, who had no doubts about Scriptural commentaries, was content to protest against their abuse. In characteristic fashion Peter hinted at this theme throughout his Biblical lectures in scattered flashes,[30] but concentrated his most thunderous objections in the *Verbum abbreviatum.*

The Chanter's chapter against prolixity of glosses is a heap of arguments piled up from Scripture, figurative analogies, the examples of the Church Fathers, and practical considerations, and is arranged with little order. For example, Peter maintained that the Bible is a vessel to transport us across life's boundless sea, which must not be laden with superfluous expositions but charged only with necessary cargo.[31] Or, Scripture is the tree of life upon which the foliage of glosses must not be allowed to choke the fruit.[32] Or again, in the vision of the Apocalypse (Rev. 5 : 1-5) where the Apostle John wept because he could not read the book closed with seven seals, Christ Himself opened the book.[33] We ourselves should not make John weep again by obscuring Scriptures with redundant expositions. Peter's own prolixity in amassing images such as these might well abuse the reader's patience, but occasionally he inserted more practical arguments which explain what specifically he had in mind. For example, he compared writers who burdened the Bible with glosses to those who preferred sumptuously illuminated codices over plain but well annotated books, just as the poet Ovid observed:

> "We are won by the dress, all is concealed by gems
> and gold; a woman is the least part of herself."[34]

Because of this penchant for ponderous books we lose precious time and energy in copying, reading, correcting, and even carrying them about.[35] Peter's objection was especially appropriate in an age when books were produced by hand.

Elsewhere in the *Verbum abbreviatum* Peter complained about commentators who indulged excessively in the allegorical sense. When we claim that all is clearly manifest in Christ's doctrine, why do we recede from the plain letter of the Gospel to the confusing interpretation of allegory? Peter reported an encounter at Reims between a Christian master and a learned Jew.[36] Although the Jew could understand the reason for interpreting the Old Testament allegorically, he could not comprehend why the same method was employed in the New. Since Christians thereby altered the Gospel according to their desires, no one observed its clear meaning. Because of this misuse of allegory, the Jew would have no part of Christianity. Not only were the Gospels inappropriate for allegorical interpretation, but even certain portions of the Old Testament presented dangers. Peter approved of a Jewish custom, mentioned by Jerome, which forbade young men under the age of thirty to read the beginning of Genesis, the beginning and the end of Ezekiel, and the Song of Solomon.[37] Although Peter did not explain his reasoning, apparently these sections containing the creation of the world, the vision of the temple by the prophet, and love poetry, posed common pitfalls for the immature interpreter. Following the warning of the Apostle to avoid myths and endless genealogies which promote speculations rather than divine training (1 Tim. 1 : 4), the Chanter judged the allegorical interpretation of Biblical numbers, genealogies, measurements, and architecture, such as the tabernacle or the heavenly temple, as yielding little profit to the theological student.[38] Although Peter did not openly name his adversaries, one can speculate over their identity. Richard of Saint-Victor and his followers, it will be remembered, emphasized the spiritual approach to Scripture.[39] Richard's works included not only allegorical commentaries to the Gospels but also spiritual expositions of the troublesome sections of Ezekiel and Song of Solomon. Most noteworthy, Richard produced elaborate treatises on Biblical chronology, genealogy, and the tabernacle and the temple of Ezekiel's vision.[40] Similarly, Peter of Poitiers composed an allegorical commentary on the Mosaic tabernacle.[41] Peter the Chanter may have had other Biblical scholars in mind, but Richard of Saint-Victor and Peter of Poitiers provided him clear targets.[42] By agreeing with the Jewish exegetes the Chanter seems to have aligned himself with Andrew, Richard's rival in the Victorine school.

Within this thicket of protest Peter nourished some positive suggestions. Referring to the interlinear gloss of Laon, he maintained that the reading of the Bible should be accompanied only by a few words such as can be contained within the lines of the text.[43] His exegetical models were Origen and Jerome who developed textual criticism, Gregory and Jerome who explained the text, and Augustine and Hilary who opposed heretical interpretations.[44] Peter's favorite example was Jerome who by explaining the sacred text through other passages of Scripture, avoided superfluous glosses.[45] With some credulity Peter asserted that Jerome clearly expounded both Testaments according to the four senses within the space of a year, but with more realism he conceded that in his own day ten years would not be sufficient for the task.[46] To the Church Fathers the Chanter added other Biblical scholars from his own century whose example of reading the Scriptures could be imitated with profit. Distinguishing two former generations of masters, he designated the "oldest" as composing Anselm and his brother, and the "old" as including Simon, Alberic of Reims, Robert Pullen, and Gilbert.[47] John of Salisbury mentioned all six names in his accounts about contemporary masters, but only some of the figures can be identified with certainty.[48] Although bare names and vague shadows to modern scholars, these writers in the Chanter's judgment were the forerunners of Biblical scholarship.

Peter the Chanter not only exhorted his colleagues about Biblical *lectio* but, as an active theological master at Paris, he practiced it himself. While preceding theologians produced glosses to portions of the Scripture, particularly to the Psalms and the Pauline epistles, he was the first Parisian master to compose commentaries on all of the books of the Bible. The commentaries of Stephen Langton, also extending over the entire Scriptures, are even more voluminous and exist in multiple versions. In most of Peter's lectures the brevity of his commentary accords with his strictures against superfluous glosses. Although he regularly employed the *Gloss* and occasionally developed the allegorical or moral sense of a passage, for the most part his comments move briskly through the Biblical text. When, however, he approached the Psalms and the Epistles of Paul, his exposition became more elaborate, depending not only on the simple *Gloss* but also on the expanded commentaries of Gilbert de la Porée and Peter the Lombard.[49] By contrast the density of Langton's commentary exceeds the Chanter's at every book of the Bible. When treating the historical books of the Old Testament, for example, his exposition pays more attention to allegorical and tropological interpretations; when dealing with the Psalms and Pauline letters, he includes the *Magna glosatura* of the Lombard as well as the Bible as text for his commentary. In these latter books, Langton's work is really a gloss upon a gloss. Peter's discussion offers little indication as to whether he would have judged Stephen's commentaries excessive, nor, for that matter, how he would have evaluated his own work on the Psalms and Epistles of Paul. Since, however, both Langton's and the Chanter's commentaries amply illustrate the prevailing temptation to increase the length of Scriptural exposition, it is evident that the Chanter's warning against superfluous glosses was concerned with a real issue.

DISPUTATIO

Disputation, according to the Chanter, was the second major activity of the theologian. In current terminology *disputatio* was closely related to the practice of *questio*, but both words lacked precision. For example, disputation could mean a discussion, a dialogue, a confrontation of theses, a comparison of texts, or an altercation, and questioning could be applied to most forms of intellectual investigation.[50] Nonetheless, during the twelfth century both *disputatio* and *questio* were employed to designate exercises generally practiced in the schools and particularly by theologians.[51] When a theologian lectured or wrote a commentary on the Bible, he might find particular problems which required further probing. The Church Fathers, Jerome and Augustine, for example, composed treatises entitled *questiones* which dealt with difficult points arising out of Scriptural exegesis. In the lectures of the twelfth century questions arose when certain passages of Scripture seemed to contradict each other or more often when Patristic interpretations were in conflict. By investigating these questions the master attempted to reconcile conflicts between opposing authorities. Not only were conflicts of exegesis involved but so also were matters of theological doctrine. As he expounded the Scriptures the theologian might inquire into a particular theological notion which demanded clear and systematic investigation. To devise rational arguments for and against certain doctrines, he was tempted to employ the tools of logic or dialectic. By the middle of the twelfth century, when Aristotle's entire logical works were available in Latin, the theologians disposed of a system of rational inquiry, applicable to the contents of the Scriptures. The *questio* approach, therefore, involved not only the harmonizing of conflicting authorities but also the introduction of logic into the domain of theology. Since *questio* was useful for solving debatable problems and for investigating all areas of theology, theologians employed these techniques widely by the close of the century.

As questioning became increasingly refined and distinguished from lecturing during the course of the century, it became further associated with *disputatio*, which eventually became a formal academic exercise. No clear picture is available of how the theological disputation was actually conducted until well on in the thirteenth century, when public debates, known as *questiones-disputatae*, involved both masters and students according to regulated procedures. The disputation provided the theologians with opportunity for exploring questions with the cooperation of their colleagues and students. During the formative period of the second half of the twelfth century, the master perhaps posed his questions, marshalled his authorities and arguments and came to his conclusions by himself. From later developments it is probable that he invited participation from students and colleagues at least on occasion, but the details are not clear. Peter the Chanter, however, provides one valuable indication of the development of the disputation. Discussing the problems of *lectio* in the *Verbum abbreviatum*, he observes that if a question arises in the text, it should be noted and deferred until the hour of disputation.[52] Since Alexander Neckam and Stephen Langton both mentioned similar procedures in their commentaries,[53] it may be assumed that by the end of the century questioning and disputations were separated from the normal sessions of lecturing and were reserved for special hours.[54] Other evidence for this practice is provided by the contemporary disputations of Simon of Tournai which were organized specifically according to days.[55] In all likelihood the distinction in time between *lectio* and *disputatio* encouraged the separate development of the disputation.

The techniques of *questio* and *disputatio* were engendered in part by the application of dialectics to theology. While most theologians were willing to allow logic to be studied as preparation for theology, many churchmen possessed grave misgivings about the direct use of dialectics for solving theological questions. Those, therefore, who fiercely opposed the penetration of dialectics into theology were also suspicious of the proliferation of theological questions and disputations.[56] As early as the eleventh century Lanfranc, for example, reflecting on his debates with Berengar of Tours, held reservations as to the validity of dialectical questions for resolving Scriptural problems. Towards the middle of the twelfth century Bernard of Clairvaux challenged the application of *questio* to the realm of faith and encouraged widespread distrust among the monastic clergy for the methods of the theological masters.[57] During succeeding decades other monks like the Benedictine Peter de la Celle contrasted the calm meditation of the cloister with the contentious disputations of the urban schools.[58] This mistrust of dialectics and theological *questiones* reached its extreme in the *Contra quatuor labyrinthos Franciae* of Wal-

ter of Saint-Victor who sharply attacked the achievements of four major
Paris theologians, Peter Abelard, Gilbert de la Porrée, Peter the Lombard,
and Peter of Poitiers.[59] At the turn of the century these themes were
reechoed by Stephen of Tournai in his often-cited letter to the pope.[60]
Writing as Bishop of Tournai, but remembering his experiences as Abbot of Sainte-Geneviève in Paris, Stephen declared that the ineffable
mysteries of God, the Incarnation, and the Eucharist were irreverently
exposed to public debate. He therefore urged the pope to restore order to
these abuses of learning and disputation. Throughout the twelfth century the theologians' efforts to devise a common method of questioning
and disputing were never without criticism.

A critic by temperament, Peter the Chanter was unable to ignore the
abuses inherent in disputation. For this reason three chapters of his
Verbum abbreviatum devoted to this subject have been occasionally linked
with Bernard of Clairvaux, Walter of Saint-Victor, and others who
were adamant against the introduction of *questio* into theology.[61] Yet
there is no doubt that Peter practiced the disputation in his own school,
because his *Summa de sacramentis* consists entirely of *questiones*. Moreover in his *Verbum abbreviatum* he maintains that since nothing can be
fully understood or faithfully preached unless it is first prepared by "the
tooth of disputation," *disputatio* provides the walls of theology.[62] As an
active master of theology the Chanter harbored no suspicion about the
legitimate role of disputation; his protests were intended rather to reform than to abolish the exercise. As in his treatment of *lectio*, Peter her-
alded his criticism in scattered passages throughout the commentaries[63]
but concentrated his arguments in the *Verbum abbreviatum*. There he
opens his discussion by distinguishing three kinds of questions found in
theological disputations:[64] Those which are useless because they treat
neither faith nor morals should be eliminated immediately. Those which
are useful and clear could be easily omitted, but those which are useful
and difficult (*scrupulose*) should be discussed with modesty and without wrangling. Some of these questions are better left to the sophists
(*sophista*) lest it be said of the theologians that they grasp for clouds and
the void. In all events, only those questions which pertain to faith and
conduct should be aired in disputation.

After these introductory distinctions Peter the Chanter devoted the first
of his chapters to assailing foolish and vain questions in theology.[65] Characteristically, he first amassed quotations from the Bible and Seneca
against such practices. For example, like the children of Israel who tar-
ried too long in the land of Rameses (Ex. 12 : 37) or wasted valuable time
in skirting Mount Seir (Deut. 2 : 1-3) before gaining the promised land,
theologians delay their advance towards truth by entertaining petty and
useless questions.[66] Although industrious in compiling authorities, Peter

was not helpful in identifying the vain questions which he deplored. His most explicit statement alluded to the logical *sophismata* among the masters of arts which has been already noticed.[67]* Nonetheless, the Chanter was sensitive to the criticism of Bernard of Clairvaux and his monastic followers against the vanities of theological questions. "We should be ashamed," he admonishes his academic colleagues, "that we make ourselves ridiculous to the monks and other discrete men who enter our schools. When they hear us retract our words, they depart believing themselves more skilled than us. Because we teach more for school than for life we deceive both ourselves and them."[68]

More serious than embarrassment from frivolous questions was the danger of rash questions which bred error and subverted the soul.[69] In the second chapter of the *Verbum abbreviatum*, again well stocked with Biblical quotations and allusions, Peter focused on this abuse.[70] Just as Moses inscribed boundaries around Mount Sinai to prevent all beasts from treading upon holy ground (Exod. 19 : 12-13), so Christ and the Fathers encircled the Holy Scriptures with limits lest anyone intrude with useless, superfluous and incautious inquiries.[71] Among these the Chanter specified the sacraments, the humanity of Christ, the paternity and the names of God.[72] Such rash disputations, Peter affirmed, spawned heresies[73] and divided theologians.[74] Unlike the secular philosophers who were divided between realism and nominalism, the theologians should dwell in unity in the house of God. According to the image of Boethius, celestial philosophy should mend her rent garments by avoiding rash and curious questions. Those masters who disputed heavenly matters in the manner of earthly and mechanical arts squandered theological learning and in the words of the Psalmist (72 : 9) "set their mouth against the heavens."[75]

Finally, in a third chapter, the Chanter offered positive advice on how disputations should be conducted. To avoid strife theologians were urged to fashion their discussions not into altercations, but into *collationes*, that is, a common research after truth.[76] Refraining from histrionic contrivances,[77] they should proceed with deliberation. In this regard Peter offered three examples drawn from the ancient church, Roman law, and the life of Aristotle. The saints and elders of the primitive church, he maintained, never responded to queries nor resolved issues without preparatory deliberation and consultation.[78] Similarly, one should consider how many judicial delays and preliminary examinations are required in Roman law before a judgment involving mere land or vineyards can be rendered.[79] Even where no personal jeopardy is involved the complete *ordo iudicarius* must be followed by examining witnesses, producing lawyers, according delays, testing the accusors, and finally rendering the sentence. If such

* See above, p. 82.

care was exercised in the courts of Justinian, how much more was demanded in the palace of the Supreme King where celestial matters concerning the sacraments are treated, matters which affect the soul's safety. The example of the physician who is accustomed to delay his solution even to theoretical exercises should put the theologian to shame.[80] As illustration Peter recounted an anecdote about Aristotle, who was in the habit of requesting delays when solving simple as well as difficult questions. On one occasion when a particularly difficult problem was posed, Aristotle asked for his customary postponement. One of his disciples, Theophrastus, imbued with youthful enthusiasm, however, promised an immediate solution. Much to the disciple's embarrassment, the answer was wrong, and the master retorted, "Your work should serve as your bridle." The Chanter was reminded that ancient theologians deferred the solution of questions until the morrow.

These chapters in the *Verbum abbreviatum* were the most extensive critique of the theological disputation of its day. Since the Chanter was merely part of a general current of protest, it is not surprising to hear echoes of his arguments in his Parisian colleagues and followers. In a Scriptural commentary Stephen Langton, for example, chastened theologians for irreverently clothing the secrets of God by disputing for the whole day the Trinity and divine properties (*de notionibus*) which provide little edification for the soul.[81] A sermon of Pope Innocent III described heretics who braid cords of subtle deceptions from theological authorities, rhetorical flourishes, and dialectical and sophistic arguments.[82] Elsewhere he objected to questions concerning the transubstantiation of the Eucharist which were more subtle than useful.[83] Among the vices depicted in Jacques de Vitry's tableau of Paris at the end of the twelfth century were the contentious disputations of scholars and the presumptuous learning of theologians.[84]

Although this criticism of the questioning method was stringent, it was never directed towards abolishing the exercise. In addition to Biblical commentaries the Paris theologians composed *Summae* which were in reality collections of *questiones*. The literary development of questioning can be traced within the writings of the Chanter's circle. Peter's own *questiones* show signs of improvisation and experiment.[85] The individual items were initially arranged according to the system of sacraments but at that of penance most formal organization is abandoned. Treatment of each separate question also varies greatly. At times the problem is stated, the arguments presented, and the conclusion attained, at other times either the arguments or the conclusions are omitted. Although Langton's *questiones* are generally fuller than his colleague's, they are often digressive, imprecise, and assembled without a controlling plan.[86] Robert of Courson's *Summa*, however, may be regarded as the final version of the Chanter's collection.[87] Attempting to complement and finish his teacher's work, he gathered all of the material within a general scheme. Although most of the individual questions and arguments were borrowed from the Chanter, sometimes verbatim, Robert standardized their presentation by recording arguments *pro* and *con* and finally their solution. Similarly, Geoffrey of Poitiers arranged the unorganized *questiones* of Langton according to a plan suggested by the *Sentences* of Peter the Lombard.[88] Both Robert and Geoffrey, therefore, attempted to rewrite their masters' *questiones* in a more readable form. The unfinished and informal character of the Chanter's and Langton's collections reflects the classroom cooperation accompanying debate. They take the form of *reportationes* by which an officially designated student (the *reportator*) wrote down the individual *questiones*. The Chanter's and Langton's work fully illustrates, therefore, the close connection between the classroom disputations and the literary form of *questio*. Since Robert of Courson and Geoffrey of Poitiers by contrast eliminated the characteristic signs of the *reportator* from theirs, they considered their *Summae* as final versions of their teachers' *questiones*.

It will be recalled that certain theological subjects such as the sacraments, the humanity of Christ, the fatherhood and names of God, were designated by Peter the Chanter as susceptible to rash and heretical conclusions. To these subjects Stephen Langton added the Trinity and the divine properties (*de notionibus*). Since the time of Abelard and Gilbert de la Porrée, however, these "presumptuous" topics had been favorite subjects for theologians inclined to abstract speculation. At the turn of the century they were regularly treated by Peter of Poitiers, Prepositinus, Simon of Tournai and Master Martin. Even Stephen Langton produced *questiones* on all of these topics including the two which he specified.[89] Since the Chanter's *Summa* was organized according to the sacraments, he could hardly avoid abstract speculation about the nature of the sacraments.[90] He also ventured into Christological controversies, but his own position of "adoptionism" was rejected by his contemporaries.[91] (Perhaps this unhappy experience chastened him about incautious questions.) The conclusion emerges that Peter's and Stephen's warnings against certain rash questions were considered as counsels of perfection which they themselves violated. Nonetheless, when compared with those of contemporary theologians the Chanter's *questiones* are seen to contain relatively little of the speculative issues which he specified. Because Courson neglected to write a section devoted to dogmatic theology, his *Summa* is free from these questions. Although not without exception, both Peter the Chanter and his student Courson represent a tendency to avoid those questions which spawned heresy and theological error.

Chapter V

THEOLOGY AND PHILOSOPHY

The employment of dialectical techniques in theology raised larger problems concerning the relations between theology and philosophy. The science of logic, after all, was merely part of a philosophical system which the Christian Middle Ages inherited from pagan Antiquity. If the liberal art of dialectics was preparatory to and useful in solving theological problems (when great care was exercised), of what value was pagan philosophy for the Christian theologian in general? Late in the eleventh century the influential Anselm of Bec established the theological program for the next century with the formula of "faith seeking understanding."[92] Following the inspiration of Augustine, he proposed that if faith preceded, understanding would follow as a matter of course. It could be assumed, therefore, that reason and logic, the instruments of understanding, could be applied to any realm in which faith had gained entrance. Since faith could be equated with theology and understanding or reason with philosophy, this formula implied that theology and philosophy were complementary and unified. To execute this program theologians such as Peter Abelard and Gilbert de la Porrée attempted to understand and solve the questions of theology with the tools of ancient philosophy.[93]

During the second half of the twelfth century, however, suggestions of a schism between theology and philosophy began to appear. Rather than regarding these disciplines as complementary, theologians began to divide their problems into two groups, those susceptible to theological argument and those susceptible to philosophical demonstration. By the end of the century the division between theology and philosophy was becoming increasingly clear.[94] Peter the Chanter and those theologians closest to him, not inclined to investigate speculative problems, took little note of the relationship between theology and philosophy. On rare occasions, however, when Peter treated a speculative subject such as the nature of Christ, he was conscious of philosophical reasons distinct from theological argument.[95] Other comments also reflected the widening division between theology and philosophy. For example, in explaining the Biblical passage (Deut. 16 : 21), "Thou shalt not plant thee a grove of any trees near unto the altar of the Lord," since the altar could be interpreted as the mystery of the Passion or Incarnation and the grove as philosophy, Peter maintained that the theologian should not dispute the mysteries of Christ with arguments of secular wisdom.[96] Although some principles were common to both realms, others were proper to each so that certain rules of reason did not apply to theology. When discussing the nature of truth in the *Verbum abbreviatum*, he noted that it was twofold: that of the statement (the logical coherence of the predicate with its subject), which is philosophical, and that of the speaker or authority declaring truth or falsehood, which is theological.[97] Others such as Raoul Ardent and Innocent III also maintained this distinction between logical-philosophical and theological realms of knowledge.[98]

The division between theology and philosophy further encouraged a distinction between the methods of faith and reason. While Anselm of Canterbury and the theologians of the early twelfth century advocated cooperation between faith and reason, those of the second half of the century under the influence of the new Aristotelian logic began to oppose faith and reason as exclusive methods. For example, Simon of Tournai declared that "with Aristotle the argument is reason producing faith, but with Christ the argument is faith producing reason. Whence Aristotle says: understand and you will believe, but Christ says: believe and you will understand."[99] Again, Peter the Chanter alluded to this distinction in discussing virtues and good works when he mentioned parenthetically that theology was not like the other faculties because there one first believed and afterwards understood.[100] Elsewhere in the *Verbum abbreviatum* he held that such propositions as the Trinity, the Ascension, and the Eucharist could be believed only by excluding human reason which proceeded from natural causes.[101] Such propositions required faithful and wholesome words, not those of the court and philosophy. Like Simon of Tournai, Stephen Langton raised the distinction between the logician and the theologian, but, more interested in such problems than the Chanter, he attempted a solution.[102] Understanding may be divided into discerning and assenting. Discerning is the means by which we understand propositions to be true or false. Assenting pertains to something which has first been discerned. Discerning understanding, therefore, precedes faith, but assenting understanding follows. Stephen's attempt to resolve the fundamental problem of faith and reason is only one of many such proposals which appeared during the thirteenth century.

The establishment of philosophy as independent from theology raised a further question: How was the medieval Christian theologian to regard the pagan philosophers of Antiquity? Peter the Chanter and Gerald of Wales, it has been seen, made abundant use of Seneca's moral philosophy and to a lesser degree of Cicero's.* Following an opinion of Augustine, Peter regarded Socrates as the founder of moral philosophy since he diverted the Greek emphasis from natural science to human behavior.[103] Since none of the sage's works were known directly in twelfth-century Paris, Socrates was only a name to the Chanter. If, however, the ancient moral philosophers presented few difficulties to the Parisian theologians, the Greek metaphysical thinkers, Plato and Aristotle, required more critical scrutiny because their theories were relevant to central Christian

* See above, p. 80.

dogmas. Except for a portion of the *Timaeus* the scholars of twelfth-century Paris knew none of Plato's writings directly, but his philosophical theories were conveyed to the Middle Ages by numerous channels, such as the Neoplatonists, Augustine, Boethius, Pseudo-Dionysius, and the Arabs. By the twelfth century there were as many Platonisms as vehicles of transmission.[104] Peter the Chanter and Stephen Langton drew their attitudes towards Plato mainly from Augustine and Jerome. Following the two Church Fathers, Peter admitted that Plato might have had some notion of the Trinity from the triune vestiges of unity, mind, and world soul.[105] When Stephen Langton perceived a discrepancy between Augustine, who maintained that the Platonists were aware of the doctrine of the word of God, and Jerome, who claimed that the learned Plato was ignorant of it, he attempted to solve the difficulty by emphasizing that it was the Platonists, if not Plato himself, who achieved this doctrine, although Plato may have received a glimpse from the books of Moses which he read in Egypt.[106] Since Plato was not known directly and his ideas were filtered through the Church Fathers, he provoked little comment from the Parisian theologians.

Of greater significance to the theological movement of the thirteenth century was Aristotle. Precisely how and when Aristotle's complete works became known to western scholars in Latin translations is still unclear, but it appears that by mid-twelfth century the entire logical writings were available in the West.[107] Since the Greek philosopher was the primary authority for dialectics throughout the second half of the twelfth century, the Parisian theologians acquiesced to the study of Aristotelian logic as preparation for theology. Nonetheless, the full measure of the ancient Aristotle included not only logic, but also natural science, metaphysics, and ethics, of which the scholars of the mid-twelfth century were largely unaware. During the second half of the twelfth century Aristotle's remaining writings gradually came to the attention of the West.[108] Some were communicated from Arabic paraphrases of Avicenna which were translated by the scholars of Toledo. Others were translated directly from Greek into Latin by James of Venice.[109] Evidence from the last quarter of the century exists for primitive Latin versions of the major scientific, metaphysical, and ethical writings known as the "new Aristotle" in distinction to the better established logical treatises. According to the chroniclers Robert of Auxerre and William the Breton Aristotelian treatises on natural philosophy and metaphysics were serving at Paris as texts at least by the first decade of the thirteenth century.[110] Just as the works of the Greek philosopher provided basic instruction for logicians, so the newly discovered treatises attracted notice from the faculty of arts. Recalling the arts textbooks at Paris towards the end of the twelfth century, Alexander of Neckham appended the *Metaphysica,*

Liber de generatione et corruptione, and the *De anima* to the logical works of Aristotle.[111] As shown by developments in the later thirteenth century, the "new Aristotle" provided a fresh authority and source of inspiration for the masters of arts.

Suddenly and quite without preparation the ecclesiastical authorities at Paris turned against teaching the new Aristotle. A council of bishops convoked at Paris in 1210 by Peter of Corbeil, Archbishop of Sens, and Peter of Nemours, Bishop of Paris, commanded that neither Aristotle's books on natural philosophy nor their commentaries should be publicly taught or privately read at Paris, under pain of excommunication.[112] According to the decree and the chroniclers, this prohibition was associated with a campaign against fourteen heretics discovered and apprehended at Paris. This group, which included a former student of Stephen Langton,[113] was implicated in the pantheistic heresies of Master Amaury of Bène and Master David of Dinant. While Amaury's connection with the Aristotelian writings is tenuous, David drew inspiration directly from the *Physics, Metaphysics* and probably the *De anima.*[114] Among those who prosecuted the heretics was Master Robert of Courson.[115] Five years later, when Robert returned to Paris with special instructions to reform the university, he renewed the decree of 1210.[116] Warning against the doctrines of David, Amaury, and a certain Maurice of Spain, he again specified that Aristotle's books on metaphysics and natural philosophy and their *summae* were not subjects for lectures at Paris although he neglected to prohibit their private reading. The condemnation of Amaury was renewed in the Lateran Council of 1215.[117] Undoubtedly this sudden hostility towards the new Aristotelian writings was provoked by the appearance of the heretics, yet the connection between the heresy and the philosopher was not altogether clear. Aristotle, the natural scientist and metaphysician, was apparently considered more dangerous than the Christianized and vaguely understood Plato.[118] Since both Peter of Corbeil and Robert of Courson were active theological masters in Paris at the turn of the century, one might turn to their circle in hopes of further understanding of this unexpected attack against the revived Greek philosopher.

Although awareness of Aristotle's natural and metaphysical writings may be found among the theologians during the last third of the twelfth century, most of the citations appear in anonymous or pseudonymous treatises.[119] Those theologians, however, who were contemporaries of Peter of Corbeil and Robert of Courson and whose names and writings can be identified, took little notice of the new Aristotle.[120] Only one quotation from *De anima,* for example, has been gleaned from the writings of Stephen Langton.[121] Peter the Chanter knew Aristotle along with Theophrastus as the "prince" of the writers of natural history, but his acquaintance was limited to the anecdotal and it is not likely that he gained it from direct reading of the natural treatises of the philosopher.[122] The writings of Peter of Corbeil have not yet been identified,[123] and the *Summa* of Robert of Courson yields no discussion pertinent to the problem.[124] Since the new Aristotle was avoided by established masters in their acknowledged works and was cited only in anonymous and pseudonymous treatises, it appears as if the Parisian theologians approached these writings with caution. Only after the decrees of 1210 and 1215 had been promulgated were comments offered by anyone remotely connected with Peter's and Courson's circle. In a turgid and mutilated prologue to the *Speculum ecclesie* written about 1216 Gerald of Wales quotes from Dominicus Gundisalvi's preface to his translation of Aristotle's *De anima*, which was certainly one of the proscribed works.[125] More important, Gerald distinguishes between Aristotle's logical works recently translated at Toledo and which were useful for doctrine[126] and his philosophical works treating natural questions which had been recently forbidden in France. Although the text is defective at the crucial lines, Gerald seems to indicate that these natural works were more subtle than useful and fostered novelties, errors and heresies. Jacques de Vitry clarifies his attitude towards the natural works of Aristotle in a sermon to students.[127] Although certain pagan philosophers were profitable to theologians, others held false and futile opinions. Since Plato asserted that the planets were gods and Aristotle dogmatized the eternity of the world, those books called *naturales* should be avoided lest the student be led astray by unprofitable investigation. The Christian faith contains many matters either above or contrary to nature, but certain individuals infected by these "natural" books refuse to believe anything unless it can be established by reason and thereby they destroy the simplicity of the Christian faith.

Because of the dearth of evidence, the historian seeking an understanding of the conditions which brought about the prohibitions of 1210 and 1215 is reduced to conjectures.[128] Since Peter of Corbeil and Robert of Courson were originally members of the theological faculty, their decisions probably reflect the attitude of their colleagues. That concurrence was widespread is suggested by the almost total silence about the physical and metaphysical treatises among the acknowledged works of the active theologians. If debate took place, it never came into the open. Although silence indicates their position, it scarcely explains their disapproval. From the circumstances surrounding the official condemnation it appears that the authorities concluded that the new Aristotle was directly responsible for the pantheistic heresy of David of Dinant, a conclusion vaguely confirmed by Gerald of Wales. If the observations of Jacques de Vitry contain any substance, the theologians not only objected to specific doctrines in the natural and metaphysical writings, but they also feared a pervasive naturalistic methodology which would threaten the supernatural character of Christian revelation.[129] Although Gerald and Jacques had possessed earlier ties with the Chanter's circle, they were remote from the Parisian scene at the time of their writing. Gerald was in England and no evidence exists that Jacques taught theology at Paris nor that his sermon was delivered prior to the decrees.[130] Not until the 1220's when a new generation of masters appeared who had no direct connections with the Chanter and his contemporaries did theologians such as William of Auxerre, Philip the Chancellor, and William of Auvergne make explicit use of the new Aristotle.[131]

PREDICATIO

According to the Chanter's blueprints preaching constituted the roof and final adornment of the theological edifice. Although he swelled his chapters in the *Verbum abbreviatum* with Scriptural passages, pious examples, and quotations from Seneca, Horace, and Juvenal, he actually offered relatively little advice which was not commonplace.[132] Compared with his treatment of *lectio* and *disputatio* his treatment of *predicatio* is less helpful in indicating abuses and remedies. Peter's first major point is that effective preaching should proceed from a holy life, an opinion universally held throughout the Middle Ages.[133] Since the book of Acts (1 : 1) declared that Jesus first acted and then taught, Peter concluded that Christ's life preceded His doctrine, thereby confirming that theology was fundamentally the science of things and not of words.[134] A recent example of the effectiveness of a saintly life was the well-known preaching mission of Bernard of Clairvaux to the Germans.[135] Although the crowds could not understand the abbot's French, they were moved to tears by his overpowering sanctity. When, however, a Benedictine monk skillfully translated the sermon into German, the words lost their original force. The sermons of the Chanter's own student, Foulques de Neuilly, were more effectively spoken than read afterwards.[136]

If a holy life was required of preachers, the practical question arose as to the extent to which sin could be tolerated before a preacher should cease his ministry. Approaching this problem by drawing distinctions between ordinary preachers and prelates, Peter maintained that those who were not prelates but whose sin was unrevealed should be permitted to preach, but sinful prelates who continued to preach were in danger of mortal condemnation even though their sin was not publicly known.[137] Their condemnation, of course, was even greater if their lives were open scandals. Other than in this initial statement Peter did not develop the implications of this distinction, but Stephen Langton approached the problem by dealing with extreme cases. Ignoring the difference between prelates and ordinary preachers and apparently assuming that occult sinners could preach, Langton asked whether a preacher should exercise his ministry in spite of scandal.[138] Even if he were a notorious fornicator, Stephen concluded that he should continue to preach because the onus to preach outweighed that of scandal. Although elsewhere adhering to the traditional emphasis, Stephen exemplifies a tendency among theologians of the later thirteenth century to stress the office of preaching over the sanctity of the preacher's life.[139]

After dealing with the preacher's qualifications, Peter the Chanter turned to the manner of preaching.[140] Employing numerous quotations and analogies he attacked rhetorical adornments as meretricious. Unlike human philosophy which requires the verbal finery of an adulterous Jezebel, the preaching of sacred Scripture, like a chaste maiden, relinquishes these embellishments.[141] Just as the sick do not select a doctor for his eloquence or beauty, but for his wisdom and skill, so listeners require preachers distinguished by their knowledge.[142] Like priests who administer penance, the preacher should imitate the doctor skillful in diagnosing illness and applying remedies.[143] Gilles de Corbeil, a practicing physician himself, further embellished this medical analogy in his *Hierapigra*.[144]

While listing the principal perversions of preaching, the Chanter also turned to the problem of remuneration. Was it permissible to preach for gain (*predicatio questuosa*)?[145] Was not preaching a spiritual function whose sale constituted simony? In his disputations Peter asked whether a preacher who campaigned in behalf of building or repairing a church could retain from one quarter to one third of the takings. Apparently this case was not easily solved within the Chanter's school because at least three different answers to it have survived. The most common version replies summarily that if the preacher delivers his sermons for the sake of raising money rather than to excite devotion among the faithful he commits simony.[146] While agreeing with this conclusion another version specifies that if the preacher does not have a regular income he may nonetheless receive remuneration; otherwise he could not perform his functions.[147] Because of the danger of confusing motives, however, a third version proposed that the church could more safely give the preacher a regular salary than allow him to retain a percentage of the funds he raised.[148]

A further problem arose if the preacher was tempted to accept ill-gotten gains. One version of the Chanter's *Summa* cites the example of Reginald, a lay convert who claimed papal authority to preach publicly in Paris for the benefit of the Hôtel-Dieu of Notre-Dame.[149] His immensely popular sermons prompted large contributions from the townsmen, including a number of usurers. Although Reginald's collections were largely devoted to the poor, could he also accept alms derived from usury for his own use? The Chanter hesitated over this question. Certainly, if the preacher possessed other means he should not accept usurers' alms for providing his clothing and shoes. But from the example of Christ Who dined with sinners in order to preach to them, it could be argued that preachers could eat with usurers for the purpose of convincing them to restore their ill-gotten spoils. On the other hand, when the Apostle collected alms from the Corinthians (1 Cor. 16 : 3), the *Gloss* explained that he took nothing before they were corrected. Therefore preachers should accept nothing from usurers before they have reformed. Ignoring the Chanter's perplexities, Thomas of Chobham maintained that although it was simoniacal to preach for temporal profit, if a preacher worked for the benefit of the church he could receive necessary sustenance from his ministry.[150] Undoubtedly to curb possible abuses, Archbishop Stephen Langton decreed in his synodical statute (1213-1214) that two reputable men should be associated with each preacher who collected contributions.[151]

The issue of preaching for gain prompted the Chanter in one version of his *questiones* to single out a particular abuse. Certain preachers, Peter complained, profited from the abominable practice of employing saints' relics for raising funds.[152] Saints who abhorred contact with money while they were living were pressed into lucrative campaigns after they were dead. While Peter would not assert that such practices were simoniacal, since they benefited most churches, neither did he deny that they consituated a temporal employment of spiritual functions. His student Robert of Courson both embellished this *questio* and put an end to the Chanter's hesitations.[153] Since the casket of Saint Gendulfus split open when it was overlaid with silver, presumably to demonstrate the saint's contempt for money, and the body of Saint Firmin of Amiens refused to budge when someone proposed to carry it on a fund-raising campaign, Robert concluded that the relics of saints should never be shown for begging money. Echoing the Chanter's and Courson's protests, Pope Innocent III attempted to deal with relics in the Lateran Council of 1215.[154] While newly found relics should not be publicly venerated without papal authority, ancient and attested relics should not be exhibited nor placed on sale outside of the reliquary. In order to curb the lies of those who sought alms by displaying relics, the council prohibited such preaching without explicit letters from the pope or the bishop. With the Parisian theologians the Pope recognized the abuse inherent in employing relics to raise money; unlike Robert of Courson, Pope Innocent preferred regulation to total abolition. Nonetheless the abuses remained throughout the Middle Ages until they provoked even severer reaction from the Protestant reformers.

Despite inherent abuses, preaching remained, in the Chanter's opinion, the crowning adornment of the theologian. For this reason Peter had encouraged Foulques de Neuilly, and preachers emanated from his circle. In his commentary to the Psalms he proposed that just as the apostles and early martyrs preached the faith to an unbelieving world so modern preachers should circulate to encourage good works and repress evil.[155] As in the primitive church, a general council should be convoked by the pope to gather preachers for this purpose. Peter's proposal undoubtedly reflected a general mobilization of preachers at the turn of the century, but his specific call was in fact answered by the Lateran Council of 1215.[156] Noting that preaching was performed unsatisfactorily by contemporary bishops, Pope Innocent III commanded all bishops to institute diocesan preachers to work among the faithful by word and deed. To the conciliar fathers as well as to the Chanter, preaching was an important remedy for the pervasive ills of the times.

But the policy of encouraging preaching was also accompanied by control. As heresy increasingly threatened throughout the thirteenth century, churchmen began to insist that preachers obtain explicit ecclesiastical authorization.[157] Although the Chanter was silent about this aspect, soon after his death the synodical constitutions of Odo of Sully, Bishop of Paris (1197-1208), insisted that no one preach until approved by the bishop or archdeacon.[158] Because of the danger of error priests were to prevent ignorant and unlettered men from preaching in their parishes and the faithful were prohibited from hearing them, under ecclesiastical penalties.[159] Priests were further urged to increase their sermons to the faithful on Sundays and feast days.[160] In the Councils of Paris (1213) and Rouen (1214) Robert of Courson, following the program of Odo of Sully, dealt with these matters neglected by the Chanter.[161] No one was to be admitted to the office of preaching without just cause and explicit letters from his diocese, and the prelates of the church were encouraged to take a more active part on feast days. Similarly, Stephen Langton affirmed the licensing of preachers in the Canterbury statutes.[162] As a part of the program to combat heresy, the Lateran Council of 1215 decreed that under the threat of excommunication no one should presume to preach either publicly or privately without the authority of the Apostolic see or the Catholic bishop of the region.[163] The ministry of preaching was to be kept closely under the supervision of the church.

The Chanter's personality, it will be remembered, animated a band of preachers who radiated from Paris at the turn of the twelfth and thirteenth centuries. Despite the abundant advice furnished in two chapters of his *Verbum abbreviatum*, Peter himself left only one sermon which can be attributed to him. Preaching on a text: "Break up your fallow ground and sow not among thorns" (Jeremiah 4 : 3), he employed the agricultural cycle from tilling the soil to storing the grain to illustrate the spiritual life.[164] Evidently addressed to clerics,[165] this sermon contains little of interest for his homiletical theories. It is furthermore conceivable that his *Verbum abbreviatum* was related to preaching because several chapters were later mistaken for sermons.[166] Extant examples of Robert of Courson's preaching are even rarer than any of the Chanter's,[167] and Foulques de Neuilly, the most reputed contemporary preacher, is survived by no sermon at all. Although a good number of Stephen Langton's and Jacques de Vitry's sermons have been recorded, these must be studied systematically before their preaching practice can be compared with the Chanter's theoretical advice. Two sermons, however, entitled *inceptiones,* which originated from the Chanter's circle, are of particular relevance to the Paris faculty of theology.

By the mid-thirteenth century candidates licensed to teach theology by the chancellor were admitted to the masters' ranks by an elaborate procedure known as inception (*inceptio* or *principium*).[168] This admittance involved prescribed ceremonies on the eve and the morning of an appointed day, and the actual performance of the candidate's duties, particularly disputations. Often these formalities were continued on the first day when the newly initiated master held his class, called the *resumptio.* On the morning of the inception, after the candidate was invested with the symbols of his office and before he publicly entertained a disputed question, he mounted his professorial chair (*cathedra*) and pronounced a discourse in praise of Holy Scripture, known as the *inceptio* or *principium* proper. Although the details of these ceremonies are not fully described until the fourteenth century, the actual *inceptio* delivered by Thomas Aquinas when he became a theological master at Paris in 1256 has survived.[169] As early as 1215 Robert of Courson refers in his statutes to the *principia* among masters of arts.[170] Perhaps Stephen Langton alluded to this procedure among the theologians when, in his commentary to Ruth (written before 1206), he remarked that the masters are to report on their students when they are called upon to preach.[171] Among the sermons of Stephen Langton and Thomas of Chobham are two, as has been seen, which purport to be their *inceptiones:*[172] "The *lectio* of Master Stephen Langton which he delivered at his inception" and "Here begins the *lectio* of Master Thomas of Chobham when he began to teach theology at Paris."[173] Since Stephen taught theology before 1187, his *inceptio* antedates that time.[174] Thomas of Chobham's is more difficult to date because his Parisian career is known only from negative evidence.[175] Although it is possible that he was a master of theology by 1189/1193, it is more likely that he delivered his *inceptio* between 1208 and 1213 or 1217 and 1228. In all events these sermons provide the two earliest extant examples of inaugural lectures at Paris.

Adopting as his text: "And the people took their dough before it was leavened, their kneading troughs being bound up in their clothes upon their shoulders" (Ex. 12 : 34), Langton creates his sermon around an elaborate moral interpretation of the Jewish exodus.[176] Egypt stands for the world, the desert for the pilgrimage of this life, and the promised land for eternal rest. As true sons of Israel, Stephen declared, before we can enjoy the fruits of the promised land, we are sustained by two kinds of spiritual food: unleavened bread from Egypt and manna from heaven. So that we may first appreciate the temporal nature of this unleavened bread, we should examine the Egyptian grain from which it was made. The ten plagues of Egypt bring to mind the numerous ills of mortal life. The changing of water into blood represents the corruption of carnal living which nips the performance of good works. The frogs are vain speakers; the lice are those who utter stinging words; the swarming flies, mundane cares; the cattle murrain, corrupted beasts; and the boils, festering pride. The hail storm represents secular power which oppresses the poor, and the locusts are adulators. Just as a locust makes noise only in heat, so the adulator is silent in adversity but is heard in prosperity. The plague of darkness stands for those who blind sinners with encouragement, and the firstborn struck by death are the powerful of this age. By feeding on unleavened bread from Egypt we are reminded of these conditions of our mortal life.

After examining the grain brought from Egypt, we should consider how the manna was collected in the desert. Since the heavenly manna stands for Holy Scripture, its properties are instructive of God's word. Just as manna appeared with the morning dew, so the Scripture comes with divine mercy. Manna was small and round-shaped like a pistil so that it could be easily gathered into little bags. Thus the letter of Scripture is ground out with the pistil of exposition so that in its smallness it can be understood by the simple and found inexhaustible by the acute. When the Jews called it manna, meaning "What is it?" this signified both the humble who asked in wonderment and the proud who despised its size. Manna was collected early in the morning because Scripture should be learned after the night of mortal sin and while one's capacities are yet fresh. It supplied each Jew according to his need, just as Scripture is sufficient for both the wise and the foolish. Manna spoiled from one day to the next but could be stored for the sabbath. Scripture may be treasured for eternal rest but when taken avariciously, becomes unprofitable. Like manna Holy Scripture has both the sweetness of honey and the qualities of oil. Not only does it delight, but it is useful for feeding the hungry, refreshing the tired, furnishing light, and healing the bruised. The bread of Scripture is broken in reading, ground with the pistil of disputation and baked in the oven of meditation.

Finally Langton considered how Holy Scripture was to be learned and taught. To the student five things are necessary: purity of life, simplicity of heart, attentiveness of mind, humility, and gentleness. Four similar qualities are required for teaching the Scriptures: knowledge, life, humility, and gentleness. Just as the prophet Ezekiel first ate the book given to him by God, before he began to speak, so the theologian must incorporate the divine word into himself before preaching. When Ezekiel prostrated himself before the divine glory, the Lord set him on his feet and enabled him both to do good works and to speak. To teach a single syllable of Scripture requires a meritorious life. Just as God had to give Jeremiah his words before he could speak, so humility is necessary in propounding the word of the Lord. Only he who is wise in knowledge and disciplined in life can dare to assume the office of teaching. He must first learn to do good works before he can be a teacher of and an example to others in all gentleness. Having summed up these four virtues required of theological masters, Langton concluded with a personal affirmation: "What am I, who have neither eminence of life nor of knowledge, to say to these matters and yet I ascend the professorial chair? Relying on the inexhaustible goodness of divine grace and not on human presumption, I transform my tongue and mind in obedience to my Redeemer and I commit myself and my resolution to His grace."

For his *inceptio* Thomas of Chobham chose the text: "When Jacob awoke from his sleep he said, Truly God is in this place and I knew it not. And being afraid he said, how terrible is this place. It is none other than the house of God and the gate of heaven" (Gen. 28 : 16, 17).[177] By meditating on Jacob's awakening from his dream Thomas distinguished six aspects relevant to the theologian: he is (1) aroused from his sleep, (2) exhorted to watch, (3) he takes notice of the place, (4) is awed by its reverence, (5) led to the gate and (6) brought into the house. Jacob's awakening leads Thomas to distinguish at length four kinds of sleep: of nature, grace, glory, and guilt, the last of which is divided into sluggishness, negligence and ignorance. The exhortation to watch is directed especially to the master who is aroused by the rods of watchfulness, of Holy Scripture, and of castigation. Just as in the Gospels (Mk. 13 : 34) the head of the family commanded the porter to watch the gate, so the teacher of Scripture shows how the heretic is to be excluded and the Catholic to be admitted into the house of God. The theological master should be especially vigilant to do what is fitting. Not only should the teacher be watchful, but he is the custodian of the place. Like the shepherds who kept watch by night, he should be mindful of the pastures where his flocks feed on green herbs. The fresh hay brought down from the mountains is the teaching of schools. The place may also be likened to mines rich in the gold of wisdom and the iron of warfare. To the Scriptural account of the Philistines who were fearful lest the Hebrews made swords and spears, the marginal gloss adds that the pagans forbade the teaching of the liberal arts to Christians and drove the protectors of churches into exile so that the Christian people could more easily be deceived. While the masters of liberal arts manufacture arms of warfare and eloquence, the masters of theology like goldsmiths make the precious vessels and ornaments of wisdom. If they were to be found in the Albigensian lands, the heretics would not have succeeded.

The reverence of Jacob's holy place should frighten away seven basic evils which beset the teacher of Scripture: hasty action, inveterate ignorance, humiliating faintheartedness, rebellion of life, desire of vainglory, perversity of doctrine, and the sting of envy. The disciple should always precede the master as a warning against haste. When Simon the magician wished to fly with artificial wings he failed because he had no natural wings. Such are those who attempt to maneuver with the artificial wings of physical questions before they have the natural wings of books and the foundation of arts. Wishing to fly to the professorial chair, they crash to the ground. Ignorance is exemplified by the Scriptural account of the Philistine god Dagon which collapsed when it was placed near the ark of the Lord. Dagon was the ignorant doctor or prelate of the church who, when brought close to Holy Scripture or his church, lost his head, (his reason) and his extremities (his good works). The examples of ancient boldness found in John the Baptist and the poet Horace should deter the wicked teacher or prelate from adulterating the word of God or the church.

As a warning against rebellion of life, it should be remembered that whose life is despised, his lecturing will be regarded with contempt. When the devil placed Jesus on the pinnacle of the temple, he indicated the place where masters and preachers were wont to vaunt their vainglory. Perversity of doctrine is twofold, consisting of excessive verbosity and vain subtlety. The brevity of the ten commandments and the moderation of the Gospel are examples against the former. Since the Lord added the ceremonial law to the decalogue as punishment for the obstinacy of the Jews, should not Christians fear to be inflicted with a multitude of Biblical glosses choking up the Gospel? Not only did the philosopher Seneca speak against such superfluity, but the Church Father Jerome provided a positive example when he succeeded in glossing the whole Bible according to the historical, allegorical, and moral senses in only one year. Similarly, nothing hurts subtlety like too much subtlety, Seneca's sharp sword which blinds the eye of neighbors. When it is read that the Lord will change the rain into dust and ashes, dust represents the vain subtleties which do not irrigate the soil of the heart but render it sterile, and ashes, the residue of fire, signify the punishment of those who refuse to learn fruitfully. Envy, Thomas concluded rapidly, has been sufficiently treated by Jerome in his various prologues so that it may be skipped over. Post-poning to another time the last two points concerning the gate of heaven and the house of God, Thomas drew his sermon to an abrupt close with a benediction.

Although Stephen's and Thomas' discourses were both expressly en-titled *lectiones*, they were not equivalent to the normal lectures of the faculty of theology. When compared with the Chanter's and Langton's lectures on Ruth, for example, it is evident that they did not follow the Biblical passage in the manner of a commentary, but rather were de-veloped homiletically. After a Scriptural text was selected, a specific theme was discussed systematically according to major divisions, each subdivided into minor points. The procedure was the rhetorical method of the ser-mon, not the literary method of the commentary. There can be no doubt that Stephen's and Thomas' sermons were predecessors of the *inceptiones* of the later thirteenth century. Not only specifically designated by that term, they contain the traditional themes in praise of Holy Scripture. Langton pursued this theme when he compared Scripture with the heavenly manna of Exodus, and then passed to exhortations to theologians in the two concluding divisions. Chobham's whole sermon is devoted to admonishing the prospective master of theology. Since Langton's *inceptio* is apparently complete, it is by far the longer of the two. Chob-ham's, which is one-half the size, was broken off with a promise to con-tinue at a future date. Most probably Thomas intended to reserve the later part of his sermon for his *resumptio*, a standard practice in the later thirteenth century. Both sermons were considerably longer than Aquinas' *inceptio* of 1256 by which time the exercise had apparently become a formality. Langton's concluding protestation of inadequacy, and prayer for divine help in all likelihood followed a common practice, because similar themes also appear in the sermon of Aquinas.[178]

In the tradition of medieval homiletics both *inceptiones* consist largely of pastiches of Scriptural quotations chosen to illustrate the major and minor themes of the sermon. The selection of Biblical passages on the basis of verbal similarities suggests that Stephen and Thomas employed Scriptural concordances or alphabetical *distinctiones* to gather their ma-terial. Over and above this preponderance of Scriptural quotations Thomas used the *Glossa ordinaria* occasionally and both he and Stephen extracted passages from Pope Gregory the Great. From profane sources Stephen cited only one line from Horace (without identification) but Thomas employed more extensive passages from Horace, Seneca, and the *Disticha* of Cato. While Langton's *inceptio* is better organized, his exhortations to theologians are more vague than Chobham's. Like those of his teacher, Peter the Chanter, Thomas' sermon abounds in practical and concrete advice to the theological master. For example, his suggestion that the Albigensian heretics would not have succeeded if there had been an active faculty of theology in the Languedoc anticipated the University of Toulouse, established in 1229 expressly for combating heresy.[179] Moreover, Thomas' *inceptio* reechoes themes of the Chanter. While protests against immaturity,[180] and excessive subtleties of masters were common to contemporary theologians, the objection against prolixity of Scriptural glosses was emphasized peculiarly by Peter. When Thomas' sermon is compared with Peter's *Verbum abbreviatum* his direct dependence becomes apparent.[181] For example, his fourfold division of sleep, his protests that glosses choke the Gospels, and the Jewish ceremonial law burdens the ten commandments, are precisely those of the Chanter.[182] Scriptural passages and quotations from Seneca and Cato are cited in common with the Chanter. Even Peter's anecdote of Jerome's glossing the Bible was adopted by Thomas.[183] Clearly then, when he composed his inaugural lecture for the faculty of theology at Paris, Thomas of Chobham had a copy of his master's *Verbum abbreviatum* close at hand.

❦ CHAPTER VI ❦

Academic Life

B Y THE END of the twelfth century the success of the schools of Paris could be felt in terms of numbers as well as of intellectual reputation. As swelling crowds of masters and students were drawn to the royal city, the academic community was forced to consider mounting problems of material existence. How were scholars to be fed, housed, protected, and even policed? The writings of Peter the Chanter and his colleagues testify to this success because they were the first masters to devote serious attention to practical problems. Their discussions, moreover, reflected conditions peculiar to Paris. The salient characteristic which distinguished the schools of Paris from those at Bologna and Salerno was that the French scholars, both masters and students, were almost entirely members of the clergy, while laymen composed an important segment of the Italian academic population. This prevailing clerical status furnished Parisian scholars with rights and privileges which significantly affected their material existence and thereby framed the theologians' discussions.

ECONOMIC SUPPORT

To the individual master or student who inhabited the Ile-de-la-Cité, the Petit-Pont, and eventually the Left Bank, the most pressing problem was that of economic support. How was he to secure enough income to feed, clothe, and house himself? The theologians' response began with the clerical status of the academic population. As members of the clergy, masters and students were entitled in principle to an ecclesiastical benefice or prebend designed to supply a regular income.[1] Since the early Middle Ages a system of benefices had been in force by which churches acquired income-producing properties to support ecclesiastics who served these churches. While in theory every spiritual office was to be supported by a prebend, in practice the number of prebends nowhere matched the clergy. While neither the Parisian churches nor those of northwest Europe possessed sufficient benefices to support the growing numbers of scholars, in theory each master and student could qualify for a prebend. The system of benefices therefore provided the point of departure for discussing academic remuneration.

This approach was further prompted by the papal policy for promoting education throughout western Christendom.[2] Since Carolingian times the popes had occasionally encouraged churches to establish schools, but at the Lateran Council of 1179, Pope Alexander III made a concerted effort by requiring each cathedral chapter to provide a benefice for a master who would give elementary instruction to poor students without charge.[3] Other churches and monasteries formerly possessing prebends for this purpose were requested to reinstate this service. Almost forty years later, at the Lateran Council of 1215, Pope Innocent III admitted that the regulation was poorly observed.[4] Renewing Alexander's program, he extended it to other collegiate churches whose chapters were sufficiently wealthy to support a teacher. Not only were the cathedral and collegiate churches to teach grammar and the elementary subjects, but each archepiscopal chapter was to support a master for more advanced instruction in theology.[5] The major churches of Christendom were therefore encouraged to supply at least one benefice in support of education.

Even if this program had been widely observed, which it probably was not,[6] it bore little relation to the existing educational facilities of western Europe and had no relevance to conditions at Paris. The institution of one master at Notre-Dame or even additional ones at Saint-Victor, Saint-Germain-des-Prés, and Sainte-Geneviève, for example, would have been ridiculous as an attempt to provide for the students of arts, nor was the chapter of Notre-Dame required to establish a master of theology because it was not of metropolitan rank. The unusual demands of Paris required unusual remedies. By the twelfth century the popes began to claim a prerogative called "papal provisions" which allowed them under certain conditions to designate prebends to clerics.[7] Beginning with Alexander III they allocated a growing proportion of benefices to clerics bearing the title of master, some indeed who were actively teaching at Paris.[8] By the time of Innocent III papal requests for prebends in support of teachers were occurring frequently. For example, one of Innocent's earliest acts was to order the chapter of York to assign the archdeaconry and a benefice to his former teacher of theology at Paris, Master Peter of Corbeil.[9] By general program and specific means the papacy endeavored to supply prebends for the academic profession.

Since the regime of ecclesiastical benefices was not restricted to scholars, the theologians at Paris discussed it not as an academic problem but in the context of the whole clergy. Assuming the general features of the system, they turned their attention to abuses such as nepotism, admission of unqualified candidates, irregularities of appointment, and separation between the spiritual office and the temporal support.[10] Since these disorders were common to all ecclesiastical benefices, full consideration of these abuses would lead us too far afield, but there were several problems of particular concern to masters and students.

An obvious temptation arising from the system of benefices was pluralism. Since prebends were lucrative sources of income, clerics might accumulate more than one out of greed and ambition. Because of the rise of prices or the manner in which the revenues were determined they might also find one income insufficient and seek additional benefices. Since ample precedents against pluralism existed in canon law, Pope Alexander III in the Lateran Council of 1179 merely forbade clerics from holding more than one church at a time.[11] In the spirit of the Lateran Council Peter the Chanter devoted several chapters of his *Verbum abbreviatum* to describing the generally harmful effects of pluralism,[12] and his theme was followed by Robert of Courson and Peter of Poitiers of Saint-Victor.[13]

Apparently, however, the exigencies of the practical world compromised the Chanter's own position, because direct testimony is furnished by Robert of Courson that Peter was himself a pluralist. Raising a number of arguments favorable to pluralism, according to the requirements of academic disputation to put the case for both sides, Robert suggested that a church often becomes dependent on a member of the chapter who cannot be easily relinquished. For example, when Peter left Reims for Paris, the chapter of Reims compelled him to retain his former prebend because of his usefulness to the church.[14] Although Robert eventually concluded that no pluralist could remain in a state of salvation, he nonetheless could think of three possible exceptions: if the prebend was insufficient according to the judgment of a good man, if the pluralist donated the income from his extraneous benefices to the poor, and finally if the pope commanded the pluralist to retain his prebend temporarily out of utility to the church, as in the case of the Chanter, whose presence would be useful to every church if it were possible.[15] Despite his high regard for Peter, Robert would hardly have counselled his master to retain two benefices because of its pernicious precedent. Apparently the Chanter's conscience was also troubled, because according to Courson, he, along with Jovinus, *écolâtre* of Orléans, Master Peter of Louveciennes, Dean of Saint-Germain l'Auxerrois, and other God-fearing men, did not dare to die holding benefices in different churches.[16]

When Robert of Courson convened the Councils of Paris (1213) and of Rouen (1214), he ignored the exceptions he had formerly proposed as a theological master, but simply forbade under threat of excommunication pluralism involving benefices to which pastoral duties were attached.[17] In the Lateran Council of 1215 Pope Innocent III both reconfirmed his legate Robert and added an important exception.[18] Learned men who should be honored with major benefices could be dispensed by the pope from restrictions against pluralism if required by sufficient reason. The pope, in effect, regularized the Chanter's position by confirming his example rather than listening to his scruples. Throughout subsequent centuries the exception, not the general rule, governed papal policy.[19]

Pluralism led directly to the abuse of absenteeism. Since a cleric enjoying multiple benefices obviously could not maintain simultaneous residence, his spiritual duties suffered.[20] The problem of absenteeism, however, was vitally important to the prebended scholar. While a distinguished master might hope for a benefice near to where he taught, many masters as well as students travelled far from their churches for the cause of learning. When the case was Paris, the local churches could hardly provide prebends for the numerous professors, let alone for the throngs of students. These conditions at Paris prompted the popes to request prebends for scholars from as far away as York in England. The pursuit of study, therefore, compelled both masters and students to be absent from their place of benefice. As early as the mid-twelfth century canonists such as Rufinus argued that students should be allowed to live on their prebends not only in nearby but also in distant schools because their knowledge eventually benefited their own churches.[21] Huguccio noted that the policies of churches differed on this matter: some permitted no support, others partial revenues, and still others full enjoyment of benefices.[22] Alexander III concurred with Rufinus' view by formally declaring that studies constituted legitimate grounds for absence from a benefice both for masters and students.[23] Similarly, Peter the Chanter proposed that even if a cleric swore to maintain residence in a church, he could be excused for the sake of study as long as this was not a cloak for avoiding expenses or for living luxuriously.[24] As part of the papal program for supporting theology at Paris, Honorius III in 1219 specifically granted to clerics studying that subject the right to be absent from their churches for five years.[25] By permitting this exception to the rules on absenteeism churchmen insured wider utilization of benefices for the support of education.[26]

As sources of revenue, benefices were susceptible to varied negotiations involving acquisition, transfer, and disposal. Although most of these transactions concerned clerics in general,[27] the theologians discussed two instances which pertained specifically to the scholars of Paris. The first was occasioned by the recent conversion of the Jewish synagogue on the Ile-de-la-Cité into the church of Sainte-Marie-Madeleine.[28] When Philip Augustus became king in 1180 his first major policy was to harass and despoil the Jews of the royal domain. By 1182 he had banished them from the Ile-de-France and confiscated their lands and immovables. From 1183 a number of royal charters disposed of this Jewish property for the benefit of the King and his favorites, among which gifts Philip gave the synagogue on the Cité to Bishop Maurice of Sully to be turned into a Christian church.[29] In other confiscated synagogues, such as at Etampes, the King ordered the creation of a chapter and prebends.[30] What specific arrangements Bishop Maurice made for the new church on the Cité are not known, except that it was dedicated to Marie Madeleine and assumed parochial functions shortly after 1183.[31] Writing about a decade after the confiscation, Peter the Chanter provides more information about the church.[32] In a discussion of prebends and confraternities he noted that seven clerics proposed to the Bishop of Paris that they be allowed to form a spiritual fraternity at Sainte-Marie-Madeleine where they would assemble their benefices. Since they knew of other comrades holding benefices at Bologna, Salerno, Montpellier, and elsewhere, who might later wish to join this society, they further proposed that the membership be extended to twenty. Should the bishop accede to their request and assign them the altar of Sainte-Marie-Madeleine? Peter opposed this scheme because later members would seek admittance to a spiritual fraternity by offering their temporal prebends, which was a form of simony;[33] rather he counselled the clerics to remain in the localities of their benefices until the required number of members was attained before they established the confraternity. In fact, Peter observed, that was where the matter stood at the time. One could conclude that this incident involved an ordinary group of clerics and had no academic relevance except for the observation that the localities from which the clerics originated also contained thriving schools. At the end of the twelfth century one confraternity, the Collège-de-Saint-Thomas-du-Louvre was established at Paris (ca. 1186) for the benefit of poor scholars, and included four beneficed canons.[34] The proposal for Sainte-Marie-Madeleine may have been a similar attempt which never succeeded.

The Collège-de-Saint-Thomas-du-Louvre, like the earlier Collège-des-Dix-huit (1180), was originally intended to support poor scholars not possessing prebends. This primary purpose was retained even after beneficed canons were added.[35] Since the original endowment provided material benefit to scholars, some were tempted to offer monetary inducement to the confraternity to gain admission. Discussing the charging of admission to lay confraternities, Robert of Courson asked whether the masters of Paris could be admitted to the hostel of Saint-Thomas by paying a certain sum.[36] This case was related to another question, whether entrance to a monastic community could be gained through monetary inducement without committing simony. Rufinus and the canonist author of the *Summa Parisiensis* had previously investigated the reverse question: whether a monastery could exact fees from those seeking admittance.[37] They concurred that although money exacted before entrance constituted simony, any gift freely offered after acceptance into membership was commendable on the part of both the giver and the receiver.

Robert merely applied this solution to the case of Saint-Thomas-du-Louvre. If the masters formed any monetary agreement before admittance, the arrangement was manifestly simoniacal. If, however, they gained membership without the intervention of money, they were then free to donate their goods to stimulate the devotion and prayers of their brothers.

Among the complex problems linked with benefices, Peter the Chanter and his circle paid relatively little attention to prebends for scholars. Since the regime of benefices pertained to the whole clergy, its application to the academic profession required no particular treatment, but, more important, the supply of prebends was not adequate for the masters and students of Paris. For these reasons the Parisian theologians devoted greater discussion to the more pertinent issue of the academic fees which constituted the chief economic support for teachers. By the twelfth century academic fees were of two types: those which a master paid to the chancellor, *écolâtre*, or other ecclesiastical authority for his license to teach, and those which the student paid to the master for his instruction. From an economic standpoint the latter fees were more significant, but problems relating to fees for the license appeared first and prompted theoretical questions about all academic remuneration.

Since education throughout northwest Europe was controlled by ecclesiastical authority,[38] the *écolâtre* or other dignitary had the right to judge the qualifications of those seeking to teach and to issue licenses (*licentia docendi*) authorizing instruction in the area of their jurisdiction.[39] At Paris these licenses, although sometimes issued by the Abbot of Sainte-Geneviève, were usually conferred by the Chancellor of Notre-Dame. In medieval times churchmen as well as laymen were sorely tempted to profit from their rights by exacting fees for bestowing privileges. This temptation permeated all segments of society, education not excepted. Since the teaching license was a source of income for a master, numerous *écolâtres* and chancellors undoubtedly felt justified in demanding a price for it. While the practice was widespread throughout northwestern Europe, it was particularly deep-rooted at Paris. Bolognese canonists who wrote at the turn of the twelfth and thirteenth centuries often selected Paris as the notorious example and specified that the chancellor demanded a mark for each license.[40]

During his long pontificate (1159-1181) Pope Alexander III waged a determined campaign against charging for the license.[41] In decretals addressed to individual churches, then to all the French bishops, and finally in the Lateran Council of 1179 the Pope not only confirmed control over the license to church officials, but also forbade exacting of fees under penalty of loss of benefice.[42] Justifying his reform program, the Pope alluded to the principle that since knowledge was something spiritual, a gift freely bestowed by God, it could not be sold, an ideal as old as the ancient Greeks.[43] From a practical standpoint it was obvious that an *écolâtre* was in fact a churchman who sold his ecclesiastical functions, which could be condemned as simony.[44] Of greatest practical significance, Alexander joined the prohibition of fees to a program to endow masters in cathedral churches with prebends.[45] The Pope most likely envisaged the beneficed master who provided free instruction to poor clerics as the *écolâtre* who licensed other masters under his jurisdiction. In all events, he who granted licenses was assumed to have a prebend, because he could be deprived of it if he disobeyed the council's canon. It was only reasonable that the official responsible for licenses should be provided with an adequate benefice to eliminate any justification for exacting fees. The provision of prebends to *écolâtres* and chancellors was the practical answer to academic simony. Although these principles were clearly enunciated, the papacy had particular trouble in applying them to Paris, so accustomed were the chancellors to collecting fees. For example, in 1174 Pope Alexander III made special exception for the illustrious Peter Comestor, who was permitted moderate fees under the supervision of the archbishops of Sens and Reims.[46] In 1212 and 1213 Pope Innocent III was still attempting to make the Chancellor of Notre-Dame renounce his charges.[47]

Despite the troublesome case of Paris the outlines of the papal campaign against academic simony were sufficiently formulated by 1179 to provide canonists and theologians with clear guidance.[48] For example, Bernard of Pavia maintained that the sale of licenses cheapened the master's dignity and impeded the student's progress,[49] and Huguccio declared that not only was it mortal sin and shameful gain for the Chancellor of Paris to exact fees, but also simoniacal if the license was for teaching theology.[50] Peter the Chanter agreed that the canonical authorities were overwhelmingly opposed to selling the schools because they constituted spiritual dignities.[51] Proceeding one step beyond Huguccio, he maintained that the sale of a license to teach the arts was also simony, because the arts were preparatory to theology. Not content to leave it there, the theologians probed deeper into the application of the papal program. To Stephen Langton and Thomas of Chobham the crucial question was: Why could a chancellor not charge a master, when, as will be seen, the master was permitted to collect fees from his students?[52] The Chanter could imagine the *écolâtre* promising the master that he would exact no charge if the latter would accept no fees.[53] To Peter and Thomas the distinction between the two positions was that the *écolâtre* or chancellor possessed a prebend, which could not be assumed of the ordinary master.[54] To cite an actual example, when Pope Innocent III conceded the chancellorship of Meaux to Master Clarembaldus in 1201, he ordered the Chancellor to be assigned sufficient revenues so that he would not be obliged to charge for the schools.[55] Even if an *écolâtre* does commit simony by selling the license, the Chanter continued, what recourse has the master who is forced to pay the price?[56] Peter concluded that if a poor cleric cannot obtain a license without a fee and if he possesses no other skill for earning his bread, he may cast his money at the feet of the *écolâtre* without committing simony because he is actually redeeming what is rightfully his. While the theologians at Paris discussed the details, the contemporary church councils renewed Pope Alexander's program. It was incorporated into the canons of the Council of London of 1200, and of the Councils of Paris (1213), of Rouen (1214), and the statutes of Parisian faculties (1215).[57]

Seen as a whole, Pope Alexander's twofold policy may have been designed to provide economic stimulus to learning throughout western Christendom. Free licenses and provision of benefices for free instruction were, in all likelihood, envisaged to encourage the teaching profession. Despite these good intentions both aspects of the program looked to a former era and were of little practical help to the problems of Paris.[58] While the elimination of the chancellor's fee should have reduced an important obstacle to poor but qualified candidates and thereby increased the number of masters, in practice even Pope Alexander found this rule difficult to enforce at Paris. The chancellor's charge, moreover, was not necessarily a quantitatively restrictive measure. As a source of income, it could have encouraged the chancellor to reduce his standards and to license as many teachers as would appear decent. Had it been carried out as intended, the Pope's policy might have been more effective in improving the quality than in increasing the quantity of masters. The second aspect of Alexander's policy, it has been seen, had even less practical relevance to Paris. To provide one benefice from each of the cathedral and collegiate chapters and to employ other benefices from more distant churches would have supported only a handful of teachers, totally inadequate for the numbers of students. Since the economic support of the newly emerging university could not be provided by prebends, the Chanter and his colleagues devoted the greater part of their attention in this matter to a system of student fees.

The Parisian theologians approached academic fees according to their different styles: Peter the Chanter formulated questions with flashes of insight scattered throughout his writings, Stephen Langton wrestled with opposing arguments on a theoretical level, and Robert of Courson provided the most comprehensive treatment of the problem. Amidst their diverse discussions at least two sets of criteria governed their conclusions: (1) Did the master possess a benefice and (2) What subject did he teach? Since the Chanter and his colleagues were concerned with problems arising at Paris they concentrated attention on masters of arts and of theology, the two principal faculties there and the two which interested them personally.

One situation envisaged by the Chanter and his followers concerned a master of arts who held a prebend: Could he charge for his instruction? Although such cases formed a minority among the masters of arts at Paris, they fitted the beneficed masters whom Pope Alexander proposed for cathedral churches. Although not without ambiguity, the Chanter's answer was that a master who is beneficed to give free instruction may not accept anything from his students.[59] Furthermore, Peter and Robert of Courson recognized that the beneficed master of arts often served both as a teacher and as the *écolâtre* with authority to license other masters. Since he could engage other sub-masters to teach in his own school, could he also demand a portion of their earnings? To the Chanter this situation was equivalent to selling the license, and must be forbidden.[60] Robert of Courson, however, probed more deeply into the case of a beneficed *écolâtre* who enlisted other masters to assist him in the instruction of his school.[61] Concerned with the question whether auxiliary teachers could in turn collect fees, Robert decided that whoever has the dignity of office should also bear its duties. If the *écolâtre* benefits from revenues pertaining to his office he should either teach or relinquish his revenues. But should reasonable cause, such as sickness, incompetence, or assignment to Rome for business of his church, prevent his duties, he may hire a qualified substitute to be supported from his own revenues. In all events the substitute master must never be permitted to take fees from students to whom the *écolâtre* owed free instruction.

More pertinent to most Parisian masters of arts were the conditions mentioned by Robert of Courson at the conclusion of his discussion: Could a master of arts who held no prebend collect fees from his students? Stephen Langton approached the question on a more theoretical level.[62] If a master of arts collected fees was he not selling spiritual knowledge and thereby committing simony? Although he did not reveal all his arguments in the tortuous course of his discussion, Langton finally concluded that such fees were licit. Similarly, Peter the Chanter maintained that neither physician, lawyer, nor teacher were selling the grace of God by accepting moderate salaries if they were in need.[63] Adopting the Scriptural principle that a laborer is worthy of his hire (Luke 10 : 7), he allowed remuneration for the teacher according to his contribution of labor.[64] Conversely, lawyers, doctors, and teachers whose fees were incommensurate with their work were robbers.[65] Even the *écolâtre*, who did not enjoy a benefice, could accept payment from auxiliary masters.[66] Thomas of Chobham declared that in contrast to the chancellor, the *écolâtre*, if he was without regular income, could accept the necessities of life from his students.[67] Again, Robert of Courson most fully developed the theme. Without mentioning the complicating factor of a benefice, Robert discussed the vital question of whether a master of arts or of authors (*auctores*) could legitimately hire his services and collect fees.[68] On the affirmative side, he noted that the teaching of foreign alphabets, such as Chaldean, of foreign languages, such as French and German, and of the liberal arts, such as geometry and arithmetic, was equivalent to the exercise of mechanical skills by the farmer, artisan, and carpenter. If these skills could be remunerated at a contract price, why not the teaching of the arts, which also involved labor? On the negative side, however, canon law forbade the sale of notorial skill, which would seem to prohibit selling the liberal arts. Robert's solution involved two sets of distinctions: first, between the mechanical arts, which could be hired, bought, and sold, and the liberal arts; the second, between those liberal arts which imparted rudimentary learning and those which pertained to matters of morality. Only the last category, the moral arts, it will be seen, could not be sold. Following his preliminary arguments, Robert associated teaching of elementary subjects with mechanical skills. Just as a farmer who plowed a field, so a master who taught the alphabet or a language could hire his services at wages previously agreed upon. Although Robert's equation of the liberal with the mechanical arts may not have been flattering to the master of arts, it yet provided him with essential justification for his support. In effect the master of arts at Paris could honorably demand fees from his students which were commensurate with labor and service contributed.

Although the theologians might justify, to their own satisfaction, the earnings of the masters of arts on the same basis as the payment for mechanical skills, was this solution appropriate to their own discipline, especially when they regarded theology as the summit of all knowledge? If it were conceded that the arts were spiritual gifts which could not be sold, how much more would this belief apply to theology, the science of God? Unlike the ordinary master, Geoffrey of Poitiers remarked, the theologian has public responsibility to witness to the truth.[69] Obviously, to a theologian the teaching of theology differed significantly from the teaching of the liberal arts. Again, it was Robert of Courson who devoted the greatest attention to the problem. Following the Chanter's suggestion that the Christian religion consisted of right faith and good morals, Robert included moral philosophy among the essential subjects of theology. To the verse of Solomon (Prov. 23 : 23): "Sell not wisdom, instruction, and understanding," he added that this prohibition rightfully applied to the sale of both moral and spiritual doctrine which proceeded from the Holy Spirit.[70] Robert turned to the intentions behind instruction to emphasize the distinction between the theologians and the other masters.[71] If one teaches principally for the sake of temporal gain he may commit mortal sin, but if he teaches spiritual and moral subjects for the same reasons he is further guilty of simony. Just as the Old Testament linked manna and unleavened bread closely together, so both Holy Scripture and moral philosophy, which they signified, could not be sold without incurring simony.

If faith and morality were spiritual matters whose instruction could not be sold, on what grounds could the theologian receive economic support? Implicit within the discussion was the assumption that ecclesiastical benefices should normally be provided for masters of theology who, as men performing a spiritual function, were appropriately entitled to maintenance from the church. Robert of Courson mentioned in passing that as for masters of arts, it was out of question for theologians possessing prebends to accept fees from their students.[72] But what about a theological master who was not so fortunate as to enjoy a benefice—a problem more pertinent perhaps to Paris? If a master of arts could collect fees, asked Stephen Langton, why not also the doctor of theology?[73] After rapidly sketching his arguments he concluded that a theologian should not because of the dignity of his subject (*propter privilegium operis*), but if he was without prebend he might accept contributions from his students provided that he made no contract for the amount. Robert of Courson concurred with his countryman, and included theoretical justification.[74] Although a theologian could not contractually sell the science of God, he was permitted to accept sufficient temporal sustenance to carry on his spiritual activities, because, as the Apostle taught (1 Cor. 9 : 7), no one wages war at his own expense. But the theologian was forbidden to enter into prior agreements with his students over fees. In effect, the theologians argued that masters of arts and theology who were without prebends could support themselves from the contribution of their students. The practical difference was that masters of arts could contract for their fees before their lessons, but masters of theology must receive their earnings as donations afterwards.

By concentrating on masters of arts and theology the Chanter's circle devised solutions of particular relevance to Paris because these two faculties dominated the university throughout the thirteenth century. Although playing a minor role at Paris, could the faculties of medicine and law also collect fees? No expression of opinion has come to light from the medical doctors and only scattered remarks from the lawyers, but the theories of the Romanists and canonists at Bologna have been carefully investigated.[75] Since Bologna was preeminent in western Europe for the study of law, the Bolognese opinions may be regarded as representing the legal discipline. Roughly contemporary to Robert of Courson[76] the Bolognese canonists and Romanists treated academic remuneration in terms strikingly similar to the theologians'. Like the theologians the lawyers

127

held their science in high regard. Since Roman as well as canon law was a sacred gift from God, and lawyers were priests and philosophers entrusted with its care, they began with the maxim that legal learning could not be sold. Having stated the ideal, they likewise felt the need to accommodate it to the economic reality of insufficient support for masters of law. Since most Romanists were laymen, they were not eligible to receive prebends. Whether Romanists or canonists, lawyers like Johannes Galensis (ca. 1210) began to ask whether masters teaching at Bologna and Paris could accept fees for teaching, if they possessed no benefice for that purpose. During the opening decades of the thirteenth century the canonists Alanus Anglicus and Johannes Teutonicus and the Roman glossators debated this problem. When they finally crystallized their conclusions they were prone to make even more distinctions than the theologians. If a master possessed a prebend, the canon lawyers, who were primarily affected, distinguished whether it was assigned for teaching or not. If it was specifically designated for teaching, the master could not demand fees from poor students but he could receive gifts from the rich. Of course, a disciple should not be prevented from making gifts out of gratitude to his teacher. If, however, the benefice was not designated for teaching, the master received fees at the risk of acting shamefully, but he did not commit simony. When the professor of law possessed no prebend or regular salary, all lawyers agreed that he could accept voluntary contributions. The canonists differed from the Romanists in that they demanded fees only from the rich students, while the Romanists felt free to exact from all according to their ability to pay.

Although differing in detail, the theologians of Paris and the jurists of Bologna agreed that the future of learning could no longer depend solely on prebends. Concurrent with the old regime of benefices they acknowledged a new system of academic fees, which broadened the universities' economic foundations in the thirteenth century. The appearance of the new academic fee in competition with the older prebend also indicates a transformation of the professional image of teaching.[77] No longer was the master regarded exclusively as a privileged, almost sacred, person secure in his benefice. Now he was increasingly viewed as an artisan of the towns who manufactured intellectual goods in the *atelier* of his school and sold them to students at prices commensurate with his skill and labor. As his artisan qualities increased, his priestly characteristics declined. This transformation was best expressed by Robert of Courson, who in an effort to justify the teacher's earnings equated the liberal arts with the mechanical skills.[78]

To Peter the Chanter the pupil who at the ringing of the schoolbell faced his teacher without his fees was an apt illustration of the sinner in terror on the great Judgment Day.[79] How were students expected to find means to pay their fees? The Chanter and his colleagues paid virtually no attention to the economic problems of the student. They may have assumed that students were entitled to prebends, but undoubtedly they were aware that such means were unavailable for the vast majority. The figure of the destitute student appears occasionally in their writings. Stephen Langton, for example, described one famished scholar who could not persevere in school longer than Easter unless God sent him relief,[80] a situation which Stephen's countryman Gerald of Wales illustrated with a personal example.[81] While in Paris during the summer of 1179, Gerald was deeply in debt, hard pressed by creditors and desirous of returning to Wales. In desperation he repaired to the newly established chapel of Saint Thomas of Canterbury at Saint-Germain-l'Auxerrois to pray for deliverance, and within the same hour messengers arrived with the necessary money. Other than this extraordinary remedy the theologians evidently proposed no concrete suggestions for the economic problems of the unbeneficed student. Maintenance by family or patrons or occupations such as copyist, tutor, or choirboy, so vividly depicted in student letters, are passed over in silence by the masters.[82]

Only when students resorted to chicanery and thievery did the theologians take notice.[83] For example, Robert of Courson warned teachers who depended on student fees to investigate thoroughly the sources of their income.[84] All masters of arts who knowingly received fees from sons of usurers and robbers owed full restitution. Nor by closing their eyes could they plead ignorance when the truth was easily ascertained. It was true, Robert admitted, that such fees may represent a mixture of legitimate and usurious money, but the master was nonetheless held to restore an estimate of what was ill-gotten. Understood in its context Courson's example may not have been entirely irrelevant because by the end of the twelfth century students had a reputation of wildness and disorderly conduct. While one is not obliged to credit most of the drinking, wenching, gambling, and thievery celebrated in contemporary Goliardic literature, not all of it can have been poetic bravado.[85] Moreover, since the chief schools were situated in towns, students were increasingly drawn from bourgeois populations whose wealth depended on commerce. It will be seen that Robert of Courson believed that wealth derived from town commerce was more implicated with dishonest usury than was income from an agricultural economy.* Because of the students' reputation for thievery and because of their bourgeois origins, Courson found it pertinent to know whether teachers were indirectly profiting from ill-gotten gains.

Other than recognizing the obvious fact that students might borrow money,[86] the Parisian theologians paid little attention to the problems of

* See below, pp. 220 and 309ff.

student subsistence. They did, however, treat the related issue of lodging. Early in the twelfth century out-of-town students were no longer permitted beds in the cloister of Notre-Dame and by the time of Bishop Maurice of Sully canons of the cathedral chapter were forbidden to rent their houses to scholars.[87] The majority of students were increasingly obliged to seek lodging in private houses and hostels on the Ile-de-la-Cité or Left Bank, where they were at the mercy of the well-known rapacity of landlords. Stephen Langton remarked that the hostels along the rue Saint-Jacques, a Left-Bank quarter eventually populated by students, advertised comfortable beds which were in reality heaps of straw.[88] At Paris the important issue was clearly the price of housing. In a passing observation Peter the Chanter decided that masters could rightfully excommunicate students who rented hostels to their fellows for unduly high prices,[89] but Robert of Courson in his statutes of 1215 granted to masters and students the right to enter agreements, supervising the rents of hostels.[90] Rent control became a valuable privilege of the Paris students throughout the thirteenth century.[91]

Academic Deportment

As moralists the theologians were prone to point gnarled fingers at the chief foibles of the teaching profession. For example, Robert of Courson consecrated one section of his *Summa* to exposing vainglory among his colleagues.[92] Just as a knight in a tourney might hire other jousters to swell his entourage, so a professor, unsure of his own ability, engaged others' services to satisfy his vanity. All teachers attracted not by sound learning but by the vainglory of mounting the professorial chair and being designated as master were not in a state of salvation. More specifically, professors who taught theology and canon law for the sake of ecclesiastical promotion, favor, or temporal advantage mentally incurred the guilt of simony. Within his discussion Robert exposed arrangements by which masters threatened, enticed, and even bought their audience. For example teachers entered agreements not to desert each other as long as one wished to lecture, or to buy the school of another whose students were not free to depart even when their new teacher was less qualified than the old. Denouncing these contracts as unworthy of free men, Courson forbade students to hire themselves as audiences—which wasted their own time as well as nurtured the vanity of fatuous teachers. In his sermons and the *Historia occidentalis* Jacques de Vitry similarly castigated masters who enticed students by pressures, blandishments, and even outright hiring.[93]

Undoubtedly the most common complaint of observers of the Parisian academic scene was that masters were too young and inexperienced, a charge which was part of a general protest against immaturity among priests and prelates. Repeatedly throughout the twelfth century reformers such as Bernard of Clairvaux described the harmful effects of youthful churchmen.[94] By the turn of the century a chorus of voices denounced the prevalence of masters who were neither sufficiently mature nor learned enough to instruct others.[95] In effect, this criticism implied that the Chancellor of Notre-Dame was not rigorous enough in examining candidates for the license to teach. As might be expected, the Chanter and his colleagues joined in this general denunciation. How could one become a master when he was not yet a disciple, Peter objected.[96] The ambition of youthful teachers was so great that they presumed to retain old men, even the "Knights of Oger the Dane," in their schools.[97] "Believe only the bearded master" was the Chanter's general advice.[98] Gilles de Corbeil found the same fault in the medical faculty where mere boys attempted to propound the laws of Hippocrates.[99]

According to most observers the chief offenders were the teachers of arts. In an effort to curb this abuse Robert of Courson decreed in the statutes of 1215 that masters of arts should be at least twenty-one years of age and have studied six years.[100] But the theological faculty was also endangered by unseasoned candidates. Peter the Chanter recalled Jewish tradition, which permitted no one to study certain controversial passages of Scripture until he had attained thirty years of age.[101] Raoul Ardent remarked that Jesus did not begin His public preaching until He was thirty.[102] When at the age of twelve He was found among the doctors of the temple He was rather listening and asking questions. With Peter of Roissy, Robert of Flamborough, and Peter of Poitiers of Saint-Victor, Raoul observed that thirty was the canonical age for the priesthood, although this requirement could be dispensed with by the bishop for reasonable cause.[103] As a theological master himself, Robert of Courson had urged maturity for professors of canon law and theology,[104] but as papal legate in 1215 he exceeded even the Chanter's suggestions and the priestly requirements by decreeing that all masters of theology should have attained their thirty-fifth year and have accomplished at least eight years of study.[105]

At no time was youthful exuberance expressed more dramatically at Paris than during the week following Christmas. The *Rationale divinorum officium* of Master John Beleth, who knew the Parisian liturgy well in the late twelfth century, indicates that four feasts were assigned to the deacons, priests, choirboys, and subdeacons, which gave vent to the unconventional energies of the younger clergy.[106] Although full proof is lacking for the late twelfth century, it is likely that the boisterous celebrations of the Boy-Bishop (previously elected on the feast of Saint Nicholas, 6 Dec.), took place on the feast of the Innocents (28 Dec.) and was relegated to the choirboys. The best known of these youthful festivities was the Feast of the Fools celebrated by the subdeacons on the day of Circumcision (1 Jan.). Consisting of town processions and special services in Notre-Dame it gave opportunity to the young subdeacons to parody the divine services at best and at worst to indulge in wild revelry. During the liturgy for that day the Gospel flight into Egypt was acted out by clerics who impersonated Mary and Joseph. The service was called the Office of the Ass because even an ass was introduced into the dramatic tableau. Since the Feast of the Fools belonged preeminently to the young clergy, it was unlikely that the students of Paris or even the young masters would have felt excluded. Saint Nicholas, moreover, whose feast initiated the Christmas activities, was the patron saint of the scholars.

Peter, Chanter of Notre-Dame, had reason to regard the annual Feast of Fools with particular concern. During the ceremony his own staff (*baculus*) and authority over the church services were transferred for the day to a subdeacon designated as "lord of the feast." He and Robert of Courson provide a new glimpse of the riotous character of the Feast of Fools in their *questiones*.[107] Discussing bodily assaults on clerics, they note that if a priest ventured too close to a spectacle of the Feast of Fools he risked being struck by an inflated chicken bladder because many were hit inside the church. Although the picture is not clear, it appears that one of the amusements of the Feast of Fools involved inflated balloons made from animal bladders.[108]

Not all of the fun of the Christmas season, however, involved harmless balloons. One version of the Chanter's *Summa* specifies that in the dramatic representations of the Feast of Fools, of Saint Nicholas, and of the Holy Innocents, actors used swords.[109] Forgetting sometimes to employ the flat of their weapons, they actually shed blood in church. In 1198, the year following the Chanter's death, Cardinal Peter of Capua, papal legate for France, reminded the Bishop and chapter of Paris of these practices, in a letter which complained of not only indecent words but the shedding of blood.[110] More concerned with verbal irreverence than physical violence, he ordered that restrictions be imposed upon the Feast of Circumcision to tame its impious practices. When Master Peter of Corbeil, one of the chapter members named in the letter, later became Archbishop of Sens, he reduced the improprieties in his own church by authorizing a more acceptable office for the Feast of Fools.[111] In 1207 Pope Innocent III wrote the Archbishop and suffragans of Gnesen in Poland to abolish masks and theatrical games in the church during the Christmas feasts, and this decretal was later included in canon law.[112] Finally, at the Councils of Paris (1213) and Rouen (1214) Robert of Courson admonished all to abstain from the Feast of the Fools where the staff of the chanter was received.[113] Apparently Robert had little hope that his directive would be followed because he applied this prohibition especially to monks and nuns. These efforts to abolish or at least to reduce excesses in the Feast of the Fools had little effect on the exuberance of the young Parisian clergy because the riotous customs outlasted the Middle Ages.

Temptations of the Flesh

Beyond these peculiarly academic foibles masters and students, of course, shared the fleshly weaknesses common to mankind. Students at Paris, Nigel Wireker observed, consumed enormous meals, imbibed without restraint, and had their girls.[114] As conscientious moralists Peter the Chanter and his colleagues could be relied on to denounce the famous trilogy of gluttony, drunkenness, and lust.[115] With the ancient poet Terence they reminded their readers that "Without Ceres and Bacchus Venus shivers in the cold."[116] To follow them into an examination of these notorious lapses of the flesh would lead far afield from academic life, but one cannot help noticing the unusual attention devoted to lust and prostitution. Clerical audiences in the Middle Ages, like male audiences at all times, exhibited an irresistible fascination for this curious subject. Found anywhere men were gathered, medieval prostitutes not only infested the cities but also the courts of princes and great barons, and even of bishops.[117] If the Chanter and his circle were directly aware of prostitution, however, it was at Paris, where the problem was relevant to the academic community. In a well-known passage describing Paris during the Chanter's time the preacher Jacques de Vitry maintained that such women swarmed the streets and squares and dragged clerics off to their lairs by force.[118] So crowded was the Ile-de-la-Cité that masters and prostitutes sometimes shared the same dwelling. On the upper floor the master held his school, lectured, and disputed, while below the women quarrelled with their procurers and exercised their unspeakable trade. Although Jacques' tableau is doubtless more interesting than true, the implication cannot be avoided that the scholars found these women distracting. Peter of Poitiers and Prepositinus, Chancellors of Notre-Dame, and directly involved in student affairs, deplored the brawls that issued from the brothels as well as their more subtle temptations.[119]

Although the Romanists and the canonists contributed the basic principles for dealing with prostitution, the theologians applied them in greater detail to a wider range of cases. In his *questiones* Peter the Chanter formulated the essential theological position which was elaborated by Robert of Courson and Stephen Langton. Even the more speculative-minded Peter of Poitiers and Master Martin joined the discussion, but the most systematic treatment came from Thomas of Chobham. In an attempt to clarify, Thomas applied the term *meretrix* or prostitute to the woman while *scortator* or fornicator pertained to the man.[120] While the word prostitute could mean any woman who committed fornication, more exactly it designated one who publicly offered herself for sale. To Thomas and the other theologians, the chief moral offense was not the factor of sale, but the illicit fulfillment of lust outside of marriage.

Since prostitution in a technical sense involved money, the Parisian theologians devoted most of their discussion to the wages. While it was unnecessary to deny that this money was immorally acquired, they nonetheless considered the question of whether the prostitute could retain her earnings, or whether she was obliged to do restitution. Under the *condictio ob turpem causam* Roman law offered a remedy whereby one could recover money given for an immoral act, but if the giver, or both the giver and the receiver, acted immorally, the money could not be reclaimed.[121] Roman law further specified that since turpitude lay solely with the giver, money offered to prostitutes could not be restored because: "a prostitute acts immorally for what she does, but she does not receive money immorally because she is a prostitute."[122] This Roman law principle was reaffirmed during the twelfth and early thirteenth centuries by canonists, Romanists, and theologians.[123] For example, Peter the Chanter, followed by Stephen Langton and Robert of Courson, maintained that public prostitutes were not held to do restitution for their ill-gotten gains in an open court of law (*ius fori*),[124] and Thomas of Chobham went so far as to declare that since these women labored with their bodies, they were legitimately entitled to their wages.[125] Although they never explicitly said so, the Parisian theologians were aware of the obvious injustice of compelling prostitutes to restore to their so-called "victims," who would have been quite content to see their money returned.

To the Roman law theory which justified the retention of prostitutes' earnings, the Chanter and his colleagues proposed one modification. If the woman employed any manner of fraud in dealing with her customer, she was obliged to restore to the extent of her deception. Peter notes that a woman might anoint her eyes with *stibio*, pretty her face with cosmetics, pretend that she is of noble birth or declare that she loves the man above all others.[126] If a man is deluded into thinking that she was a simple girl and loses between thirty and one hundred shillings in the affair, must she be held to restitution? Peter admitted that such cases were difficult, but in principle the girl must be held to restitution if she has deceived the man. If, however, he had defrauded her and satisfied his lust, she owed him nothing. More practical about the matter, Thomas of Chobham opined that if in her natural form the prostitute would have received only a halfpenny but because of her make-up she gained a penny, she was obliged to restore the difference.[127] Robert of Courson emphasized that the prostitute owed full restitution to an undiscerning boy defrauded of his inheritance, but nothing to the mature man.[128] For these reasons the Chanter held that the private courtesan was more fraudulent than the street woman and so more liable to claims for restitution.[129]

In addition to that of restitution medieval churchmen raised a further problem: could prostitutes legitimately offer alms from their earnings? Although this question did not arise directly in Roman law, the Romanist doctrine of restitution nonetheless provided a basis for its solution. Among the canonists Huguccio pointed out that if restitution of the prostitute's money was not required, she was entitled to her wages and could rightfully contribute alms.[130] Contrasted with usury, prostitution became the classic example in canon law of ill-gotten gains which could be licitly retained and from which alms could rightfully be given.[131] The Parisian theologians accepted by and large the canonists' conclusions,[132] but offered modifications in detail and emphasis. Thomas of Chobham, for example, maintained that if prostitutes were free from fraud, they might contribute their money to pious causes as a part of penance and conversion.[133] Had not the Lord accepted the ointment of Mary Magdalene purchased from a life of sin?[134] Robert of Courson was even willing to accept alms from secret prostitutes who had not yet renounced their shameful ways in hopes of hastening their repentance.[135] Not content to leave the matter there, Peter the Chanter reiterated in his *Summa* that such women not only *may* but *must* give alms. Although not obligated to restore in an open court (*ius fori*), they were not permitted to retain their ill-gotten gains in the confessional (*ius poli*).[136] In a burst of indignation Peter exclaimed: "Why should we require a usurer to part with his gains and not a prostitute? The prostitute kills two souls, the usurer only one. The prostitute sells what she should deny, the usurer, what he should concede."[137] Since the man cannot reclaim the money and the woman should not retain it, Peter concluded that the money should be given to the church for use by the poor.

The Parisian theologians' concern with prostitutes' donations to the church was somewhat more than theoretical; it was closely related to an event of their day. The construction of Notre-Dame and accompanying problems of finance, it will be remembered, was a major preoccupation of Bishop Maurice of Sully.* Without mentioning particulars, Peter the Chanter noted that certain women actively practicing prostitution during his day desired to present chalices and stained-glass windows to the church.[138] Elaborating on Peter's observation, Thomas of Chobham reported that the prostitutes of Paris offered a magnificent stained-glass window to Notre-Dame.[139] While commenting on Deuteronomy 23 : 18: "Thou shalt not bring the hire of the whore," Stephen Langton discussed prostitutes' oblations to the tabernacle and what would have been his policy were he a prelate of the church.[140] Although Maurice of Sully was

* See above, p. 65.

never named, the relevance of these discussions to the Bishop's building program would not have been missed by contemporary Parisians. In the judgment of all three masters Bishop Maurice was morally free to accept donations from such women, but they offered advice as to how these gifts should be received. Since such donations were a delicate matter susceptible to misunderstanding by the faithful, Peter and Stephen maintained that they should be presented privately in order to avoid public scandal. In other words, only gifts which could be offered discreetly were acceptable. Robert of Courson, however, objected that public women could not make any offerings, but the secret prostitute could tithe those of her earnings gained without fraud.[141] If Chobham's report may be trusted, Bishop Maurice, mindful of the theologians' advice, refused the prostitutes' magnificent donations because public acceptance would have seemed to approve their way of life.

That the theologians permitted the church to accept offerings from prostitutes in no wise condoned the turpitudes of the profession. Peter the Chanter assumed that such women were under the ban of excommunication, but was hesitant as to how this penalty cut them off from the faithful.[142] To be sure, prostitutes were excluded from the Eucharist, but they were not debarred from the church for the kiss of peace and the offering of prayers. Thomas of Chobham confirmed the Chanter's picture by reporting that at Notre-Dame prostitutes were allowed to mingle with other women at the presentation of candles to the altar at Sunday vespers although they were never admitted to the mass.[143] To Thomas this relatively lenient treatment implied that the church tolerated prostitutes because of human weakness and in order to prevent worse abuse, just as Moses permitted divorce to the Jews.[144] Assuming a firmer stance, however, Robert of Courson urged bishops and parish priests to excommunicate all public and incorrigible prostitutes named by legal confession, conviction of witnesses, or notoriety of fact.[145] If such measures were ineffectual, Robert advocated their expulsion from the city.[146] As papal legate for France Robert implemented this last proposal in 1213 at the Council of Paris, where he forbade under pain of excommunication all public prostitutes from residing within the city and enjoined their segregation according to the custom for lepers.[147]

Although the masters were preoccupied with questions which resulted in mulcting and harassing prostitutes, they were responsible for at least one effort which expressed pity towards these unfortunate women. During the twelfth century numerous preachers both orthodox and heretical were known to be effective in redeeming women of ill fame,[148] but none had the reputation of Foulques de Neuilly. At the turn of the twelfth and thirteenth centuries most of the chroniclers in France and England recorded his amazing deeds performed among the prostitutes.[149] Not only possessing a remarkable gift for persuading women to renounce their sin, he also displayed an understanding of their problems unusual for his day. During his preaching at Paris in 1198, for example, he founded the Cistercian convent of Saint-Antoine on the outskirts of the city to shelter repentant women who desired to abandon their former life,[150] but for those who feared that they could not continue chastely Foulques proposed another solution. A significant obstacle to legitimate marriage and an important incentive to prostitution was, in all probability, that poor girls could not easily raise the required dowries. To permit these fallen women to marry honorably Foulques raised a fund to provide the necessary money. According to Otto of Saint-Blaise, the scholars of Paris contributed 250 pounds in silver and the bourgeoisie over a thousand pounds.[151] Concurrent with Foulques' program Pope Innocent III issued a general letter to the Christian faithful declaring that all who rescued women from brothels and led them in marriage performed a meritorious work for the remission of their sins.[152] No evidence has come to light of direct collaboration between the Pope and the preacher at this time,[153] but the papal decretal and the preacher's program certainly complemented each other. As if in answer to the papal exhortation to redeem prostitutes by honorable marriage, Foulques de Neuilly provided them with dowries.

ACADEMIC DISCIPLINE

The ebullient energies of youthful students and masters crammed into the Ile-de-la-Cité and the Left Bank confronted the public authorities of Paris with evident problems of order and discipline. Since the academic population was largely clerical, these problems pertained primarily to the ecclesiastical regime, although they also concerned the king and royal provost in charge of Paris. Peter the Chanter and his colleagues considered various means to insure academic discipline, ranging from exhortation through spiritual penalties to physical coercion by secular authority.

The simplest remedy was to urge scholars to good behavior by preaching. Though the Chanter himself is survived by few sermons, he provided inspiration for a celebrated preacher, Foulques de Neuilly. Chiefly effective among the illiterate laity, Foulques was not ideally suited for preaching to learned audiences since his own education was acquired late. As has been seen, when the masters and students transcribed his words in their notebooks, they discovered that the force of his sermons lay in his personality, not in their content.[154] Although Foulques' talent was more appropriate for the market place of Champeaux, Peter the Chanter made him preach to a learned audience at the church of Saint-Séverin on the Left Bank.[155] The substance of his sermon is not known, but according to Jacques de Vitry the scholars were impressed with his preaching. The chronicle of Otto of Saint-Blaise, however, noted that on another occasion Foulques invited a certain Master Peter to join his ministry and exhorted other teachers to pay closer attention to their academic responsibilities,[156] advice then current among the Chanter and his associates. Canonists, theologians, logicians, and masters of arts were urged to eliminate the useless, lengthy and sophistic in their lectures and disputations. Undoubtedly other preachers addressed similar exhortations to academic audiences in Paris at the turn of the century. Among the preachers enumerated by Jacques de Vitry who were currently active at least two, Stephen Langton and Robert of Courson, were members of the theological faculty.[157]

Jacques himself has left two examples of sermons preached to scholars. From the text of Ecclesiasticus 6 : 36: "And if thou seest a man of understanding, go to him early in the morning and let thy foot wear out his door steps," the one exhorted students to take great care in selecting worthy teachers.[158] By employing the Scripture and Seneca, Jacques outlined the standard moral defects of masters, such as vain curiosity, fraud, envy, and contention, and piously concluded that masters of understanding should be attentively heard, their doors frequented and their steps worn down for the benefit of their sound doctrine. From the Old Testament account of the Hebrews despoiling the Egyptians (Ex. 3 : 21, 22) the second sermon considered the study of the liberal arts and ancient philosophy, which, as has already been seen, Jacques recommended as long as they were held in due subordination to divine truth.[159]* In the thirteenth century this kind of academic preaching increased considerably.[160] Already at the beginning of the century the theologians claimed that there was no dearth of moral preaching at Paris. Robert of Courson, for example, maintained that a peasant who acted immorally might be excused by ignorance and remoteness from teachers, but certainly not those at Paris who benefited from an abundance of masters.[161] Stephen Langton similarly chided the people and scholars of Paris who heard the word of God so often and yet were barren in good works.[162] Obviously measures stronger than preaching were required to eradicate the vices of students and masters.

By reason of their clerical status masters and students were particularly subject to church sanctions. Through the confessional and the church courts they could be coerced with penitential penalties ranging from liturgical recitations to solemn excommunication.[163] Although such spiritual sanctions were perfectly in order, problems arose from assigning jurisdiction over the academic classes. Spiritual jurisdiction was traditionally distributed by parishes and dioceses so that parish priests were authorized to discipline ordinary matters and the bishops major affairs.[164]

* See above, p. 79.

While this system was designed for the laity who were relatively immobile, it was less suitable for clerics who moved about more often. Although teachers, once having established their schools, were inclined to remain fixed, students were expected to travel great distances in search of worthy masters. Just as Ruth forsook her native land to reap in the fields of Boaz, the Chanter observed, so theological students left their homes and families for the sake of study.[165] The increased fame of the Paris schools during the twelfth and early thirteenth centuries resulted in an international composition of the student body. Remembering the former days of Peter the Chanter and Foulques de Neuilly, Jacques de Vitry enumerated clerics from England, the Ile-de-France, Germany, Normandy, Picardy, Burgundy, Brittany, Lombardy, Rome, Sicily, Brabant, and Flanders.[166] Since the scholars were far from their local priests and bishops, who claimed jurisdiction over their spiritual life and moral conduct?

By the turn of the century several solutions were being applied concurrently to this problem, the simplest of which was to allow the Bishop and the parish priests of Paris to exercise diocesan and parochial jurisdiction over foreign clerics in the confessional. The Chanter advised students to go to the bishop for confession or to whatever parish priest the bishop designated as his substitute.[167] Maintaining that hospiced clerics and scholars were subject to the parish priest or bishop of their domicile, Peter of Poitiers of Saint-Victor could not understand how a cleric unlike a layman could claim exemption from his parish.[168] More troublesome was the problem of granting absolution to students excommunicated by their home priests. The Chanter's solution was simply to send the cleric back to the priest who had pronounced the sentence, particularly if he was the home priest,[169] but by the second decade of the thirteenth century the problem had become more complicated. The anonymous Saint-Victor penitential from this period claims that the Bishop of Paris or his substitute could temporarily modify penance enjoined by the home priest until the cleric returned and received full absolution.[170] If, therefore, a student fell under a general ban of excommunication, upon promise of amends his sentence could be relaxed temporarily by the Paris authorities until he returned home, especially if he came from a remote region and could not send a messenger without difficulty. If, however, a student was excommunicated by name by his home authority, he must obtain notice of absolution at home either personally or by messenger before he could be absolved by a confessor at Paris.

In effect, the Bishop of Paris or a designated parish priest exercised ordinary spiritual authority over the Paris students. As the academic population grew during the first two decades of the thirteenth century this jurisdiction was gradually shared by the Abbey of Saint-Victor on the Left Bank.[171] In an amusing *exemplum* attributed to the year 1199 Caesar of Heisterbach told how a particularly contrite student who confessed his overwhelming sins to the Prior and Abbot of the church, received absolution directly from God Himself.[172] At the time of Courson's *Summa* Saint-Victor's parochial jurisdiction over students cannot have been fully established because Robert maintained that the canons of the church could not impose penance except by the Bishop's command.[173] When in 1208, however, Cardinal Gallo published his disciplinary measures at Paris, he provided that those who were thereby excommunicated could receive absolution from the Bishop and, in his absence, from the Abbot of Saint-Victor.[174] In 1212 Pope Innocent III granted to the Abbot the right to release students from automatic excommunication incurred from assaulting clerics.[175] An office of *penitentiarius* was created within the Abbey and assigned to a canon, Menendus, who in 1218 wrote to a certain Ralph, his counterpart in the papal curia, asking advice on questions involving penance for the masters and students of Paris.[176]

This increased assuming of parochial responsibility for the academic community was likewise reflected in the Victorine guides to confessors. Robert of Flamborough's *Penitential*, written between 1208 and 1210, makes almost no mention of students or academic problems. The guide of Peter of Poitiers of Saint-Victor, composed shortly after 1215, however, contains a few allusions to students and to the role of the Abbey as their confessor. For example, when the Bishop of Paris wished to fill a vacant prebend, he consulted the confessor of Saint-Victor about several students under consideration.[177] Finally, the anonymous compiler of the penitential of Saint-Victor from the second decade of the thirteenth century not only excerpted the works of Robert and Peter but also added sections specifically relevant to student affairs,[178] while Menendus' letter of 1218 likewise posed questions of importance to scholars.

With the Bishop, the Abbot of Saint-Victor, and designated parish priests, the masters themselves also shared jurisdiction over their students. Precedent for this authority was provided by Pope Alexander III who about 1170/1172 heard a case in which a priest of Bourg-Saint-Remi near Reims roughly handled and later excommunicated a group of scholars who had jeered and disrupted a church procession.[179] Although the students clearly provoked the disturbance, the Pope forbade excommunication of the scholars as long as they wished to remain under the jurisdiction of their masters, who were responsible for judging the guilt and assigning the punishment. Perhaps familiar with the Saint-Remi affair from his Reims days, Peter the Chanter queried in one version of his *questiones* whether a master could excommunicate his clerics for theft, purloining of books, or rent discrimination.[180] Even if the clerics were not subject specifically to the master, Peter nonetheless allowed him this authority, unless the clerics placed themselves directly under the Bishop of Paris. In the statutes for the faculties of Paris of 1215 Robert of Courson stated summarily that to each master belonged the court (*forum*) of his student.[181] Since masters were not necessarily ordained priests, they did not normally hear confessions and impose penance, but they did share with the bishop jurisdiction over students in more serious crimes which required court adjudication and excommunication.

Since ecclesiastical discipline touched only the student's soul, whether by mild penance or stern excommunication, were there other provisions for applying coercion to their bodies? Such measures as there were might vary from petty birchings within the schools to mutilation and death administered by secular authorities. To lay hands physically on a cleric, however, was fraught with grave consequences, because by the second quarter of the twelfth century the persons of all churchmen were protected by an immunity known as the *privilegium canonis*. In 1130 the Council of Clermont decreed that all who laid hands on clerics or monks were guilty of sacrilege and automatically excommunicated,[182] to which the Councils of Reims of 1131 and 1148 and, most important, the Lateran Council of 1139 added that except when death was imminent such excommunication could not be remitted by a bishop until the guilty party presented himself before the pope and obtained absolution.[183] Under this unqualified decree, to strike a cleric involved sacrilege, automatic excommunication, and a penitential journey to Rome.

The contingencies of real life were too complicated to permit full enforcement of clerical inviolability. When actions prompted by playfulness were not distinguished from those intended to harm, when the term *clericus* comprised not only the mature priest but also the schoolboy under puberty, it soon became evident that extensive modifications were demanded if the general principle was to have practical effect. In particular qualifications were required in the schools, where the problems of disciplining youthful clerics were urgent. John of Salisbury relates that as early as the Reims council of 1148 Pope Eugenius III informally offered restricting interpretations.[184] For example, whoever struck clerics in performing their just duties, such as a doorkeeper holding back a crowd or a teacher disciplining a pupil, were exempt from the penalties. It was not until 1171/1172 that the papacy issued an official enumeration of exceptions to the *privilegium canonis*. In the decretal *Sicut dignum* to the canonist Bartholomew, Bishop of Exeter, Pope Alexander III specified cases involving the assault of clerics which released the excommunicated party from seeking papal absolution.[185] Huguccio systematized the papal list of exceptions under eight categories: (1) those under the age of puberty, (2) those acting in playfulness, (3) teachers disciplining students, (4) those acting immediately in self-defense, (5) those discovering clerics in immoral acts with members of their families, (6) fights involving monks and regular canons within the cloister, (7) clerical doorkeepers exercising their duties, and (8) lay officials performing their just functions.[186] Huguccio exceeded Pope Alexander by recommending that the first five types of offenders be immune from excommunication altogether and that the last three, while excommunicated, be absolved by their bishops or abbots without papal permission. With slight changes the Victorine writers of guides to confessors proposed similar lists of exceptions.[187] While not drawing up formal schemes, Peter the Chanter, Robert of Courson, and Thomas of Chobham applied in detail the exceptions proposed by Pope Alexander. Robert of Courson concluded that only those who laid violent hands on clerics and with harmful intention should fall under the *privilegium canonis*.[188]

It would lead us far afield to examine those cases which pertained to all clerics, but a number were more directly relevant to the schools. To take the simplest example, clerical schoolboys indulging in a brawl were not compelled to seek papal absolution according to Alexander III nor even excommunicated according to Huguccio by reason of their age.[189] Robert of Flamborough designated fourteen years as the age limit.[190] If schoolboys were engaged in games which injured a priest either as a participant or as a bystander, they were free from the ban or at least from the requirement of papal absolution.[191] In this connection the Chanter and Courson maintained that if anyone swatted a priest with an inflated bladder during the Feast of Fools he was not guilty of clerical assault.[192] If one played a game with immoderate violence, for example, by hardening his snowball into ice, he fell under the ban. Of greatest importance to academic discipline, however, was Pope Eugenius' interpretation that teachers who administered corporal correction were not fully guilty of assaulting clerics. Among the theologians hesitation arose as to whether the penitential visit to the pope was remitted,[193] but Peter the Chanter, and Peter of Poitiers of Saint-Victor agreed with Huguccio that the teacher was also free from excommunication.[194] Raising the case of an *écolâtre* troubled by idle and unruly pupils disturbing his school, the Chanter decided that even if these clerics were deacons, the master could punish them by flogging provided that he preserved a righteous attitude.[195] Similarly Courson permitted corporal punishment by the teacher if it was performed without malignant intention, as emphasized by Pope Alexander.[196]

After Pope Alexander III formulated certain cases granting absolution for assaults in the schools, the next step was to extend this benefit to all assaults committed by students. Before 1212 Pope Innocent III had granted to the Abbot of Saint-Victor this authority over all students in Paris,[197] and from that time only the most flagrant cases of excommunication for clerical assault were sent to Rome for absolution. In a letter of 1218 to Menendus of Saint-Victor, who requested clarification, Ralph the papal *penitentiarius* replied that the serious cases to be sent to Rome should be judged according to the gravity of the injury and the importance of the person assaulted,[198] that Menendus had jurisdiction over students who committed assaults even on pilgrimages to Saint-Denis, Notre-Dame, and other sanctuaries, that he did not have authority to absolve beadles and other lay servants of students, that he could absolve students assaulting clerics who were not students, but not vice versa, and finally that this authority to absolve could not be extended retroactively.[199] This increased attention to clerical assaults indicates that student brawls occurred frequently enough to cause concern among the church authorities.

The mounting pressure of university population in Paris at the turn of the century only aggravated the problems of student discipline. If it is known that students were fighting among themselves more frequently, it may be further suspected that they were also involved in brawls with the Parisian bourgeoisie, since the *privilegium canonis* rendering students inviolate would hardly discourage their aggressions against lay neighbors. Indeed, King Philip Augustus was once reported to have marvelled that clerical boldness exceeded that of knights.[200] While knights fight only in armor, clerics spring into the fray brandishing knives but with no helmets to protect their clean-shaven pates. In truth, the King had little cause to wonder since he knew full well that the tonsure, the unmistakable sign of clerical status, was more effective protection than the helmet. Not only was assault of clerics an act of immense gravity,[201] but the services of the Abbey of Saint-Victor to adjudicate such affairs were not available to townsmen. Of course, if a cleric assaulted a layman the ecclesiastical penalties were not nearly as severe.

The protection of the townspeople as well as the maintenance of public order was the responsibility of the Provost of Paris, the chief royal police officer. How his duties were complicated by the increased numbers of privileged students was dramatized by the well-known student riot of 1200.[202] As told by the English chronicler Roger of Hoveden, the affair developed according to a pattern which became classic in the thirteenth century. A number of German students were involved in a tavern brawl in which the tavern was wrecked and the owner severely beaten. In retaliation Thomas, Provost of Paris, attacked the German hostel with an armed band of citizens, and killed several students in the melee. Protesting to the king, the masters of Paris demanded redress of injuries. Although this incident is the first clearly documented student riot involving royal authority, one may suspect that it was not a novelty. Walter Map tells of a disturbance between clerics and laymen of the royal court during the reign of King Louis VII without specifying whether the clerics were students.[203] About 1192 Stephen of Tournai recounted a riot between students and the men of Saint-Germain-des-Prés in which a student was killed, but the account implicates the Abbot of the church and not the King.[204] However, in a Biblical comment, composed before 1197 and probably decades earlier, Peter the Chanter suggested that such affairs were not new either to the King personally or to his reign.[205]

The Chanter intimated that King Philip had been tempted in times past to evict the troublesome scholars from Paris, but in 1200 (according to Roger of Hoveden) he was afraid that the masters and students would desert the city, and so he came to terms with them by issuing a charter in their favor.[206] The first section of the charter dealt with the punishment of Thomas the Provost and the other lay malefactors. While the scholars proposed that the Provost and his accomplices be whipped in the manner of schoolboys and then restored, the King reserved the fit punishment to himself. Thomas was imprisoned for life unless he chose to submit to the water ordeal. If he failed, he was to be put to death, but if he won, he was to abjure the realm.[207] Similar procedures were imposed on the accomplices, who were arraigned by special inquest. If they fled the city, they were judged guilty and condemned.[208] After dealing with the immediate issues, King Philip declared privileges for the future protection of students. The first of these was to provide royal enforcement of the students' *privilegium canonis* by requiring of the bourgeoisie of Paris that if they saw any layman assaulting a student, except in self-defense, they were to apprehend the malefactor, hand him over to royal justice, and present testimony of his crime. Moreover, the Provost was empowered to conduct inquests and to bring to justice those suspected of clerical assaults notwithstanding their denial or their offer to purge themselves by duel or the water ordeal. In effect, the King assigned the secular judicial machinery to the defense of the student's person against assaults by laymen. Finally, the King required the Provost and the people of Paris to swear to observe these measures. The Provost was to take his oath before the scholars in a church on the first or second Sunday after assuming office. Fifteen years after the royal charter, however, Robert of Courson as papal legate was not entirely satisfied with the royal guarantees. In the statutes of 1215 he decreed that in default of royal justice the masters and scholars could enter into mutual agreements sanctioned with oaths and penalties to deal with killing, mutilation, or other gross injuries.[209] In other words, if the royal remedies were ineffectual, the scholars could take appropriate action, such as threatening to leave Paris.[210]

The closest that the canonists and theologians came to discussing the maintenance of public order against turbulent clerics was in their treatment of doorkeepers and officials, who were two exceptional cases proposed by Pope Alexander to the *privilegium canonis*.[211] If a clerical doorkeeper malignantly mishandled a cleric while performing his duties, he fell under the ban but could be absolved by the bishop unless the cleric was gravely injured. A lay official, however, who manhandled a cleric could be absolved only by the pope because no authority over the clergy was permitted to the laity. If, however, he accidentally injured a cleric while attempting to control an unruly crowd, he could be absolved by local church authorities. Huguccio's interpretation of these cases closely agreed with the papal decretal.[212] Writing after the events of 1200, Robert of Courson and Robert of Flamborough followed Huguccio by declaring that lay agents who inadvertently injured clerics while maintaining public order among crowds were not excommunicated or if they were, could be absolved by the local bishop.[213] Raising the issue of the ruler's complicity, Courson stated that if a prince commanded a subject to assault a cleric, he as well as his agent fell under the ban, just as King Henry II of England shared the guilt with his knights for murdering Thomas Becket.[214] None of these opinions, however, were directly pertinent to the events of 1200 since the Provost of Paris and his company had not acted inadvertently and the King disavowed his responsibility.

Clerical status provided scholars not only with the *privilegium canonis,* but also with the *privilegium fori* which furnished them immunity from secular justice.[215] By reason of their ecclesiastical status the students of Paris demanded freedom from the royal courts and submission to their masters' justice or to the diocesan courts. During the last decade of the twelfth century Pope Celestine III reminded the Bishop of Paris that all clerics involved in secular cases should be judged according to canon law.[216] Although ecclesiastical courts exercised criminal jurisdiction over the clergy, they were not permitted to hand down penalties involving the shedding of blood so that clerics who committed gross crimes such as murder, rape, and robbery were immune to the punishment by death and mutilation customarily meted out in the secular courts. Adequate punishment of criminous clerics became a serious problem to the conscientious prince responsible for the peace of his realm.

The issue of criminous clerics was dramatically exposed by the confrontation between King Henry II of England and Thomas Becket, Archbishop of Canterbury.[217] Claiming to follow the customs of England, the King outlined in the Constitutions of Clarendon of 1164 a procedure for prosecuting felonious clergy. All clerics accused of serious offenses against the king's peace were to be summoned before the royal court, and then transferred to an ecclesiastical court to be tried according to canon law, though in the presence of a royal officer. If found guilty, they were to be degraded, that is, stripped of their clerical status, and returned by the officer to the king's court where they were to be punished as laymen. By combining royal and ecclesiastical jurisdiction the King hoped to insure the public peace and yet to safeguard the clergy's *privilegium fori*. At a time contemporary to Henry's proposal, the position of the canon lawyers on criminous clerics was not altogether clear. While Gratian's *Decretum* furnished precedents for degradation and delivery in specific cases, Henry's initial arraignment before the royal court and the presence of the royal officer were unknown to canon law. In effect Henry attempted to transform the isolated cases of canon law into regular procedure.

For his part, Thomas Becket contested all semblance of royal jurisdiction over accused clerics, not only by opposing the initial arraignment, but also by refusing to deliver degraded clerics to secular authority for punishment. Since, in his view, degradation constituted a fit penalty for their crimes, further penalties in the royal courts would have amounted to double punishment for the same crime, which was forbidden by the Scripture: "God does not judge twice in the same matter."[218] If a degraded cleric committed a second crime he could no longer, of course, claim clerical protection. Although the Archbishop's position found some canonical precedent and some support among the canonists, the uncompromising character of his refusal to deliver degraded clerics to secular punishment, like Henry's attempt to regularize the procedure, produced an effect novel to canon law.[219] Thomas Becket defended this and other principles with his own life at the hands of Henry's knights. The Archbishop's martyrdom and acknowledged sainthood influenced Pope Alexander III to confirm Becket's stand in a letter to the Archbishop of Salerno, about 1178.[220] Echoing the argument against double punishment, the Pope forbade turning over to secular judgment clerics degraded for serious crimes.

The dispute between the King and the Archbishop which was climaxed by Thomas' brutal death in 1170 reverberated in Paris during the succeeding decades. If the *Dialogus miraculorum* of the Cistercian Caesar of Heisterbach can be trusted, a disputation was held at Paris in the early 1170's over this issue between a certain Master Roger and Master Peter the Chanter, the former contending that Becket merited death as a traitor to the kingdom, the latter declaring that he was a martyr for the liberties of the church.[221] Although it is difficult to authenticate an incident reported perhaps fifty years later, the defender of the royal cause may have been Master Roger the Norman, who was a canon of Rouen as early as 1166, resided in Paris in the 1170's, claimed the title of master, was learned in Roman law, became Dean of Rouen in 1199, and died in 1200.[222] While connections can be established between this particular Roger and the English royal family, one can only conjecture as to his arguments.[223]

On the other hand, Peter the Chanter is not only well known, but he has also provided a clear statement on the central issue of criminous clerics. This problem was apparently debated within the Chanter's own school. One collection of *questiones* poses the case of a cleric degraded by the bishop for homicide or some other serious crime, in which the particular question of concern is whether the secular judge could immediately apprehend and hang the malefactor without falling under excommunication for clerical assault.[224] Although it was maintained that such action seriously prejudiced the church because deposition was sufficient punishment, it was further argued that the judge was not liable to excommunication because the degraded cleric no longer benefited from his clerical privilege. Although this *questio* lacks a clear resolution, the principal collections of the Chanter's *Summa* include another *questio* which does come to conclusion.[225] In considering churches which handed over to secular authority clerics degraded for major crimes, Peter gravely warned that such customs betrayed the cause for which Thomas died. The Chanter presented, however, the clearest case for Becket's principle in the *Verbum abbreviatum*, where he declared that Saint Thomas of Canterbury incurred the wrath of the King because he refused to deliver to the royal court a cleric convicted by the church.[226] Maintaining that the crime was sufficiently punished by degradation, Thomas would not turn the cleric over immediately to the executioners because "the Lord does not punish twice in the same matter." If afterwards the degraded cleric committed another crime, he merited punishment by the secular arm because he then pertained to secular, not ecclesiastical justice. Whether Peter the Chanter actually debated the issue with Master Roger the Norman at Paris or not, he was nonetheless an outspoken defender of the principle of the martyred Archbishop. About 1215 when, as will be seen, Becket's position was less popular among churchmen, the Chanter's arguments were still being rehearsed in England by Thomas of Chobham.[227]

If the secular authorities were debarred from punishing criminous clerics, were they thereby denied any role in suppressing clerical crime? The Chanter's school considered a provost who apprehended and jailed a cleric caught in the act of robbery.[228] When the bishop requested that the cleric be turned over to ecclesiastical authorities for judgment, the provost refused because the malefactor was manifestly guilty. The Chanter decided that at the moment when the provost refused he was guilty of mistreating the clergy and automatically excommunicated, but he emphasized that before the bishop's request the provost acted rightly because secular authorities can apprehend and hold criminous clerics. In the Chanter's view the secular police suppress clerical crime by arresting and detaining malefactors until they can be judged by church authorities.

The issue of criminous clerics was not unrelated to the problem of student discipline in Paris at the turn of the twelfth and thirteenth centuries. How was the royal provost to suppress serious crime when an important element of the population claimed clerical privileges? Little is known about royal procedures before 1200, but the riot of that year induced King Philip to include in his charter to the scholars a resolution of the problem. Only a decade previously, King Richard of England, embroiled in a dispute with the Norman clergy over felonious clerics, adopted Becket's main principles whereby ducal justice could arrest churchmen accused of murder, but must turn them over immediately to the church courts.[229] Since no mention is made of subsequent punishment and condemnation, one must assume that the case was terminated with the ecclesiastical sentence. As Becket had insisted, the handing over of criminous clerics to secular justice was abolished. Perhaps under pressure from the Becket party in Paris, King Philip Augustus followed the Norman solution in his charter of 1200 by promising that the royal justice would not lay hands either on a scholar or on his chattels (*capitale*) without urgent and apparent necessity.[230] If such an arrest was necessary the student was to be delivered immediately to ecclesiastical justice, which would attend to satisfying the king and the injured party. If the arrest took place when ecclesiastical justice was inaccessible, the provost should detain the scholar in a student hostel until the church court was able to take custody. Particular care was to be exercised in avoiding physical injury unless the apprehended scholar resisted arrest, and all complaints of violence were to be investigated.[231] What is significant is that no mention is made of royal participation in justice after the offending cleric had been delivered to the ecclesiastical authorities. As the Chanter had observed, the sole function of the police was to apprehend the felonious student. Since his subsequent trial, judgment, and sentence was the church's responsibility, there could be no question of returning him to the provost. Both in Normandy in 1190 and at Paris in 1200 secular justice was obliged to respect Thomas Becket's principles. Ten years later King Philip further limited royal arrests of clerics by specifying murder, adultery, rape, housebreaking, assault and battery with stick, stones, and pointed weapons as the only legitimate pretexts.[232] As in 1200, the offenders were to be turned over immediately to ecclesiastical authorities unless the offense was at night, when the cleric was to be detained in an honorable abode, kept separate from brigands and other malefactors.

The consistent refusal to deliver degraded clerics into secular hands was evidently a policy too rigid to be accepted for long by both the church and royalty.[233] Modifications were introduced as early as 1184 when Pope Lucius III (in the famous decretal *Ad abolendam*) gave permission for convicted heretics, clerical as well as lay, to be punished by the temporal authorities.[234] Similarly, Pope Celestine III (1191-1198) permitted such coercion for incorrigibly felonious and obstinately rebellious clerics,[235] and in 1201 Pope Innocent III applied it to forgers of papal bulls.[236] Al-

148

though these cases might appear exceptional because they involved crimes particularly odious to churchmen, in 1209 Pope Innocent III sent a decretal to the Bishop of Paris which gave general sanction for the degrading of criminous clerics in the presence of royal officials and permitted their delivery to secular justice.[237] Not only were popes willing to make accommodations, but in France the royalty also demanded concessions to enforce the public peace. In 1205 King Philip Augustus and his barons came to agreement with the French clergy over the issue of criminous clerics.[238] Between the princes' demands for immediate delivery and the clergy's claim to complete freedom a compromise was achieved: while the church court should not hand the degraded cleric over to the secular authority neither should it degrade him in a church or a cemetery where he could not be taken subsequently. Rather he should be released in a place where the secular justices could apprehend him and render justice without incurring the church's anathemas. In effect the French clergy conceded to King Philip the essential demanded by King Henry but refused by Thomas Becket.

@ CHAPTER VII @

Epilogue: Masters of Renown

AS PETER the Chanter and his colleagues examined academic life in their lectures, disputations, and sermons, they evoked the names and memories of specific masters who flourished in the past and in their own day. Not only did they cite their theological and moral opinions, as has been seen, but they occasionally referred to their deeds as well. Their purpose in recording these examples was less to satisfy their students' curiosity about past teachers than to teach lessons. The Chanter's circle were firmly convinced that *res* were more important than *verba,* that deeds spoke more eloquently than words. Since throughout the Middle Ages the primary justification for writing history was moral edification, the theologians were justified in drawing *exempla* from the lives of famous masters. Because their basic motive was the moral lesson, they were less concerned with the literal truth than with the underlying message. For this reason historical accuracy suffered. Although their accounts are often confused or in error, they nonetheless indicate the current repute of renowned masters.

The schools of Paris grew out of an educational revival originating in France in the eleventh century. Ecclesiastical writers who wrote before this epoch were usually designated as "authorities," while those who wrote after it were distinguished by the modern term of "master." The earliest examples of modern teachers to occur to the Chanter's circle were the two eleventh-century adversaries, Master Lanfranc of Bec (d. 1089), and Master Berengar of Tours (d. 1088). In a commentary to the Psalms and in two versions of the *Verbum abbreviatum* Peter rehearses an anecdote about them which Robert of Courson repeated with embellishments.[1] Master Lanfranc, the most learned man in all of Gaul, had retreated in an act of self-abasement to an impoverished monastery. In an effort to appear unlearned to his fellow monks, he deliberately distorted his speech by shortening long syllables, and lengthening short syllables. When, however, the faith of the church was threatened by the Eucharistic doctrines of Master Berengar, Lanfranc suddenly appeared at the Council of Tours, where he refuted his opinions in open disputation. Confronted by this unidentified adversary the astonished Berengar exclaimed: "You must be either Lanfranc or his good or evil spirit." To which Lanfranc replied: "I am neither spirit, but Lanfranc himself." Not without charm, this story, however, presents historical problems. It is true that on the eve of Lanfranc's arrival the monastery of Bec could qualify as "poor." Moreover, the story about Lanfranc's humility echoes Milo Crispin's *Vita Lanfranci* which claimed that he kept his identity secret for three years, even submitting to an illiterate prior who mistakenly corrected his Latin pronunciation.[2] But the rest of the story is uncertain. Although Lanfranc opposed Berengar's theses in writing and in person at the synods of Rome (1050) and Vercelli (1050), there is little evidence that he was present at the synod of Tours (1054/1055).[3] The dramatic confrontation, therefore, between the two adversaries rests on the authority of the Chanter. The point of the story, however, was to illustrate Lanfranc's humility in contrast to Berengar's self-esteem, since it was commonly assumed that false doctrines arose from inordinate pride. Although simple humility was the immediate lesson, contemporaries may have found further significance in the account. Opinion in the eleventh and twelfth centuries, reflected in this *exemplum*, considered Lanfranc as a preeminent dialectician.[4] Since he was considered one of the "modern" founders of dialectics, the anecdote further implied that because of the dangers of presumption dialecticians like Lanfranc should be especially humble in order not to fall into false doctrine.

The tradition to which the Chanter and his colleagues belonged stemmed ultimately from the leadership of Master Anselm (d. 1117) of the school of Laon at the turn of the eleventh and twelfth centuries. Not only did the Chanter's circle make ample use of the scriptural *Glossa ordinaria* produced at Laon, but they often quoted the opinions of Anselm and his school. Anselm had lived during the tumultuous epoch of Gaudri, Bishop of Laon (1106-1112), whose vicious life, according to the testimony of Guibert of Nogent, included murder and whose scandals provoked the commune of Laon to revolt and to assassinate the Bishop himself.[5] In a commentary to Psalm 118 : 115, "Depart from me, ye evildoers, for I will keep the commandments of my God," the Chanter recalled that the unsettled conditions of Laon had prevented Anselm from completing his gloss.[6] We should weep, he remarked, that Master Anselm could not perfect his great work because the canons, whose dean he was, and others distracted him from his studies by their adulation, their ceaseless litigation, their chapter affairs, and their oppression of the weak who were his responsibility.

Those chaotic times at Laon also elicited from Peter another story about Anselm, which he brings into the *Verbum abbreviatum* as an *exemplum* while discussing the temptation of rewarding one's kin, in relation to the Biblical account of Joseph.[7] When the innocent as well as the guilty were accused of Bishop Gaudri's assassination, Master Anselm cast himself at the feet of Stephen, at that time chancellor of the king (seneschal, according to other versions), and with his identity concealed requested an unnamed favor. When this was granted, he asked that his nephews who had never been party to the atrocity be released from prison. When the royal chancellor suddenly perceived that it was the illustrious Master Anselm who was before him, he fell on his knees, protesting that he had rectified all injustices in his life except only this one. Although he could never give full satisfaction for Anselm's humiliation, he would order that the nephews be restored immediately, that they be endowed with his own goods, created knights, and granted noble girls in marriage. To these extravagant proposals Anselm refused assent. Coming from poor and peasant families, those boys should never be advanced to knightly rank. Anselm concluded that he would rather forego teaching Holy Scripture than see them tempted to pride beyond their station. Although the Chanter originally included this *exemplum* to illustrate refusal of family advancement, it also served to portray Anselm's personal humility. To re-inforce this second theme Peter continued that Anselm once made the claim that he was the son of a deacon and thereby illegitimate of birth in order to prevent his elevation to the prelacy. On another occasion he exhibited a small scar which he carried on his thumb from infancy. Pretending that it was a stigma received from the altar, he attempted to scandalize the people and discourage their electing him, but nonetheless he was chosen for the archbishopric of Canterbury.

In this last episode the Chanter has obviously confused Anselm of Laon with Anselm of Bec, who was elected Archbishop of Canterbury in 1093, but the rest of the story remains plausible. As far as can be told, Anselm was *écolâtre* at Laon by the 1090's, dean by 1106/1109 and archdeacon in 1115.[8] According to Guibert of Nogent he was continually troubled by the outrages during the episcopacy of Gaudri, and after the latter's as-sassination in 1112, he was sufficiently respected by the people of Laon that they permitted him to retrieve the bishop's mutilated corpse and to give it decent burial.[9] The office of royal chancellor was held by Stephen of Garlande from 1108 and to this he added the title of seneschal in 1120.[10] Although Stephen was not yet seneschal at the time of the assassination, his later dual role explains the confusion in the different versions of the Chanter's account. Although Stephen's part in punishing the conspira-tors finds no confirmation apart from the Chanter's, Guibert of Nogent remarked that the chancellor was interested in the bishopric for himself, but when this preferment proved impossible, he gave it to the Dean of Sainte-Croix of Orléans so that he could annex the deanship for him-self.[11] Although the story about the confrontation between Anselm of Laon and Stephen of Garlande must rest on the Chanter's word alone, it does fit what is known about the principal personages.

The death of Master Anselm, which occurred less than five years after this alleged event, prompted Robert of Courson to recount another story. Discussing a question formulated by Augustine, whether those who sought moral perfection were permitted to lie, Robert recalled that three days after Anselm's death his students told his mother that he had been promoted to an archepiscopacy in order to spare her a shock which might have precipitated her own death.[12] With the notable exception of Abelard, who clashed with Anselm at Laon, the theologian of Laon enjoyed the highest reputation among contemporaries. To the many epitaphs composed in his honor may be added one from Peter the Chanter, who in the words of the Apostle (Rom. 10 : 10) characterized Anselm as a man who believed with his heart unto righteousness and with his mouth confessed salvation.[13]

The schools of Reims where Peter the Chanter received his early education were linked with Laon through the person of Master Alberic of Reims. A student of Anselm of Laon,[14] Alberic engaged Abelard and Gilbert de la Porrée in theological controversy.[15] By 1123 he appears in the charters of Reims as a master;[16] by 1131 he held the dignity of archdeacon. Bernard of Clairvaux unsuccessfully supported his candidacy to the bishopric of Châlons, but in 1137 he was chosen as Archbishop of Bourges, where he died in 1141. Although Alberic flourished at Reims at a period probably anterior to the arrival of the Chanter, Peter recalled one story about the master which took place when Reims was afflicted by a severe drought.[17] When after three days the Christian efforts to produce rain by solemn procession of holy relics had proved a failure, the Jews of the city asked permission to test their scrolls and Torah in a similar fashion. If rain did not appear within three more days, the Jews promised to convert to the Christian faith. Many Christians were tempted to accept the challenge, but Master Alberic refused to allow the trial.[18] The prospect of converting the Jewish community did not justify a contest which constituted a clear case of tempting God.

Another master found in the pages of the Chanter's circle is the heretofore elusive figure of Robert *de Camera*.[19] First appearing in a charter of 1149,[20] Master Robert was well established in a house at Reims by 1157.[21] In 1165 he was designated as a cleric of Notre-Dame of Reims on the eve of his election to the bishopric of Amiens, which he held until his death in 1169.[22] Apart from the information provided by the Parisian theologians little is known about Robert *de Camera*,[23] but within the Chanter's circle he was the earlier master who excited the most comment. Not only did they frequently quote his theological opinions, but they recited numerous anecdotes which illustrated his career both as a teacher at Reims and as Bishop of Amiens. Because of the vivid impression which Robert *de Camera* made upon Peter the Chanter, he is the most likely candidate to have been Peter's teacher at Reims. For example, while preaching at a certain bourg, Master Robert discovered that his audience held doubts about the real presence of Christ in the Eucharist.[24] By asserting his own learning and by swearing an oath he convinced his listeners of the orthodox doctrine.

But it was as a lawyer and a judge that Robert *de Camera* was best remembered by the Parisian theologians. While Master Robert was lecturing at Reims, he agreed to defend a servant of a close friend who was accused of counterfeiting.[25] Although the client was successfully acquitted of the charges, Robert felt obliged to do penance for homicide because during the trial a judicial duel was employed and the plaintiff was hanged for false accusation. As a lawyer Robert was accustomed to warn his prospective clients that he would plead their cases only so far as they were just.[26] If he found guilt, he would reveal it to their adversaries. When he became Bishop of Amiens he was particularly zealous in compelling lawyers and judges to restore compensation to their clients for unjust advocacy and judgments.[27] When asked why he expended so much effort in such matters, he replied that if restitution was not performed, he would feel personally responsible for indemnifying the defrauded. On another occasion the bailiffs of Amiens brought before the bishop an apprehended brigand.[28] When the *vidame* asked what should be done, Robert replied ambiguously: "Do what you have to do." Shortly thereafter, repenting of his reply, Robert spurred messengers with promises of reward to prevent the execution. When they arrived too late, the bishop did penance for homicide. According to one version, executions always caused the bishop great distress, which became aggravated as the hour of death approached.[29] Even though he was only indirectly involved with matters of life and death, he nonetheless assumed personal responsibility in them. For example, when he heard that a young boy had drowned in a fish pond which he had ordered to be dug, he was once more prepared to perform penance as if he were guilty of the death.[30] But the bishop was spared the drastic action this time, because the victim was resuscitated. This trait of agonizing scrupulousness often appears in the sketches of Robert *de Camera*. The Chanter reported that Master Robert always warned those who came to him for confession to be mindful of what they said because what things should be concealed, he would conceal, but he would not hide what should be revealed.[31] Similarly, Gerald of Wales reported that as a bishop Robert was extremely scrupulous in assigning prebends and dispensing emoluments for ordinations.[32] It is not unreasonable to conjecture that Peter the Chanter's own sensitive conscience was inherited from Master Robert *de Camera* in Reims.

A final master from Reims who appears in the pages of the Chanter was a certain Foulques who later became Dean of Reims. In a chapter of the *Verbum abbreviatum* which protested proliferating masses for the dead, Peter remarked that Master Foulques, Dean of Reims, requested the chapter to celebrate his own anniversary without additional masses.[33] It is difficult to identify the career of this particular Foulques in the documents of Reims, because there were several masters who bore the name of Foulques;[34] nonetheless, this particular Master Foulques was most likely *écolâtre* by at least 1165[35] before he was dean between 1168 and 1175.[36] Although his obituary notes in detail the donations for his anniversary, it unfortunately makes no mention of this special request.[37]

The traditions of the schools of Paris went back to the early twelfth century when the illustrious masters Peter Abelard (d. 1142) and Gilbert de la Porrée (d. 1154) attracted disciples to their rival camps. Although Peter the Chanter never referred to Abelard's theological opinions by name he recalled two anecdotes about the famous theologian. Discussing the accepting of gifts derived from illicit gains, the Chanter recalled that when Count Thibaut of Champagne distributed presents to his comrades, Master Peter Abelard refused to accept them unless they were drawn from pure revenues; otherwise they should be cast to dogs and beasts.[38] In another chapter of the *Verbum abbreviatum*, which protested favoring the rich, the Chanter cited the example of Abelard along with others.[39] Although he did not explain the allusion, in this passage, in a comment to James 2 : 4, the classic Biblical authority against "respect of persons," Peter further noted the example of Abelard entering the cloister of Clairvaux.[40] Apparently the incident was often told at Paris for Stephen Langton, referring to the Chanter's gloss, explains that when Master Peter Abelard wished to visit the order of Clairvaux he first applied alone and shabbily attired, and was placed among the poor.[41] On the morrow, however, when he arrived with a change of raiment and was received with honor, he rebuked them with the verse from James.[42] Although Abelard's troubles with the Cistercians were well-known, the authenticity of this last account stretches one's credulity. These anecdotes which appear two or three generations after the alleged events place Abelard in an unaccustomed light. Rather than as the brilliant but disputatious theologian, he is represented as a crusader against moral abuse. Other members of the Chanter's circle pictured him in his more normal role. For example, Gerald of Wales recounts a debate which he held with a Jew,[43] and Jacques de Vitry narrates a delightful if dubious tale about his teaching.[44] When the king of France became exasperated with Master Peter Abelard, he forbade the theologian from lecturing in his land. Abelard promptly climbed a tree and assembled his disciples below. When the king extended his ban to the air as well, Abelard installed himself in a boat and the king good-naturedly resigned himself to Abelard's presence in the royal city.

Gilbert de la Porrée, whose theological positions the Chanter adopted and whose opinions were often cited by name, also provided moral examples for the Parisian masters. Peter numbered Master Gilbert with Bernard of Clairvaux and others who protested excessive monastic exemptions.[45] Master Gilbert called all abbots schismatics who claimed freedom from episcopal jurisdiction. As Bishop of Poitiers himself, he denied that the abbot's consecration was of an unusual character which conveyed special privileges. Like Abelard, Gilbert de la Porrée was also remembered for his disputes with the Jews,[46] and he too performed acts of exemplary piety. For example, according to Thomas of Chobham, Master Gilbert once accompanied a bishop who never distributed alms when he celebrated the hours.[47] The theologian rebuked the bishop by retorting: "You say the hours, but I practice them," thus illustrating the principle dear to the Chanter's circle, that deeds are more precious than words.[48]

Peter Comestor and Maurice of Sully are the two masters from the immediately preceding generation of scholars at Paris whose deeds are mentioned by the Chanter's circle. Often linked together in later accounts, Master Peter Comestor was Chancellor of Notre-Dame between 1164 and 1168 and died about 1179, and Master Maurice of Sully taught theology at Paris before becoming bishop of the city (1160-1196).[49] Not only was the Comestor frequently quoted in Biblical and theological matters, but his *Historia scholastica*, as has been seen, served as a text for the lectures of Stephen Langton. In an anecdote resembling one reported for Abelard, Peter the Chanter described a certain French monastery which, although endowed with rich rents, appeared to be languishing.[50] When Master Peter Comestor investigated why this cloister was unable to flourish, he discovered that its revenues were drawn from usury. Because of corrupt foundations, the house was threatened with collapse. On the other hand, the Chanter never referred to Bishop Maurice by name, although he discussed the construction of Notre-Dame and the redivision of the parishes, two of the Bishop's favorite projects. But if the Chanter did not pronounce the name of his Bishop, his followers were not troubled by the same inhibition. An important source for the early life of Maurice of Sully originates from an *exemplum* of Jacques de Vitry.[51] According to the preacher, when Maurice first arrived in Paris, he was so poor that he had to beg for his bread.[52] His talents nonetheless won him the title of master of theology. When the bishopric of the royal city fell vacant in 1160, the chapter presented two candidates, Master Peter Comestor and Master Maurice, for royal approval. King Louis VII inquired of the canons who was the better cleric. When it was acknowledged that Peter was more learned than Maurice, the King replied: "Let him teach others, but make Maurice bishop." Jacques' word is the only guarantee for this story, but it appears to fit the facts better than a rival story from Caesar of Heisterbach.[53] During the Bishop's pontificate Thomas of Chobham reported that Maurice excommunicated the Provost of Paris when he refused to allow priests to serve the Eucharist to condemned criminals in prison.[54] But the one event which made the deepest impression on the Parisian theologians was a miracle which took place while Maurice was dying. According to the earliest account (by Robert of Courson), when the Bishop was on his deathbed in the Abbey of Saint-Victor where he had retired, the canons brought him unconsecrated bread fearing that he could not receive the real host without danger.[55] But inspired by the Holy Spirit, Maurice perceived the deception, and demanded the truly consecrated sacrament, which he recognized immediately although he could not receive it because of his weakness. This story was retold by Thomas of Chobham, Gerald of Wales, Jacques de Vitry, as well as by Caesar of Heisterbach.[56]

PART

THREE

PRINCES

ᕲ CHAPTER VIII ᕲ

Regnum & *Sacerdotium*

WHEN Peter the Chanter directed his gaze from Notre-Dame westward across the rooftops of the Ile-de-la-Cité, he could easily distinguish the tall stone tower of the royal palace at the other end of the island. Since this structure was frequently a residence of the king, it must have served to remind the theologians of the realm of government. In the days of Peter the Chanter King Philip Augustus was not the sole and absolute ruler of France. After centuries of feudalism political authority in France was splintered into complex fragments. Great barons such as the counts of Flanders and Champagne ruled their fiefs with equal if not more effectiveness than the king himself. Well over half of the kingdom was in the hands of the Plantagenet King of England who claimed the titles of Duke of Normandy, Count of Anjou, and Duke of Aquitaine. In a confused web of feudal ties these barons shared their authority with innumerable lesser lords and castellans. Moreover, the rulers of the church also participated in the secular functions of government on a broad scale. For example, in Paris itself the king shared rights of police and justice with the bishop and the abbots of Saint-Germain-des-Prés and Sainte-Geneviève. An illustration of this confused political organization is that the king was forced to distinguish between his kingdom, over which he was nominal suzerain, and his royal domain, a small cluster of land in the Ile-de-France, which he governed directly. Since this distinction was commonplace to his contemporaries, the Chanter used it to elucidate a Biblical text.[1] Attempting to explain the geographical terms of "Midian" and "Judean" in particular and general senses, he reminded his students that the word "France" could designate either the area around Paris or the kingdom in general. To avoid the complexity of contemporary politics the theologians rarely distinguished between the titles of king, duke, count, and lord, based on dignity and honor; rather they were inclined to use the functional terms of princes (*principes*) and prelates (*prelati*), that is, those who ruled the temporal and spiritual realms respectively. Since princes and prelates were those assuming the responsibilities of government, they performed many functions in common and could be treated together.

As moral theologians, the Chanter and his circle viewed government chiefly in terms of personnel and functions. For example, among governmental personnel they distinguished chancery clerks, judges, lawyers, and soldiers, and among political functions they examined secretarial service, justice, war, and revenue. This predominantly practical attitude rendered the Chanter's group less inclined to discuss the more theoretical issues of politics such as the origin and nature of authority, the distinction between the spiritual and temporal spheres and the nature of civil obedience—issues which attracted the attention of the Roman and canon lawyers. Only Stephen Langton, Simon of Tournai, and Master Martin, on the perimeter of the Chanter's circle treated the more abstract problems of political theory, but even their contributions are little more than echoes of the jurists' opinions.

At the end of the fifth century Pope Gelasius I opened the medieval era of political thought by formulating two propositions: (1) All authority is divided into two spheres, the *sacerdotium* (spiritual) and the *regnum* (temporal) which are distinct according to a division of labor. The spiritual rules the souls of men while the temporal governs their bodies. (2) Of the two the *sacerdotium* is superior to the *regnum* in dignity. In brief, Gelasian theory postulated two principles, duality and superiority, which, if extended to extremes, were incompatible and whose friction generated one of the central debates of the Middle Ages. By the turn of the twelfth and thirteenth centuries the jurists had accepted the two propositions and were attempting to resolve their contradictions.[2] As might be expected two positions emerged from the debates. On one hand was the "hierocratic" view which, emphasizing the principle of superiority, postulated a unified system of political authority in which all authority flowed from God to the pope and thence into the spiritual and temporal realms. According to Alanus Anglicus, who represented this position, the *regnum* received its authority from and was subordinate to the *sacerdotium*. On the other hand was the "dualist" position, best defended by Huguccio who, emphasizing the principle of division, maintained that God instituted the two realms separately. Although the spiritual was superior to the temporal in dignity, as Gelasius had said, this proposition did not imply total subordination. *Regnum* was fundamentally independent of *sacerdotium*, although under divine providence the two were intended to work closely in cooperation. In the confusion of debate these two tendencies were not always clearly distinguished and on a practical level the distance between opposing positions was often narrowed; nonetheless, the central problem of *sacerdotium* and *regnum* was being approached from two directions at the turn of the century.

In the thirteenth century one device for expressing the relations between the *sacerdotium* and *regnum* was the analogy of the sun and moon. Just as the sun ruled over the day and the moon over night, so priestly authority governed men's souls and royal power their bodies. The metaphor was particularly apt because it expressed the fundamental ambiguity between the duality of the two realms and the superiority of the spiritual over the temporal, since the moon received its light from the sun. Coined in the early Middle Ages and last employed by Pope Gregory VII,[3] the analogy was revived by Pope Innocent III during the first year of his pontificate (1198).[4] Among the occasions on which the Pope employed the expression, were two when he did so to emphasize the superiority of the spiritual over the temporal.[5] In similar terms Stephen Langton employed the analogy in his commentary to Joel 2 : 13: "The sun shall be turned into darkness and the moon into blood."[6] Although Stephen's passage is not explicit and exists in two variant versions, it nonetheless poses the political problem. After establishing the relationships between the sun and moon and between prelates and princes, and noting that the moon receives its light from the sun thus implying the superiority of *sacerdotium*, he abruptly asserts that the conclusion is questionable. That the moon derives light from the sun Langton interpreted not in terms of political authority but rather of doctrine and faith, explaining in one version that princes receive *spiritualia* from the prelates. His next step was to return to the eclipse portrayed in the Scriptural text. While Innocent considered the consequences of a "lunar eclipse," that is if the emperor was negligent,[7] Stephen discussed the effects of a solar eclipse as well. Just as the sun can be obscured by the moon, so prelates can be changed by sin into darkness, and as the moon can be eclipsed by the shadow of the earth, so secular princes can lapse into plunder. Since Stephen's commentaries cannot be dated with precision,[8] the relationship between this passage and Innocent's letters cannot be determined. Moreover, metaphors such as the sun and moon cannot be pressed too hard to reveal precise political theories; nonetheless, certain comparisons can be made between the discussions of the Pope and of the professor. In contrast to Innocent, Langton avoided drawing conclusions from the sun-moon analogy which emphasized the subordination of *regnum* to *sacerdotium* but rather maintained their essential duality.

The dominant mode for expressing the relationship between *sacerdotium* and *regnum* in the Middle Ages was the allegory of the two swords which represented the two governing authorities of the world. First applied to political theory during the eleventh-century controversies over church reform, this Scriptural image was revived and endowed with a hierocratic interpretation by Bernard of Clairvaux. By the second half of the twelfth century questions such as whether the pope has both swords or whether the emperor has his sword from the pope constituted a literary genre for discussing political theory. Debating these questions of the swords from hierocratic or dualist positions, the canonists came closest to producing a general theory of politics. Among the theologians at Paris at the turn of the century four gave the question a passing glance, three of whom came to "hierocratic" conclusions.

Considering whether the prince has the temporal sword from the pope, Simon of Tournai answered affirmatively on two grounds.[9] The prince should obey the pope by reason both of his person and of his dignity, which confers on the pope a superiority implying the right to give orders. Moreover, the oath which binds subjects to the prince is under the jurisdiction of the priest who has the right to judge its validity. Master Martin posed the question of the pope's temporal authority when he investigated the more specific problem of a prelate's exercise of police powers.[10] On the basis of Peter Damian's well-known affirmation that Christ conferred upon the Apostle Peter rights to the temporal as well as to the spiritual kingdoms, Martin concluded that the pope held the temporal sword. Like Master Martin, Robert of Courson also approached the church's political authority by asking whether a bishop could exercise police powers.[11] Adopting the distinction between *auctoritas* and *administratio* proposed by Rufinus,[12] Robert declared that while the prelate held both the authority and the execution of the spiritual sword, he claimed only the authority of the temporal sword; its execution was delegated to a layman. His chief justification for assigning temporal authority to the church was the famous Donation of Constantine, which claimed that the Emperor Constantine delegated to Pope Silvester the imperial rights (*iura*). At a later time, Robert continued, Pope Hadrian conferred the execution of these rights on Charlemagne, and similarly Pope Leo on King Otto. A forgery of the early Middle Ages, the Donation of Constantine was inserted into Gratian's *Decretum* by the decretist Paucapalea in the mid-twelfth century, whence it attracted notice from the canon lawyers.[13] The conferring of the administration of the kingdom on Charlemagne was inspired by the Henrician forgeries of the eleventh century, likewise found in Gratian's *Decretum*.[14] This theory was closely related to Pope Innocent III's notion of *translatio imperii*, which claimed that the pope withdrew the empire from the Greeks and transferred it to Charlemagne.[15] The distinction between authority and administration, the Donation of Constantine, and the translation of empire—arguments well known to contemporary canonists—were employed by Robert to demonstrate that the church held the authority of the temporal sword.[16]

If Stephen Langton's use of the sun-moon image suggested the independence of the *sacerdotium* and *regnum*, his discussion of the allegory of the two swords confirms his adherence to the dualist position.[17] Like Master Martin and Robert of Courson, Langton prefaced the specific question of whether a prelate could exercise police powers[18] with the general problem of whether the church has both swords. Two parties dispute this question, the "Romans" who answer affirmatively like Courson from the Donation of Constantine and the translation of empire, and the "Lombards" who defend the imperial cause by responding in the negative. Stephen's own resolution of the controversy contains three major elements. In the first place it is founded on a distinction between the church broadly conceived as the whole congregation of the faithful, including both laity and clergy, and the church interpreted narrowly as the prelates alone. Secondly, only in the broad sense can it be maintained, says Stephen, that the church transmits the temporal sword to the prince because it is only by the consent of the faithful, both clergy and laity, that the king is placed at the head of their government. Just as clerics elect bishops so all the faithful of the realm, both clergy and laity, place the emperor in authority over them. The prince, therefore, received the temporal sword from no prelate, not even the pope. Finally, the primate or archbishop, because of his dignity in the kingdom, could in the name of all the faithful confer the temporal sword on the ruler. Only as a representative of the people could a prelate transmit temporal authority.

The allegory of the two swords was not the most satisfactory vehicle for exploring the relations between the spiritual and the temporal realms. The canonists found it more effective to apply general conclusions to practical matters and to enumerate the specific rights of popes and emperors. The attention paid by the Parisian theologians to the abstract theories of *sacerdotium* and *regnum* is relatively slight when compared with the jurists' controversies. Master Martin's, Courson's, even Langton's, main concern was to investigate the prelate's exercise of police powers. Moreover, the component elements of their treatment were freely borrowed from the canonists. Although, on the whole, their discussions have little intrinsic merit, the subsequent role of Stephen Langton in English politics as Archbishop of Canterbury lends significance even to his most casual theories on *sacerdotium* and *regnum* pronounced by him as a professor at Paris.

One preliminary difficulty in considering Stephen's position arises from chronology. Although his discussion of the two swords is phrased as a scholastic *questio* and therefore was presumably completed before he left his academic career in 1206, his forced retirement during the years 1207-1213 and 1215-1218 provided him with opportunity to revise his earlier writing. One can never be sure whether this particular statement stems from the Parisian master or the exiled prelate. Moreover, Langton's terminology is both unusual and awkward. His use of "Romans" to designate the papal position and "Lombards" to identify the imperialists or dualists is uncommon among the canonists. The terms "empire" and "kingdom," "emperor" and "king" were employed indifferently, although this lack of precision was engendered by the canonists, who about 1200 formulated the principle that "the king is emperor in his own kingdom."[19] From the standpoint of spiritual-temporal relations it could be argued that the titles of emperor and king were interchangeable. Furthermore, Langton's assertions that the king did not receive the temporal sword from the prelate and that the primate acted in the name of the faithful cannot be squared with existing coronation ceremonies. Like the other Parisian theologians Stephen constructed his solution from elements current among contemporary canonists, particularly the dualists. The conception of the church as the congregation of the faithful, to be distinguished from the prelacy, may be found, for example, in Huguccio.[20] Like Langton Huguccio argued that the emperor received the temporal sword not from the pope but by election of the people and the princes. Langton's conclusion, therefore, that temporal authority was not transmitted through the prelacy, but by all the faithful closely resembles the Bolognese canonist's.[21]

Despite this lack of originality Langton's treatment of the two swords is of interest because of its relevance to English conditions. Whether writing as an English master at Paris who recalled and drew upon his native traditions or as the actual archbishop, Stephen underscored the importance of Canterbury's role in English affairs. Not only was the archbishop's presence necessary to the royal coronation, but his advice was required on all important measures.[22] To be sure, Stephen envisaged the archbishop's coronation role as conferring temporal authority on the king in the name of the faithful. But if Langton thought of the archbishop as the people's representative in crowning the king, could he not also extend this role to the important business of the realm? Although the chronicler Roger of Wendover exaggerated Langton's contribution to the Magna Carta, the Archbishop nonetheless provided the baronial party with leadership in the negotiations with the King during the months preceding June 1215.[23] Could he not have justified his participation in the baronial movement as action in the name of the faithful? Furthermore, did not Langton's conception of the church as the congregation of the faithful, both clerics and laymen, resemble the baronial notion of the community of the realm? Just as Stephen derived temporal authority from the congregation of the faithful so the barons viewed their program as representing the community of the realm.[24] Unfortunately, since Langton's discussion is terse and the barons' notion of community is only vaguely implied in their specific proposals, no definite correlations can be drawn, but the possible connection is too tantalizing to be excluded.

Brief as this academic treatment of the two swords is, it nonetheless reveals the tenor of mind of the Archbishop of Canterbury. Although Stephen owed his entire career as cardinal and archbishop to the Pope, his former acquaintance and contemporary at Paris, he was never an unquestioning papal agent. Not only did Langton ill disguise his disgust when King John yielded up England as a fief to the papacy, but he also openly sided with the barons, whom he refused to excommunicate when so commanded by Innocent. Assigned the task of mediating between the King and the barons by the Pope, the Archbishop succeeded in pleasing neither King nor Pope.[25] After Magna Carta was drawn up, he found himself suspended from office by Innocent. As Archbishop, Stephen Langton attempted to steer an independent course which inevitably was misunderstood by both sides. Hardly the king's man, neither was he a papalist. His actions accorded with his theories, which stressed the duality of the two swords and which claimed temporal authority to be derived from the community of the faithful.

Another problem central to political theory was that of civil obedience or, to phrase the question negatively, does one have the right to disobey constituted authority? The Scriptures offered two opposing answers to the medieval Christian. On one side was the principle of the Apostle Paul, "Let every soul be subject unto the higher [governmental] powers, for there is no power but of God" (Rom. 13 : 1); on the other was the reply of the Apostles to the authorities at Jerusalem, "Whether it be right in the sight of God to hearken unto you more than unto God, judge ye" (Acts 4 : 19). While the theologians at Paris ignored the theoretical issues underlying this dilemma, they considered one concrete case to which it applied.

The crucifixion of Christ provided medieval thinkers with an occasion for discussing varied problems, but the Chanter's circle used this episode to approach the question of civil obedience. What were the obligations of the various actors in the drama to obey Pilate's command to execute Christ, which in Christian terms was manifestly unjust? The theologians distinguished three groups of agents who were involved. First were the public officials (*lictores*), or in this case the executioners, secondly the ordinary people, in this case the Jewish multitude (*minores judei*), and finally, by extension to their own times, what would be the obligation of bishops as leaders of the people, faced with a comparable situation?

Peter the Chanter approached the obligations of public officials by posing the case of a jailer who knew of the innocence of a prisoner committed to him by a prince.[26] Was it his duty to set the man at liberty when such action would obviously jeopardize his own life? Because of the consequence for the jailer, the Apostle Paul refused to escape from prison when opportunity was provided (Acts 16 : 25ff). As a practical rule, therefore, the jailer—relying on the prince's responsibility—must receive prisoners. If as an ordinary man he does all within his power to improve their lot, he may in good conscience believe that he is not sinning. If, however, he knows with certainty that the prince has imprisoned someone unjustly, the jailer retains him at the risk of mortal sin. The Chanter's confused and contradictory discussion was rephrased by Robert of Courson in more categorical terms.[27] Punishment by imprisonment was replaced by the death penalty, the jailer was transformed into an official, and the practical consequences for disobedient officials were ignored. Against arguments that the Lord commands obedience to duly constituted authority and that the condemned was convicted under due process of law, Robert concluded that the official who was certain of the innocence of the condemned should not carry out the death penalty, because earthly lords should not be obeyed in unlawful affairs. In effect, the Chanter and his student both took up the Apostle's position from the book of Acts.

In treating of the obedience due to prelates, Stephen Langton also raised the example of public officials at the crucifixion of Christ.[28] Probing the obligations of the executioners, he added a number of refinements to the discussion. Only if the injustice of the death penalty was publicly known could the official refuse to carry out the sentence. If, however, it was known only to the official, the alternatives were limited: he should attempt either to avoid the command or to resign his office, or if both these were impossible, he should execute the sentence as a last resort. This solution was also accepted by his student Geoffrey of Poitiers.[29] Despite these modifications, Langton's and Geoffrey's final answer was opposed to that of the Chanter and Courson. Only when the injustice was common knowledge did Langton and Geoffrey urge the official to defy the prince. Relying ultimately on the principle of Paul, they supported the authority of government to require obedience from public officials.

From the specific case of public officials the masters turned to the more fundamental question of political obedience required from the people. The Chanter cited the crucifixion of Christ and Augustine's commentary which condemned the Jewish people for permitting this miscarriage of justice.[30] From this authority, Peter reported, some have concluded that when the prince is grossly delinquent in exercising justice the people have the right to liberate the condemned. Against this position the Chanter interpreted Augustine as blaming the Jews not for failing to rebel against their superiors, but for urging the crucifixion which might have been in their power to prevent. By proposing the opposite example of Saint Andrew, who refused to allow the faithful to rescue him from unjust condemnation,[31] Peter concluded that the people do not have the right of insurrection in such cases. Seeking to make the Biblical example more relevant to his own day, the Chanter further inquired whether in a similar case the bishop should propose a rebellion, thus provoking daily altercations between the episcopacy and royalty. While it was the bishop's duty to represent popular opinion in a peaceful effort to free those un-justly condemned and to insure the right of a just judgment to all ac-cused, the Chanter denied him the recourse of armed sedition. In effect the bishop as leader of the faithful was to prevent royal injustice by all means short of armed violence. In a passage which reflected his teacher's views, Thomas of Chobham employed the cases of the crucifixion and Saint Andrew to formulate the same conclusions.[32]

After examining the obligations of the executioners, Stephen Langton likewise turned to the people present at the crucifixion.[33] Because he was persuaded that the Jewish people really believed in Christ, Stephen felt that in one sense they were obligated to liberate Him from the cross, but in practice they were permitted to persuade the king by prayers and pe-titions. Although Langton agreed with the Chanter and Chobham in denying violent insurrection to the people in face of injustice, he placed greater emphasis on the judicial process. If, for example, the king con-demned someone to death without a judicial sentence, the people accord-ing to Stephen had a greater right to release him. If, however, an injustice resulted from a judicial sentence, the people had the right neither to discuss the decision nor to hinder its execution. Although Langton's mean-ing is not altogether clear, he placed the greatest importance upon judicial procedure. Geoffrey of Poitiers had difficulty in untangling the sense of his master's arguments, but when he arrived at a conclusion he agreed with Langton that popular resistance to unjust acts should be limited to the persuasion of public opinion.[34] Since recourse to violent rebellion against an unjust government was denied to the people, the Parisian theologians must in the last analysis be seen as supporting Paul's princi-ple, which made political obedience a divine command.[35]

As political theory these discussions of civil obedience are wanting in coherency and completeness. Peter the Chanter, for example, neglects to explain how he could counsel disobedience to the public official but obedi-ence to the people when both were confronted with the same injustice. Only Langton, relying on the Pauline principle, devises obligations for public officials compatible with those of the people. Moreover, to satisfy more speculative minds the theologians would have had to consider such fundamental questions as: What is the nature of royal authority? How do spiritual obligations impinge on political duties? Who are the peo-ple? These are issues which did not receive their attention.

Although deficient in theory, the theologians' discussions were none-theless relevant to practice. On occasion bishops did become leaders of the faithful who assumed responsibility for opposing royal injustice, if not by force, at least by marshalling public opinion. According to the chron-iclers at least one bishop, Baldwin of Worcester, performed this service.[36] When Gilbert of Plumpton was maliciously and unjustly condemned to death in 1184 by the English justiciar Ranulf Glanville, Baldwin rallied a crowd who by public demonstration obtained a stay of execution and the eventual release of the accused.

When as a master at Paris Stephen Langton urged the king to make no decision without a judicial sentence, he enunciated a principle which not only governed his own actions but was important in contemporary England. Again, it must be remembered that since the chronology of Stephen's *questiones* is not precisely known, the relation between his ideas and actions cannot be determined. It is nonetheless of interest that when King John led a campaign to punish the northern barons in September 1213 the Archbishop maintained that he could only proceed by judgment.[37] Similarly in August 1215 he refused to give up his castle of Rochester, insisting that he could not be deprived without judgment.[38] Obviously Langton's defense of legal judgment was neither new nor exclusively his. Recently interpolated into manuscripts of two English legal codes,[39] it possessed precedents as old as an imperial constitution of 1037.[40] Even King John, under pressure from the barons, in May 1215 promised that he would neither disseise them nor proceed against them with arms without a judgment in his court.[41] Echoing the King's promise, Pope Innocent III urged in June 1215 and again in August that the dispute between King and barons be settled in the royal court according to the customs of the realm.[42] This principle of no seizure without judgment headed the list of the so-called "Unknown Charter" produced by the preliminary negotiations between the King and barons in 1215.[43] Inserted into the Articles of the Barons, it was finally formulated in the famous Article 39 of Magna Carta where King John promised that he would abide by lawful judicial procedure in proceeding against any free man.[44] Although not alone in his espousal of due process of law, Stephen Langton not only emphasized this principle as a professor in Paris but as leader of the barons he helped to incorporate it into the customs of England.

Peter the Chanter and his followers also devoted attention to the practical question of how those who governed the *sacerdotium* and *regnum* were chosen. On the church's side they were not so much concerned with the selection of the more remote papacy as with the ecclesiastical election regulations applied to prelates close at hand. One account survives of how Peter expressed his opinion on this subject in his characteristically personal way. Sometime before 1227 Stephen of Gallardon, a former cleric of the chancery of Philip Augustus, left the royal service to become a canon of Bourges. Employing his skills acquired in the chancery, he composed a cartulary of the chapter of Bourges for his own use in which he inserted items of personal interest. Among these is the record of a conversation between King Philip Augustus and Peter the Chanter on the subject of bishops, which Stephen had most probably heard.[45] Apparently the incident began when the King patiently submitted to the Chanter's harangue on how he should rule himself and his kingdom. With a sly smile Philip suddenly interrupted the cleric: "Lord Chanter, tell me why it is that in ancient times bishops were saints such as Saint Marcel of Paris, Saint Germain of Auxerre, Saint Euverte of Orléans and Saint Sulpice of Bourges while today no bishop could scarcely be considered a saint?" But Peter would not easily relinquish the attack and responded with an enigma: "Lord King, wisdom does not come unless called, but foolishness always arrives unbidden." "By the lance of Saint James," growled Philip, "what does that have to do with my question?" Then the Chanter continued to lecture the King that the Holy Spirit comes only with great fasting, shedding of tears, contrition of heart, and humility, such as accompanied ancient elections, but modern elections, which are accompanied with revelry, drunkenness, pride, avarice, and simony debase the quality of bishops. Echoing these arguments, Peter contended in his *Summa* that perfect men were no longer found for the modern prelacy because apostolic severity was undermined by the weaknesses of his day.[46] When, however, the Chanter dealt with the selection of prelates his discussion amounted to little more than moral exhortation.[47] Following the Scriptural analogy (John 10) that only the shepherd enters the sheepfold by the door, he enumerates four gateways to the prelacy. The three ancient accesses by miracle, voice from heaven, and designation by lots are superseded in modern times by canonical election. This pattern was followed by Robert of Courson and Gerald of Wales, but neither the Chanter nor his circle devoted much space to elaborating the technical regulations governing free canonical elections.[48] By their time, over a century after the Gregorian reform program, these procedures were familiar to all churchmen.[49]

Of immediate importance was the intrusion of lay magnates into the selection of prelates. In both France and England the royalty made its will felt by selecting bishops who were agreeable to the king. While Louis VII and Philip Augustus may have shown respect for the forms of canonical election, they nonetheless managed to secure an episcopacy in royal sees who suited their tastes.[50] The Plantagenets characteristically participated more directly in the choice of their bishops. This inveterate royal habit of intervening directly or indirectly in episcopal elections provoked churchmen's opposition. In 1140 Gratian was still hesitant on the matter, allowing some latitude to lay action, but by the second half of the century the canonists had found sufficient precedent to agree on the principle of the laity's total exclusion from canonical election,[51] an opinion naturally shared by the Parisian theologians.

In language suspiciously reminiscent of the episode between the Chanter and Philip Augustus, Gerald of Wales recounted a conversation between King Henry II and a certain bishop. To the King's question of why holy bishops could scarcely be found, the prelate responded that while in former days churchmen were chosen through canonical election, now kings create bishops with a nod of their heads.[52] The Chanter himself alluded to the question in his commentary to Numbers, where he declared that kings who choose bishops are like the strangers who usurped the Levites' functions and were therefore put to death.[53] In similar terms he designated candidates forced upon churches through the violence of secular princes as the *Coriti*, so named after the followers of Korah (Num. 16) who were swallowed up by the earth because they contested Moses' authority by intruding into the priesthood.[54] In his own day Peter noted that their chief intrusions resulted from simony and nepotism. Robert of Courson and Gerald of Wales recalled the example of their hero, Thomas Becket, who resigned his appointment to Canterbury into the hands of the pope because he had received it through royal favor.[55] So adamant was the Chanter against these *Coriti*, that he was willing for simony to be risked in order to insure their exclusion from the church.[56] If, for example, a church which has already completed an unanimous election is threatened by an additional candidate supported by a prince, should it buy off the disturber? On the principle that dire necessity makes its own laws and on the precedent of the church of Trier which in ancient times bought its liberty from the emperor, the Chanter conceded this exceptional remedy. But if the disturber appears before the election, should the church likewise pay for its freedom? Here the Chanter's answer was inconclusive. While, on one hand, this recourse is simony, on the other, to purge a defect in a church was justified by Pope Alexander.[57]

Reflecting on the English church, Gerald of Wales also treated the Plantagenet abuses of free elections; yet he recalled two instances, Baldwin to Worcester and then to Canterbury and Hugh to Lincoln, where royal interference was beneficial to the church.[58] The canonist program to exclude laymen from church elections, seconded by the Parisian theologians, received final formulation in the Lateran Council of 1215 where Pope Innocent III invalidated elections made through secular interference, and fashioned sanctions against ecclesiastics participating in such affairs.[59] In the thirteenth century, however, the papacy was more concerned with enforcing the conciliar decree in the empire than elsewhere. In France and England the victory was more formal than real. While the French and English kings perhaps became more scrupulous in respecting canonical procedures, they continued to see that candidates favorable to their interests were chosen.[60]

Some practical problems in selecting rulers for the *regnum* also attracted the attention of the Chanter's circle. A leading question was whether the king should be chosen by hereditary succession or by election. Although both procedures competed in the early Middle Ages, by the time of Peter the Chanter the question had been substantially solved in both France and England. Associating the royal son with the reigning father, the Capetian dynasty continually reduced the elective element to assure their hereditary claims to the French throne. In 1179 Louis VII was the last monarch to associate his successor; his son Philip Augustus found no need to continue the practice. Close behind the Capetians, the Plantagenets also clarified the rules of hereditary succession (at the accessions of Richard, John, and Henry III). Similarly, the Hohenstaufens attempted to retain their rights to the imperial crown by pressing dynastic claims. Election, however, was the principle *par excellence* of the church. The popes of the late twelfth and early thirteenth centuries, preoccupied with imperial affairs, attempted to establish it in the empire. In his Biblical commentaries Peter the Chanter notes that ancient kings were chosen by the people.[61] According attention to Joshua as ruler of Israel, he points out that the choice was governed neither by acclamation nor by hereditary kinship, but God Himself elected Joshua because of his spiritual qualifications and his friendship with Moses.[62] When Peter, therefore, treated the problem of dynasty versus election in the form of a *questio* he referred to Joshua's example.[63] Since royal hereditary succession often obligated the people to accept wicked princes, Peter believed that God had ordained the elective principle for the Empire. The Chanter's preference for election over hereditary succession was clearly a clerical and not a French point of view. What is noteworthy about his discussion is that as late as the reign of Philip Augustus a prominent cleric at Paris yet dared to criticize one of the major Capetian achievements—the establishment of the hereditary principle.

The point at which churchmen became involved in the making of kings was the royal consecration.[64] Traditionally considered a sacrament in Carolingian times, this ceremony imparted a sacred character to the early medieval king which distinguished him from other rulers of feudal society. Under pressure from the church reformers, however, by the twelfth century the royal consecration was no longer considered a true sacrament but rather a lesser *sacramentale*. Even in this debased condition, the religious consecration provided essential support for royal authority in France and England. Peter the Chanter and his followers inquired into two aspects of royal anointing. First they asked whether it was simony to sell a kingdom or duchy considering that this involved the sale of a religious consecration. It could be argued from the analogy of marriage that just as a bride could be sold without affecting the conjugal benediction, so a kingdom could be bought without debasing the royal benediction. One version of the Chanter's *questiones* rejects the analogy on grounds that the sacerdotal blessing did not constitute the substance of marriage, while kingship was not possible without consecration.[65] The majority of the manuscripts, however, do accept the validity of the analogy.[66] Robert of Courson likewise concluded that kingdoms could be sold if one treated them as material property apart from the spiritual ceremony, which could not be sold.[67] The question, however, was of little practical significance because no kingdom or fief involving a religious consecration had been formally purchased in western Christendom within recent memory; nonetheless, the Chanter's and Courson's response places them among contemporary churchmen who sought to minimize the effects of royal consecration.[68] In a similar vein both Stephen Langton and Thomas of Chobham attempted to differentiate priestly from royal anointing.[69] Whether a true sacrament or merely a *sacramentale*, royal consecration nonetheless required the cooperation of the priest. The Chanter's second question, therefore, was of more practical significance: If royal succession produces a candidate for the throne who is yet a child or lacking in merit, does a prelate sin who consecrates him?[70] Combining the Apostle Paul's example of severity and Christ's presence at the marriage feast of Cana, which He would not have attended had He not approved of the wedding, Peter concluded that since the prelates' presence implied consent, they should not attend an unworthy consecration. In effect the Chanter urged an ecclesiastical boycott against anointing unfit kings, but this measure was seldom followed by the prelacy of his day.

❧ CHAPTER IX ❧

Service in the Court

WHEN Peter the Chanter and his circle turned from political theory to the actual operation of government, they entered a realm more congenial to their interests. Since government was yet a crude affair in their day, no one thought to analyze the political structure, but modern historians have often described the functions of medieval government as threefold: administrative, military, and financial. Although rarely acknowledged in medieval writing, governmental service was in fact performed in the court, and in the field, and with the purse. These three political functions will be useful for approaching the discussions of the theologians at Paris.

Court service was the realm where the cleric made his chief contribution to medieval government. The courts of princes as well as of prelates contained important numbers of ecclesiastics in attendance. As clerics themselves the Parisian masters naturally approached administrative functions from the point of view of their class, but in their discussions they considered matters also relevant to laymen. Since there were similarities between the *prelates* and the *principes*, the lords spiritual and temporal to whom God had entrusted the world, clerics who served in the courts of prelates shared common problems with those in the courts of princes. To illustrate this similarity, Peter the Chanter pointed out that prelates and princes sin not only with their own but also with the hands of their ministers.[1] On their deathbeds they should place their agents under oath to discover the misdeeds for which they as magnates must assume responsibility in their confession. Although medieval terminology here is characteristically imprecise, one can distinguish two terms, *officialis* and *curialis*, often employed to designate the court service of clerics.

In the secular and ecclesiastical courts of the twelfth century *officialis* was an unrestricted term.[2] Equally applicable to laymen as well as clerics, it usually referred to any type of governmental functionary. Within church circles during the second half of the century, however, the term acquired a second and more restricted sense when it was applied to clerics who increasingly assumed the judicial tasks of the prelate. By the turn of the century many bishops in northern France and England had an *officialis,* a special judicial officer, who presided over the episcopal court of law. Since these "officials" gained a reputation for venality, rapaciousness and extortion, Peter the Chanter and his circle were concerned with their remuneration. The Chanter dealt with the *officialis* both in the general and in the specific sense. In his *questiones* he asked whether a church such as Reims which had many officials (provosts, deans, stewards and castellans) could sell these offices without incurring simony.[3] Perhaps recalling student days, Peter reported that the question had been disputed at Reims before a great assembly of prelates and that a judgment had been rendered by Master Philip of Caune, an exiled partisan of Thomas Becket who was then teaching in the city.[4] His solution was confirmed by a letter of Pope Alexander III which was treasured by the church of Reims. On the authority of Pope Urban II's well-known decretal *Salvator*[5] Philip of Caune concluded that the selling of these positions was simoniacal. Continuing from this general proposition, Peter distinguished between "intrinsic" officials, or custodians of churches and altars whose offices doubtless could not be sold, and "extrinsic" officials, who managed the temporal property of the church. Even these secular offices, however, could not be sold without incurring simony because they were supported by ecclesiastical benefices and were immune to royal obligations because of the liberty of the church.

In the *Verbum abbreviatum* the Chanter used the term *officialis* not only in the broad but also in the specific sense. Dealing with clerical avarice, he distinguished three kinds of officials who aided prelates: the confessors, rural provosts, and *questores* of the episcopal palace.[6] Although the first two abused their duties, the last was open to greatest excess. As supervisor of the bishop's court, the *questor* was the *officialis* proper. His rapaciousness devised such expedients as employing excommunication and absolution for extorting money, profiting from blessing the water in the ordeal, and manipulating affinity regulations to procure divorces for those who were willing to pay. Expressing his disgust in an anecdotal fashion characteristic of his day, Peter quoted a certain cleric that if he wished to offend God more than any other sinner, he would become an *officialis* or *questor*. These officials were the prelates' leaches who fattened themselves on the blood of the faithful. Popular among his followers, portions of the Chanter's diatribe were incorporated by Gerald of Wales into his *Gemma ecclesiastica* and Gilles de Corbeil converted certain passages into verse.[7] As papal legate Robert of Courson inserted canons into the Councils of Paris and Rouen to curb the exactions of officials, in both the general and the specific scope of the term.[8] Chamberlains, butlers, marshals, and seneschals were not to extort money and *officiales* proper were to do justice freely and impartially.

If *officialis* referred to almost any kind of functionary, *curialis* more specially designated those who served in the *curia* of princes. These princely entourages inspired in France and England a literature to describe their activities and a genre of rhetoric to castigate their peccadilloes. Walter Map, who composed one of these treatises, found the princely court eminently comparable to Hell.[9] His colleague and friend Gerald of Wales prefaced his book on kingship with an elaborate contrast between the delusions of the court and the wholesome benefits of the schools.[10] Obviously Gerald's refuge in the world of study was in part motivated by disappointments suffered at the Plantagenet court. As Walter Map rightly pointed out, the prince was the sole focus around whom all others revolved according to his pleasure. Similarly, another countryman, Stephen Langton, noted that the proximity of one's seat to the king was an indication of royal favor.[11] Since the prince was the prime mover of the courtly universe, adulation was the chief temptation of *curiales*. In his *Verbum abbreviatum* Peter the Chanter devoted to this abuse a long chapter which consisted of little more than a mosaic of generalities supported by numerous Scriptural and classical quotations.[12] The campaign against flattery possessed a hoary tradition, to which Peter added little, except perhaps to complain about its pernicious effect on grammar. In a *questio* he maintained that full restitution of benefits gained through flattery was necessary for absolving a courtier seeking penance,[13] and Robert of Courson extended this principle to detraction as well.[14]

Although clerics legitimately served as *officiales* in the courts of prelates, clergymen who served as *curiales* in the retinues of princes were open to question. Ecclesiastical writers had two minds on the subject, but occasionally someone such as Master Peter of Blois, then archdeacon of Bath, conceded the practice, as when he defended the clerics at Canterbury from the reproaches of the grammarian Master Ralph of Beauvais.[15] These men were not curial clerks in the worst sense of the word as Ralph had accused, because they were engaged in the useful task of aiding their archbishop contribute to the political welfare of England. In lectures, debates, and judgments of litigation, they gave their learned opinions on the difficult questions of the realm. In another letter, addressed to the clerics of King Henry II, who were technically *curiales*, Peter pointed out the valuable contributions performed by royal clerics.[16] Their assistance to the king in promoting the public welfare by aiding the poor, defending religion and the church, and promoting equity was not only to be tolerated but even commended. Among Peter's letters another was addressed by Hubert Walter, Archbishop of Canterbury, to the chapter of Salisbury requesting permission for a certain Master Thomas of Essenben to absent himself in the king's service.[17] To Hubert Walter royal service was comparable to attending school or undertaking a pilgrimage which excused one from canonical residence. At other times, however,

Peter had second thoughts about curial clerics, as when he wrote letters to royal clerks warning them of the pitfalls to their high calling as servants of God.[18] Peter later confessed that he wrote one of these letters at a time of personal despondency,[19] but these lapses probably reflect more faithfully the general opinion of churchmen that service to princes was not a worthy occupation of the clergy. Peter's saintly contemporary Hugh, Bishop of Lincoln, for example, denied a prebend to a royal favorite and refused to allow his own clerics to engage in royal business.[20]

After the Lateran Council of 1179 clerics were frequently warned against becoming the agents of secular princes.[21] It is not surprising that many of these admonitions were issued from councils in Plantagenet lands where the practice of recruiting clerics into royal service prevailed.[22] When Pope Alexander III addressed a decretal to the Archbishop of Canterbury on the subject he specified the chief grounds against curial clerics.[23] The Council of Toledo in the seventh century had maintained that clergy involved in "blood judgments" were not fit to handle the sacraments, and were impeded from advancing into holy orders.[24] Since attendance at court implicated clerics in blood affairs, they served princes only at the risk of obstructing future ecclesiastical promotion. To be applied realistically, however, such a broad restriction required qualification. Canonists such as Rufinus and Huguccio proposed distinctions for interpreting the term. According to Huguccio, *curiales* in the broadest sense meant any of those who were bound to the court of a prince, and included knights, lawyers, judges, officials, and court entertainers.[25] In a more limited sense, it referred to those who exercised honorable functions, such as the *decuriones*, but in the narrowest sense, it comprised those who executed court sentences involving the shedding of blood. At this level of interpretation the term *curialis* was derived from *cruor* (bloodshed).[26] Only those who were *curiales* in the strictest sense, who were directly implicated in blood or who performed shameful practices such as actors, were absolutely barred from church advancement. All others could be promoted upon release from their obligations to the court. Lawyers and judges, for example, who dealt with civil cases, found no impediment to their advancement. The Parisian theologians who considered the general problem of *curiales* merely adopted the canonists' distinctions. Robert of Flamborough's discussion, for example, was directly taken from Huguccio.[27] Although Robert of Courson's *questio* on the subject was elaborate, his solution also was largely inspired by the canonists.[28] Robert observed, however, that the pope often dispensed with the impediment of *curialis* to promotion, even to those who qualified under the strictest meaning. As a matter of fact in many regions of his day it was scarcely possible to receive advancement without being a *curialis*. Following the guidance of the canonists, the theologians began to identify the chief functions of court service in an effort to apply more realistically the restrictions against *curiales*. Among their list they devoted special attention to chancery clerks, judges, lawyers, and entertainers.

While the clergy could conceivably refrain from the normal courtly duties, they could not, of course, neglect their spiritual ministry to the prince and his entourage. Among their spiritual duties was the hearing of confessions, which rendered precarious their immunity from court politics. Moreover, the sacred obligation to the seal of the confession, which prevented the clergy from divulging information gained through confession, undoubtedly produced bewildering perplexities for the court chaplain. As some more serious examples Peter the Chanter cited cases involving treasonous court conspiracies of which a priest learned through confession.[29] What was the priest's obligation to the prince and the public welfare threatened by sedition known only to him? Peter explored a number of possible solutions. If the priest warned the prince to protect himself without revealing the basis of his warning, the prince would probably not believe the priest. If he admitted that his knowledge was gained through a certain confession, the prince would cruelly punish the malefactor. If the priest exacted a guarantee from the prince not to harm the conspirator, the prince would nonetheless hold against the culprit a hate jeopardizing his own salvation. Of course, the priest was fully justified in dissuading the traitor, but if the conspirator refused to desist from his intended violence, could the priest refuse to accept his confession and threaten to reveal the plot? While the culprit probably would have repented under such pressure, the Chanter agreed with Master Robert *de Camera*, who taught that forced penances were not legitimate. Finally, if the confessed and repentant traitor was part of a group who were still determined to conspire, what should the priest do? Peter concluded by posing a number of specific cases without coming to any final solution, but the drift of his discussion indicates that he would have chosen the inviolability of the seal of confession even under the most perplexing circumstances. His follower Peter of Poitiers of Saint-Victor in his brief treatment was doubtful whether a bishop informed of a plot by a priest could in turn warn the king.[30]

CHANCERY CLERICS

Effective government requires the service of the pen. Political administration which attempts more than the most rudimentary tasks demands some kind of secretariat, or in medieval terms, a chancery. Since most churchmen were assumed to be literate in an age of widespread illiteracy, one of their obvious contributions to the courts of princes was their skill of writing. Emerging from the court chapel in Carolingian times, the chancery produced some of the earliest forms of governmental bureaucracy.[31] The course of this development is illustrated by a change in terminology. From the ninth century the secretariat was indicated in the documents by its chief officer, the chancellor (*cancellarius*), but during the second half of the twelfth century it was also designated by the impersonal term chancery (*cancellaria*). That a bureaucratic body had formed by this time is shown by the fact that in France, for example, the office of chancellor was often kept vacant while the chancery continued to function. By 1216 the direct supervision of the papal chancery was assigned to a lesser official, the vice chancellor, and specific rules were drawn up for personnel and procedure.[32] From all indications these groups of governmental clerks were large in size. When Thomas Becket, for example, was the English royal chancellor, it is said that he was assisted by at least fifty-two clerics.[33] Even if not all of these worked directly in the chancery, they represented a sizeable group by contemporary standards. Modern knowledge of the chancery is facilitated by the near-simultaneous appearance of collected records from Rome, England, and France at the turn of the twelfth and thirteenth centuries. Although the papacy kept registers, now lost, from early times, the first continuous extant series dates from the pontificate of Innocent III (1198-1216). Surviving English chancery enrollments begin with King John (1199), and Philip Augustus initiated the Capetian registers in 1204. Although the survival of these voluminous records has been conditioned by historical chance, they nonetheless show modern scholars that chanceries in Rome, England, and France attained a comparable development at about the same time. Since Peter the Chanter and his colleagues were exact contemporaries, they were well situated to observe the functions of the chancery.

In occasional passages from his Scriptural lectures the Chanter indicates his particular familiarity with chancery clerks. At one point, for example, he distinguishes a wide range of connotations of the terms *notarius* and *librarius*.[34] At one end of the scale the two are identical and designate copyists; at the other, the *notarius* signifies one who copies the books, the *librarius* one who corrects and takes care of them. More important, Peter also discussed the uses of the seal, whose custody was one of the principal functions of the chancellor. Prefacing his commentary to the Psalms with an allusion to the Apostle John's vision of a book closed with seven seals (Rev. 5 : 4), he took this occasion to distinguish five ways in which chanceries customarily employed the seal.[35] First of all, a seal may both authenticate and close a letter, such as one issued by the pope. Secondly, it may authenticate but not close the letter, if it is sent open. Or thirdly, it may close but not authenticate the letter, if the seal is ungenuine or if, for example, someone seals a letter with a piece of money. Fourthly, the seal may be enclosed within the charter as in the privileges of the king, or finally, the charter may be enclosed in itself as in the letters of the English king. Although the Chanter's purpose was not to describe chancery practices, but to provide an object lesson for his Biblical lecture, it is nonetheless possible to identify the first three uses of the seal with fair certainty from contemporary procedures. With little doubt the second category designates the diploma or letter patent with a pendant seal which was regularly sent open by the chanceries of the pope and the kings of England and France.[36] The first category indicates the letter close for which we have abundant evidence from the English, but also a few examples from the French and the papacy.[37] Of course, the third class—forgery—was widely practiced, and some examples are known of the coins used as seals.[38] Because of the brief nature of Peter's remarks the last two categories cannot be identified with the same assurance. The fourth type probably refers to the older Capetian practice of placing the seal directly on the diploma,[39] and the last reference may indicate the English manner of sealing letters close by using a strip partly detached from the bottom of the parchment.[40]

More important than these scattered observations, Peter the Chanter and Robert of Courson debated in their *questiones* two problems which were fundamental to the operation of the chancery: (1) How were chancery services to be rewarded? and (2) Under what conditions could the clergy participate?[41] On these issues of economics and personnel Peter characteristically outlined the major issues in a somewhat confused array, which Robert coordinated in a single *questio*. In treating the economic problem they first distinguished between ecclesiastical and secular chanceries. Enumerating specific cases among the former, they considered the ecclesiastical chancellor who held a benefice. As a church dignitary would he not be committing simony if he sold the appurtenances of his office, such as wax, pen, and notarial skill, which were compensated by his prebend?[42] To support this contention Robert collected authorities drawn from canon law,[43] but he and Peter the Chanter based their answer primarily on the example of Thomas Becket. Apparently disgusted with bureaucratic rapacity from his experience as royal chancellor, when Thomas became Archbishop of Canterbury, he forbade under oath his own chancellor, Master Arnulf,[44] to accept the smallest recompense—not even a knife—in discharge of his duties. Becket's restriction may indeed have been effective because "Master Arnulf, Chancellor of the Archbishop" was listed among the debtors of the notorious English usurer, William Cade, as owing three marks.[45] Thomas' example clearly made a vivid impression on the Chanter's circle for allusions to this deed are repeated throughout the Chanter's own works and echoed in the writings of Robert of Courson and Gerald of Wales.[46]

Beside Becket's example Peter also placed the response of Luke, Archbishop of Gran (1161-1179) in Hungary, who burned a valuable papal privilege because his archdeacon paid a customary three shillings to the papal clerks for expediting the document.[47] This archbishop is identical with the Luke whom Walter Map knew from former days in the schools of Master Gerard Puella in Paris.[48] By the end of the century a tradition accumulated at Paris around this former student for Walter Map's account complements and elaborates the Chanter's story. According to Walter, Luke had been imprisoned at the time by the King of Hungary for refusing to comply with his coronation. The papal letters, therefore, which Luke refused to accept because money (one shilling according to Walter) had been paid for them, were written by Pope Alexander III to procure the Archbishop's own release! But the pious Archbishop had no need for simoniacal documents because he was miraculously liberated from prison by the Lord Himself. On the basis of canon law confirmed by the recent examples of two saintly archbishops, the Chanter and his followers concluded that an ecclesiastical chancery endowed with benefices should not accept anything for its seal or other services.[49] Robert of Courson embedded this simple, almost bald, solution in the canons of the Councils of Paris in 1213 and of Rouen in 1214.[50]

Such a conclusion, however, was a counsel for perfection and not necessarily strict law. Both the Chanter and Courson recognized that the custom of charging fees was widespread,[51] nor could they avoid the fact that Rome, the model for all church chanceries, although well endowed with benefices, was notorious for fees and for the exorbitant size of gifts which were required.[52] For these reasons Peter and his followers were led to consider qualifications to the general principle. From the beginning the Chanter distinguished two groups of church documents: *littera depreciatoria* and *littera citatoria*.[53] Although these are not normal terms, his classification was evidently based on "letters of grace" and "letters of justice" of the papal chancery.[54] The first category comprised beneficial documents such as confirmations of property and privileges, letters of protection, ordinations to churches, dispensations, and other sacramental affairs. To sell such letters was in Peter's opinion clearly simoniacal and encouraged intolerable abuse. Otherwise one was tempted to bribe the notary to strengthen or improve the wording of the letter or even to place one's name on the list of candidates to be installed in churches. The second group consisted of administrative correspondence, chiefly delegation of cases and perhaps summons to justice. While those who charged for these letters were certainly not committing simony, the Chanter was not persuaded that they were wholly blameless. Nonetheless he conceded that prelates who held temporal justice were tempted to charge for writs of summons as this was commonly practiced by lay lords.[55]

The premise underlying the Chanter's position was that the chancellor and his staff were adequately endowed with benefices. To pose a second case, what if these resources were lacking, and the prelate was forced to hire a scribe at a daily wage? Under such circumstances Peter conceded that the prelate might charge for the parchment, ink, and labor of the scribe, but he could not demand a fee for his seal, which would have been equivalent to selling his mitre, crozier or other priestly insignia.[56] Robert further developed this concession of his master. Interpreting Pope Gregory's prohibition of fees for the notary, he pointed out that the Pope had in mind excessive charges which did not eliminate recompensing the just price for the wax, parchment, ink, and the copyist's labor.[57] If chancery clerks were without regular income, they were permitted moderate fees, provided that they did not enter into contracts for their payment but received remuneration as gifts after the work had been completed. In sum, chancery clerks' fees were justified on the same grounds as those for masters of theology.[58]

After treating those issuing chancery documents, Peter the Chanter briefly considered a third case, of one receiving such instruments.[59] What should a cleric do who has been promised a church for which the notary has refused to write the letter of grace without a fee? Although this resembled the situation of Luke of Gran, the Chanter hesitated to suggest the saintly archbishop's solution to the ordinary cleric. His response was to counsel casting the money at the notary's feet, thus receiving the letter but refusing to accept responsibility for the simoniacal transaction.

The ideal of gratuitous chancery services even as modified by the Chanter and Courson was too lofty for the chancery at Rome, not to speak of lesser ecclesiastical bodies throughout western Christendom. Some evidence exists, however, that influential figures at Rome were disturbed by current practices and undertook remedial measures. About the time of Innocent III there appeared the first regulations governing the conduct of papal chancery clerks.[60] Moreover, the anonymous but contemporary biographer of Innocent states that the Pope, troubled by the venality of the *curia* decreed that no official should exact payment for his services although he might accept a tip if it were freely offered.[61] Two important exceptions were the chancery scribes and officials administering the seal, who were allowed fees according to a rate schedule, established about 1207.

Since few details survive about these fixed rates from periods before the middle of the thirteenth century,[62] it is impossible to ascertain how Innocent's practice corresponded to the theologians' principles. Obviously a system of fixed fees overlooked Courson's prohibition of contractual agreements, but it could have allowed for the Chanter's distinctions between letters of grace and letters of justice and the remuneration of materials and labor. The Chanter, however, would not have permitted charges for the seal as Innocent permitted. When evidence becomes clearer at a later date, there is little relationship between the masters' theories and the practice of Rome. At the beginning of the century both the theologians at Paris and Pope Innocent III, nonetheless, possessed a common desire to curb the notorious venality of ecclesiastical chanceries, although they differed as to means of reform. By adopting a fixed schedule of fees the Pope, in effect, followed a system close to that of the secular chanceries of England and France.

Chancery revenues were equally precious to the secular princes of France and England. Although the earliest recorded French rates come from a source a century later, there is evidence that fees were exacted during the reign of Philip Augustus.[63] More significant, King John at his accession in 1199 issued a solemn charter which restored the rates of the English chancery to the level of his father, thus abolishing the increases demanded by his brother Richard.[64] Roughly contemporary to these measures, Peter the Chanter also treated exactions demanded by lay chanceries.[65] Since ecclesiastical dignities were not involved in this case, secular chancery fees did not raise the question of simony; rather, Peter fixed his attention on the actual rates. Just as a bishop cannot increase the synodical dues from his clergy, he asked, how can a prince rightfully double or triple the revenues of his seal? On the other hand, who sets the rates? Are they not the responsibility of the prince who in modern times possesses unlimited authority? Although the Chanter's discussion is ambiguous, he concludes that the assessments for the seal should be fixed; otherwise the pope would have just cause for intervention. While it was clear that whoever raised the charges committed sin, the Chanter was doubtful about the precise manner in which penance should be performed. Particularly was he hesitant about the case of a courtier who doubled the rates of the seal in behalf of his sovereign. After considering several alternatives of restitution, he finally decided that the best recourse was to abolish the innovations themselves. Since public services were performed through the seal, Peter was opposed to arbitrary exactions, but he advocated a program of fixed fees to recompense the chancery. In a sense then, he would have approved of King John's action, which returned the fees to the traditional rates of his father. The charter itself explicitly states that the reform was produced by ecclesiastical pressure. Hubert Walter, royal chancellor and Archbishop of Canterbury, originally proposed it to the King, and it was enforced by ecclesiastical as well as political sanctions.[66]

The skills of reading and writing remained one of the important services rendered by the clergy to political administration. Although the chanceries of princes and prelates in Mediterranean lands employed laymen, those of northwest Europe, even the secular chanceries, were dominated by clerics. The chancellorship of the French and English kings was invariably held by an ecclesiastic who accumulated clerics in his service. Literate laymen, to be sure, were not excluded,[67] but their numbers were not as significant as those of the clergy. Employment in a secular chancery, however, presented problems peculiar to the clergy which the Chanter and Courson quickly perceived.[68] To be specific, a cleric might be required to draft letters ordering execution, mutilation, imprisonment, or imposing unjust fines which involved mortal sin. Associations with blood judgments, as has been seen, endangered a cleric's future promotion to holy orders, but how these issues pertained to chancery clerks attracted only slight attention from the canonists. Gratian included the case of one who "dictated" a legal petition (*preces dictans*) for capital punishment, and concluded that since the ultimate decision of condemnation or absolution pertained to the judge, the "dictator" was immune from responsibility even when the judgment was unjust.[69] The canonists who commented on this canon were undecided as to the person to whom this "dictator" referred, but Huguccio in discussing the possibilities suggested that it was the notary who wrote the petition.[70] If the notary was a layman, he was free from responsibility, but if he was a cleric, he sinned even if the accused was justly condemned, because a cleric is not allowed to become involved in judgments of blood.[71] The Paris theologians applied the distinction directly to clerics serving as notaries in secular chanceries. The Chanter, seconded by Courson, counselled princes to assign to literate laymen rather than to clerics the duties of drafting documents involving blood judgments.[72] This specific advice was adopted by the Lateran Council of 1215 under the direction of Pope Innocent III.[73] Interpreting the principle for actual practice, Peter the Chanter, however, recommended modifications.[74] Clerics could draw up letters commanding the destruction of malefactors in general terms or even the condemnation of specific individuals with monetary fines. Only the drafting of individual sentences decreeing death or mutilation were denied. In effect, therefore, the Chanter permitted to the clergy most of the duties demanded of notaries in the chanceries of princes.

JUDGES

The dispensing of justice was the chief function of the medieval court. From the national monarch to the petty seigneur the lords of France and England heard suits in their courts and enforced the law within their jurisdiction. When the theologians considered this function of court service, they distinguished two groups of agents, the judges and the lawyers. Since the masters were themselves clerics, they envisaged the problems of the judge from the standpoint of ecclesiastical lords. Although the prelates' primary duty was to preside over the church courts in spiritual and religious affairs, they frequently possessed the authority to judge tem-

poral matters as well. Many bishops and abbots were in fact political
lords exercising temporal justice in their seigneuries. In other words, prelates often held *regalia*, lands from which secular justice and military service was required. To choose one example, but one which also occurred
to the masters, the king shared temporal justice in Paris with the bishop,
the abbots of Saint-Germain-des-Prés and Sainte-Geneviève, the canons
of Saint-Merry and others.[75] When Stephen Langton became Archbishop,
he discovered that the see of Canterbury claimed jurisdiction over criminals in certain lands.[76] Peter the Chanter remarked that the bishop was a
dual (*biformis*) person who often exercised the functions of a count.[77]
Echoing the complaint of Bernard of Clairvaux,[78] he maintained that
since duels were held and thieves were hanged in episcopal courts, all
bishops were damned. Their time was more occupied with suits involving peasants' land than with their spiritual welfare. Caesar of Heisterbach reported the similar opinion of an unnamed cleric of Paris, that a
German bishop could not be saved because he judged criminal cases
and waged war, and the saintly Hugh, Bishop of Lincoln, complained
that the only difference between a town bailiff and a prelate was that the
former decided secular disputes every day and the latter every other day.[79]

Not only were churchmen judges by reason of temporal rights, but
often they were enlisted by monarchs to serve as agents of royal justice,
particularly in the Plantagenet lands, where prelates were appointed jus-
ticiars and itinerant justices. In a well-known account the English chronicler Ralph of Diceto described Henry II's reliance upon the churches of
Winchester, Ely, and Norwich for incorruptible justices. Writers at the
end of the twelfth century recalled the examples of a Roger of Salisbury
or a William of Ely who served in such capacities.[80] This practice was
further justified by the Lateran Council of 1139, which permitted kings
and princes to do justice with the counsel of archbishops and bishops.[81]
Because legal business preoccupied the life of a contemporary prelate,
Robert of Courson felt it useful to include a brief *ordo judicarius* in his
Summa for the benefit of ecclesiastics.[82] Although the masters were more
concerned with the ecclesiastical than with the secular side of justice, attention will be confined to their consideration of the ecclesiastic as a temporal judge, which illuminates the administration of secular justice.

Temporal justice invariably involved the prelate in criminal cases or
police jurisdiction where penalties requiring the shedding of blood were
demanded by customary law. The major question facing the theologians,
therefore, was to what extent it was legitimate for churchmen to judge
criminal cases. Discussed extensively by the canonists,[83] this problem also
attracted attention from the theological masters. Peter the Chanter and
Thomas of Chobham raised practical problems, while Robert of Courson
devoted the question fullest treatment by agonizing over perplexities

which arose in practice and to which he could find no decisive conclusion.[84] His discussion consists of tentative conclusions each rejected in turn. Parts of his work were adopted by Geoffrey of Poitiers. Approaching the issues from the theoretical side, Stephen Langton, Master Martin, and Simon of Tournai formulated solutions which fitted their abstract views on temporal authority. Moreover, the question seems to have been debated with the heretics because it is found in the *Summa contra hereticos* ascribed to Prepositinus.[85]

Examining the general justification for churchmen handling criminal cases, Robert of Courson constructed a full scale *questio* which aligns authorities for and against the proposition. His arguments in favor consist of examples not only from the Old and New Testaments,[86] but also from contemporary practice. The Roman curia commissioned bishops and legates to enlist armies for defending the Holy Land and who were thereby implicated in the shedding of blood, and in fact it was the custom of most churches to punish malefactors through their officials.[87] In opposition Robert assembled other Scriptural passages, including the Lord's prohibiting David to build the temple because he had shed blood.[88] It will be seen that the conclusion to this debate involved the relationship of the prelate to his secular ministers. For Stephen Langton the justification of ecclesiastical police jurisdiction was also a matter of reconciling Scriptural texts (and he included authorities also cited by Robert[89]), but his inclinations towards abstract theory led him to focus on the nature of the political authority which permitted prelates to handle criminal cases. It will be remembered that when he dealt with the question of whether the church possesses both swords, Stephen adopted the dualist position. By the close of the twelfth century the canonists were interpreting the metaphor of the secular sword either broadly as meaning temporal authority or narrowly as designating physical coercion.[90] After employing the term sword in the broad sense, Langton turned to its specific use, in the right of an individual church, such as Paris, to punish malefactors.[91] The tortuous route of Stephen's argument need not be followed too closely, but as a dualist he merely assumed that the prelate received the police power from the king. The crux of his argument centered on a twofold understanding of power (*potestas*) as authority and as ability. Applying this distinction, he concluded that a bishop has the power, interpreted as authority (*potestas juris*), to kill malefactors, but not the actual ability or faculty (*potestas facti*) to execute this power. Approaching the question from the hierocratic position, Simon of Tournai and Master Martin simply argued that since the prelate transmitted the secular sword to the king at the royal anointing, he himself originally possessed it.[92] Like Langton, however, they also made a twofold distinction by maintaining that the prelate had the power to commit the sword to the prince but not to bear it himself. Starting from the unitary hierocratic premise, Simon and Martin could easily demonstrate that since temporal authority flowed directly from God to the prelate, who finally conferred it upon the prince, the temporal sword was originally possessed by churchmen. The involutions of Langton's argument indicate the difficulties of a dualist who must explain how political authority flowed from God directly to the prince and was finally bestowed upon the prelate as a "power" but not as a faculty. Both dualists and hierocratics, however, concurred that churchmen possessed police jurisdiction *de iure*.

Following the canonists, the theologians, whether dualists or hierocrats, agreed that the police powers of ecclesiastics should be executed *de facto* by lay ministers.[93] Geoffrey of Poitiers summed up his masters' teachings that such officials should be zealous in enforcing human laws,[94] and Thomas of Chobham advised prelates to hire discreet seneschals to execute justice.[95] Assuming a dualist position, Thomas further maintained that such ministers punished criminals not on the prelate's authority but according to the law of the prince who delegated this power to the ecclesiastic. It was precisely this delegation of authority, however, that troubled Robert of Courson.[96] Arguing as a hierocrat, Robert assumed that the temporal sword was committed to laymen by the church. If the authority to kill criminals came from the bishop, was he not implicated in shedding blood? After considerable discussion Robert came to his first conclusion, that the ecclesiastic resembles a lord lacking a hand who orders his servant to perform what he cannot do. Nonetheless, how is the prince's position to be distinguished from a prelate's?[97] If the former kills through his ministers, why not the latter? Robert's final solution was that the official of a prince has the authority to punish both generally and at the specific command of his lord, while the ecclesiastical minister has general authority and the prelate cannot advise him in individual cases. In similar terms Master Martin and Simon of Tournai envisaged both prelates and princes to have ministers who execute justice, but the prelate's minister pronounces death sentences in his own name, although he has his power from the prelates.[98]

If churchmen exercised criminal justice through lay ministers, the question nonetheless remained of their personal participation. Was any role permitted to the ecclesiastic in judging criminals? Could they avoid being involved in the decisions of their courts? By considering these questions the theologians were drawn to a closer examination of the prelate as a judge in criminal justice. Peter the Chanter directly posed the question of whether prelates can command their agents to execute criminals.[99] Supported by two examples, his immediate response was negative. The first episode was a rebellion which Pope Lucius faced at Rome, but which strictly speaking involved the bishop's right to wage war. The second and more pertinent example was furnished by Master Robert *de Camera,* who as Bishop of Amiens was confronted by his *vidame* with an apprehended thief. Robert's immediate reply to his minister was to do what had to be done. Although he later repented of his words, the news of the reversal did not reach the gallows in time to save the felon, and the Bishop did penance for homicide. By this example the Chanter implied that ecclesiastics should totally abstain from such decisions, but elsewhere he offered a more qualified response. If outside of the court a judge should inquire from a cleric whether a certain crime was worthy of death, the cleric may reply in such a way as to enunciate a general principle, but never may his response be applied to a specific judgment.[100] If, for example, a prince brought a criminal into the lecture room and asked whether those convicted of a certain crime should be killed, the master in the presence of the criminal person was not free even to quote an appropriate Scriptural passage. Scholars, however, in their theological disputations could debate whether homicide should be punished with death, because their discussion did not result in individual shedding of blood.

The Chanter's solution of allowing churchmen to contribute general but never specific advice was widely adopted among his followers.[101] Thomas of Chobham accepted it completely,[102] and Stephen Langton concluded that bishops may declare the law but may never render a sentence.[103] Although Robert of Courson began and ended with his master's principle in a long and vacillating discussion, he was troubled by objections which arose in practice. After listing relevant authorities, Robert proposed as a preliminary solution that an ecclesiastic could not participate in a specific judgment but should commit to a lay official the execution of justice according to the customs of the realm.[104] But this solution was merely verbal and did not solve realities. Often the bishop's bailiffs are confronted with a prominent malefactor whom they dare not punish without the express command of their lord, thus presenting to the ecclesiastic the dilemma of involvement in blood judgments or permitting lawlessness.[105] This case occurred at Paris in 1201 when the notorious heretic Evrard of Châteauneuf, convicted of heresy in a church council presided over by the Cardinal Octavian, was handed over to the secular authority for punishment. According to Robert, the prince refused to execute the condemnation until the council specified the penalty. Replying that it was not within their competence to define the punishment, the council declared that the prince possessed codices of Roman law enumerating criminal penalties. But Robert was dissatisfied even with this reply. To say "Consult the codices," was in effect to advocate the death penalty, because the codex says nothing specifically about the punishment of heresy. Such verbal solutions obscure realities and deceive the simple-minded. Nor can the dilemma be avoided by simply assigning competence in corporal punishment to the laity and in others to the clergy, because boundaries cannot be precisely drawn.[106] Through their counsel the clergy nonetheless indicate to the prince whether the death penalty should be inflicted. Thus Robert returned to the solution of the Chanter, also shared by a certain Master *R. Modici passus*:[107] clerics may counsel their ministers as to which penalties are suitable for various crimes, but they may never participate in specific judgments.

In the foregoing discussion Robert assumed that the prelate was served by laymen in his court. In another passage he considered the perplexity of a prelate who did not possess such ministers or was otherwise forced to judge a felon in his own person.[108] A certain archbishop of Rouen was reported to have solved this dilemma in a crude fashion by blinding the criminal, but the more gentle Sanson, Archbishop of Reims, maintained that once the criminal was introduced into his presence he could not be executed. Robert himself rehearsed most of the arguments already considered, but in this case he accepted the opinion of the Archbishop of Reims. Since it was impossible for an ecclesiastic to render a death sentence, his most severe alternative was to commit the felon to prison, a solution adopted by Geoffrey of Poitiers.[109] Thomas of Chobham, however, applied this solution to English conditions, where ecclesiastics were often employed by the king as itinerant justices.[110] If the prince guaranteed the defendant immunity from death and mutilation, bishops, priests, and deacons could hear criminal pleas and pronounce imprisonment and exile. Only in this manner could churchmen personally serve as judges in secular justice without jeopardy to their order.[111]

A final question concerning criminal justice arose directly from current practice. The cartularies of churches contain numerous examples of contested jurisdiction between lay and spiritual lords, in which lay magnates encroached on the churches' rights of secular justice. One case debated in the school of Peter the Chanter concerned a notorious brigand captured on a seigneury whose justice pertained to Notre-Dame of Chartres.[112] A lay magnate, however, who did not possess jurisdiction, seized and threatened to execute the criminal. The ecclesiastical lord must choose between acceding to the usurpation of the layman or defending the rights of his church. The former would result in a public service at the expense of the church's jurisdiction; the latter would uphold the church's rights at the cost of allowing the criminal to escape punishment, because the church could not decree a death penalty. The answer offered was to acquiesce to the magnate's encroachment, thus sacrificing the church's jurisdiction to the public good.

In the Lateran Council of 1215 Pope Innocent III reaffirmed that no cleric was to be involved in blood judgments on the pain of ecclesiastical censure, which merely restated the premise of the theologians' discussions.[113] The Council also declared that just as laymen should not usurp clerical rights, neither should the clergy intrude upon secular jurisdiction.[114] When applied to churchmen exercising criminal jurisdiction, this decree summed up the matter rather baldly. It was the kind of solution which Robert of Courson complained did not recognize the complexities of the problem. Although he and his colleagues at Paris were not always successful, they attempted to apply general principles to the perplexities of the real world, but these two canons of 1215 did little to recognize their efforts.

Remuneration of the judge was another problem which the Parisian theologians treated briefly. Peter the Chanter quoted an opinion from Augustine which was the point of departure for all discussion: "A judge should not sell a just judgment nor should a witness sell true testimony although a lawyer is permitted to sell just defense and a jurisprudent right counsel."[115] The canonists justified this distinction by observing that while lawyers are committed to one of the contending parties, judges and witnesses have the duty to be neutral.[116] If they accept money from one party they are in danger of defrauding the other. Although a judge is entitled to a salary to recompense his labor, Huguccio explained, he may not accept money for a judgment.[117] If he does sell his judgment, he sins gravely but does not, strictly speaking, commit simony. Among the theologians, the preachers relished citing examples of bribes influencing a judge's decision. Jacques de Vitry, for example, explained how litigants in fact "greased the palms" of avaricious judges.[118] After quoting the Augustinian statement, Peter the Chanter emphasized that judges as public officials should be supported by independent resources.[119] If you are a judge, he continued, you should be careful to have sufficient income. Even if you are in need, you cannot sell a judgment because—in contrast to Huguccio—such transactions are simoniacal. Following the Chanter, Thomas of Chobham likewise declared the sale of judgments to be simoniacal.[120] Since judges customarily enjoyed large revenues attached to their dignities, they should demand nothing for their services. In the opinion of Peter and Thomas judges belonged to those spiritual dignities who should be sufficiently supported by independent income so that they would not be tempted to sell their services.

Although in the *Verbum abbreviatum* the Chanter enunciated Augustine's condemnation of selling judgments, in his *Summa* he devoted *questiones* to cases in which judges did charge for their services. For example, he noticed that delegated judges in Italy exacted a compensation for their travel, labor, and expenses, called procuration.[121] They even hired "assessors" or councillors from the contributions of the litigants. Peter was undecided as to the legitimacy of these exactions. Moreover, some judges, often ecclesiastics holding manors, exact from litigants before the trial two and a half shillings which is called the "penny of justice."[122] Is this not judicial simony? Similarly, it was customary for judges to accept two or three shillings from parties after achieving a settlement.[123] Was this payment a salary which the judge received for his labor? Augustine's condemnation also raised the question of exactions by officials who performed auxiliary services in the court. Peter cited the examiners of witnesses who charged for recording testimonies or even for speeding up their services.[124] He would have dared to assert that such practices were simoniacal were it not for the fact that they were customary at the Roman court. Thomas of Chobham referred to minor officials (*apparitores*) who summoned men to judgment.[125] Since they expended labor in their duties, they were accustomed to receive wages exacted from the parties.

These fragmentary passages of the Chanter and Chobham hardly solved the complexities of remunerating judges and their officials. The two theologians made little effort to distinguish between ecclesiastical and secular judges. Although they may have assumed that ecclesiastical judges enjoyed benefices, they scarcely acknowledged that lay judges often depended on the revenues of justice for subsistence. They failed to distinguish clearly between the judge delegate and the judge ordinary; they only hinted at the difference between the judge and his subordinate officials. Most important, they attempted no resolution of the discrepancy between judicial fees considered as the sale of justice, which was prohibited, and as remuneration for labor and expenses, which was legitimate. As might be expected, many of these issues were more adequately handled by the canonists.[126] Nonetheless, Peter the Chanter and his circle joined their voices to a common protest against the sale of justice, which found echo in the synodical statutes of Stephen Langton[127] and the baronial charters of England,[128] but no one, at the time, was clear how the general prohibition applied to actual practice. In a decretal of 1198, however, Pope Innocent III clarified the question of judge delegates raised by the Chanter.[129] Alluding to Roman law and to Augustine's prohibition, the Pope forbade ecclesiastical judge delegates from exacting a customary tenth of the suit as security on a salary. Although judicial decisions were to be rendered gratuitously in principle, the decretal permitted procurations and fees for auxiliary assessors.

LAWYERS

In contrast to their spasmodic treatment of judges, the Chanter's circle devoted more sustained attention to lawyers. Although occasionally distinguishing between the learned jurist (*jurisperitus*) who provided expert counsel and the advocate (*advocatus*) who pleaded in the courts, the Parisian theologians tended to envisage the legal profession as a whole and to consider problems common to lay as well as to clerical lawyers.

In medieval times lawyers were often the object of popular hostility, a reaction which they have endured since the origins of their profession.[130] This prevailing distrust permeates the writings of the theologians. In a chapter of the *Verbum abbreviatum* entitled "Contra advocatos" Peter the Chanter notes that the lawyers' vileness has been acknowledged since ancient times, when their profession was numbered among base occupations such as those of pugilists, couriers, and heralds, and Robert of Courson placed them in company with surgeons, mongers, pimps, and adulating courtiers, whose dubious professions required special penitential instruction.[131] Like their contemporaries, Peter and Robert were convinced that the besetting sin of pleaders was inordinant cupidity, which prompted other misdeeds. The Chanter charged that just as the prostitute sets a price on her bodily members so the lawyer sells his tongue,[132] and Courson exhausted the possibilities of this indelicate comparison.[133] To elaborate the theme of the lawyer's venal tongue Peter recounted *exempla* which were multiplied in the popular sermons of Jacques de Vitry.[134] Such protests against the lawyers' avarice, however, were not uncommon. Even Peter of Blois, who himself claimed legal expertise, belabored this theme.[135]

To expose the lawyer's greed with colorful rhetoric and amusing anecdote is a simpler task than to devote sober analysis to the problem of just remuneration for the legal profession. Naturally the canonists could be expected to give serious attention to the problem, and in a similar manner the theologians also turned to the constructive side. Peter the Chanter, Stephen Langton,[136] and Thomas of Chobham briefly treated the matter, and Robert of Courson devoted to it a systematic *questio*. Despite divergence at particular points the theologians' discussions agreed in broad outline with the canonists' position.

The theologians' main avenue of approach was through judicial simony. If the advocate received his talents and knowledge freely from God was he not sinning by selling his counsel?[137] Although Robert of Courson collected Scriptural authorities affirming this proposition, both he and the Chanter opposed it with Augustine's statement which permitted lawyers and jurists to sell their pleading and counsel.[138] In contrast to judges and witnesses, who were required to be impartial, lawyers and jurisprudents could accept remuneration from their clients. The theologians' case for the lawyer followed closely their justification of teachers' salaries. Considering, first of all, the factor of benefices, which did not arise in the canonists' discussion,[139] they forbade the advocate from accepting fees if he possessed a prebend or other regular support.[140] For example, it was clear to the Chanter that a jurisprudent should freely offer his counsel if

he possessed ample means, if he could do it without undue consultation of books, study, and effort, and especially if the client was poor.[141]
Since this preliminary condition concerned clerical lawyers who enjoyed
benefices, it primarily affected those who pleaded in ecclesiastical courts.

If the lawyer lacked regular income—in other words, if he was a cleric
without benefice or a layman without regular salary—he could accept
fees from his clients under certain conditions. According to the Scriptural principle (Luke 10 : 7) that "the laborer is worthy of his hire," both
the canonists and the theologians maintained that the advocate's chief
title to remuneration was labor expended in study and defense of the
case.[142] The obvious corollary was that legal fees should be commensurate
with work. Like doctors and teachers, lawyers who exact fees greater
than warranted by their labor are thieves and robbers.[143] Peter the Chanter illustrated this corollary with a specific case:[144] if a celebrated attorney
demands more for his services than others of his profession, he sins
mortally, since he aids his client no more than his less famous colleagues.
This relationship between labor and remuneration was to be regulated
"according to the proportion of the just price" or what was "due" or
"moderate."[145] To illustrate these criteria the theologians occasionally cited
specific figures. At Paris Robert of Courson considered ten pounds an
exorbitant fee for an ordinary case, and three pence per day was specified
as moderate in a marginal notation to the *Verbum abbreviatum*.[146] To
these moderate fees Robert of Courson added a further corollary: like
the theological professor and the chancery cleric, the lawyer should not
enter into a contract over his price before his work is completed.[147]
Just as the medical doctor is not paid until his care is completed, so a lawyer cannot demand his wage before the final decision so that the true
value of his labor can be assessed. Certain canonists, however, disagreed
with this extension of the principle which equated legal fees with the
advocate's labor. While Huguccio, for example, objected to the lawyer
contracting for a percentage of the claims in monetary cases, he nonetheless insisted that the lawyer arrange a fixed fee at the beginning of the
case which could not be altered during the litigation.[148] In contrast to
Courson's scheme the advocate was guaranteed his remuneration notwithstanding the brevity of the proceedings or the outcome of the decision.
Undoubtedly the opinions of the canonists were of greater consequence in shaping actual practice in the ecclesiastical courts, but Robert
of Courson attempted to impose his views on clerical lawyers. At the
Councils of Paris in 1213 and of Rouen in 1214, he restated his position
and enforced it with ecclesiastical sanctions.[149]

In the theologians' opinion the lawyers' greed was not only vicious
in itself but also spawned other temptations. The preachers associated with
the Chanter seldom let slip an opportunity to expose the ruses and deceits

of the legal profession.[150] Noting the practice of pleaders to overwhelm the courts with the din of their clamors, Peter the Chanter claimed that Pope Eugenius III once silenced the advocates in order to hear the plain facts from the litigants themselves.[151] The lawyer's principal temptation, however, was to defend causes which he knew to be unjust.[152]

The problem of lawyers undertaking unjust causes was considered by the canonists as well as the theologians. Huguccio, for example, simply advised the advocate to abstain from such cases.[153] Remembering the well-known difference between judges and lawyers, Peter the Chanter observed that the judge was bound by strict impartiality to base his decision on allegations from both parties.[154] Since the lawyer was obligated only to his client, he was responsible for the justice of his case. If the advocate won an unjust decision, he was held to do penance in the confessional and make restitution of damages to the other party. This conclusion was followed by Robert of Courson and Thomas of Chobham. At the Councils of Paris and Rouen Courson summarily exhorted clerical lawyers to be diligent in the truth and legality of their cases.[155] Beyond the general principle the Chanter offered specific advice to the practicing lawyer. Warning that it was always dangerous to accept the case of a friend, because if it turned out to be unjust the advocate was in an embarrassing position, he cited the example of Master Robert *de Camera* who from the outset averted his clients that if he discovered anything unjust with their claim he would reveal it and transfer his services to the adversary.[156] Although it was assumed that the advocate could know with certainty the justice of the cause, more likely in practice he merely suspected the falseness of his client's plea. In such cases the Chanter concluded that it would be prudent to abstain, because as a general rule it is better to support neither side than to run the risk of causing unjust injury.[157]

Up to this point the advice offered by Peter the Chanter and his followers could be applied to laymen as well as clerics, but there were problems peculiar to the clerical lawyer, especially the cleric who pleaded in secular courts. Because of the canonical prohibition against clerical involvement in blood judgments, the clerical advocate was discouraged from accepting criminal cases, but presumably civil cases before lay tribunals were still open to him. During the twelfth century, however, obstacles to clerics pleading in secular courts were increased. In the Lateran Council of 1179 all clergy in major orders and those in minor orders holding benefices were excluded from serving as lawyers in lay courts except in cases involving their own interests, the interests of their churches, or the causes of defenseless classes (*miserabiles persone*).[158] Although this last exception was based on canon law, which permitted the clergy to undertake the business and legal affairs of widows, orphans, and wards,[159] it obviously conflicted with the principle concerning blood judgments. The question therefore arose as to whether a cleric could defend a *miserabilis persona* accused before a secular judge, especially when canon law also contained a statement of Pope Gregory I which declared that it was the clergy's duty to defend the innocent accused of crimes punishable by shedding blood.[160] Eventually therefore the canonists and the theologians were faced with the question of whether clerics could plead for defendants in criminal cases.

Inclined to approach this question in a technical fashion, the canonist Huguccio reported two points of view in a long gloss to a canon which forbade priests to serve as curial lawyers.[161] The first group, represented by Johannes Bassianus,[162] applied this prohibition only to clerics representing plaintiffs and not to advocates for defendants. The second party objected that the counsel for the defense was no less guilty of involvement in blood judgments because the successful defendant could prosecute his accuser for *calumnia* in retaliation. Johannes' replies to this objection included such arguments as: prosecution for *calumnia* did not always follow and the intention of a defendant's advocate was not to punish the plaintiff but to absolve his client. Aligning himself against Johannes Bassianus, Huguccio concluded that clerics who pleaded for either plaintiffs or defendants should be barred from advancement in holy orders. He therefore interpreted Pope Gregory's statement to mean that only after a blood judgment has been rendered may clerics intercede for the condemned.

The theologians' treatment was less technically formulated than Huguccio's and more concerned with particular situations. In the *Verbum abbreviatum* Peter the Chanter exhorted lawyers to undertake the defense of the *miserabiles persone*,[163] but in his *questiones* he cited two cases which specified judgments of blood. One involved a theologian who was present in a bishop's court exercising police jurisdiction.[164] When three men were presented for the death penalty on charges of theft, the theologian, uneasy about his presence, wished to withdraw and urged the bishop to follow. The bishop, however, insisted on remaining until he could determine whether the accused could be defended, explaining that his presence was necessary to insure just verdicts. Taking courage from the bishop's example the theologian resumed his place, defended the men, and won their acquittal, and Peter the Chanter wondered whether it was not advisable for priests skilled in secular law to attend criminal trials in order to liberate the innocent. The answer to this question was suggested in the other case. Although a cleric cannot serve as judge, assessor, plaintiff, witness, or lawyer in blood judgments, he can be a *defensor* according to the example of Saint Nicholas, who rescued three youths from the death penalty by reopening their cause before the magistrate and demonstrating the injustice of their conviction.[165] In this case the prelate is not a judge or assessor (councillor to the court) who must decide impartially, but rather is a "semi-judge or assessor" who attempts to secure the liberation of one of the parties.[166] Essentially, this is what Baldwin, Bishop of Worcester, did when in 1184 he rescued Gilbert of Plumpton from an unjust condemnation by the English Justiciar Ranulf of Glanville.[167] The problem inherent in these two cases was restated by Robert of Courson.[168] In support of clerics serving as lawyers in criminal cases, Robert assembled arguments based on the clergy's duty to defend the helpless,[169] and he concluded that if a clerical lawyer snatched destitute orphans, wards, and widows from the executioner's hands and defended them in just causes, he was performing a meritorious service.

Defending the innocent from blood judgments, however, was not without pitfalls for the clergy. Speculating about alternative sequels to the Saint Nicholas story, the Chanter asked whether, if during the retrial of the three youths the plaintiff established clear evidence of their guilt, it was right for the lawyer to continue their defense and to attempt to pervert justice? Although the Chanter believed that under such circumstances Saint Nicholas would have withdrawn, even such action would not have disentangled the cleric from blood judgments. Withdrawal by the clerical lawyer would prejudice the defendant's case in the eyes of the judges, who would interpret this action as a sign of manifest guilt. Nonetheless the Chanter felt that it was safer for the advocate to step down than to remain. Rehearsing the example of Saint Nicholas, Thomas of Chobham emphasized the dilemmas involved and therefore warned clerics of the dangers.[170] Indeed the seriousness was further illustrated by an example of Master Robert *de Camera* reported by the Chanter.[171] When Master Robert taught at Reims, he agreed to defend the servant of a friend accused of counterfeiting. When the servant, however, elected to prove his innocence by judicial battle and won his decision, the accuser was hanged in retaliation.[172] Although Robert's client had been successfully defended, Robert himself had become implicated both in an ordeal and in a death sentence.

The incident of Master Robert *de Camera* furnished a case in point in the canonist debate between Johannes Bassianus and Huguccio. Since Robert's defense had associated him with the condemnation of the plaintiff, lawyers for the defense could not always avoid blood judgments, as Huguccio had warned. Huguccio therefore limited clerical intervention to interceding for the innocent after an unjust sentence had been pronounced. Accordingly, Peter the Chanter described Saint Nicholas' role in liberating the three innocent youths not as lawyer but as *defensor*, but in subsequent episodes it is not clear whether the saint also intervened during the normal judicial procedure. Robert of Courson, however, ignored the special term of *defensor*, but assumed that the clerical lawyer should plead for helpless defendants at all stages of the criminal trial. While Peter the Chanter and Thomas of Chobham may have been inclined to Huguccio's position, Robert of Courson appears to have been among the supporters of Johannes Bassianus.[173]

At the Periphery of the Court: Entertainers

Since the canonists defined *curialis* as anyone attached to the court, the term included those who provided amusement.[174] Such a classification was not without foundation because undoubtedly professional entertainers circulated at the peripheries of the courts of princes and prelates.[175] These people are designated by a rich variety of names such as jongleurs (*joculatores*), actors (*histriones*), mimes (*mimi*), and buffoons (*scurre*), which could be employed interchangeably, and this imprecision of terminology reflects contemporary realities.[176] The professional entertainer displayed a remarkable versatility of talents as musician, storyteller, actor, dancer, acrobat, and juggler. Not only a performer, he may also have been a troubadour, one who composed his own tales and music.[177] Nor were his audiences less varied, ranging from the magnates' courts to the crowds of the marketplace, towns, and pilgrim routes.[178] His *métier* was to entertain an audience wherever one could be found to contribute to his support. Undoubtedly Peter the Chanter and his circle took notice of this profession because of their concern with morality, but perhaps their interest was more personally involved. Since the schools were a major source of recruitment for performers, many a bright student, despairing of employment in church, state, or schools, may well have been tempted to venture his wit and luck in amusing others. By the end of the twelfth century students contributed to a new genre of literature known as Goliardic poetry, which celebrated the vagrant life of entertainers.[179] With vivid hues and undoubted exaggeration these poems depict the success and failures of the wandering jongleur, replete with glorious escapades of drinking, gambling, and wenching.[180] Whether or not jongleurs or Goliards attended the theologians' lectures, Peter the Chanter and his followers were nonetheless admirably situated in place and in time to observe the activities of the entertainer. Since modern scholars are agreed that the golden age of the jongleur appeared with the opening years of the thirteenth century,[181] the contemporary observations of the masters help to illuminate a crucial epoch in the history of drama and literature.

From ancient times the attitude of churchmen towards the entertainment profession was unrelentingly hostile. Even in pagan Rome not only were theatrical performers stigmatized with infamy and prohibited from marrying into senatorial families, but actresses were relegated with prostitutes in law.[182] From at least the second century A.D. the realistic performance on the Roman stage of actions considered unquestionably immoral by Christians was hardly conducive to the sympathy of the Church Fathers. Jerome's asceticism generated vigorous protests against the theatre of his day, and Augustine's repentance of his former dissolute life was accompanied by a violent aversion to the theatre which he had loved so passionately.[183] Throughout the early Middle Ages churchmen prolonged this hostility in the decrees of councils.[184] By the middle of the twelfth century the ecclesiastical position was expressed in canonical authorities assembled in the *Decretum* of Gratian.[185] Defamed as in Roman law, actors were prevented from bringing accusation in ecclesiastical courts.[186] They were refused the Eucharist and denied ordination in the church.[187] The canonists Rufinus and Huguccio underscored the infamous character of performers and their attendant disabilities.[188] Professional entertainers incurred whatever legal penalties were generally imposed on prostitutes.[189]

The canonists clarified this association between the entertainer and the prostitute when they defined the character of the latter. In essence the members of both professions put their bodies to shameful use. Rufinus declared that actors (*ystriones*) were storytellers (*ystoriones*) who by transforming their visage and clothing represented images which provoked laughter, and thus told a story (*ystoria*) with their bodies.[190] For Huguccio an actor was one who by bodily movement and transformation of the face represented the actions of others, thereby exercising wantonness.[191] Adopting terminology close to Huguccio's, Peter the Chanter asked whether the definition of the actor should also extend to those who recited monstrous or effeminate songs without bodily gestures.[192] Were not those who followed the camps of princes with their shameful tales equally worthy of infamy?

Among the theologians, Thomas of Chobham offered the most detailed description of the actor's functions.[193] Elaborating the definitions of the canonists and the Chanter, Thomas divided the acting profession into three general categories. First were those designated by the canonists who transformed their bodies by shameful dancing or gestures, by disrobing wantonly, or by wearing terrifying costumes (*lorice*) or masks. The second kind resembled those described by the Chanter who had neither steady employment nor domicile but circulated among the courts of the magnates recounting abuse and scandal. Finally Thomas designated a third classification of actors, who played musical instruments for the delight of men. Certain of these frequented public drinking bouts and roguish gatherings in order to sing bawdy songs inflaming men's desires. Although Thomas denounced these categories of actors in unmistakable terms and urged the priest to deny penance until they abandoned their profession, it will be seen that musicians in the last category could be tolerated.* Thomas' threefold division of actors represented the moralist's attempt to comprehend the social complexities he wished to evaluate. He did not insist that these distinctions were clearly evident among actors of his day but rather proposed this scheme as a means for judging the entertainment profession more realistically.

The moralist often finds it easier to denounce an evil than to define it precisely.[194] Following the traditional hostility, Peter the Chanter devoted a chapter of his *Verbum abbreviatum* to the rhetorical censure of the entertainment profession, which Gilles de Corbeil later embellished with verse.[195] Those whom Peter singled out for attack included prostitutes, magicians, gamblers, and tournament champions, but it is evident that his principal concern was with actors, mimes, and jongleurs. The first half of the Chanter's chapter strung out a long array of Scriptural and Patristic texts against such occupations. Scriptural authority was marshalled against entertainers by equating them with the *curiosi* found in the Bible and its glosses. Passing from arguments of authority to those of practice, Peter declared that there are no human occupations totally devoid of utility.[196] Although imposters and rogues remove filth from cities, and even brothels are necessary because they prevent worse debauchery, the acting profession stands alone as an exception. To it Martial's epigram—"something useful was found in that evil"—cannot be applied. The Chanter's unqualified denunciation led him to demand the appropriate ecclesiastical sanctions. In the *Summa* he insisted that under no circumstances should notorious prostitutes and actors be given the Eucharist, although they were permitted to enter the church to pray.[197] Neither should they be received at one's table except in extreme necessity because hospitality encouraged their errors and contributed something which could be expended in dishonorable use. This last advice was implemented by Robert of Courson at the Councils of Paris (1213) and Rouen (1214) and by Stephen Langton in his diocesan statutes (1213/1214) when they charged the clergy to prohibit actors, mimes, and their instruments from being heard at their tables.[198] In the Lateran Council of 1215 Pope Innocent III similarly forbade all clerics from paying attention to mimes, jongleurs, and actors.[199] Since entertainers were in effect excommunicate, the faithful were to avoid all contact with them.

It was nonetheless clear to the canonists and theologians that the normal penalties were not sufficient to rid society of entertainers,[200] but sanctions threatening their economic support might be employed with more effect. In the twelfth and thirteenth centuries those who amused society depended on contributions from their audiences.[201] These varied according

* See below, p. 203.

to the skill and luck of the performer and ranged from passing one's hat in a crowd to receiving regular support from the court of a lord. Most fortunate were those, of course, who found favor from princes or prelates. In the twelfth century the Plantagenets, especially King Richard and his mother Eleanor of Aquitaine, were reputed as being liberally disposed to entertainers,[202] and undoubtedly other great lords in England and France paid well for their amusement. It is not surprising therefore that the duty of *largesse* or unreserved generosity was incessantly encouraged by troubadours while niggardliness was held in contempt.[203]

Peter the Chanter recorded anecdotes in his *Verbum abbreviatum* which illustrate the good fortune of contemporary performers. At least two deserve retelling. One entertainer boasted that he could count on the contributions from certain rich prelates and cities as if they were fixed annual rents.[204] Proceeding to enumerate three prelates and three cities according to their value, he claimed that from the gifts and promises of the French prelates alone he could expect an annual income of a hundred pounds. On another occasion a certain prince bestowed a gift of fifteen pounds on an actor.[205] In the meantime the prince was approached by a knight captured in a tournament (or perhaps he was even a crusader, the Chanter wasn't sure) who sought the customary aid from the prince to procure his ransom. The prince, however, regarded him with suspicion and subjected him to humiliating questions. When the knight finally demonstrated through witnesses the truth of his story, the prince begrudgingly conceded him forty shillings. At this point the actor, who had observed the incident, could no longer contain his indignation and upbraided the prince for his double standard. To the actor, the vilest of men, the prince had given a handsome fifteen pounds without hesitation or proof. To the knight, who unquestionably benefited the public, he had offered a mere forty shillings and not without scrutiny. With a gesture worthy of his profession the actor turned over his fifteen pounds to the knight. According to the Chanter the incident vividly impressed the prince's entourage, and even Peter conceded that actors often respect men who refuse to support them more than those who encourage their wicked ways.[206] The historical veracity of the Chanter's *exempla* need not trouble one unduly, but they illustrate the esteem in which entertainers were held within aristocratic society.

If performers could not exist without contributions, clearly the most effective sanction was to discourage audiences from making gifts. Gratian's *Decretum* included texts from Augustine which declared that giving to actors was not virtuous generosity but sin.[207] The canonists Rufinus and Huguccio interpreted these statements to mean that one should not give to an actor for the sake of his fame or the exercise of his vices, but only out of charity and in cases of necessity. In other words, one could not contribute to actors as actors, but only as human beings.[208] Recalling the words attributed to Jerome that to give to actors was to sacrifice to demons, Peter the Chanter accepted the canonists' proposals.[209] Robert of Courson contested the right of mimes, jongleurs, actors, and other flatterers to sell their services because they deceived their listeners and thereby received their money fraudulently.[210] Thomas of Chobham dryly remarked that if actors received no contributions they would abandon their profession.[211] Apparently the Capetian kings of France were the one conspicuous example of magnates who adhered to this policy. From the middle of the twelfth century more than one troubadour complained of the stinginess of the "king of Saint-Denis" (probably Louis VII) in contrast to the king of England or the counts of Blois and Champagne who knew how to reward poets handsomely.[212] Somewhat later the Capetian historian Rigord described the contemporary custom of kings and princes to lavish gold, silver, horses, and rich garments on actors for their blandishments.[213] So extravagant were these garments, worth twenty to thirty marks of silver, they could have nourished twenty to thirty poor souls for an entire year. But King Philip Augustus, according to Rigord, remembering the teaching of holy men that to give to actors was to sacrifice to demons, promised all his garments to the poor, thus providing a pious example to the minor princes of the realm. Although these holy men are not identified, it is evident that the royal practice corresponded closely with the counsel of the Chanter's circle.

A further question concerned the restitution of ill-gotten gains. If an actor did penance for his sins, what were his obligations to restore the money he had received? Both Peter the Chanter and Robert of Courson placed mimes, actors, and other adulators in the same category as prostitutes, whose earnings were dishonorably acquired but could be licitly retained.[214] Unless they employed unquestionable fraud, they were permitted to retain their gains. For example, Robert specified that whatever was received through blandishment from youths and simple-minded folk must be restored, but whatever was given by mature men aware of the devices of actors was not subject to restitution.

In voicing these opinions the canonists and theologians merely implemented the traditional ecclesiastical hostilities against all entertainers without distinction. Towards the end of the twelfth century, however, fissures appeared in this wall of opposition. After condemning actors, the canonist Huguccio considered those who played lutes and other musical instruments.[215] Was it sinful to listen or to give to those whose instruments could praise God and serve His ministry? If, of course, musicians played to excite one's lustful desires, their music was condemned, but if they performed for God or the body's health, they could be heard and supported with little danger of sin. The theologians likewise devised concessions to musicians. In his *Summa* Peter the Chanter distinguished instrumental music which provided recreation from that which provoked lust.[216] After denying licit wages to mimes, jongleurs, and actors, Robert of Courson turned to the lutist who supported his wife and family from music. Since the Biblical examples of David, Miriam (the sister of Moses), and other revered men commended the playing of lyres, lutes, tambours, and organs, it was permissible to gain one's livelihood from music.[217] Elsewhere Robert discussed the organist (*magister organicus*) in particular.[218] His art was illicit if he played scurrilous and effeminate music for the corruption of youths and the uninstructed. Prelates who bestowed benefices on such musicians to perform in churches incurred simony. If, however, organists played decent pieces on solemn occasions according to the custom of the land without mixing scurrilous notes, their services were to be tolerated.

Not only conceding a certain value to music, the theologians of Paris also took a further step. If the entertainer rehearsed edifying stories accompanied with instrumental music or even if he sang these stories alone, his services were likewise justified. Peter the Chanter distinguished two kinds of performers called jongleurs.[219] One, deforming the image of God, earned his living from the wantonness of his body. Others, however, who sang of deeds with or without instruments for the recreation, or better, the instruction of others, were exonerated. Elaborating the distinction of his master, Thomas of Chobham applied the name *jongleur* to those musicians whom he approved.[220] In contrast to the pernicious kinds who, as has been seen, performed for lascivious gatherings, these true jongleurs sang of the deeds of princes and the lives of saints for men's solace in sickness and sorrow. In the opinion of Peter and Thomas, if these performers sang their tales without resorting to physical obscenities they merited gifts and maintenance. In illustration, both theologians recount an *exemplum* about a jongleur who inquired of Pope Alexander (III?) whether he could save his soul if he supported himself by this profession. According to the Chanter's account the Pope expressed neither permission nor refusal, but would have granted leave except for his fear that this concession would encourage greater license.[221] According to Chobham, Alexander first inquired whether the jongleur knew any other skill, and when the entertainer admitted that he didn't, the Pope permitted him to live by his profession as long as he refrained from shameful acts.[222]

There can be little doubt that Peter and Thomas referred to the jongleurs who recited martial *chansons de geste* and pious saints' lives in vernacular dialects,[223] although none of the songs or stories were identified by them. In a totally different context, however, the Chanter did produce a list of *chansons* (*cantilene*), in his *Verbum abbreviatum*.[224] Probing simony committed by priests, he objected to the multiplication of the forms of the mass in order to increase the offerings of the faithful. These priests, he continues, are similar to jongleurs who change their tales to suit the audience. When they see that the "chanson de Landri,"[225] for example, does not please their listeners, they immediately begin to sing of Antioch.[226] If the deeds of Alexander[227] are unpopular, they turn to Appollonius[228] or to Charlemagne.[229] The short version of the *Verbum abbreviatum* retains the "chanson de Landri" and substitutes the tale of Narcissus for the others,[230] while Gerald of Wales exchanges the latter for the song *de Wacherio*, in his rendition of this passage.[231] Although his terminology is not clear, he may have been referring to the now lost "chanson d'Auchier." The stories about Charlemagne were apparently favorites because Thomas of Chobham complained that parishioners knew the *chansons de geste* about Charlemagne and other princes better than the doctrines of the faith, or the deeds of the Savior and the saints.[232] The theologians' oblique references do not necessarily indicate titles of literary works but rather themes popularly demanded of jongleurs. Although such a list represents only a small sample of the extant contemporary *chansons de geste*, it furnishes testimony of what themes came readily to the mind of a contemporary observer.

These *chansons de geste* recited in France and England during the lifetime of Peter the Chanter and Thomas of Chobham were of great importance in the development of vernacular literature. In effect the Chanter and Chobham provided moral justification for the poets and performers who created and sang these new songs. By distinguishing an approved kind of jongleur and by constituting him an exception to the ecclesiastical condemnation of entertainers, the theologians in their own way contributed to vernacular literature. Perhaps it was their defense of the jongleur which encouraged King Louis IX, whose piety was above reproach, eventually to reverse the former Capetian hostility and to make the French court brilliant for its patronage of minstrels of song.[233] Since the Chanter and Chobham were by no means prepared to exonerate other species of entertainers, nor to offer concessions to the skill of acting,[234] their contribution was small. Their step was nonetheless necessary, and moved opinion in the direction of Thomas Aquinas, who less than a century later asserted that the acting profession was not illicit in itself.[235]

@ CHAPTER X @

Service in the Field

W HEN churchmen formulated their political discussions in terms of the allegory of the sword, they thereby acknowledged the dominant preoccupation of medieval government. The foremost political function was, in fact, to wield the sword. Service in the field was ostensibly the occupation, *par excellence*, of the noble classes on whom governmental responsibilities rested. Since Peter the Chanter, like many contemporary clergy, originated from a knightly family, he could not be indifferent to the conditions of this warrior aristocracy. Moreover, the Chanter and his followers at Paris were well informed about the contemporary exploits of their sovereigns Philip Augustus and Richard the Lionhearted in the Holy Land or the departure of the barons to Constantinople. Closer at hand were the conflicts raging between the Capetians and Plantagenets on French soil.[1] Hostilities which began with the accession of Henry of Anjou to the English crown in 1154 reached the tempo of total war after 1194 when Richard returned from the crusade to defend his lands from the determined aggressions of Philip Augustus. By 1204 the Capetian king had wrested Normandy from the hapless John; in 1214 his victory was secured at the Battle of Bouvines. The French and Norman Vexin downstream from Paris suffered ravage and bloodshed for decades. In one way or another this conflict personally touched the university masters. Peter the Chanter's family lands at Hodenc in the Beauvaisis lay exposed to the hostilities of the Vexin. Although Stephen Langton, Robert of Courson, and Thomas of Chobham were English subjects they studied and taught at the French capital. The bitter contest between Capetian and Plantagenet formed the historical backdrop to their discussions of contemporary warfare.

As theologians the Parisian masters naturally approached warfare from the churchman's point of view. Although the duties of ecclesiastics were theoretically remote from the exigencies of battle, prelates often in fact exercised the temporal sword. In contemporary terminology prelates held *regalia* or lands which required not only justice, as has been seen, but also military service. Since numerous bishops and abbots held lands in France and England for which knight service was due, they were thereby implicated in the military regime. For example, in the English royal survey of 1166 fifteen bishoprics and twenty-four monasteries were recorded as owing knight service to King Henry II.[2] Although the evidence is less precise for France, the numbers of ecclesiastical vassals were at least comparable if not larger than for the English,[3] and these examples do not include the prelates' military obligations to other feudal magnates. Although the primary concern of the Parisian theologians was to investigate the military duties of prelates, they could not avoid considering conditions pertinent to the lay aristocracy as well. Magnates and prelates shared much in common in military service, but in this case as in so many our information about a secular affair—here, the obligations of warfare —depends heavily on ecclesiastical sources.[4]

THE JUST WAR

Underlying the discussions of the Chanter's circle was the doctrine of the just war, whose principal elements were forged in the fifth century by Augustine, and were assembled in the twelfth century by Gratian in the *Decretum*. This textbook and its canonist commentaries formed the point of departure for the theologians.[5] When Gratian summarized the Augustinian passages he singled out two elements constituting a just war: an authoritative edict and the avenging of injuries.[6] The first element originated from the ancient Roman conviction that war was unjust unless declared by public authority. Enunciated by Cicero, this idea was transferred to canon law by Isidore of Seville.[7] According to ecclesiastical doctrine, since a just war must be officially proclaimed by constituted authority, it was removed from private and individual initiative. Augustine elaborated the second element of avenging injuries as chastising a city or nation which had neglected to punish aggressors or recovering goods which were violently usurped.[8] While certain kinds of offensive action might be implied in chastisement, the texts collected by Gratian primarily envisaged the just war as defensive. When a public authority defended itself against aggression it was undoubtedly waging a just war. The canonists who commented on the *Decretum* began to construct a more generalized theory from these Augustinian elements. Rufinus, for example, enumerated three categories of participants in his definition of a just war: those who declared, waged, and were the object of hostilities.[9] Those who declared hostilities should possess constituted authority. Those who conducted the campaign should act with righteous zeal and in an honorable manner, and those who were the object of hostilities should merit the attack.

It was evident, however, that Rufinus' three criteria did not explicitly rule out offensive warfare. While defense against aggression was usually considered a just cause, did not other causes justify an offensive war? Relevant to this question were, of course, the Old Testament examples of aggressive campaigns waged by the Israelites with explicit divine approval. Gratian included passages which offered two different interpretations of these Biblical wars. One text, originating from the Greek Father Origen of Alexandria, maintained that since they were only figures of spiritual conflicts for instructing Christians, they lent no sanction to actual hostilities.[10] Another text briefly excerpting a passage from Augustine judged the Jewish conquest of the Amorites (Num. 21 : 21-24) to be a just war.[11] Gratian himself understood this passage to mean that the Jews waged a just war because the Amorites had denied them the harmless right of transit which in human society should be open to all. Nonetheless, anyone familiar with Augustine's full passage could also conclude that the conquest was justified by God's direct command. This second interpretation was directly confirmed by another Augustinian text, immediately preceding.[12] By the beginning of the twelfth century, therefore, churchmen had developed a notion of the holy war sanctioned by God which was by that title also a just war. The crusades, which were offensive campaigns against pagans and heretics, were legitimate because they were commanded by divine authority through the church and the pope.[13] In the minds of many churchmen, however, the patently offensive action of the crusades was further justified by the defensive criterion of the just war doctrine. These early crusades were envisaged as protecting the Byzantine provinces or the eastern churches from Muslim aggression, or as avenging the injuries of heretics.[14] Even aggressive holy wars were thereby included in the theories of the just war.

These canonist notions of the just war were neither totally coherent nor helpfully explicit, but the *Decretum* nonetheless provided a framework for the Parisian theologians. Unlike the canonists, however, the Chanter's circle preferred to enumerate specific cases in which to apply principles rather than to construct comprehensive theories.[15] In all of their discussions they assumed that the just war was predominantly defensive in character. For example, Thomas of Chobham maintained that knights should follow the king in a just war for the defense of the country and for the preservation of justice.[16] The defense of the church or kingdom against aggression justified extraordinary military service from ecclesiastics as well as laymen. Contemporary royalty and prelates also emphasized the defensive war. When Philip Augustus, for example, summoned special levies from the chapter of Reims in 1197 to put down the rebellion of the Count of Flanders, he admitted that the request was unusual, but excused himself as defending the crown.[17] From such precedents the Capetians developed a doctrine of defense of the realm to justify extraordinary measures.[18] Prelates were also tempted to distinguish between defensive and offensive warfare, but for the opposite purpose of reducing military obligations. In England, for example, the Bishops of

Lincoln and Salisbury and the Abbot of Saint Edmunds, who owed regular knight service to the king, refused in 1197-1198 to contribute to campaigns in Normandy on the grounds that their military obligations were limited to England.[19] Although King Richard succeeded in quelling their resistance, it is plausible that the prelates attempted to reduce their military service by the doctrine of the defense of the realm.

In comment to the book of Joshua, Peter the Chanter found occasion to consider briefly the legitimate authority for declaring war.[20] It was the same Old Testament passage that prompted Augustine to formulate his best known definition of the just war, which Peter incorporated into his commentary. In contrast to this Biblical war waged on God's authority, Peter continued, contemporary wars are declared by a judge who decides between contending parties. Obviously the Chanter was thinking of a vassal's obligation to seek a decision in an overlord's court before defending his cause by arms. If, however, two parties such as the French king and the German emperor have no overlord, they should resort to the pope as their superior judge. Thomas of Chobham declared in similar terms that wars among Christians were unjust when undertaken without judgment and the counsel of the realm.[21] By discussing the problem of constituted authority for declaring war Peter and Thomas gave tacit acknowledgment to the judicial character of warfare in the twelfth century. Seeking justice in a lord's court was the necessary preliminary and battle was the frequent sanction to the judge's decision.[22]

As Biblical scholars the theologians were led to consider the relevance of the Old Testament wars to the conflicts of their own day. Robert of Courson, for example, approached offensive warfare through Biblical cases. In a section of his *Summa* devoted to perplexing situations, he raised the same examples which Augustine had taken from the book of Numbers.[23] On the one hand, when the Israelites' request for transit was denied, they proceeded to invade and possess the Amorite land (Num. 21 : 21-24). On the other hand, when they made the same petition to the Edomites and received the same response, they carefully skirted the kingdom (Num. 20 : 17-21). The only difference between these seemingly identical cases was that God had promised the land of the Amorites to the Jews, but not that of the Edomites. Although the conquest of the Amorites was just, an attempted invasion of Edom was not. In another section Robert asked whether the Biblical examples of divinely inspired conquest justified contemporary princes to invade other lands, expel the legitimate heirs, and turn them into dependencies from which to enfeoff knights as they wish.[24] His response involved a series of distinctions: Did the prince act on his own or on the authority of the church against its enemies? Were the invaded Christians or infidels? Was the war just or not? Although Robert was not entirely coherent in applying these conditions (he did not, for example, elaborate upon the factor of the just war), he was clear that a prince was justified in conquering the infidel on the authority of the church. A crusade to the holy land for liberating the eastern Christian provinces was legitimate because it regained the church's rightful inheritance. Just as God's promise justified the Hebrew conquest of the Amorites, so the present "land of promise" could be rightfully taken by Christians. If, however, princes like Alexander the Great, Nebuchadnezzar, and Sennacherib occupy other lands in hate and unjust war, dispossessing their heirs, they will be held to restitution.[25] A holy war, such as a crusade, was the sole justification for conquest.

In these brief remarks the Parisian theologians merely elaborated the canonists' principles. When these principles were broad and vague, grave doubts and serious arguments arose as to the legitimacy of actual and specific conflicts. Since constituted authority in itself was insufficient to render a conflict just or holy, an important question arose over the "subject's" right to discuss publicly the justice of his prince's cause. The answer to this question turned on who was the "subject." Employing the broad term "subject" (*subditus*), Robert of Courson briefly examined the tradition of human law which denied subjects the right of discussing a prince's war.[26] Robert flatly concluded that this human tradition was contradicted by divine authority. Although defending the right of discussion, he was unclear as to those to whom it extended. Similarly when Thomas of Chobham pronounced a war unjust which was waged without judgment and counsel of the realm (*regnum*), he thereby implied the right of discussion, but did not specify who was included in the realm.[27] Peter the Chanter, however, considered the specific case of bishops.[28] Assuming that bishops were vassals because they possessed *regalia*, Peter declared that they were responsible to inquire into the justice of a particular war, but he did not mention whether this right was extended to lay vassals. It was Stephen Langton, however, who provided the most specific answer.[29] It will be remembered that when Stephen discussed political obedience he refused to allow the "people" (*populus*) to act against a court sentence which unjustly condemned a man to death.* He also applied this finality of the judicial procedure to warfare. If the decision to wage war was adjudicated in the prince's court, he concluded, even though it was unjust, the people have no right to discuss it. Here Stephen appears to have distinguished between the people outside the court who were ineligible to discuss the prince's decision and the members of the court who presumably deliberate with the prince. In general, therefore, the theologians defended a right to discuss a prince's wars, but they were unclear whom this right included. In all probability they conceded it to

* See above, p. 169.

the ecclesiastical and lay vassals of the prince's entourage, but only Langton specified that it was denied to the "people" beyond the prince's court.

Although the Parisian theologians generally assumed that those who owed military service were obliged to follow the prince in a just war, the principal question remained whether these subjects should fulfill their obligations in an unjust war. Clearly this problem involved a conflict between political obedience and refraining from unjust acts. Peter the Chanter had two minds on the subject. In one section of his *Summa* he advised the bishop possessing *regalia* not to obey the king's summons to an unjust war in order to provide an example to lay knights.[30] In another place, citing the Gospel authority of rendering unto Caesar the things that are Caesar's (Matt. 22 : 21), he concluded that just as misuse of governmental revenues does not excuse paying taxes, so an unjust cause did not exonerate a prelate from providing his quota of knights.[31] His student Robert of Courson, however, overlooked this second interpretation in favor of the first. Just as a judge should not condemn those whom he knows to be innocent, so a knight should not follow his prince's standard in an unjust war.[32]

The Chanter's hesitancy was experienced by others of the Parisian group. Stephen Langton acutely sensed the dilemmas involved in a summons to an unjust war and attempted to bridge them with practical remedies. Obviously referring to the aggression of King Philip Augustus against the Plantagenet holdings in France, or perhaps even to the conquest of Normandy, an example which would have occurred to Englishmen, Stephen outlined a situation in which the king of France waged an unjust war against the king of England.[33] He examined the dilemma of a single knight and of an entire host who owed service to the French king. By following the king they sinned against divine precepts, but if they refused they were traitors and guilty of scandal because they refused to perform their political obligations. In a tortuous discussion Stephen wrestled with the question of whether treasonous guilt and scandal could be assigned to individuals or only to the group, but his solution for the individual knight was clear. A knight should answer a summons to an unjust war, but withdraw at the time of battle or at least remain without fighting. Thomas of Chobham likewise oriented his discussion towards first the entire group and then individual knights.[34] Bishops should exhort the people to withdraw from an unjust war, he stated, if the people were unanimous and if it could be accomplished without schism and sedition. Individual knights were advised to follow their prince in an unjust conflict as long as they could avoid rapine and shedding of blood. When it came to killing Christians and plundering goods, these knights should disobey and even resist with force. In another *questio* Stephen Langton sought to apply a solution analogous to the administration of the sacrament.[35] Just as a priest will publicly serve the Eucharist to a certain communicant who is in mortal sin but not privately, so a knight will aid his sovereign publicly but not privately in an unjust aggression. An extreme example of public assistance occurred when the king was clearly outnumbered by the enemy. If the knight deserted his lord in a disadvantageous battle, would he not clearly be a traitor even if his lord's cause was unjust? At this point Stephen introduced a second pair of distinctions: between offensive and defensive action. A knight was wrong to serve his lord in an unjust and aggressive campaign, but if he defended his king, he was not guilty of sin, even when the cause was unjust. By distinguishing between public and private and offensive and defensive, Langton attempted to accommodate the principles of the just war to the perplexities of actual practice.

Ecclesiastical proposals which advocated abstention on the grounds that the war was unjust were, of course, opposed to customary practices of feudal society. To refuse to answer a summons to the host was a felony, punishable by the forfeiture of lands from which military service was due.[36] To follow the theologians' advice would cost the possessions of a knight or prelate who held *regalia*. Moreover, the actual world provided little agreement as to the justice of a specific conflict. Then as now most wars must have appeared as hopeless mixtures of just and unjust elements. Faced with those confused conditions Robert of Courson offered one piece of concrete advice.[37] If a knight was confronted with an unjust war or even a partly just war, he could avoid the dilemma by electing the middle course of the crusade. By assuming the cross in promise to defend the Holy Land he was absolved from his military responsibilities in an unjust war and the lands of a crusader became inviolate under protection of ecclesiastical sanctions.[38] As a matter of fact, Robert observed, a number of barons had recently embarked for the Holy Land for this very reason. Perhaps he had in mind the Counts of Flanders, Blois, and Perche who departed on the Fourth Crusade (1202-1204). According to two chroniclers they took the cross to divert the revenge of King Philip Augustus for having allied themselves with King Richard who had recently died, in 1199.[39] Although the crusader's status had afforded Richard little protection against Philip Augustus, the lands of Flanders, Blois, and Perche were unmolested while these counts were on the crusade.

In addition to the doctrine of the just war by which churchmen attempted to regulate warfare under normal conditions, ecclesiastics at times imposed special conditions. Popes and prelates could intervene in warfare by excommunicating one or more of the belligerent parties. Since this sanction isolated the excommunicated prince from his associates,[40] the question arose of whether a vassal should obey an excommunicated lord, or to be more precise, whether he should follow him into battle. Two opposing sets of authorities in Gratian's *Decretum* provoked canonist debate over this problem in the twelfth century. On one side were the statements of Popes Gregory VII and Urban II which forbade subjects to observe their oath of fealty to an excommunicated prince.[41] On the other stood the authority of Ambrose who counselled Christian soldiers to defend the commonwealth in obedience to the Emperor Julian, although he was apostate and therefore excommunicated, and another pronouncement from Pope Gregory VII which modified the excommunicated person's isolation by allowing his family, household, and servants to associate with him.[42] Although the canonists' discussions involved the fundamental relations between spiritual and temporal authority,[43] they frequently focused on the practical question of warfare. Distinguishing between oaths of fidelity made in respect to persons and in respect to dignities, Rufinus nonetheless declared that in both cases an excommunication nullified the service of subjects.[44] In practical terms a knight was never obligated to follow an excommunicated lord into battle. Simon of Bisignano added a further distinction between legitimate and illegitimate affairs.[45] Although a subject need not obey an anathematized lord in illicit matters, he could cooperate in legitimate affairs as Ambrose and Gregory VII suggested. This cooperation, furthermore, was limited to the lord's immediate household; all others were to shun his service to bring him to his senses.

It was Huguccio, however, who treated this issue of excommunication most extensively if not most consistently.[46] Inquiring in the first place whether the bond of fealty remained between a vassal and an excommunicated lord, he followed the analogy of marriage and concluded that just as adultery does not break the conjugal relationship, but only hinders its exercise, so excommunication does not sever fidelity, but rather prevents its execution. As long as the lord is excommunicate, the vassal cannot serve him, but as soon as he is reconciled with the church, the normal fealty resumes. Having established this theoretical framework, Huguccio turned to its practical consequences.[47] As to whether vassals are held to pay to an excommunicated lord taxes and tributes resulting from their fiefs, he answered in the affirmative. Just as one who has sworn to do so is bound to pay interest to an excommunicated usurer,[48] so a vassal must pay to an excommunicated prince his obligations based on oaths. Whenever reasonably possible, a subject should avoid normal contact with the lord in visiting or attending his court, in accompanying him on journeys and eating at his table. Among these activities to be avoided was included military service. While it is not quite clear how Huguccio distinguished paying tribute from serving in the host, his final advice was to dissuade the vassal from following an excommunicated lord into battle.

Citing the authorities found in the *Decretum*, the theologian Master Martin adopted Huguccio's solution which maintained the bond of fidelity but forbade its use while the lord was under ban.[49] He also rehearsed Huguccio's argument for paying taxes to an excommunicated prince based on the precedent of usury. Since Master Martin accepted the canonists' position that a vassal should not follow an excommunicated lord into battle, he interpreted Ambrose's opposing advice as an exceptional case.[50]

The conclusions of Master Martin and the canonists were not fully shared by Peter the Chanter and Robert of Courson. In one version of his *questiones* Peter raised the dilemma of a vassal summoned to the host by an excommunicated lord under penalty of forfeiture of fiefs.[51] The Chanter decided that the vassal was free to respond, just as a servant out of necessity must minister to an excommunicated master. Noting in another passage the example of a city under ecclesiastical ban which was unjustly besieged by enemies, Peter assumed that those responsible for its protection could come to its defense without incurring excommunication.[52] Although Peter did not dispute the canonical sources, Robert defended this opposing position by taking cognizance of the canonists' arguments in a full-scale *questio*.[53] A prince who was justly excommunicated summoned to defend the realm his liege men bound by fealty to serve bodily in his army. Since their service rested on three grounds: oath, obligation to defend the realm, and duty to protect the church endangered by impending invasion, should these vassals follow their lord? To explore the problem Robert collected the standard canonical authorities, to which he added corroborating Scriptural passages.[54] Not satisfied with the solution of Huguccio and Master Martin, he proposed a twofold distinction based on the doctrine of the just war.[55] While in one case the excommunicated prince actually defends his own errors, attacks the church or unjustly dispossesses another, in the other he gathers his subjects for the defense of his kingdom or the church in a just war. In the first example the vassals naturally owe no service, but in the second, they are obligated to follow their lord. At this point Robert revived Huguccio's argument drawn from usury. Just as one is held to pay usury promised by oath, so one is bound to military service based on fealty. Unlike Huguccio and Martin who limited this obligation to taxes, Robert applied it also to personal service in the host. Vassals are therefore held to follow an excommunicated lord in a just war for the defense of realm and church because, irrespective of the person of the excommunicated, their obligation relates to the welfare of the church and the kingdom.

In a section of the *Summa* devoted to perplexing situations Robert applied these principles to a historical event.[56] He reported that the pope had dispatched a certain legate to France with instructions to excommunicate all knights and barons who followed the royal standard in the war which then raged "between the kings" and to command the bishops of the realm to enforce this order with excommunication and interdict. In the meantime, however, a new factor appeared in the dispute of which the pope was unaware. If he had known, he would not have issued the original order. Under such circumstances the bishops were faced with two sets of quandaries. Either they must obey the pope's expressed command or they must seek what they understood to be his underlying intent. More important, these prelates served dual roles both as barons having liege men and as pastors caring for their souls. Implicit in these two positions was a conflict of loyalties between king and pope. If as lords they counsel their vassals not to serve the king in legitimate defense of the realm, they deprive their sovereign of his regalian rights. If as pastors they excommunicate those of their men who follow the king they cause them to break their oaths of fealty and commit perjury. If they do not, they are disobedient to the pope, for which they themselves incur excommunication. To solve the dilemma of such a conflict between obligations to king and pope Robert employed the doctrine of the just war. If the war is unjust then neither the bishops nor their vassals owe service to the king. If the war is just, however, the prelates should not dissuade their liege men from following their lord especially in defending the kingdom and the church. In this case the pope has no authority against the Pauline command to obey one's lord. The principle of the just war, therefore, takes precedence over the special condition of excommunication. As to the initial quandary concerning the pope's expressed statement and his underlying intent, Robert advised the legate to await further indication of the pope's mind rather than to execute the command because a change of causes might produce a change in instructions.[57] These conclusions were summarized by Geoffrey of Poitiers.[58]

Robert of Courson does not reveal precisely what historical incident he had in mind, but it is evident that his reference to the war in France waged "between the kings" can only refer to the Capetian-Plantagenet conflict. Among the papal legates who served in France during these hostilities Peter of Pavia negotiated between Louis VII and Henry II in 1177 and Peter Capuano intervened between Philip Augustus and Richard in 1199. Since Robert's account lacks specific details, it is possible that he referred to either one of these possibilities, but there was a third legate, Gerald, Abbot of Casamari, whose mission in 1203-1204 would have been yet vivid when Robert wrote and whose features fit the outlined circumstances. At the time when Philip Augustus was intent upon the conquest of Normandy from John, Pope Innocent III dispatched Gerard to stop what appeared to be overt aggression.[59] The legate was empowered by a letter of 31 October 1203 to excommunicate Philip if he refused to deviate from his course, a sanction which was made known to certain bishops as well as repeated in a general letter to the French prelates assembled at Meaux in April 1204.[60] In resulting correspondence with the Pope, Philip Augustus protested that the war was justified by a judgment of his court in 1202 which had found John in default of feudal justice over the Lusignan affair. Perhaps this was the new and mitigating circumstance to which Robert referred, but a more likely possibility is the death of Arthur, Count of Brittany.[61] Ralph of Coggeshall reports that during the spring of 1204, Philip Augustus became convinced that Arthur had been murdered by John. While this fact appeared at a time when the conquest of Normandy was assured and was therefore of little consequence for Philip's beginning the war, it could have served to justify the French policy before the Pope in 1204. Alleged evidence that John had murdered Arthur, which appeared precisely at a time when the threat to excommunicate Philip and his followers was renewed at Meaux, may well have been the new case to which Robert referred and which, he maintained, would have changed the Pope's mind. The following year Innocent did in fact acquiesce to the French conquest when he wrote to the Archbishop of Rouen and his suffragans allowing them to acknowledge Philip Augustus as Duke of Normandy.[62]

WARFARE AND FINANCE

During the twelfth century warfare became intimately connected with finance in France and England.[63] Actual or threatened war became the ruler's leading justification for exacting revenue from his subjects. Under the feudal regime lords were expected to raise their armies from the personal military service of their vassals. By the twelfth century, however, and particularly in England, the royalty devised ways to commute this personal service into cash payments called "scutage." Money could be transported more easily than feudal levies to the Plantagenet monarch across the Channel, where it was converted into mercenary armies to defend the continental holdings. To the English royalty money was more useful than knight service.[64] Moreover, cash payments provided the ecclesiastical vassal with a convenient means for discharging military obligations. Since canon law forbade clerics from participating actively in warfare, prelates either provided knights who served in their behalf, or transformed their service into money. In England, for example, during Richard's reign most churchmen preferred to pay scutages or fines in lieu of providing men.[65] Whether in the form of knight service or in cash, ecclesiastical contributions formed an important part of the royal armies.

In England the church supplied about one-seventh of the total royal host.[66] While documentation is not complete for France, churchmen there contributed perhaps even more to the royal armies.[67] Not only did the French and English monarchs require men and money from their direct vassals, but during the twelfth century they also demanded extraordinary war taxes from all free subjects. It will be seen that the crusades provided ecclesiastical precedents for these new levies and from them the English royalty devised a national system of taxation.

Whether in their ordinary or extraordinary form, these war levies were usually designated by ecclesiastical writers as tribute (*tributum*), which was the technical term for war taxes in ancient Roman law.[68] As churchmen the Parisian theologians were chiefly concerned with the war levies imposed upon prelates. The governmental right to tax churches for war was only part of the broad issue of the church's duty to contribute money to secular authority, upon which there were conflicting arguments. On one hand were the examples of Christ, Who taught His disciples to render to Caesar the things which were Caesar's in specific reference to tribute money (Matt. 22 : 17-22) and Who paid this tribute with a coin miraculously found in the mouth of a fish in order to avoid scandal (Matt. 17 : 24-27). On the other hand, there had appeared by the twelfth century a canonical doctrine to the effect that since church lands were sacred to the works of charity, they were immune from taxation.[69] Although Gratian assembled authoritative statements which reflected this controversy over taxation,[70] he was concerned specifically with ecclesiastics contributing to war efforts.[71]

To investigate the normal regime whereby ecclesiastical vassals contributed to war efforts, the canonists first considered the *regalia*. Since Gratian assumed that military aid was due from regalian lands, he attempted to isolate as much as possible other lands immune from political service from the *regalia*.[72] Following Gratian the canonists usually agreed that prelates holding *regalia* owed military service to the king although some insisted on the additional condition that papal consent must be obtained.[73] Similarly, when the Parisian theologians discussed the *regalia,* they assumed that the prelate was also obligated to contribute to the king's war. For example, one version of the Chanter's *Summa* suggests that the bishop who was a count should carefully separate his regalian obligations from all other revenues which supported the works of charity and the bishop's necessary expenses.[74] Robert of Courson, however, in one passage attempts to nullify the obligation of military service derived from regalian lands.[75] Arguing that Christ's example of paying tribute no longer applied to ecclesiastics, because the Emperor Constantine liberated all *regalia* from tribute, he declared that the church bore the yoke of war contributions only because of prelates' servility. In unjust wars, or even in partly just wars, churchmen owed no subsidies to princes from either their free or their regalian lands. Robert's reference to Constantine was probably a confusion of Constantius and Constance, Constantine's two successors who granted immunity to the church in a text found in the *Decretum*.[76] But a solution which eliminated regalian service was too radical even for Robert, and elsewhere he found occasion to temper his conclusion. Envisaging a normal situation, Robert inquired whether princes could compel churches to pay subsidies from regalian lands in wars against Christians.[77] The mitigating circumstances of holy wars against pagans or heretics were eliminated, and the contributions were clearly demanded from land originally given for military service. Among canonical authorities marshalled for and against, Robert repeated the argument which granted full immunity to cathedral churches according to the dispensation conferred by Constantine. Robert resolved the question by making a historical distinction. Those churches benefiting from Constantine's grant of immunity owed no regalian military service except in holy wars against pagans or heretics. Those, however, which had received towns, manors, and fields with regalian obligations since the time of Constantine, owed military service for those lands, but nothing beyond the required amount. As a practical matter, the latter lands were more significant than the former, because it is doubtful whether many churches in France or England could successfully claim donations extending beyond the time of Constantine. In effect, therefore, Robert acquiesced to the church's payment of aids for warfare from regalian lands.

During the second half of the twelfth century the Plantagenets initiated the practice of bypassing their tenants-in-chief to collect war revenues directly from subvassals. While scutages were normally taken from the direct vassals, the new aids such as the tax on moveables and carucage were taken directly from the undertenants.[78] Although French practice is less clear, it is probable that the Capetians followed their example, especially in collecting aids from ecclesiastical vassals. In all events, Robert of Courson observed that when a prince waged war justly or unjustly he usually demanded aid directly from the men of bishops and abbots.[79] If refused, he plundered their lands. Under this pressure churches tallaged their manors for war. By permitting these exactions to the prince, they believed themselves relieved of further responsibility. Decrying this complaisance, Robert advocated that prelates should resist these extortions with ecclesiastical censures. If the prince persisted in plundering the church's undertenants the guilt was his and not the prelate's. Robert thereby maintained that prelates bore responsibility for contributing to their overlord's wars and they could not avoid this simply because their prince collected directly from their undertenants. Since these regalian lands were burdensome to both ecclesiastics and their subvassals, ways were undoubtedly explored for disposing of them. Robert cited the case of an abbot who held a regalian manor on which an annual tallage was owed to the king.[80] Could the manor be redeemed from this tallage, and if so, should the abbot or the king receive the price? Assuming that liberation was possible, Courson advised the men of the manor not to buy their freedom from the abbot because of the danger of revocation by the abbot's successor; rather they should obtain their liberty directly from the king in a grant certified by the royal seal which would be valid in the future as well.

In addition to the normal military obligations of the *regalia*, the prince could declare a state of emergency produced by a just war, the need for defending the realm, or a crusade. At the turn of the twelfth and thirteenth centuries Roman and canon lawyers began to declare that urgent necessity or common utility justified extraordinary taxes from all subjects.[81] For example, the Lateran Council of 1179 permitted the Italian communes to tax the clergy when necessity and utility became evident, a concession renewed by the Council of 1215 with the provision that the pope first be consulted.[82] Where this state of emergency affected ecclesiastics most directly was in their non-regalian lands, normally immune from military obligations. Although the canonist author of the *Glossa Palatina* declared that bishops without *regalia* followed their prince in a just war only if they wished,[83] the Parisian theologians indicated that the prelate's choice was not entirely free. In a brief gloss to 1 Samuel Peter the Chanter asked why churches and monasteries not possessing the *regalia* were compelled to pay war taxes.[84] As far as can be determined, he did not prepare a reply, but Stephen Langton explored the ramifications in a full *questio*.[85]

Among conflicting authorities Stephen framed two situations which faced a bishop who, possessing no *regalia*, derived his support from ecclesiastical tithes and offerings.[86] In the first case a king who had embarked upon unjust aggression demanded revenue from the bishop. In support of the king's exaction was Ambrose's opinion that prelates should give money but not churches to the emperor and the argument that refusal to pay tribute will cause scandal, which is a mortal sin. In opposition were arguments that the bishop would be aiding an unjust cause, which is also a mortal sin, and would be depriving the poor of their due sustenance to which the king had no right. In this case Stephen concluded that the bishop should refuse the king, but what if the same bishop were confronted by the king with an unusually just cause? Such an exceptional case might be turned into a harmful precedent which would scandalize other churches. Nonetheless Stephen decided that on the assurance that no precedent would be created and because of the justice of the particular royal cause, the bishop might support the king from the church's goods. As an example Stephen cited the cooperation of the English church in paying the ransom for King Richard in 1193. Extraordinary measures were adopted to raise the huge sum of 150,000 marks of silver, including, for example, a tax on moveables and revenue from all laymen and clerics, but Richard in fact promised that this emergency action would not create a precedent.[87]

Robert of Courson raised a similar situation and arrived at a similar conclusion to Stephen's.[88] Observing that monasteries supply horses and wagons (*charrettes*) from goods designated for the poor, and that the bishop's men contribute annual war subsidies, Robert concluded that these churchmen share responsibility for ravaging manors, villages, and monasteries. His examples recall the royal document from the reign of Philip Augustus entitled *Prisia servientum*, which listed the number of sergeants and *charrettes* provided by monasteries and other communities in the royal domain.[89] While these services fulfilled the obligations attached to *regalia*, Robert's example envisaged immune lands. His advice to ecclesiastics was to distinguish between two situations. If the kingdom or church is threatened with destruction by pagans or heretics, churchmen are held to aid the prince to the full extent of their resources. If, however, the prince's wars are unjust, that is, against other Christians and of no benefit to the church, ecclesiastics sin mortally who contribute goods designated for the poor and must do full restitution.

The theologians agreed that churchmen's contributions to normal warfare were limited to their regalian holdings, but that national emergencies justified extraordinary measures implicating all resources, both regalian and free. When the masters wrote, the most pertinent example of such an emergency was the defense of the Holy Land. It is not surprising, therefore, that the crusading movement produced in France and England an extraordinary war revenue—the tax on moveable property. Perhaps as early as 1147, but certainly by 1166, there was instituted the general aid for the crusade which consisted of a broad impost on moveables and revenues of both laity and clergy. Renewed in 1185, this aid was most effectively employed on both sides of the Channel in the famous Saladin tithe of 1188.[90] In England the exceptional measure was transformed by degrees into a regular source of royal revenue. In 1193 it was employed to raise King Richard's ransom. By 1207 the tax on moveables had become an established feature of the English fiscal system.[91] As Gerald of Wales correctly observed, because of these extraordinary taxes Henry II and his sons were able to bear the financial strain of their numerous wars.[92] It was the Saladin tithe of 1188, however, which first attracted widespread attention and provoked the strongest reaction from churchmen. Consisting of one tenth of moveables and revenues, the highest rate to its date, it was effectively collected by Henry II, but Philip Augustus encountered widespread resistance and eventually abandoned it. Undoubtedly reflecting public opinion, Gerald of Wales recorded Margaret of Bohun's bitter criticism against King Henry II's part in the Saladin tithe and attributed his death soon after to divine retribution.[93] Ecclesiastics such as Stephen of Tournai in France and Peter of Blois in England argued that these exactions impoverished the church.[94]

When Robert of Courson composed his *Summa*, the Saladin tithe and the English levy of 1207 were already established facts. When he spoke of the aid for the crusade, his object was not to protest against it but rather to investigate the source of revenue. While the regalian revenues were drawn almost exclusively from landed incomes based on agricultural products, the new taxes on moveables included town wealth produced from trade as well. As will be seen, ecclesiastics regarded commercial wealth with suspicion because of its implication with usury.* For this reason Robert felt obliged to probe the moral legitimacy of the crusading levies based on moveables. Posing a preliminary question, Courson inquired whether a prince is charged with the defense of his kingdom and the church against the invasion of enemies and if he has no other means for raising an army, he can accept aid from towns.[95] His dilemma consists in knowing, on one hand, that his cause is just, but on the other, that these urgent contributions are drawn from usurious commercial gains which he has sworn in his coronation oath to punish and to restore. From this question Robert passed to the main problem of the crusading prince who possessed the privilege of demanding aid from moveable property.[96] What is his responsibility in accepting goods which have originated from theft and dishonest gain? For the defending prince and the departing crusader Robert's solution was the same.[97] Both may temporarily accept illicit aid as if it were a loan. After completing their mission they are responsible for restoring these ill-gotten goods as quickly as possible. Courson's discussion of the tax on moveables touched one of the vital fiscal issues of his day. Although contemporary princes taxed the towns without hesitation, Robert's conclusion represents a provisional yet significant acceptance by a churchman of a form of taxation which was to play an important role in the royal government of England in the thirteenth century and of France in a later age.

MERCENARIES

The chief explanation for the close nexus between war and finance was the mercenary army.[98] Although hired soldiers were employed before the twelfth century, their widespread and systematic use has been attributed to Henry II. Shouldered with the defense of vast Continental holdings, Henry recognized the limitation of the ordinary knight who served by

* See below, pp. 271ff.

feudal tenure, and substituted in his place the mercenary. Henry's lesson was learned not only by his sons Richard and John, but also by his antagonist Philip Augustus. At the turn of the century the wars between Plantagenets and Capetians became contests between hired armies led by professional captains. Mercadier and Louvrecaire for the English and Cadoc for the French represented a new age, which contemporaries viewed as a match between the pound sterling and the pound tournois. If Philip Augustus finally won and drove John out of Normandy, it was in large measure due to superior finances.[99] Churchmen possessing regalian obligations could not extricate themselves from mercenary warfare. English prelates, for example, discharged their military obligations either in revenue or in knights. Although they normally contributed money which was immediately employed to raise mercenaries, even if they elected to supply their quotas directly, they often experienced difficulties in inducing their knights to serve overseas and were forced to hire substitutes in their place.[100] Because the ecclesiastical contribution invariably ended in the mercenary's pocket, the Parisian theologians took particular interest in this problem.

At the Lateran Council of 1179 Pope Alexander III pronounced on one aspect of mercenaries. Certain groups designated as Brabançons, Aragonese, Navarese, Basques, Cottereaux, and Triaverdini were anathematized and treated as heretics because they attacked churches and defenseless people, sparing neither age nor sex.[101] It is evident that the Council referred to groups generally known in the contemporary chronicles as Brabançons or Cottereaux who made their living from the profession of arms.[102] Readily hired into the mercenary armies, they easily slipped into brigandage when unemployed. Since they were the scourge of France, the English kings rarely introduced them on the island during the second half of the twelfth century.[103] Recalling the severe anathemas of the Lateran Council, Robert of Courson ranked the Cottereaux with other excommunicates, and advised princes not to employ them even in the defense of the realm.[104] In this regard Robert singled out Benedictine and Cistercian monks who associated with these men anathematized by the church.[105]

Since the designation Cottereaux or Brabançon was ill defined, it could be used as an abusive term against any warrior whom one wished to defame. Nonetheless, in ecclesiastical terminology it clearly did not comprise all mercenary soldiers. Philip Augustus' financial accounts for the year 1202-1203 distinguished several kinds of hired soldiers ranging from knights to sergeants and crossbowmen on horseback and on foot.[106] Since Robert of Courson was careful to separate hired knights from the Cottereaux,[107] the Parisian masters recognized a kind of mercenary who could legitimately seek his hire. After all, in the Gospels (Luke 3 : 14) John the

Baptist explicitly commanded soldiers to be content with their wages. Peter the Chanter referred to this legitimate category when he cited the case of a city under interdict which was unjustly besieged by an enemy.[108] Could knights accept employment without incurring excommunication? He decided if the knights were dependent on wages for their subsistence and if there was no other available employment, they could sell their services without falling under censure. Although the Chanter's example bore the complicating factor of an excommunicated employer, the normal situation was clearly stated by Robert of Courson: If a war is just, knights may receive their due wages, but anything taken beyond this amount is robbery for which restitution is required.[109]

The Chanter's and Courson's view of armies in which soldiers received fixed wages accorded with the practice of the Plantagenet and Capetian kings.[110] King John's campaigns amply illustrate, however, that princes were ever tempted to draw from the spoils of warfare to pay the armies.[111] These practices, therefore, prompted the theologians to consider whether booty was a legitimate source for paying mercenaries. Peter the Chanter approached this problem in his commentary to Genesis 14 : 17-24 where Abraham led an expedition to rescue his nephew Lot and to restore posessions plundered from the king of Sodom. When the king of Sodom offered to reward Abraham with the goods recovered, Abraham refused remuneration except for what his companions had eaten on the expedition. Following the *Glossa ordinaria*, Peter concluded that although the faithful should wage wars not for gain but for charitable service, the exception demonstrated that legitimate wages could be derived from the spoils of battle.[112] Although soldiers should not fight for the sake of pay, they cannot fight without it. In their penitential manuals Robert of Flamborough and Thomas of Chobham reached similar conclusions. By means of a dialogue between a priest and a soldier seeking penance, Robert decided that if the war was just and waged with the authority of the prince, the soldier was permitted to retain plunder unless it was taken from the defenseless or from ecclesiastics.[113] Thomas' advice followed the same lines with the sole difference that if the helpless or clerical parties had resisted with arms, the soldier was entitled even to what he took from them.[114]

These conclusions were not meant, of course, to exonerate all wartime plunder. Peter alluded to cases of pillage for which restitution was due, even by those who did not actively take part, but he was not specific about the examples.[115] Although Robert of Flamborough and Thomas of Chobham envisaged exceptional protection for ecclesiastics and the defenseless, Robert of Courson found it difficult to separate wages legitimately derived from plunder from those gained by unmerciful despoiling of the poor and churches in time of war.[116] Even if the prince summons to a just war, everyone knows that unjust ravaging of churches will result. The knights and bailiffs of the prince are confronted with the usual dilemma of deciding between obedience to their divine and obedience to their earthly lord. As in similar cases, if they refuse to follow the prince they risk forfeiture and bear responsibility for the destruction of the church and kingdom. Nonetheless, Robert concluded that mercenaries should follow the superior command of God by imitating the emissaries of Saul (1 Sam. 22 : 17) who refused to obey the royal command to slay the priests of the Lord.[117] While Courson was inclined to allow mercenaries their due wages, which were presumably drawn from public revenues,[118] he was highly skeptical of payment taken from booty. As a practical matter he was convinced that such sources were inevitably implicated with the pillaging of churches and the poor, which could be justified under no circumstances.

Although the military functions of mercenaries varied from those of simple combatants on foot to those of armored knights on horseback, one skill, that of the crossbowman, made a special impression on contemporaries. Robert of Courson, for example, included arbalisters along with the Cottereaux and hired knights.[119] It is probably true that each age possesses an "ultimate weapon" the propriety of whose use is for many a question of conscience. In the twelfth and thirteenth centuries the crossbow was such a weapon. Effective in piercing armor, it was reputed to be a highly lethal instrument. Since the crossbow bolt struck without discernment, could be poisoned, and was discharged by non-noble warriors, the crossbow was considered unfair by the noble classes whom it rendered vulnerable. In the Lateran Council of 1139 Pope Innocent II forbade under anathema its use against Catholics and other Christians —although it was presumably condoned against pagans and heretics— a prohibition which was renewed in canon law compilations and provincial councils.[120] Although the conciliar decree had little effect in England and the Empire, it may have been respected in France. Louis VII was reported to have employed crossbowmen before the Council, but at the turn of the century the chronicler William the Breton claimed that the crossbow had only been rediscovered of late in France.[121] Profiting from experience gained on the crusade, King Richard reinitiated the French to its use and it was widely used in the Plantagenet-Capetian struggle.[122] In contemporary documents it is difficult to distinguish crossbowmen from artillerymen who manned siege engines because the term *balistarius* is used for both, but there is evidence that the English and French royalty courted crossbowmen with property and pensions.[123]

When the theologians at Paris considered the crossbow they followed the established canon law traditions and offered only slight modification. Peter the Chanter cited the crossbowman as a prime example of a profession in which one lost salvation because he received his entire living from killing innocent victims.[124] When this warrior has no intention of renouncing his profession, under no circumstances should he be served the Eucharist. Apparently Peter was impressed with the effectiveness of the crossbow, since he made no effort to square this opinion with his more tolerant attitude towards other forms of military service. Discussing useless professions in another version of his *Summa* he inquired into the manufacture of such articles as dice and crossbow bolts,[125] such as Philip Augustus produced at Paris.[126] Although he would have wished all such articles to be burned, he allowed Christians to use crossbows against pagans and Cathars but not against Christians. In this passage, which was closely followed by Robert of Courson,[127] Peter stands within the traditions of canon law. Elsewhere, however, the Chanter added one slight but significant modification. Quoting a certain bishop he maintained that crossbows could be employed not only against Saracens but also in a just war.[128] Similarly Courson conceded that crossbows could be legitimately manufactured for defending both the Holy Land against pagans and the realm. Since these qualifications nullified the traditional prohibition of use against Christians, both Plantagenets and Capetians must have welcomed this enlarged justification of the crossbow.

At the Periphery of Warfare: Tournaments and Hunting

If warfare was the vocation of the noble classes, their avocation consisted of tournaments and hunting. By the end of the twelfth century tournaments had become the rage of French and English feudal society.[129] In some regions of France a tourney was held in one place or another about every fortnight. As the kings and great princes discouraged private warfare in their domains, the popularity of tournaments increased for venting energies as well as providing training for the profession of knighthood. From external appearances there was little difference between actual battle and the tourney, which consisted of general melees where all the accepted practices of war were exercised. Not until a later age were these contests regulated to reduce the dangers, transforming tournaments into jousts. The tourneys gave opportunity not only for exercising knightly skills, but also for exhibiting prowess. Here the knight won the glory so essential to the chivalric ethos. Moreover, tournaments also provided income to the victorious from the ransoms of those vanquished on the field. Many a knight, such as the young William the Marshal, gained his livelihood by traveling from tourney to tourney risking his skill and luck in the lists.[130] So lucrative were these contests that even royalty shared in the business despite repeated fulminations from the church. Desperately in need of funds in 1194, King Richard the Lionhearted licensed tournaments in England as one of many schemes for augmenting the royal treasury.[131] Tournaments in twelfth-century France and England provided a service in feudal society similar to that of rodeos in American frontier society. The broncobuster winning glory and prizes was the latest heir of the medieval tourney champion.

These fierce contests which Walter Map aptly described as torments rather than tournaments can hardly be expected to have met with ecclesiastical approval.[132] From 1130 numerous church councils, including three Lateran Councils under the papacy, prohibited tourneys under pain of automatic excommunication.[133] Although the viaticum could not be refused to those mortally wounded in tournaments, they were deprived of Christian burial. To this clearly defined papal position the canon lawyers[134] and theologians had little to add. Jacques de Vitry pictured tourneys as the arena where seven mortal sins were committed, of which vainglory was foremost.[135] The pertinence of this attack against prowess, the heart of the chivalric ethos, is obvious. Despite the clamor of councils and preachers, the historical records and the literature of the twelfth century testify that many knights took little heed. Since Peter the Chanter and his followers were well aware of the gap between ecclesiastical theory and the nobility's conduct, this discrepancy prompted them to investigate practical measures for enforcing the prohibition.

Since all participants of tournaments were automatically excommunicated, the faithful were to avoid contact with them under risk of incurring the censure themselves. When such outcasts were numerous, awkward situations arose in normal social intercourse. Peter the Chanter raised the problem in a brief comment,[136] but Robert of Courson dealt with it seriously by posing a concrete situation.[137] Recalling the sentence of excommunication promulgated by the papal legate in the French church, he pondered the alternatives open to a cleric in a magnate's palace or at a feast who met a knight fresh from a tournament. He was forced either to incur the censure or to create a scandal. Moreover, the cleric's prelate in order to ingratiate himself with the magnates might associate with the outcast, commanding the cleric to follow his example. The cleric's dilemma was thereby compounded with disobedience to his superior. After rehearsing the standard arguments *pro* and *con*, Robert decided that since the decree of the pope and his legate was more authoritative than the prelate's, the cleric should avoid contact with the transgressor. One should not denounce such individuals on vague suspicion, but only on indisputable knowledge. The family, servants, and the unaware may associate with the excommunicated without censure, according to the decree of Pope Gregory VII.[138] Although recognizing practical difficulties, both the Chanter and Courson supported the full rigor of the anathema against tournaments.

In the Lateran Council of 1179 Pope Alexander III renewed the prohibition of the rites of Christian burial to those killed in tournaments, although the sacrament of penance should not be denied to those requesting it.[139] Apparently this last qualification gave rise to practices which tempered the rigor of the decree. Since certain signs, such as a gesture of the hand or the striking of the breast, were taken as evidence that a victim was repentant in the throes of death, the body might be interred in holy soil. Thomas of Chobham cited a case in which a knight killed in a tourney and buried in unconsecrated ground was found by his friends to have his right hand over his face in the form of a cross.[140] When the pope was apprised, he ordered the body to be transferred to a church cemetery. These practices may have been the result of popular pressures on the priesthood to modify the prohibition, but the Chanter nonetheless resisted them. While he did not deny penance to the dying nor forbid the faithful's prayers for the dead, he refused to concede Christian burial.[141] In his opinion the stigma of non-Christian burial served to deter this social evil.

Finally, the theologians considered the lucrative side of tourneys. Since some knights drew their livelihood from them, could the church legitimately demand alms and tithes from their gains? The problem was raised in a *questio* from the Chanter's school where it was decided that the custom of accepting oblations from tournaments resulted from priestly cupidity and should not be tolerated.[142] Reversing the decision, however, Robert of Courson maintained that the profits from tourneys were equivalent to those from prostitution.[143] Although ransoms taken in tournaments were illicitly gained, they could be licitly retained, because they involved an unlawful transaction by both the taker and the giver. As in prostitution such income rightfully should be tithed.

Among the passions of the nobility hunting closely rivalled fighting. Employing dogs and falcons, the feudal classes missed few opportunities to indulge in the pleasures of the hunt. Since it is also clear that prelates shared this contemporary enthusiasm,[144] the canon lawyers' chief interest was to restrict churchmen's participation in hunting. Shortly before Huguccio two canons forbidding ecclesiastics to hunt with dogs and falcons were inserted as *paleae* into Gratian's *Decretum*, and later included in the *Compilatio prima* by Bernard of Pavia.[145] While discussing restrictions on ecclesiastics the canonists formulated principles applicable to laymen as well. As an exegete Peter the Chanter found the appropriate occasion for discussing the hunt in the Scriptural personage of Nimrod "the mighty hunter before the Lord" (Gen. 10 : 9).[146] Beginning with the analysis of the canonists he noted that hunting was illicit according to the three categories of person, time, and cause.[147] Although it was forbidden to clerics during Lent and for the sake of pleasure, a poor layman was permitted to hunt to feed his family. While these qualifications inhibited not only the clergy but also the lay nobility, who hunted for pleasure rather than from necessity, the Chanter proceeded further. Although he allowed hunting fowl with crook and bird call, he objected to falcons and other superfluous means, but with the one important exception of the king. Just as silken garments are permitted the king, not for their own sake but to enhance the royal dignity, so the falcon was a sign of the king's prerogative. Robert of Courson limited his restrictions on hunting to the clergy. The Council of Montpellier (1215) advised the regular clergy to avoid the hunt.[148] The secular clergy including bishops, canons, and clerics holding prebends were forbidden to keep falcons in their residences.[149] If they accompanied laymen, they were not to carry the birds on their own hand. In the Lateran Council of 1215, however, all clerics were not only enjoined to abstain from keeping dogs and falcons, but were altogether forbidden to hunt and fowl.[150]

The nobility's passion for hunting affected peasants whose fields and crops undoubtedly suffered in the wake of horsemen and dogs. In his *Summa* Peter outlined a situation which was probably not an infrequent occurrence.[151] Someone who kept hunting hounds for pleasure permitted his dogs to cross a field and to terrify a team of plough horses which bolted the traces and smashed the plough. Was the owner of the dogs, Peter queried, responsible for the damages? Although the response is lacking, an answer can be hazarded from the Chanter's discussion in the Biblical commentary. Since dogs maintained for pleasure were illicit, full restitution should be required of the hunter. The treatment of this problem is brief and fragmentary but it represents a glimmer of sympathy towards the peasants, who rarely received such consideration even from churchmen.

⊗ CHAPTER XI ⊗

Service with the Purse

BESIDES the extraordinary levies of warfare, the medieval prince relied on normal revenues for the operation of government. During the early Middle Ages, however, the ancient channels of revenue were radically altered. The regular systems of taxation in the Roman Empire all but disappeared from western Europe by the tenth century. With a decline of the money economy and a shrinkage of political jurisdiction princes increasingly relied on landed estates, known as domains, which provided the principal support for all levels of government from the king to the local seigneur. The ruler demanded a great variety of services from the inhabitants of his domain: labor to provide food, shelter, and other needs, produce in fixed amounts or in percentage of harvests, and a great number of imposts and levies. In effect, the inhabitants of the domain bore the costs of government. Closely connected with the domain was an accumulation of rights also enjoyed by political lords. Whenever anyone exercised a right in the Middle Ages, he was sorely tempted to profit from it, or in other words, to sell its exercise for as much as possible. It has been seen, for example, that rights over justice were especially profitable to rulers. Medieval princes claimed other jurisdictions over their subjects at all levels of society, which were also viewed as revenue. For example, over their peasants they exercised monopolies of mills, ovens, and winepresses; from merchants and traders they demanded road tolls and market dues; over noble vassals they claimed wardships and marriages. In sum, the normal revenues of a medieval ruler consisted of a composite and variegated bundle of lands and rights.

In their lectures and debates the theologians naturally had no intention to investigate systematically governmental revenues such as might have been enumerated by the royal exchequers of the Plantagenets and the Capetians; rather their attention was drawn to financial arrangements considered illicit and sinful, and which they often designated as recent customs in contrast to more ancient and legitimate sources of income. The theologians treated these matters only sporadically, and then only to protest abuses. Although Peter the Chanter, joined by others, investigated numerous revenues, it was Robert of Courson who provided the most extensive treatment by discussing forms of robbery by which the prince plundered his subjects. From these scattered comments a list of revenues may be compiled which included the retention of tithes by laymen, *tailles,* tolls, *droit de prise,* coinage, treasure trove, shipwreck, wardship, marriage, and regalian rights over ecclesiastical vacancies.

TITHES

The two leading forms of illegitimate revenue undoubtedly consisted of usurpation of ecclesiastical tithes by laymen and the exaction of *tailles,* both of which originated in the customary practices of the early Middle Ages and were dearly cherished by princes in the twelfth and thirteenth centuries.[1] Since the lay holding of tithes was clearly a trespass on ecclesiastical rights, it met the most vigorous protests of the theologians. Originally an ecclesiastical institution founded on the Old and New Testaments, the tithe first appeared in practice in the fifth century.[2] By the second half of the eighth century the Carolingian rulers had extended the obligation to all Christians of western Europe, enforced it by political sanctions, and assigned to bishops control over its perception. Thus universalized and strengthened, the tithe became the most widespread and valuable form of taxation in western Europe. In theory the tithe consisted of a yearly tenth of all economic gain. In practice the percentage often fell below the ideal, and sometimes was as low as one-fortieth.

During the chaotic centuries which followed the collapse of the Carolingian world the lay lords found this lucrative taxation a temptation too great to resist.[3] Whether by outright usurpation or by ecclesiastical donation (which usually amounted to the same) a large part of church tithes fell into laymen's hands, thus transforming them into a secular revenue. When the papal reform party in the eleventh century reacted against the laity's control over the church, one of their specific programs was to abolish lay retention of tithes.[4] After Pope Leo IX returned to Rome from his famous trip to Reims where he was directly confronted with flagrant abuses, he forbade the possession of ecclesiastical revenues by laymen in a council of 1050. His energetic successor Pope Gregory VII in the council of 1078 designated the lay holding of tithes as sacrilegious and perilous to the soul. Viewing tithes as spiritual in nature, whose misuse by the laity constituted the crime of simony, the papal reformers reaffirmed the right of bishops to supervise their collection. Once pronounced by the papacy in the eleventh century, the reform program against lay possession of tithes was perpetuated by the councils and canonists of the twelfth century. While the Lateran Council of 1123 mentioned ecclesiastical revenues in general,[5] the Lateran Council of 1139 specified tithes and commanded their restitution to bishops on pain of excommunication.[6] Although the Lateran Council of 1179 merely restricted the transferring of tithes among the laity,[7] synodical statutes of the early thirteenth century reminded them of ecclesiastical censure and of danger to their souls if they did not relinquish these revenues.[8] Gratian included the essential text of Pope Gregory VII in his *Decretum*, which canonists interpreted in their commentaries.[9]

Peter the Chanter and his colleagues approached the problems of tithes on a broad front. The Chanter himself devoted a number of scattered *questiones* to the subject in his *Summa*,[10] which Robert of Courson coordinated in two books of his *Summa*.[11] Stephen Langton composed a *questio* on the same theme[12] and the issue appears in the guides to confessors.[13] Since their interest in tithes extended to a wide range of topics, their observations were often pertinent to the practices of their day. For example, they voiced few complaints about the laity's willingness to meet their normal tithing obligations,[14] but they did notice resistance in some regions to paying "small tithes" (*minute decime*).[15] They also participated in disputes which erupted during the pontificate of Alexander III over the exemption of the Cistercians, Templars and Hospitallers from tithing obligations.[16] Robert of Courson further demonstrated a sense of sympathy when he considered how a peasant's crops should be tithed after his fields had been ravaged by a knight.[17] Among these varied questions the chief issue, however, was the lay holding of tithes.

Although the papacy had threatened lay possessors of tithes with excommunication since the eleventh century, Peter the Chanter and his circle provide unanimous testimony that these anathemas were widely ignored at the turn of the twelfth and thirteenth centuries. As Pope Leo IX had discovered on his journey to Reims, the French knights were still the chief offenders. Speaking as a Frenchman the Chanter was dismayed by the numbers who were guilty,[18] and his experience was direct. Undoubtedly he himself had inherited from his family the small tithes of Hodenc which he donated in 1183 with the consent of his brother and nephews to the church of Hodenc and the Hôtel-Dieu of Beauvais shortly before becoming Chanter of Notre-Dame.[19] When the Welshman Gerald of Wales searched for notorious examples, the French knights came readily to mind.[20] Robert of Flamborough and Thomas of Chobham, who wrote guides for English use, also attested to large numbers of laymen guilty of possessing tithes.[21] Churchmen in England as well as in France found great difficulty in wresting tithes from the laity.[22]

The immediate problem posed by the Chanter's circle was whether the ordinary priest should serve the Eucharist to laymen known to possess tithes.[23] The priest's dilemma was further complicated by the compliance of the prelacy, because, as the Chanter pointed out, knights possessing tithes often held their fiefs from bishops who by communicating with these men in the act of homage consented to their iniquity.[24] Robert of

Courson envisaged the problem in explicit terms:[25] What should a parish priest do who is confronted by such a knight seeking the sacrament on Easter Day? Although the whole neighborhood knows that he holds tithes and the knight is aware of his excommunication, the bishop none-theless receives him. Robert's solution proposed a series of distinctions. First, the priest should determine whether the knight holds the tithes against the protests of the bishop or whether he does not claim the right of tithes but only holds their fruits with the bishop's consent. (It will be seen that the latter arrangement was permissible.) If the knight him-self was unsure of his holding, the priest should not deny him the Eucharist. If, however, the knight forcibly held the tithes, he should in the second place be admonished according to the Biblical procedure of threefold fraternal correction.[26] If the knight remained incorrigible, the prelate should publicly denounce him. If, however, the bishop defended him or simulated ignorance, the priest should have recourse to a higher prelate and finally to a council. Robert's advice to the parish priest pointed a difficult and impractical path to pursue, but the theologian's discussion nonetheless illustrates the prelacy's obstructions against the reform program.

More serious than the compliance of the prelacy was the ambiguity of the papacy. If the chorus of protests from Paris can be trusted, the popes of the late twelfth and early thirteenth centuries found practical pressures too great to insist on full enforcement of the reform program. Peter the Chanter, Gerald of Wales, and Robert of Courson all declared that the popes refused to take notice of such practices. By simulating ignorance they in effect abrogated the former decrees.[27] Both the Chanter and Cour-son refused to admit that the silence of the papacy excused laymen from the mortal sin of holding tithes.[28] The Chanter moreover accused the Roman curia of actively investing knights with tithes,[29] and Courson indignantly refused to recognize the authenticity of any papal letter which dispensed laymen from the due penalties.[30] Reporting that such letters were once presented to judge delegates at Paris, he advised them to be rejected as forgeries because such commands could not emanate from the pope's conscience even if he actually sent them. In another *questio* Robert refuted a further argument in favor of lay retention of tithes.[31] It could be maintained that when Charles Martel summoned the knights of the realm to protect the church against the pagans, he did not have sufficient wages, and therefore confiscated tithes from prelates who re-fused to aid him, distributing them to his knights. In this incident Rob-ert recalled the famous despoiling of the church by the Frankish king in the eighth century to raise an army to repel the Saracens,[32] but again Rob-ert refused to accept the historical explanation. Just as good ends can never justify evil means, so Charles was not justified in robbing the church to defend it.

The weight of practice which encouraged the papacy to simulate ignorance or even openly approve also placed pressure on the theologians to make accommodations. As realistic thinkers they could not avoid the fact that so many laymen ignored the church's policies on tithes. Wrestling with the problem in several *questiones* without arriving at clear solutions, Peter the Chanter noticed that the Count of Saint-Gilles collected tithes from the church of Saint-Gilles and the noble Roman senators took the oblations of Saint Peter.[33] If one church could transfer part of its tithes to another without conferring the accompanying rights, why couldn't a church similarly assign the material substance of tithes to the laity? If this were possible then the tithes could be enfeoffed by laymen and held by hereditary right, but if the Count of Saint-Gilles, and the Roman senators held tithes in their own name, this amounted to conferring on them a spiritual right which was unlawful.

Elsewhere the Chanter considered a knight who asked for certain payments (*sub pensione*) from tithes for protecting a church.[34] If laymen were conceded the positions of custodian and churchwarden for their services, why not also for tithes if they were granted only for one year, two years, or even for life? Peter reported that this question was argued for a long time at Reims.[35] In the same connection he observed that at Châtenay certain payments from tithes were held in a quasi-hereditary form because they could be sold.[36] Similarly, Stephen Langton inquired whether a prelate could sell a tithe to a knight for a year or two or even for lifetime by paying a fixed annual sum and whether this tithe could thereby be inherited by the knight's heirs?[37] In this manner the French knights could possess their tithes justly. After admitting the possibility of selling a tithe for two or three years, but not perpetually, Stephen, like the Chanter, was unable to resolve the question. Inconclusively the Chanter and Langton were groping for ways to distinguish a temporary and licit form of tithe-holding from the perpetual form, which was forbidden. At about the same time the canonist Huguccio proposed a distinction between the *ius spirituale* which constituted the ecclesiastical authority to levy tithes and the *ius percipiendi* which involved the collection of the fruits of tithes.[38] While the former could not be possessed by the laity under any circumstances, the latter might be granted to the laity, even in fief, if required by necessity and explicitly conceded by ecclesiastical authority. Although Huguccio's solution lacked clarity, later canonists understood him to allow the bishop to confer tithes to the laity in some form.[39]

One version of the Chanter's *Summa* declared that the counsellors of the realm decided at Reims that the fruits of tithes could be temporarily conceded to laymen for life or even for three generations, but not perpetually.[40] By combining this suggestion with Huguccio's dual distinction,

Robert of Courson formulated a clear solution to lay possession of tithes. While in one passage of his *Summa* he distinguished the right (*ius*) from the fruits (*fructus*) of tithes,[41] in another he delineated the case of a knight who held a certain tithe, but was prepared to obey the bishop.[42] Since the knight was already poor he would further impoverish his family if he relinquished the tithe. He therefore petitioned the bishop to grant him the fruits of the tithe for the remainder of his life. Robert concluded that from a sense of mercy the bishop could concede to the knight not the right but the fruits, extending to the fourth generation. Since tithes were spiritual, however, they could never be possessed by laymen in hereditary succession. The right remained with the church, but the fruits were temporally permitted to the laity for legitimate reasons. Later, at the Council of Bordeaux in 1214, Robert specified one of these reasons.[43] Laymen who offered their services to the church on a crusade might retain the use of their tithes with the prelate's permission, but at their death the tithes must revert to the church. This attempt to recognize realities by distinguishing between rights and fruits was followed by other theologians. Like Stephen Langton, Robert of Flamborough allowed priests to sell the temporal part of tithes to laymen for two or three years, stressing that the concession must be temporary and justified by urgent considerations.[44] Similar to Courson, Thomas of Chobham emphasized the difference between the right to collect tithes which belonged to the church and the fruits which could be conceded to laymen.[45] Following the solutions of his masters, Geoffrey of Poitiers clarified Langton's discussion by incorporating passages from Courson.[46]

Despite these accommodations, the reformers' major object was to restore tithes to the church. Although threats of excommunication were of some effect, churchmen often found that more material inducements were helpful in recovering tithes. Since laymen regarded tithes as secular revenue, they were willing to exchange them for something of economic value, sometimes simply selling the tithes back to a church.[47] Redemptions of tithes, however, might be misunderstood. How could a church pay money for a spiritual right which was originally hers without incurring simony? A canon from the Council of Worms in 829 included in Gratian's *Decretum* required bishops to prohibit the redemption of tithes which the laity refused to restore.[48] Huguccio, however, refused to interpret this canon as preventing all redemption of tithes, and maintained that the guilt of simony was attached to the seller, not the buyer.[49] Similarly, Peter the Chanter understood the canon to apply only when other ways of regaining tithes were available.[50] If no other means were possible, they could be redeemed by the church. Following Huguccio, Robert of Courson simply maintained that the prohibition assigned guilt to the laity who sold, but not to the clergy who bought.[51]

In practical terms, however, the question whether churches could legitimately redeem their tithes was of little importance. As any ecclesiastical
cartulary will testify, most churches were actively engaged in retrieving
their tithes by all possible means.[52]

From the outset of the reform movement it was apparent that churchmen were more concerned with extricating tithes from laymen than with
restoring them to the original parish churches.[53] Throughout the twelfth
century a large proportion of the restored tithes fell into the hands of the
monastic rather than the secular clergy.[54] Offering an illustration, Peter
the Chanter discussed a certain knight in need of money who offered to
sell his tithes back to the church for one hundred pounds.[55] When the
church to whom the tithes rightfully belonged was unable to pay the
price, a more wealthy church asked the bishop for permission to redeem
and retain these tithes. Although Peter did not specifically designate
the second church, most redeemed tithes were actually taken over by
monks who considered them revenues much as did the former lay holders.
Peter's example illustrates another element in the process of recovering
tithes from laymen. Although tithes need not be restored to the original
church, the transfer must always be under episcopal supervision. Tithes
should never pass from laymen to a church except by explicit consent
of the bishop. When the Chanter himself donated the tithes of Hodenc
he resigned them into the hands of Philip, Bishop of Beauvais, who then
conferred them on the Hôtel-Dieu of Beauvais and the church of
Hodenc.[56] After this Carolingian principle of episcopal control was revived by the reformers, popes, councils, and diocesan synods kept it alive
throughout the twelfth and thirteenth centuries.[57] When the Chanter,
Courson, and Robert of Flamborough, noted this episcopal supervision,
they followed a well-known principle.[58]

Closely related to this problem was a case which must have occurred
frequently in practice. Peter the Chanter cited a peasant who for a long
time and by stealth withheld tithes from the knight who possessed them,
perhaps with the intention of restoring them to the church.[59] When the
peasant came for confession, should the bishop advise him to return them
to the knight or to the church? On the one hand it could be argued that
since the church permitted the knight to collect tithes, the peasant sins
if he fraudulently withholds them. On the other hand, if one steals a
horse from a second party who has stolen it from a third, he is required
to restore it to the original owner. Similarly, why should the peasant return to the knight what the latter has stolen from the church? In the
principal version of his *Summa* the Chanter expressly left the solution in
doubt, but Peter of Poitiers of Saint-Victor and an anonymous Victorine
penitential report that the Chanter decided for the second alternative,
provided that it could be performed without scandal.[60] Peter of Saint-

Victor and the anonymous penitential also refer to another group of masters who defended the first position. Among this group was the Chanter's student, Robert of Courson, who decided that the peasant was not exempt from excommunication for withholding tithes, not because he did not pay his full tithes to the knight but because he acted on his own authority, thus endangering the church with schism.[61] To the peasant who had scruples about paying to a layman, Robert advised that he cast his tithes on the ground so that they could be collected by whoever dared to claim them. For the peasant who withheld tithes and was required to restore to the knight, Robert proposed one device to shield him from the knight's vengeance. The peasant should make restitution to the knight through the priest, who could refuse to reveal the offender's identity.

TAILLES

A second source of domanial revenue which provoked the protests of Peter the Chanter and his circle was the *taille*.[62] In the tenth century at the same time that the tithe was being usurped by laymen, this exaction originated from seignorial exploitation. When it appears in eleventh-century charters it is designated by numerous terms, which have been rendered by modern historians as *taille* in French or tallage in English. As bewildering as its terminology is the variety of forms which the *taille* assumed. It could be levied according to territory or to person, demanded from the free as well as serfs, be fixed or indeterminate in size and regularity, yet beneath this multiplicity historians have discerned common features which distinguish it from other seignorial exactions. As a rule the *taille* was imposed on peasants, townsmen, and Jews who belonged especially to the lord's domain. In forms varying from absolute commands to polite requests it was imposed by a ruler exercising direct authority over his subjects. Since the *taille* was often occasioned by the lord's urgent need for aid, its outstanding characteristic was arbitrariness. Unlike the *gîte*, the *cens*, and other domanial revenues it was neither fixed in amount nor regular in collection, but depended totally on the lord's will. Even in England, where tallage of the royal domain became a regular feature of the king's finances, its arbitrary character is evident in that it was assessed each time by an individual bargain between the royal commissioners and the local men. Undoubtedly the capricious and uncontrolled features of the *taille* rendered it odious to peasants and townsmen. Except in England, where it was normally accepted, numerous complaints were voiced against this revenue. Whenever subjects were able to muster sufficient opposition, lords were compelled to renounce it formally in charters.[63] To the peasant and bourgeois the *taille* was robbery.

Adopting this common attitude, the theologians of Paris sustained the accusation of robbery with numerous reasons. In a series of sketchy *questiones* Peter the Chanter sniped at the *taille* with Scriptural arguments. Recalling the Gospel passage (Luke 3 : 13) where John the Baptist commanded tax collectors to "exact no more than what is appointed to you" (*nichil ultra quod constitutum est faciatis*), he inquired whether the *taille* had been legitimately appointed.[64] He found no justification for it either in the laws of God or in written law (that is, Roman law), but only from customary practice. Since Roman law maintains that unreasonable customs cannot stand, the Chanter concluded that it was reasonable to enjoin knights in the confessional to renounce the *taille* except in extreme necessity. Elsewhere, Peter confronted the argument that since kings have authority to perform matters not specifically prescribed, they can establish a *taille* on whomever they wish.[65] Again, he concluded that kings commit mortal sin if they exact *tailles*, since they are not prescribed by law. It will be seen that the only possible concession to these exactions had to arise from dire necessity. Since the *taille* was equated with robbery restitution must compensate damages. Posing the example of a prince who extorted *tailles* from the peasants of a certain church, Peter reported that, desiring to do restitution, the prince returned the proceeds to the canons of the church who endowed a new prebend.[66] The Chanter, however, insisted that satisfaction was not fulfilled until the exactions were restored to the peasants. Similar was the case of a prince who stole from the Carthusians.[67] Wishing later to make amends by offering the *tailles* of his subjects, his settlement was refused because the Carthusians would not accept stolen goods. To Robert of Courson the *taille* was likewise plunder, committed by princes and prelates at the prompting of courtiers.[68] For him, these evil customs transgress natural law, which teaches us not to do to others what we would not have them do to us.[69] Even if established by former rulers, they should not be followed by their successors, as illustrated by the Biblical example of Belshazzar whom God punished for retaining the wicked practices of his father Nebuchadnezzar.

Despite this theoretical opposition to *tailles*, the theologians were willing to consider conditions which might excuse the custom. Peter the Chanter allowed them in times of extreme emergency, but the necessity must be reasonable. To demand a *taille* to pay superfluous expenses was not sufficient excuse.[70] One's needs must be measured with an equitable standard. To illustrate this necessity Peter recalled the action of Count Thibaut of Champagne (d. 1152) during a severe famine.[71] This great baron, who was celebrated for his pious generosity, was reported to have compelled the rich to support the poor under threat of exacting *tailles*. Inquiring whether this compulsory poor relief was licit when Augustine maintained that one cannot steal to support his father and the Apostle Paul (Rom. 3 : 8) had declared that one should not do evil that good may result, Peter argued to the contrary that it was wrong for the rich to allow the poor to die of hunger. Since the count could punish them for this wickedness, could he not also prevent this consequence by forcing the rich to contribute to the poor?[72] In the Chanter's opinion the extreme necessity of famine justified Count Thibaut's tallages. When Peter considered a prelate in similar circumstances, however, he hesitated to approve these exactions without the consent of the subjects.[73] By assembling and adding to the Chanter's conflicting arguments, Robert of Courson constructed a *questio* on whether princes and prelates can compel their subjects to give alms in times of famine.[74] Although he included the example of Count Thibaut in favor of such measures, he gave serious attention to opposing arguments. His final conclusion devised a twofold distinction which tempered his master's solutions. Either the subjects were the true owners of their goods, such as laymen or clerics possessing their own inheritances, or they were merely stewards (*dispensatores*), such as ecclesiastics whose goods belonged to the church. The first group could only be induced to contribute alms, but never coerced. Those who were stewards of the church might not only be admonished, however, but also compelled to distribute their goods, just as in the time of famine mendicants were obliged to share their alms with those perishing from hunger. In effect Robert concluded that prelates and princes like Count Thibaut of Champagne could impose compulsory poor relief only on churchmen who administered the wealth of the church, but not on laymen and other ecclesiastics who possessed their own property. In the Lateran Council of 1215 Pope Innocent III took exception to Courson's conclusion. After anathematizing laymen who imposed tallages on churches, Innocent conceded that in great necessity bishops and their clerics could contribute to public needs providing that these subsidies were offered without coercion and with prior consultation of the pope.[75] In the council's view no one could impose tallages on the church without its full consent.

In addition to the condition of necessity Robert of Courson introduced a social distinction, whether the subjects were freemen or serfs. Although freemen, such as the bourgeoisie, should be excluded from the *taille*,[76] Robert designated three kinds of serfs, only one of which was exempt. Since the classification of serfdom has been one of the more complicated tasks of medieval history, modern historians have found it nearly impossible to rely on terminology alone. It is too much to expect to identify what classes Robert had in mind, but his brief observations represent an early discussion of servile classes by a university professor. First of all, referring to the "native serfs" (*nativi servi*) on whom the *taille* was assigned (*conscripta*) from birth, Robert concurred that the prince could collect this exaction because all of the serf's goods belonged to his lord.[77] Since the term "native serf" was one employed in charters from Robert's England, this particular servitude may apply to English villeins.[78] Elsewhere he devised a twofold distinction in classifying serfdom.[79] Some serfs might be considered as "bound and sold" (*ascriptii et empticii*), such as Robert believed could be found in Apulia and Sicily. Here Robert was thinking of something close to chattel slavery because the serfs could be bought and sold like sheep and cattle.[80] Since these serfs owned no property and all their possessions belonged to their lord, their master was free to impose *tailles* and exactions. Although it is not clear whether Robert distinguished this chattel serfdom from the former category of "native serfs," he nonetheless maintained that in contrast to southern Italy nearly everywhere in France a different class of servitude could be found, known as *censive* serfs because they supplied their lords with fixed payments (*census*). Since these serfs were protected by defined and regular obligations Courson concluded that their lords could not levy *tailles* above the owed rents. Although Robert's description of southern Italy may not be valid, there can be little doubt that in France Robert referred to the growing number of *censive* peasants who transformed their servile and labor obligations into fixed rents.[81]

Courson's countryman, Robert of Flamborough, also distinguished *tailles* according to social divisions.[82] Like the English royal commissioners, Flamborough reduced the whole population to two classes, servile and free. Although in his judgment it was sinful to impose arbitrary tallages on free men, as upon serfs, he concluded by neither counselling nor opposing such exactions. If a lord reduced his peasants to dire straits through tallages, he was obliged to support them at his own expense.[83] Both Robert of Courson and Robert of Flamborough in effect justified *tailles* from unfree classes, such as the slaves of southern Italy and the villeins of England, but free men and *censive* serfs were to be free from these exactions.

Originating in the tenth century, *tailles* underwent a radical transformation during the second half of the twelfth century. French and English seignorial charters attest that a significant number of lords commuted their *tailles* to a regular and fixed money rent[84] as part of a growing tendency to convert rights and services into money payments. Since the peasants and bourgeoisie preferred these regular rents to the former arbitrary exactions, the *taille* rapidly became a regular *census*. Aware of this contemporary movement, the Parisian theologians raised the question of whether a lord could legitimately accept this commutation. Since they judged the *taille* to be illicit, it was difficult to concur with its transformation into another form of payment. Citing peasants who wished to free themselves from the *taille* by promising an annual revenue, Peter the Chanter oscillated between two answers and was unable to arrive at a definite solution.[85] With a little more conviction Robert of Courson declared himself doubtful whether a knight could receive a monetary redemption for something to which he had no right.[86] He then proceeded to distinguish between the chattel serfs of southern Italy and the *censive* serfs of France, as has been seen. According to this reasoning Robert could only approve of commuting the *taille* on chattel serfs. Bound by their logic on the illicit character of the *taille*, the Parisian theologians could not concur with a movement beneficial to the peasants of France and England.

Although opposed in principle to tallages and to their transformation into rents, the theologians did not object to the regular payment as an alternative to arbitrary revenues. Robert of Flamborough, for example, considered the application of the *taille* to *hôtes*, who were brought in to settle a new territory. Since these colonists did not originate from this land and since they came from free and servile backgrounds, they presented conflicts of seignorial jurisdiction.[87] To which lord did they belong: the old or the new? To which lord did they pay the *taille*? Robert's example concerned a lord who granted land to an *hôte* and desired to impose a tallage whenever and however he chose.[88] It has been seen that Robert acquiesced in this arbitrary exaction if the *hôte* was a serf, but if he was free, Robert proposed an alternative solution. If the *hôte* realized an income of a hundred pounds from the land each year or two, he should regularly pay a rent of forty shillings. Unless the payment was fixed in amount and in time Robert judged it to be robbery. It is not clear whether he intended the rent to be set at a certain amount or percentage, but in his example the rent amounted to two per cent of the land's yield. Flamborough's *hôte* resembled Courson's *censive* serf who likewise paid a regular rent and was immune to the *taille*.

Robert of Courson also proposed that fixed rents be substituted for arbitrary *tailles* imposed on townsmen. Acknowledging that princes justify tallages on towns by protecting townsmen in their own territories as well as in other lands, Robert contended that the prince should demand from his bourgeoisie no exactions above the just rent and decreed revenues due from the town.[89] If, however, the prince projected expensive fortifications, he could induce contributions from the bourgeoisie by converting the customary tallages into moderate annual rents.[90] Beneficial public projects, therefore, justified the commutation of *tailles* into fixed revenues. Finally Robert of Courson raised the real problem of lords who were so dependent on their *tailles* that they were unable to abandon these unjust exactions. What advice should be offered to knights and noble ladies who, possessing no regular revenues (*census*) from their domains, lived entirely from *tailles*?[91] In a solution resembling his advice to towns, Robert proposed that these lords redeem their tallages by constructing poor houses, common pastures, aqueducts, and undertaking other enterprises useful to the community. For whatever arbitrary exactions could not be converted into regular revenues, the next recourse was to employ them in public works.

TOLLS

While the *taille* produced revenue for the seignorial lord from the peasants and burghers of his domain, tolls on roads, rivers, bridges, and markets were his profits from merchants. During the early Middle Ages local and long-distance trade was seriously harassed by innumerable customs and imposts levied on the routes and junctures of transportation.[92] These commercial taxes constituted a jealously guarded income to lords great and small in France and Germany. Robert of Courson recognized the similarity between tallages and tolls and investigated how tolls were employed to plunder merchants.[93] Enumerating three kinds of commercial imposts: the general toll (*pedagium*), the sales tax (*tonleatio*), and the more specific toll on wagons (*roagium*), Robert believed that these levies were justified originally by the lord's protection of the merchant. Since traders travelling from fair to fair were seriously menaced by brigands in former days, when France was heavily forested, castellans and princes had been obliged to hire armed sergeants to conduct them safely through their lands, for which the lord rightfully demanded compensation in tolls. But in his own day, Robert continued, the highways were free from danger, and princes no longer hired men to protect trading caravans. Because the lord performs no service he has no right to impose exactions. Rulers who continue to extort tolls are damned, and prelates sin mortally who do not publicly oppose them and withhold the sacraments from them. Where the lord contributed no service, but robbed the trader with unjust customs, he was held to restitution. A certain prince, for example, decreed that if a teamster set down a wine cask in the road because he broke a wheel or tongue of his wagon, he was to pay sixty shillings. Since the lord robbed rather than helped the unfortunate wagoner, he must restore his exactions. If, however, the lord continued to perform genuine services of protection—that is, if he supplied guards for traders coming and leaving the fairs and markets, and indemnified merchants suffering pillage—he might legitimately collect tolls and sale taxes according to the just and ancient rates. When Robert of Courson visited the south of France as papal legate in 1214, he inserted canons into the Council of Montpellier which implemented his theories.[94] Following the Lateran Councils of 1139 and 1179, he forbade under anathema the creation of new tolls, or the raising or transferral of old ones.[95] Moreover he admonished local lords to attend seriously to guarding the public routes for which they received imposts. If any merchant or traveller suffered damages through violence, the lord to whom he paid tolls must take vengeance. Until the lord satisfied these losses, he was prohibited under censure from collecting further tolls. In Courson's judgment the prince's primary justification for exacting toll was his service of protection. Certain lords in France and England (notably the royalty) regarded these duties seriously at the turn of the twelfth and thirteenth centuries. The merchants of Ypres, who were one of the principal groups trading in the fairs of Champagne, were protected by King Philip Augustus in 1193 when travelling in his lands.[96] By 1209 the king extended the royal safe-conduct to all merchants going to the fairs of Champagne, thereby performing an invaluable service to this center of international commerce.[97]

Droit de Prise

Another seignorial tax on merchants which was indirect but arbitrary was the *saisimentum* or *droit de prise* by which the Capetian kings provisioned their household from the market at low prices or even gratuitously.[98] Peter the Chanter observed that princes employed an official called the "estimator" (*appreciator*) who was authorized to set the prices of supplies purchased for the princely household.[99] Inquiring into the moral aspects of this position, Peter asked whether the official was not committing robbery if he decreed a price of two shillings for something that a merchant would have sold for three on the marketplace. If he sought advice in the confessional, should the priest advise him to resign his position? Peter noticed that in episcopal cities such as Beauvais bishops regulated the prices of poultry, cattle, firewood, and shoes.[100] If the estimator adjusted his prices to the regulated prices he did not sin, and in other markets where prices were uncontrolled, if he followed the current prices, his functions could be tolerated. In other words, the Chanter condoned the estimator as long as he did not impose disadvantageous prices on the merchants, but under such circumstances the prince could no longer consider the office as lucrative.[101]

Coinage

Coinage constituted a further source of revenue derived from commercial origins.[102] Although the authority to mint money had been widely dispersed among the French barons, King Philip Augustus took measures to reestablish royal control. After his conquests over the Angevins, Philip attempted to coordinate royal currencies under the two systems of Paris and Tours. The Capetian monopoly over coinage at the turn of the century, however, was limited to the royal domain. In contemporary England royal currency circulated without rivalry throughout the kingdom. Princes profited from minting by collecting seigniorage (a charge for producing the coins) and by manipulating the value of money. Although the theologians did not devote sustained attention to currency problems, their brief discussions did envisage, if only tangentially, these two sources of revenue.

Peter the Chanter and Robert of Courson both posed the academic question of whether money could be minted from illicit sources, and it is in this connection that the subject of seigniorage is treated by them, though somewhat indirectly. The Chanter offers the example of a town which coined all of its money from bullion (*plate*) obtained in trade with the king of Sicily.[103] Since Peter believed that the Sicilian treasury consisted entirely of plunder, he queried whether such material could be used as currency.[104] If not, then all contracts, rents, salaries, and the like would cease. Since all worldly affairs would thereby come to a halt, he was forced to conclude that corrupt currency could be employed of necessity in contracts and debts only if no legal liability was incurred. Peter's example skirted the question of whether town governments could demand seigniorage from minting such coins, but presumably the profits of coinage were disqualified in the same way that the currency was invalid for contracts.

Approaching the problem with a different example, Robert of Courson offers a more probing inquiry.[105] A certain prince accumulated through *tailles* and usury a sum of tainted money which he melted into bullion and transported to the fairs to be reminted. Not only did the prince profit from the seigniorage of reminting, but this new money circulated through the hands of merchants and money-changers. What are the responsibilities of a merchant who knows for certain that the current money is derived from robbery, or even knows, for example, that despoiled citizens of four cities are seeking redress from the prince? Can this illicit money serve as a medium of exchange? From one point of view, it would seem that all loans, sales, and donations based on this currency would be invalidated, because this money must be considered as stolen goods whose ownership cannot be legally transferred, as required by these contracts. Just as a blighted root corrupts the whole tree, so the blemish of robbery remains in the bullion of currency until it is rightfully restored. On the other hand, all transactions of the fairs would cease, as the Chanter had pointed out. Rather than acceding to exigencies as his master had done, Robert attempted to solve the problem by proposing two sets of distinctions to be applied in the penitential forum. The first involved the knowledge of the merchant. If he knew with certainty that the currency was derived directly from plunder, he must refrain from transacting his affairs with this money. If, however, after reasonable investigation he remained ignorant of the illicit character, his transactions remained valid. Apparently Robert believed that this *bona fide* ignorance would be shared by most merchants, thereby preserving the business of the fairs. In the second place Robert distinguished between the purposes of the transactions. If the business was conducted for the merchant's own pocketbook, such money could not be employed. If the transactions were in behalf of the church or out of necessity, these goals justified the use of tainted currency. Although Courson's solutions bore little practical effect in the real world of commerce where the individual merchant would find it impossible to distinguish licit from ill-gotten currencies, his discussion was obliquely relevant to the princely right of seigniorage. In his view rulers could not profit from currency based ultimately on robbery.

A prince also profited from coinage by changing its value. If he wished to reduce his debts, he debased his money, but if he was primarily concerned with his rents and fixed revenues, he would attempt to keep his money stable or even to raise its value. By the end of the twelfth century numerous lords in France and England were commuting domain labor services and payments in kind into fixed money rents.[106] As rents increased proportionally among governmental revenues, the ruling classes became increasingly attentive to the value of money and the manipulation of currency. Beginning with King Henry II the Plantagenets led the way in establishing a relatively stable currency, a step followed by Louis VII and Philip Augustus in France.[107] By the turn of the century, therefore, the English and French monarchs aimed towards a currency uniform in weight and fineness of silver, thereby, emphasizing the intrinsic value of money. The great movements to debase coinage in France and England did not arise until the fourteenth century. The royalty's interest in a stable currency was shared by the contemporary Roman lawyers who queried whether, for example, if a borrower had received a loan and afterwards the currency had been devalued, he should repay the nominal sum or compensate for the debased currency.[108] Placentinus, Pillius, and Azo concurred that a debtor was obligated to repay in the equivalent measure or money of the time when the debt was contracted. Following Huguccio's lead, the canonists adopted the Romanist doctrine of the intrinsic value of money, and in a celebrated decretal of 1199 to Alphonse, King of Aragon, Pope Innocent III ordered the King to restore the debased coinage of his father to its former value.[109]

Less concerned with debasement, which occupied the contemporary Romanists and canonists, Peter the Chanter turned to the other side of monetary manipulation, the appreciating of currency to increase seignorial revenues.[110] If peasants on a domain, for example, owed a fixed rent to a prince, could he double the value of currency and receive the same nominal amount of rent? In this case one hundred shillings of the new money would be worth two hundred of the old. If peasants owed their lord one hundred measures of grain, this increase would be the same as if the lord doubled the size of the measure. Or it would be equivalent to doubling the time of knight service owed by vassals. Peter concluded that a prince sinned mortally if he exacted from his subjects in a new currency any more in value than what they formerly paid. In other words, since the value of obligations should remain constant, compensations should be made for currency fluctuations. The Chanter then applied the intrinsic principle to a number of situations. If an older money which was formerly equal to the new money should have in the meantime depreciated, may the peasants continue to pay their rents in the devaluated money? In this case the prince may raise the value of the old currency as long as he does not exceed the value of the rents owed by the peasants. If certain simple folk contract an obligation with an oath to pay each year a hundred shillings in Parisian money without taking into account a future rise in the value of money, what should they pay in the third year, when the value of Parisian currency has increased? Just as prices should be determined according to place, Peter affirmed, so should they be reckoned according to time. If you sell me something in England for a hundred shillings, you are held to pay in sterling wherever you settle. Similarly, you are obliged to pay the equivalent value of the hundred shillings at the time of contract.

Peter's examples of increasing the value of coinage may seem academic because evidence of contemporary rulers making this change is extremely rare. On the contrary, the few manipulations which took place were towards devaluation. Nonetheless, the Chanter suggests two conclusions from his illustrations: In general he adhered to the intrinsic value theory of money, thus following the contemporary Romanists and canonists and, more specifically, he taught that princes cannot rightfully profit from the manipulation of currencies.

TREASURE TROVE AND FORESTS LAWS

A further source of income discussed by the theologians was treasure trove. During the twelfth century many lords in France and England claimed all treasures found on lands under their jurisdiction. Although it is difficult to ascertain how lucrative this right was to its possessor, King Louis VII claimed it at least once in the Ile-de-France, and in England the concealment of treasure-trove was among the offenses vindicated by the royal courts.[111] Lest its contemporary significance be missed, it must be remembered that King Richard lost his life at an obscure castle in the Limousin defending his rights over treasure-trove. In opposition to Roman law, this claim to treasure originated from medieval customary practice. The Romanists defined treasure-trove as a valuable moveable, usually money, which had been hidden for so long that its former ownership could no longer be determined. According to Justinian if one discovered the treasure on his own land, it belonged to him.[112] If he accidentally discovered it on another's land, he divided it with the property owner, but if he intentionally searched another's land, he had no claim. In all events, the right of a suzerain to treasure was unknown in Roman law, unless it was discovered in a public place, in which case the finder shared it with the public treasury. The essentials of this Roman law theory were perpetuated by the legists of the twelfth century.[113]

The twelfth-century canonists and the Chanter's followers considered treasure-trove in the larger context of the obligation to return things which have been found. Gratian included in his *Decretum* Augustine's dictum that one commits theft unless he returns what he has found. By the time of Huguccio this statement prompted the canonists to discuss the ramifications of restitution.[114] Huguccio decided that the finder must exhaust all means to ascertain who was the former owner. If the owner is known, it should be returned; to his heirs, if the owner is deceased; or to the church, if the heirs have died out. In the last case the church should apply the proceeds of the recovered article to good works which will benefit the souls of the deceased owners. If the identity of the former owner is doubtful, the finder may retain the article until the question of ownership is cleared, when final restitution should be arranged. Only when it becomes impossible to determine the original owner, may the finder keep the lost article. At this point Huguccio adopted the solutions of Roman law.[115] Peter the Chanter, Alain of Lille, Stephen Langton, Robert of Courson, and Peter of Poitiers of Saint-Victor likewise emphasized the church's role in discovering the former owner and adjudicating the settlement.[116]

A number of the masters, however, proceeded from the problem of returning lost articles to the issue of the customary right of treasure-trove. Noticing the contrast between Roman law and contemporary practice, Peter asked what confessional advice the priest should offer to a poor man who found such a treasure.[117] If the prince was a tyrant who violently enforced his claims, he decided that it would be prudent for the man to turn over the treasure to his lord. In a *questio* which expanded the Chanter's passage Robert of Courson considered the same situation.[118] Robert observed that in almost every realm such treasures belonged to the kingdom. If the priest counselled the peasant to conceal his discovery, he endangered him with the customary punishment of hanging for theft. If he advised him to hand it over to the prince, he acceded to a wicked custom which deprived the church and the poor of their rights. Not acquiescing to the practice as did his master, Robert counselled the peasant to hand the treasure over to the church or to a respected ecclesiastic who would allocate its proceeds to the church or to the poor. As to the peasant who faced the prince's wrath, Robert proposed that the church undertake his defense since he was obeying its command. In effect Courson applied to treasure-trove the principle of his fellow theologians, which assigned to the church the major role in restoring lost goods. The church's duty was to oppose the custom of treasure-trove and to assume responsibility for distributing such goods for charitable purposes. Thomas of Chobham also was familiar with the English practice which condemned those who concealed the discovery of treasures on their lands.[119] Rather than acceding to custom as did the Chanter, or proposing an alternative as had Courson, Thomas merely advocated the replacement of the customary practice with Roman law, but offered no suggestion how this change was to be effected. Raoul Ardent came to a similar conclusion.[120] After rehearsing the alternatives open to one who found a treasure, he conceded that he could keep it if it were done without scandal and for good purposes.

The Parisian theologians noticed similarities between the arbitrary character of treasure-trove practice and the forest laws, which demanded that subjects hand over to their lord objects which they found and to which they would have been entitled under Roman law. Under the forest laws the lord claimed that all wild beasts of the forests, particularly the deer, belonged exclusively to him. As will be seen, no one could hunt these wild beasts without incurring savage punishments or severe fines.* Quoting Ovid, Peter the Chanter declared that those elements which were common by natural law were converted to private use by iniquity.[121] If the ground is for treading, the air for breathing, and water for drinking and bathing, why are hunting, fowling, and fishing not permitted to all? Elsewhere he specifically questioned fishing rights claimed by monasteries and hunting prohibitions in the forests.[122] The problem was acutely felt in England where vast territories were designated as royal forests in which the king possessed exclusive rights over the wild beasts.[123] Like the Chanter, Thomas of Chobham also protested that the birds and beasts of the forest were common to all men by natural law.[124] Discussing the returning of lost animals, he maintained that in many regions wicked custom has changed sound laws.[125] Kings and princes compel forest inhabitants to swear an oath respecting the peace of all wild animals which they enforce with severe penalties. If a subject takes a beast in secret, Thomas queried, does he sin mortally, or must he return it to the prince? To this problem the masters had two solutions. If the subject's oath to the prince was without duress, he should both do penance for perjury and restore the animal. If, however, the subject made the oath under threat of imprisonment or loss of possessions, he need only do penance for perjury. Restitution is unnecessary because the prince is not lord of the beasts but has usurped this authority. By this distinction Thomas of

* See below, p. 320.

Chobham offered to forest inhabitants justification for circumventing the royal monopoly over wild animals.

SHIPWRECK

Like those governing treasure-trove the medieval customs concerning shipwreck departed radically from ancient Roman law, and were considered lucrative revenue by numerous rulers in France and England. Roman law extended protection over the remnants of shipwreck to the surviving owners or their rightful heirs.[126] Those who took advantage of the misfortune to requisition the remaining goods were treated as robbers and punished with fines four times the value of the cargo. The imperial officials were forbidden to intervene or to make exactions. By contrast to ancient Roman procedure, customary practices in the early Middle Ages permitted the prince to seize all goods from shipwrecks upon his shores. In effect the ruler was granted the pillage forbidden in Roman law. Apparently some princes were troubled over the propriety of these ruthless practices, because during the course of the twelfth century Henry I, Henry II, and Richard I, renounced their rights of wreck in England and granted the remaining goods to the survivors and their heirs.[127] But these reforms were not altogether permanent because they were frequently renewed. There is little evidence of such renunciations in France, where jurisdiction over the coasts and rivers was shared by innumerable lords.[128]

Churchmen, however, denounced this form of pillage without hesitation. In the Lateran Council of 1179 Pope Alexander III attacked shipwreck customs in measures to further the crusades.[129] Those who despoiled Christians shipwrecked upon their shores when they should have extended their aid were to be excommunicated until they restored the plunder. During the early years of the thirteenth century two British masters, Robert of Courson and Gerald Wales, renewed these protests in explicit terms. Raising the subject of shipwreck while discussing robbery committed by princes, Robert noted that whenever a vessel damaged at sea seeks refuge at a port, the prince customarily seizes it and confiscates its goods.[130] Brittany and certain parts of Poitou and Lombardy were particularly notorious for such practices, since prelates as well as lay princes there participated in the plunder. By denying aid to the distressed these lords were guilty of murder as well as theft. Robert's solution was to urge the prelates of his day to refuse the sacraments without dispensation or dissimulation to all who exercised such rights. In a section of the *De principis instructione* devoted to the ancient Roman emperors and the superiority of their laws, Gerald of Wales treated the issue no less explicitly than Robert.[131] Mentioning the coasts of England, Wales, and Ireland as his examples, Gerald, like Courson, blamed prelates as well as lay princes. Not only if a ship was broken on the rocks, but even if it was merely stranded on a sand bar and remained intact, it was declared wrecked and mercilessly despoiled because it could not achieve its destination. Such customs heaped affliction on the afflicted and endangered seafarers with two tribulations. What survived the fury of the sea was ravaged on land. Gerald's response was more academic than Robert's. Quoting from the *Digest* to demonstrate the superiority of the Roman law of shipwreck over contemporary customs,[132] he claimed that ancient laws of former good kings of England were more equitable because they recognized the rights of survivors and their heirs. In contrast to these ancient precedents, modern culprits were worthy of punishment without mercy. Gerald advocated penalties ranging from twofold to fivefold, reminiscent of Roman law, but unfortunately he gives no hint as to how these reforms were to be instituted.

WARDSHIP AND MARRIAGE

Among the rights highly prized by the lords of France and England were certain prerogatives over their vassals designated as feudal "incidents." Robert of Courson specified two of them, wardship and marriage, which were probably the two most lucrative. Wardship and marriage rights were justified by the military character of feudal relationships. When a fief which entailed military service was inherited by a minor boy or woman who could not perform this duty, the lord had the right of wardship over the heir and the fief. This right entitled the lord to the fief's income above what was required to maintain the heir until the boy became of age or the girl married and the military obligations were again met. The revenue was the lord's compensation for the temporary loss of military service. Since political alliances were usually formed along family lines, it was also important to a lord that his vassal marry into friendly families. To safeguard his interests the lord claimed the right to consent to his vassal's marriage. The feudal incident of marriage, which was closely allied to that of wardship, stipulated that a lord could marry the sons and daughters of his vassals to whomever he wished. Whenever someone vindicated a right, he was sorely tempted to profit from it. Rich heiresses could be placed on the auction block by their lords and married to the highest bidder. It took little imagination to see how "incidents" of wardship and marriage were open to serious abuse.

Robert of Courson pointed to obvious abuses when he observed the Anglo-French custom that whenever barons died and left minor heirs, the prince confiscated their goods and married the heirs and heiresses to spouses of lesser nobility.[133] In the case of wardship the lord profited from pillaging the fief with heavy exactions. In the case of marriage he exercised his prerogative by commanding a disparaging union[134] and profited from selling the nobility (*generositas*) of the heir to a mate who was willing to pay for the advantageous match.[135] Although such rights were approved by the customs of the realm because a prince could claim remuneration for protecting the heir and his inheritance during minority, Robert found that they were contrary to Roman law which maintained that a guardian was forbidden to alienate his ward's goods but rather was responsible for preserving them for future use.[136] Robert's final judgment was to abolish these customs infected with greed and to restore goods confiscated from wards and the sale of marriages. Princes were, however, permitted to deduct legitimate expenses in administering the affairs of their wards.

Courson specifically affirmed that these customs flourished in the French and English regions. By the French region (*Gallicana regio*) he perhaps thought of Normandy, where they were well known. It is less likely that he referred to the Ile-de-France because there wardship was usually assumed not by the feudal lord but by a relative.[137] In all events, one need look no farther than Robert's native England to find a historical context for his discussion.[138] In contemporary England and Normandy the Angevin kings vigorously asserted rights known as "prerogative" wardship and marriage because their claims took precedence over those of other barons. It is possible that Robert had this English prerogative jurisdiction in mind when he referred to "the prince of the land" (*princeps terre*). By mulcting great sums from wardships, by marrying highborn heiresses to mercenary captains of humble and foreign origin, and by selling marriages at handsome prices, King John profited from wardship and marriage to a degree hitherto untried at a time contemporary to Robert.[139] Courson's complaints were also shared by the English barons. When the barons forced the king to concede in *Magna Carta* that the guardian should not devastate the lands of his ward, but maintain them in good repair, taking for himself only reasonable produce, customs, and service,[140] these terms resembled Robert's protest against confiscation, and approximated to his concession of due expenses to be deducted by the guardian. When the king further promised to arrange marriages without disparagement and with the knowledge of the nearest kin,[141] this echoed Robert's protest against the prince who married wards to less noble spouses. But the measures of the baronial charter were not as radical as those of the theological *Summa*. Courson unconditionally denounced sale of marriages and demanded restitution, but this reform was unthinkable to the barons of England.

Regalian Rights

A final revenue specified by Robert of Courson was analogous to wardship. Just as a feudal lord could profit from a military fief when the vassal was a woman or a minor, so kings claimed the revenues of certain cathedrals and abbeys between the death of the prelate and the investiture of his successor. Although this privilege was designated "regalian right" in France and England, it referred to a restricted sense of *regalia* which differed from a broader use of the term in the Empire.[142] In this limited sense regalian rights were twofold: a claim to the revenues of a vacant ecclesiastical fief, called the temporal *regalia*, and the right to assign prebends which became available during the vacancy, later designated as the spiritual *regalia*. In England the temporal regalian rights were introduced by the Conqueror, widely abused by William Rufus, and vigorously claimed in the Constitutions of Clarendon by Henry II.[143] At the beginning of the thirteenth century King John, driven to desperate financial expedients, profited from the regalian rights to an unprecedented extent. Exercise of the spiritual *regalia*, however, was not common until the reign of Henry III.[144] In France the temporal *regalia* was first claimed early in the reign of King Louis VII.[145] Profiting widely from it, King Philip Augustus used it, for example, to pillage the bishopric of Auxerre in 1207.[146] Royal exercise of the spiritual *regalia* appeared in Capetian lands at the turn of the twelfth century.[147] Contemporary to the exploitations of King John and Philip Augustus, Robert of Courson raised a voice against both temporal and spiritual regalian rights.[148] Inquiring whether princes could confiscate the goods of vacant churches and whether the bestowal of prebends during these vacancies was valid, Robert listed canonical authorities for and against from Gratian's *Decretum*.[149] Although these arguments referred specifically to the emperor's right to elect the pope, he applied them to the *regalia* and concluded that the prince owed restitution for all confiscations and assignments of prebends. Unless the prince possessed special papal authorization (*speciale privilegium*), all episcopal goods and cathedral prebends should be reserved for the future bishop. Gerald of Wales, however, had doubts about the legitimacy of regalian rights even when they were specially granted by the pope.[150] Citing the example of King Louis VII, Gerald reported that a certain cleric recently returned from Rome presented a papal privilege allowing the King to enjoy the revenues and assign the benefices of the vacant cathedrals in his custody. Avowing that such liberties were dangerous to the soul, Louis thrust the letter into the fire. There is little chance of corroborating Gerald's account, but if it has any substance, it is more appropriate to the latter half of Louis' reign when the King was more susceptible to ecclesiastical opinion.

In contrast to Robert's and Gerald's protests the contemporary canonists were reticent to discuss[151] and the papacy reluctant to prohibit the temporal and spiritual *regalia* as practiced in France and England. For example, in 1210 when Master Thomas d'Argenteuil, who was granted a prebend by the King during the vacancy of Laon, was contested by another candidate, Pope Innocent III refrained from judging the validity of the case but asked the King to have the affair decided by a local commission of legal experts.[152] Although the Lateran Council of 1215 forbade the laity to dispose of ecclesiastical goods, it did not specify regalian practices.[153] Elsewhere it attempted to limit the vacancy of cathedrals and abbeys to three months, which would have curbed but not abolished the abuse.[154] Although during the thirteenth century the Plantagenets gave no sign of foregoing their rights, these privileges came under increasing criticism in France during the reign of Philip Augustus.[155] Protesting against the spiritual *regalia* in 1208 and 1209, the bishops of Troyes and Amiens persuaded the King to renounce his claims over their sees. More important, between 1189 and 1209 Philip Augustus withdrew temporal regalian rights over the bishoprics of Autun, Arras, Langres, Auxerre, Nevers, and Mâcon. The protests of Robert of Courson and Gerald of Wales reflected, therefore, an effort among the French clergy to be free of this lucrative royal right.

@ CHAPTER XII @

Epilogue: Contemporary Princes

PETER the Chanter and his colleagues approached political questions as casuists. Although such developments as the formation of
feudal monarchy or the Capetian-Angevin rivalry over Normandy
formed the context of their discussion, they wrote not as historians but
as moralists. Not content merely to describe their world, they analyzed it
for the purpose of judging its moral standing. Their task was to apply
general ethical principles to particular cases, but their interest in the individual event was less concerned with who performed the deed than
with what action should be taken. For this reason they chose an impersonal
style to phrase their problems. *Quidem princeps, quidem miles, quidem*:
"a certain prince," "a certain knight," "a certain person," was their characteristic mode of expression. Dealing with specific cases, they seldom
mentioned names or offered clues to identify the figures they may have
had in mind. It is true that when referring to ecclesiastics they more
frequently named a famous prelate or a notable master, but only on rare
occasions do they identify a contemporary prince. When such a name is
pronounced, the prince is noted not so much for his political acumen
as for his piety, beneficence, or besetting vices—qualities which churchmen might be expected to applaud or condemn. Like those of famous
masters, the deeds of contemporary princes were made to serve as moral
exempla to embellish the theologians' teachings.

The one striking exception to this approach may be found in Gerald
of Wales.[1] Throughout his voluminous writings he provides scores of
colorful sketches of contemporary political celebrities. Gerald's studies in
Paris, his duties as archdeacon in the British Isles, and his missions to
Rome acquainted him with a wide circle of notables. His frustrating failure to secure the bishopric of Saint David's, which was the underlying
fact of his life, sharpened his sensibilities to personalities. Unafraid
either to mention names or to voice decided prejudices, Gerald displayed
hostility towards the Plantagenets and almost treasonable admiration
for the Capetians, attitudes which have been well known to subsequent
historians. Most of his observations on contemporary princes are recorded
in the *De principis instructione*, composed late in his career, when the
disillusioned Gerald was farthest removed from his days in Paris under

the Chanter's influence and most inclined to nourish idiosyncrasies. His comments alone therefore cannot be taken as representative of the opinions of the masters at Paris.

Set within French history the Chanter's generation spanned the last decades of King Louis VII (1137-1180) and the first decades of King Philip Augustus (1180-1223). As students and masters they found themselves in a city which became the true capital of France during their lifetime. Peter the Chanter's services were employed by Philip Augustus on several occasions, and it is known that the theologian had personal conversations with his sovereign.[2] The contacts between the other masters and the Capetians, however, can only be left to conjecture.

Louis VII is only briefly seen in the pages of Robert of Courson.[3] Not only was Robert concerned with his divorce from Eleanor of Aquitaine, as will be seen,* but he also found occasion to remark upon the pious king's austerities. After 1149, when Louis returned from the humiliating failure of the Second Crusade, his fastings and other religious observances became common knowledge. The chronicler William of Newburg reported Eleanor's reproach that she thought she had married a king but found herself bound to a monk.[4] Declining in old age the king increased his austerities, which aggravated his ill health. In a passage treating conditional vows Robert of Courson inquired whether a vow of continence or fasting could be dispensed with for overriding considerations.[5] For example, could a monk of royal lineage leave the cloister to provide an heir for a kingdom whose dynasty was threatened with extinction, or could someone be released from a vow of fasting because of danger to health? To illustrate the last case Robert remembered that King Louis was dispensed from his vow of fasting on bread and water on Fridays because he was so weakened that he was incapable of doing justice on that day. In Robert's opinion this dispensation was justified by its evident utility to the poor and the church. Gerald of Wales was also aware of Louis' Friday fasts, which the king persisted in despite his counsellors' warning that they endangered the kingdom.[6] To Louis' virtue of abstinence Gerald added continence, which similarly imperilled the King's health in the opinion of his doctors.[7] When his advisors proposed a young girl for the royal recovery, Louis steadfastly refused for the love of his queen Adèle.

Despite Louis' reputation for continence Gerald judged that the King's supreme achievement was to have fathered a son, the future King Philip Augustus. After waiting twenty-one years Louis finally received his long desired heir on the night of 21 August 1165. Philip's birth left a telling impression on the memory of Gerald, who was a young man at the time pursuing his studies in Paris.[8] In old age Gerald recalled the noise

* See below, p. 335.

and excitement of the night, the pealing of the bells, the bonfires in the squares, the rejoicing in the streets, and the prophetic utterance of a poor woman: "Tonight is born to us a boy who will be a hammer to your king." The eventual triumph of Philip Augustus over the Plantagenets came constantly to Gerald's mind as he composed his *De principis instructione*, particularly because it was already accomplished in many respects.[9] His explanation for the Capetian success was their superior personal virtues and respect for the church's rights.[10] In glowing terms he expatiated upon the justice, the modesty, the sobriety, even the marital faithfulness (!) of the French kings, in contrast to the blackness of the Plantagenet soul. Instead of lions and other ferocious beasts the French house had appropriately chosen a flower to emblazon their standard. Contrasting the peace and justice of France with the war and tyranny of England, Gerald concluded the book with a treasonable suggestion that the two kingdoms be united under one monarch.[11]

By comparison to Gerald's effusive adulation, the other masters are nearly mute about Philip Augustus. Peter the Chanter, who probably knew Philip better than the others, offers only one comment on the king.[12] Discussing the avoidance of unseemly swearing, Peter commends his sovereign (*rex noster*) for purging his court of ignominious oaths on God or the saints by fining the rich five shillings to be paid to the lepers or by commanding the poor or under-aged to be dunked fully clothed. Following the royal example other princes had instituted similar penalties in their courts. After reporting Philip's action, Peter proceeded to decry the notorious swearing of gamblers.[13] The royal historians Rigord and William the Breton also testified that the young king had a special distaste for the swearing of gamblers in courts and taverns. Overhearing such profanity on one occasion, he ordered dunking and immediately issued an edict against blasphemous oaths.[14] Many years later, in a letter to the Archbishop of Reims, Pope Innocent III supported the King's measures against ignominious oaths with ecclesiastical sanctions.[15] By the early thirteenth century the Capetian aversion to swearing had become proverbial. Gerald of Wales contrasted it with the Plantagenets' infamous habit of swearing by the members of God,[16] and Jacques de Vitry further embroidered *exempla* to illustrate Capetian sobriety.[17] Over a half century later Philip's illustrious grandson Louis IX renewed the ordinance against blasphemy which, according to the legist Beaumanoir, was enforced throughout the French kingdom.[18]

The rulers of France comprised not only royalty but also a great number of local lords ranging from great barons to the most petty seigneur. Although vassals or subvassals of the king, they were for practical purposes princes in their own lands. Again, when the masters discussed contemporary princes they rarely mentioned specific names. One baron, however, of a preceding generation assumes the stature of a secular hero in their writings. This is Thibaut (1090-1152), Count of Blois, Sancerre, Meaux, and Provins and later (1125) of Troyes, Vitry, and Bar-sur-Aube, but generally styled as Count of Champagne. Since Thibaut lived when the house of Blois were rivals of the Capetians, the Count openly conflicted with King Louis VI and Louis VII. Thibaut was also lord over the Cistercian monastery of Clairvaux, and the Count became the friend and protector of Bernard its abbot. Undoubtedly this association with the great abbot raised Thibaut's estimation in the eyes of the theologians.

Count Thibaut's image as reflected in the pages of the Chanter's circle was that of a feudal baron whose virtues were rough and ready. For example, the Chanter pictures him in the *Verbum abbreviatum* as doing speedy justice with a minimum of formalities.[19] Following the precept of Moses (Deut. 19 : 15): "at the mouth of two or three witnesses shall the matter be established," the Count shut off the clamors of contending parties and quickly decided suits by hearing the oaths of the plaintiffs' neighbors. In the short version of the *Verbum abbreviatum* Thibaut is picturesquely described as rendering judgments while standing on one foot.[20] Presumably when the other foot touched ground the trial was over. The Count was remembered for his program of compulsory poor relief when during a severe famine he threatened the rich with heavy *tailles* unless they contributed to the poor.[21] In the masters' opinion Count Thibaut's conspicuous virtue was his generosity and spontaneity in giving alms.[22] To illustrate, the Chanter recounted the following *exemplum*:[23] When the Count of blessed memory left the monastery of Pontigny, he prepared a sumpter horse burdened with shoes and ointment which he personally distributed to the poor, kissing the hands of each recipient. To the monks' inquiry why he did not dispense alms through his servants, Thibaut offered three reasons: "I engender in myself greater love for the poor; I excite among them greater devotion and gratitude so that they will pray for me more frequently and fervently; and I implant a more vivid impression in their hearts." The Count's almsgiving clearly contained an element of spontaneity which exceeded conventional bounds. Jacques de Vitry employed the Chanter's anecdote in his sermons[24] and by the thirteenth century it circulated widely as an example of charity.[25] Somewhat incongruously Gerald of Wales linked Count Thibaut with the Capetians and celebrated the baron's alms to the lepers of Chartres.[26] Just as Louis VII's piety was seen to have its rewards in the exploits of his son Philip, so the advancement of Thibaut's children was regarded as the just recompense for their father's virtue. Three of his sons, Henry of Champagne (d. 1181), Thibaut of Blois (d. 1191) and Stephen of Sancerre (d. 1191) became magnates of France; a fourth, William of White-Hands, became Archbishop of Reims (d. 1202), and a daughter Adèle married King Louis VII to become the mother of Philip Augustus.

Despite the praise lavished on Count Thibaut of Champagne, his liberality had one drawback, at least as it affected Thibaut's friend, Bernard of Clairvaux. The saintly abbot's hostility towards sumptuous buildings in his own order was well known.[27] According to the Chanter, Bernard once bitterly complained to the Bishop of Auxerre that when the Cistercian buildings were thatched cottages, the monks' piety had been effective, but now that Count Thibaut has enlarged them one hundredfold into magnificent stone edifices, the power of God had departed.[28]

Although the circle of theologians who studied and taught at Paris included a number of men from the British Isles, their writings, with the exception of Gerald of Wales', provide even rarer glimpses of contemporary English princes than of those of France. Discussing the repression of lusts (in his commentary to the Psalms) Peter the Chanter enumerated cases of hermits and holy nuns who mutilated themselves to discourage unwanted attention.[29] Along with a tale of nuns near Jerusalem who amputated their noses to foil pagan ravishers, Peter included the example of the fair nun of Fontevrault who blinded herself because the beauty of her eyes attracted the unwelcome attention of the King of England. This story was undoubtedly popular for it was repeated in a contemporary collection of *exempla*, and by Jacques de Vitry and others.[30] (Later in the thirteenth century Stephen of Bourbon identified the King as Richard.)[31] Although the *exemplum* of the holy nun who sacrificed her eyes to cool the ardor of an enflamed suitor was as ancient as the *Vitae patrum* of the fourth century,[32] the Chanter and his followers attached it to the Plantagenets since it conveniently illustrated the common report that the kings of England were a lusty breed whose passions respected few boundaries. Although Peter's allusion conveys no invidious comparison between Plantagenet promiscuity and the Capetian chastity, Gerald of Wales at a later date spared few pains to depict the debaucheries of King Henry II, contrasting them with the continence of Louis VII.[33]

King Henry II's sole deed to become deeply embedded in the memory of the Parisian masters was his involvement in the murder of Thomas Becket, Archbishop of Canterbury. It will be recalled that early in his career Peter the Chanter had defended Thomas' reputation as a martyr for the church in public debate against Master Roger the Norman, who accused the Archbishop of having betrayed the King.* Later, while treating in his *Summa* the problem of consent to an immoral act, Peter raised the specific example of the assassination and rehearsed its events as narrated by Becket's hagiographers.[34] Enumerating the Archbishop's injuries

* See above, pp. 146, 147.

against the King, Henry had complained that he had badly trained his court if they did not avenge him. Since certain of his courtiers had seized this occasion to kill Thomas, was not the King guilty of the murder? In another version of his *Summa*, while discussing the similar question of committing illicit acts through intermediaries, Peter again turned to Henry and Thomas.[35] If the King dispatched a command ordering the death of someone overseas, but later revoked it because it had been issued in a moment of passion, was he not still guilty of the crime if his counter-command arrived too late? Recounting the pertinent facts of the Arch-bishop's death, once again the masters condemned King Henry as responsible. Gerald of Wales expressed his rancor towards the monarch by praising the martyred Thomas who had steadfastly resisted tyranny to the end of his life.[36] Writing after Becket's elevation to sainthood in 1173, the Chanter and his followers adopted the saint as their foremost hero, whose deeds were a continual inspiration, but the Thomas of their writings was not the chancellor, the man of politics, but the converted Archbishop and holy martyr.[37]

The austerity of Louis VII, the sobriety of Philip Augustus, the benefi-cence of Thibaut of Champagne, the lechery and tyranny of Henry II—such characterizations offer no new insights into the personalities of con-temporary princes, but rather merely repeat common contemporary views. Although revealing little about the rulers of their day, these *exempla* are nonetheless further evidence of prevailing public opinion.

PART
FOUR
MERCHANTS

❧ CHAPTER XIII ❧

The Merchant and His Activities

AS RESIDENTS of Paris the Chanter's circle were not only at an emerging university and the capital of France, but also within a lively commercial environment. The largest urban concentration in northwest Europe at the turn of the century, Paris contained an important gathering of merchants. Across the Seine on the Right Bank the masters could observe the quays where wares were incessantly loaded and discharged, the newly constructed Halles where weekly markets were held, and the honeycomb of streets bustling with mercantile life whose very names evoked the variety of trades. To the southeast of Paris lay the renowned fairs of Champagne which served as the foremost juncture in the north-south trading axis connecting the Mediterranean with northwest Europe. Here the merchants of northern France and England regularly encountered the Italians who were the leading innovators of medieval commerce. The fairs of Champagne represent a stage in commercial development which historians call the age of the travelling merchant, when the long-distance trader accompanied his goods and managed his affairs directly. It was an era in which not only the quantitative volume of distant commerce increased perceptibly, but also qualitative techniques involving investment, exchange, and banking were created and perfected. By the beginning of the fourteenth century the Italians had devised commercial practices sufficient to permit the enterprising merchant to remain at home and to conduct his affairs through agents, thus ushering in a new age of the sedentary merchant. Although the Paris theologians were not concerned with the quantitative aspects of economic life, they did take notice of the qualitative changes, and their writings shed valuable light on the commercial techniques which they witnessed.

Within the medieval universities the academic consideration of business pertained primarily to the Romanists. Roman law contained the most sophisticated treatment of sale, barter, hire, loan, and partnerships. These Roman legal principles were not always and everywhere followed in practice, but they presented a point of departure for academic discussion. Since church writers also dealt with such aspects of mercantile life as dishonest gain and usury, the canonists similarly developed theories on these subjects. By the twelfth century, therefore, the lawyers, both Roman and canon, had created a legal framework for the scholarly discussion of commercial techniques. The theologians of the early twelfth century were not generally concerned with such mundane matters. The reluctance of Peter Abelard, Gilbert de la Porrée, or Peter the Lombard to treat these problems was inherited at the end of the century by theologians more inclined to abstraction. Peter of Poitiers, for example, the foremost exponent of the Lombard's school, preferred to leave usury and similar matters to the canonists.[1] Since the practical interests of Peter the Chanter's group encouraged them to investigate all spheres of human activity, like the canonists they lectured on and debated issues relevant to the merchant. In the realm of business, however, they clearly followed the lawyers' steps. While the Romanists and canonists outlined a framework, the theologians provided a richness of detail concerning commercial activities.

By the twelfth century the merchant profession still labored under a traditional onus of social hostility in western Europe.[2] The ancient Graeco-Roman civilization harbored ambivalent feelings about the business man which tended to be less than complimentary. When the father of fair Nausica in Homer's *Odyssey* wished to add insult to injury to the half-drowned Odysseus, he called him a merchant. While both Plato and Aristotle recognized the usefulness of trade to society in a general way, yet in specific instances they forbade commerce to their first-class citizens because of its inherent dangers towards avarice and immoderation.[3] Although conceding a certain respectability to wholesalers, particularly if they acquired landed estates like good Romans, Cicero despised petty retailers because of their inveterate lies and thievings.[4] Since Classical civilization was pervaded with this distrust, it is not remarkable that the Church Fathers interpreted Christ's enigma about rich men and "eyes of needles" and His action of expelling the merchants from the temple in a sense unfavorable to men of commerce. From the pens of the Greek Fathers Basil the Great and Gregory Nazianzus and the Latin Tertullian and Jerome flowed reproach for merchants and their besetting sins.[5] In a passage reminiscent of the poet Horace, Ambrose of Milan regretfully observed the merchants' ships which like the wind churned the seas in restless pursuit of gain.[6] In sum, the spokesmen of pagan and Christian Antiquity accused commercial classes of two characteristic failings: Their search for profit led to both unquenchable cupidity and the irresistible temptation to employ fraudulent means.

The twelfth-century collections of ancient authority picked up these notes and reechoed them as shibboleths against merchants.[7] In canon law Gratian's *Decretum* reproduced a statement of Pope Leo I that it was difficult to transact commercial affairs without committing sin.[8] In another place Gratian fashioned a rubric which baldly stated that buying cheap to sell dear was shameful gain.[9] Later canonists inserted passages called *paleae* into the *Decretum*, such as Cassiodorus' accusation that merchants burden their wares more with perjuries than with prices,[10] and an apocryphal homily entitled *Ejiciens* originating from the fifth or sixth centuries, but falsely attributed to the Greek Father John Chrysostom.[11] Commenting on Christ's expelling the merchants from the temple, the author concluded that no merchant can please God. Also rehearsing these hostile notes, Peter the Chanter quoted Horace's line about the indefatigable merchant who rushes to the Indies.[12] Like Ambrose he was doubtful about the merchants of his own day who braved peril and brigands to reach the fairs and to make their profit. Robert of Courson included those of merchants and retailers among morally dubious professions requiring special attention in the confessional.[13]

These obloquies prompted the canonists to investigate more thoroughly the moral aspects of the commercial profession.[14] Beginning with Rufinus and culminating with Huguccio the canonists analyzed the merchant's functions in an effort to devise a moral justification for his place in society. As a preliminary to their analysis, they distinguished the artisan from the merchant. The artisan was defined as one who bought materials and improved their quality through additional expenses and labor. Since the sale of this merchandise at a higher price was fully justified as remuneration for his contribution of labor and expenses, these artisan activities were permitted to the laity and even to those clergy whose ecclesiastical income was not sufficient. Although most theologians took little notice, this preliminary definition of the craftsman was fully accepted by Thomas of Chobham.[15] To distinguish the artisan from the merchant, the canonists, again followed by Chobham,[16] defined the merchant as one who bought wares cheaply and sold them at a high price without material improvement. Although the commercial activity of pure buying and selling was forbidden to the clergy, it was permitted to the laity.

From the time of Augustine churchmen recognized that the merchant's chief service to society was transportation.[17] This theme was occasionally heard in the twelfth century,[18] but it was Thomas of Chobham at the beginning of the following century who reexpressed it with new force.[19] Explaining that merchants performed the necessary function of finding goods in areas of abundance and carrying them to areas of scarcity, he stressed that distribution was their chief social contribution. Since "a laborer is worthy of his hire," according to Augustine, the merchant should be permitted profits to compensate labor and provide a livelihood.[20] The canonists constructed a justification of mercantile profits by elaborating these suggestions. Considering the economic origins of these gains, Rufinus proposed that if a merchant contributed expenses and labor to his ventures, he could realize his income honorably.[21] Only the absence of expenses and labor, as for example in affairs of pure speculation, vitiated such gain. On the other hand, Huguccio investigated the intentions of the merchant.[22] If he conducted his affairs to provide for himself and his family, he was permitted a profit. If, however, he engaged in business solely for gratifying an insatiable greed, his earnings were judged immoral. Rufinus' scheme of allowing mercantile profits to compensate for expenses and labor was incorporated by Thomas of Chobham.[23] In effect Chobham followed the canonists by providing moral justification for the mercantile profession. Since the merchant's functions were precisely defined and distinguished from artisans', since his services of distribution were appreciated, and since under specified conditions he was entitled to mercantile profits, in the considered opinion of such ecclesiastics the merchant could live with honor in medieval society. During the twelfth and thirteenth centuries the merchant was engaged in business so important that historians have termed this period the "Commercial Revolution." During the same period the churchmen provided the mercantile revolutionary with essential social and moral justification.

Although the canonists and theologians disentangled the merchant's profits from the implications of avarice, they also had to deal with charges that the mercantile profession was irresistibly drawn into fraudulent practices. Augustine suggested a solution to this problem by distinguishing between the trader and his trade:[24] if perjuries and deceptions arise in commerce, they are due to human frailty and not necessarily to the profession of trade. Other artisans such as shoemakers and farmers are capable of fraudulent dealings, yet their professions are not considered evil. Beyond this preliminary distinction, however, further clarification was required. In Roman law contracts of sale, barter, hire, and the like were normally considered *bona fides* actions which excluded all forms of *dolus* or fraud.[25] When *dolus* was defined in Justinian as "any cunning, deceit, or contrivance used to defraud, deceive, or cheat another,"[26] one of the problems of the medieval Romanists was to determine how such fraud affected a contract of sale.[27] In the first half of the century a scheme was devised to divide fraud into two basic kinds: intentional fraud (*dolus ex proposito*) and a mistake or error of fact (*dolus re ipsa*). Intentional fraud, or *dolus* proper, which gives rise to a sale, nullifies the contract altogether and it is no longer binding. Intentional fraud which is incidental to the sale—that is, the fraud did not cause the contract, but without it the parties would have agreed to different terms—does not nullify the contract, but the damages suffered, even of the smallest order, may be remedied. Unintentional fraud or mistake in fact, which is not true *dolus*, has no remedy in law, unless the damages in certain kinds of contracts are unusually large. This Romanist scheme for analyzing fraud in commercial contracts was adopted by the canonists by the beginning of the thirteenth century.[28]

Since churchmen are against sin, the Parisian theologians, of course, can be counted in the battle against commercial fraud. From the Chanter's circle preachers such as Jacques de Vitry denounced the chicaneries of the marketplace,[29] sometimes with a touch of humor. "For seven years I have been buying my meat from you," related Jacques of a customer who hoped to obtain a more reasonable price from his butcher. "Seven years of eating my meat," responded the butcher in amazement, "and you are still alive!"[30] It is a simple matter to be against fraud; to define it is more difficult. While the theologians did not directly follow the legist's elaborate distinctions, they yet arrived at similar conclusions. Referring to the Romanists and canonists, Peter the Chanter distinguished merchants who traded with good intent from those who sold with fraudulent designs.[31] Robert of Courson declared that retailers who fraudulently sold above the just price were held to do restitution above the just value according to the estimation of a priest.[32] Elsewhere noting the common temptation at the fairs to swear falsely, he maintained that any merchant who perjured himself for the sake of a higher price was guilty of mortal sin.[33] What Peter and Robert had in mind approximated the intentional *dolus* of the Romanists, and mortal sin and restitution beyond the just price were the theological equivalents to the Roman law remedies of voiding the contract and seeking full redress in law.

In addition to conscious deception over prices, the theologians also recognized the Roman law principle which obliged sellers to reveal latent defects in the goods.[34] The Chanter offered specific advice to priests who resided in commercial quarters and administered penance to butchers and other retailers.[35] If a butcher deceived an unwary buyer with tainted meat not only should he restore the price, but also perform penance for homicide because he had endangered the life of his customer. Even merchants who attempted to deceive buyers by dyeing cheap cloth to resemble better material were required to restore what they gained from such practices. Elsewhere Peter inquired how far the responsibility of the original seller extended in subsequent resales of defective goods.[36] Robert of Flamborough insisted on penitential satisfaction for concealing flaws,[37] and Robert of Courson proposed that prelates supervise the markets to prevent the sale of defective items such as lame horses and spoiled meat.[38] If their efforts were unavailing, policing the market should be delegated to the prince, as was often the practice in contemporary France and England. Since Carolingian times, moreover, secular and ecclesiastical authorities had made provisions to inspect weights and measures,[39] and on occasion princes had attempted to standardize units of measurement. For example, in 1197 the chief justiciar issued an assize to make uniform throughout England the weights and measures of common commodities such as bread, wine, and ale, an enactment which was renewed in Magna Carta.[40] When Raoul Ardent, Robert of Courson, Peter of Poitiers of Saint-Victor, and Thomas of Chobham demanded restitution of all gains derived from fraudulent units of measurement, they were thus repeating a commonplace.[41]

In addition to supporting secular remedies against fraudulent practices, churchmen devised other commercial restrictions which were religious in nature. The most widespread was the prohibition of Sunday commerce, derived from the Old Testament. Although ecclesiastical measures forbidding Sunday markets appeared in the Carolingian era, they often fell into disuse during the subsequent centuries. It is apparent that by the twelfth century Sunday markets were commonly being held in France and England. In a brief discussion of labor permissible on the Lord's day Peter the Chanter made no reference to commercial activities,[42] but there is evidence of a sabbatarian campaign which can be associated with his circle. In 1200 and again in 1201 Eustace, Abbot of Saint-Germer-de-Fly, conducted a crusade against Sunday markets in England with such force that it aroused the chroniclers' attention.[43] Although his first effort had little effect, his second mission caused a number of English markets to switch their dates from Sunday to other days in the week. The sabbatarian movement gained momentum in England during the reign of King Henry III and may even have had influence in France.[44] Since the abbey of Saint-Germer-de-Fly was located in the diocese of Beauvais not far from Hodenc, the birthplace of the Chanter, it received benefactions from the lords of Hodenc.[45] The chroniclers Roger of Hoveden and Ralph of Coggeshall associate Abbot Eustace with the preaching of Foulques de Neuilly, who, as has been seen, was directly inspired by the Chanter.[46] In another passage Roger of Hoveden added to these preachers the names of Peter of Roissy and Robert of Courson, who worked intimately with Peter the Chanter.[47] Whether directly inspired by the Chanter or not, Eustace of Fly's sabbatarian reforms found later support from the English members of the Parisian circle. Gerald of Wales took notice of Eustace's work in England, which reinforced former attempts to abolish Sunday markets during the reign of King Henry II.[48] Thomas of Chobham was likewise against Sunday commerce, although he allowed specific concessions.[49] Since those who transported merchandise and who ran kitchens could not always avoid working on Sundays and other feast days, they should make other compensations for the holy days which they violated. In the diocesan statutes for Canterbury Stephen Langton admonished parish priests to forbid Sunday commerce with ecclesiastical sanctions.[50]

The theologians also discussed merchants' responsibility for selling merchandise of a dangerous nature. For example, Peter the Chanter declared that a merchant who sold poison for antidotal use should inquire into the buyer's credentials or demand an oath that the buyer would not illegally employ the poison against others.[51] Similar guarantees should be exacted from purchasers of swords. Failure to take these precautions would render the vendor guilty in the penitential forum of homicide and liable to restitution if misdeeds resulted. Finally, in the age of crusades, churchmen devised their equivalent of "trading with the enemy acts." In the Lateran Council of 1179 Pope Alexander III decreed that Christians who sold arms to the Saracens or transported merchandise for the infidels were to be excommunicated and their goods seized by Christian princes.[52] The churches in the maritime cities were responsible for publishing this ban. Recalling an incident which involved this prohibition, Peter the Chanter reported that certain Christian merchants intended to sail from Marseilles to Alexander with a cargo of arms for the Mohammedans.[53] Although the citizens of Marseilles were unable to prevent the traders' departure, three bishops who were passing through the seaport on pilgrimage to the Holy Land formally declared them excommunicate. The merchants' ship had not sailed more than two leagues from the port when it suddenly sank and all were drowned. To the Chanter this incident demonstrated the efficacy of a righteous sentence of excommunication, even when the bishops had no parochial jurisdiction, but the story also illustrates the difficulty of preventing trading with the Saracens by normal means. Peter also considered the perplexing problem of Christians inhabiting Mohammedan lands who were compelled to manufacture arms against their fellow believers.[54] Since resistance would have entailed death, the Chanter concluded that martyrdom was not required of the ordinary Christian unless it was the general will of the faithful. In this case overpowering coercion exonerated the individual Christian from the penalties of the Lateran Council.

By means of well-defined contracts of sale (*emptio-venditio*), barter (*permutatio*), lease (*locatio-conductio*), and loan (*mutuum*) the medieval Roman lawyers distinguished the varied activities of the merchant. With the important exception of loans, the canonists had by the end of the twelfth century adopted the Romanist analysis of these contracts.[55] Among these, sale was undoubtedly the most necessary to ordinary commercial life. By and large the Romanists and canonists of the late twelfth century accepted the ancient Roman legal principle of freedom of bargaining which declared any price freely agreed upon by buyer and seller without fraud as the legally sanctioned price which could not be rescinded under normal circumstances.[56] The only recourse for wrongs suffered in a free bargaining was provided by the doctrine of *laesio enormis*, which stated that contracts in which the price was grossly unfair could either be rescinded or adjusted to the fair value.[57] The limits for this exceptional remedy were set at below one-half the just price or above the just price raised to its half. According to the Romanists and canonists, therefore, *bona fides* prices which did not exceed these extreme limits had no remedy in law and stood as agreed in the bargain.

Among the theologians of Paris only Peter the Chanter and Thomas of Chobham paid attention to the lawyers' theories of price determination. Referring to the laws and canons on sale, Peter alludes briefly to *laesio enormis*[58] and Thomas includes a succinct outline of the theory in his *Summa confessorum*.[59] More important, the theologians begin to distinguish their theory of sale from that of the legists. The Chanter noted that according to the laws one was required to do restitution for prices beyond the limits of *laesio enormis*, but according to the canons restitution was required even within those limits.[60] Although the term "canons" does not necessarily refer to the canonists, Peter differentiates his theories from those of the lawyers by distinguishing between canons and laws. Elsewhere, in a passing reference, Peter mentions the excommunication of an *épicier* who sold his wares for more than the just price, a punishment unintelligible under the Romanist and canonist system.[61] Other theologians underscore the differences suggested by the Chanter. Within a list of questionable commercial practices Robert of Courson places merchants who are accustomed to selling wares above the just price, and elsewhere he states that those who sell above the just price commit mortal sin.[62] Finding contracts of sale and of loan comparable, Stephen Langton notes that just as a seller who receives more than the just price sins mortally so one who receives more than he has loaned is guilty of usury.[63] Among the requirements of a just contract of sale Raoul Ardent lists the just price.[64] Expressing the difference between the two theories most clearly, Thomas of Chobham declares that although human law requires restitution only if the price is beyond one-half the just price, divine law demands restitution even if the mistake involves a mere pittance.[65] While the Romanists and canonists refused to remedy any price set in a free bargain unless it exceeded the limits of *laesio enormis*, the theologians insisted that the price represent the fair value of the commodity. In contrast to the legists, the theologians at Paris insisted on the full enforcement of the just price.

One important problem remained: How was the just price or fair value of goods to be determined? Not only necessary to the legists for determining the limits of *laesio enormis*, the estimation of the just price was central to the theologians' theories. In addition to sale it served many other purposes. As a preliminary matter, Romanists, canonists, and theologians all recognized the obvious fact that prices differed according to place and time and could only be determined for specific instances.[66] According to the Romanists at the turn of the century "a thing was valued at that price for which it could be commonly sold." In brief, the just price was the going or current price which included both free competitive prices and officially regulated prices according to the actual market.[67] While the contemporary canonists employed the factors of labor and expenses to justify mercantile profits, when they estimated the just price they accepted the current or market price.[68] They made no attempt to correlate their theories of justifying profit with methods of determining the just price.[69]

Although the theologians disputed the legists' neglect of enforcing the full just price, they nonetheless accepted the current market price as the fair value of commodities.[70] Peter the Chanter frequently assumed that the true value of goods was their going price on the market.[71] When Stephen Langton investigated whether a seller who profits beyond the just price should restore to the buyer or to the church, a corrector of one of his manuscripts supplied the following marginal notation: "some people say that a thing is worth as much as it can be sold."[72] Another corrector added that this opinion was shared by the Chanter of London, who was Benedict of Sansetun, later Bishop of Rochester (1214). One cannot be certain that Langton agreed with Benedict of Sansetun, but Robert of Courson, his colleague at Paris, did accept the market price as the just price. In discussing a special problem of selling priories, he equated the usual course of the market with the just estimation.[73] Elsewhere, Robert advised the merchant to observe prices closely as they fluctuated according to time and place.[74] If he valued his goods at ten shillings and estimated his labor at an additional shilling, he could wait until he found a market on which to sell his wares for eleven shillings. Robert's discussion represents an attempt to reconcile the theory that profits were justified by labor and expenses with the theory that just value was the current market price. Implicit in this statement was the observation that the going price must remunerate labor and expenses or in other words, that production will not continue below cost. In the long run the current price tends to coincide with the cost price. If the market price falls below cost, some producers will drop out; if it rises above, others will be induced to supply the market. Although these implications of Robert's statement anticipated what economists in the nineteenth century called the "law of costs," little notice was taken of the concept until the modern era.[75]

◎ CHAPTER XIV ◎

Credit, Investment, and Exchange

IN ONE FORM or another some element of credit is present in any economic system, however primitive.[1] Even under the most rudimentary agricultural conditions such as existed in early medieval Europe peasants borrowed seed, provisions, implements, or cash at the time of planting to pay back at harvest. During the twelfth century not only agriculture but also industry and commerce expanded rapidly, which increased the demand for credit. Craftsmen and merchants required credit to purchase raw materials and merchandise which they intended to repay after realizing their profits. This need for capital was most strikingly apparent in the towns of western Europe where industry and commerce were concentrated. Moreover, others possessing surplus cash or goods were tempted to invest them in industrial or commercial enterprises to realize more profit. At the turn of the twelfth and thirteenth centuries the expanding demand for credit, capital, and investment prompted varied techniques, many of which were developed by the Italian merchants. Partnerships were formed; payment was deferred in sales; exchange banking was employed to extend credit; and loans were issued in which interest was charged either openly or in various guises. Profit from lending, which in modern terms is called interest, was denoted as usury (*usura*) in the Middle Ages, while interest (*interesse*) had a more restricted meaning, as will be seen. In medieval times the subject of usury demanded special attention because the church forbade all remuneration from loans. Since the ecclesiastical position on usury had wide ramifications, the Parisian theologians' views concerning credit and investment must be seen within its context.

Although the churchmen's definition of usury was relatively vague until the second half of the twelfth century, the papacy began, with Alexander III, to pay attention to these matters, which in turn stimulated the church lawyers. In the late twelfth and early thirteenth centuries it was chiefly the canonists who formulated the major principles of usury.[2] When the theologians considered the problem of credit, they entered territory well occupied by the canonists. Working within the legal context, they applied the canonists' rules to concrete situations which arose in commercial practice. After decrying the evils of usury in rhetorical terms in his *Verbum abbreviatum*, Peter the Chanter proposed that the hidden aspects could be more conveniently elucidated in disputation.[3] Undoubtedly he was referring to his own *questiones*, where he probed commercial activities for traces of usury. His followers similarly discussed concrete examples in the light of the canonists' principles which not only reveal their theories on credit but also cast light on contemporary commercial practices.

THE DEFINITION OF USURY

Like the canonists, the theologians made a preliminary distinction between spiritual and corporal usury.[4] The first kind, which multiplies the spiritual benefits of God's grace, is laudable, but corporal usury which involves economic activities is forbidden. In the *Decretum* Gratian collected Patristic authorities which broadened the definition of corporal usury. Augustine stated that usury consisted of demanding back more than what was given.[5] Jerome termed it any form of superabundance,[6] and Ambrose devised the formula that usury was "anything which exceeds the principal" (*quodcumque sorti accedit*), which was adopted by Gratian.[7] Since this latitude of interpretation implicated all forms of economic gain, the canonists found it necessary to introduce qualifications. In general they agreed that usury consisted of any increment realized from a loan (*mutuum*), thereby exonerating profits from other contracts such as sale, hire, and the like.[8] When the Parisian theologians proposed definitions of usury they invariably accepted one of the Gratian formulations, but they always understood it in terms of a loan.[9]

By and large the twelfth-century canonists took few pains to justify the church's position against usury on rational grounds, but were content to cite the Old Testament prohibitions and the Gospel command to "lend freely expecting nothing in return" (Luke 6 : 35).[10] One exception may be found in the *palea Ejiciens* which was inserted into the *Decretum* some time before the time of Huguccio.[11] In somewhat confused fashion this authority suggested three arguments which were followed by the Parisian theologians. In the first place the usurer gains from the work of others. Whether discussing teachers, judges, lawyers, or merchants, time and again the Parisian theologians justified economic profit in all professions on the grounds of labor. To Peter the Chanter and his followers the usurer was immoral because he profited without labor, making a livelihood even while sleeping.[12] Furthermore, *Ejiciens* implied that the usurer sold something which belonged to God alone, which the Chanter and Chobham interpreted as the sale of time, a divine gift to all men.[13] Finally, *Ejiciens* suggested that money was essentially sterile. Thomas of Chobham maintained that unlike a fruitful vineyard, money lying in a chest produces no natural yield.[14] Stephen Langton

271

similarly held that usurious practices were contrary to natural law, but he did not specify in what manner.[15] Only one version of the Chanter's *questiones* elaborated natural law arguments against usury. Since a loan (*mutuum*) was fundamentally a benevolent contract provided by natural law for aiding the destitute, any attempt to profit from someone else's need was a violation of natural law.[16] But Langton's and the Chanter's arguments were only the rudimentary beginning of an elaborate philosophical justification based on reason and natural law which was constructed by the theologians of the thirteenth century.[17]

The canonists and theologians had no doubt that a lender who demanded remuneration from a *mutuum* committed mortal sin, but what of a borrower who paid usury? A decretal of Pope Alexander III to the Archbishop of Palermo seemed to allow no exception.[18] Asked whether it was permissible to borrow at usury to redeem captives held by Saracens, the Pope replied that the clear teaching of Scripture granted no dispensation for usury. If this statement implied that the borrower as well as the lender was involved in mortal sin, it was contradicted by papal practice. On one occasion Pope Alexander himself ordered the archpriest and canons of Pisa to borrow at usury if money could not be obtained gratuitously, and he or his successors would repay the loan.[19] Ignoring the isolated prohibition, the canonists followed the papal practice. Huguccio declared that the borrower was involved in mortal sin only if he borrowed at usury when other alternatives were available.[20] Succeeding canonists exonerated the borrower's guilt if he was driven by dire necessity to seek a loan at usury, a solution which was followed by the theologians.

Peter the Chanter offered preliminary observations[21] which Robert of Courson amplified. After considering arguments which associated the borrower with the guilt of the lender, Robert of Courson envisaged three situations.[22] The first involved a borrower in need of money who enticed a lender with promises of reward, such as contemporary prelates who offered benefices to the sons of usurers. This sort of borrower knowingly and willingly participates in the sin of the usurer. A second case concerned merchants not in need of money but who for the sake of trade borrow at usury and thereby sin. Finally, when a needy borrower asks a lender for a gratuitous loan according to the Gospel command and is refused except at usury, he can throw the increment at the usurer's feet and be free from complicity. To illustrate this last situation Robert cited the example of a bishop who having made a crusading vow was unable to secure sufficient sums except on usurious terms.[23] If the bishop exhausted all alternatives, he could in the last instance resort to a usurer. Thomas of Chobham[24] and Stephen Langton[25] were in accord with Courson that necessity must be the determining factor in judging a usurious transaction. Langton and Master Martin advised the borrower first to proceed with the formalities of seeking the loan gratuitously in order to clear his intentions.[26] It was a greater sin, Langton added, to seek credit from a novice usurer than from an established one, just as it was more wicked to frequent a young rather than a seasoned prostitute.[27] Similarly it was more sinful to pay usury to a Christian than to a Jew.[28] The importance of necessity to justify the borrowers' recourse to usurious loans is illustrated by surviving charters. In Normandy and Flanders during the twelfth and thirteenth centuries, where credit operations have been studied, borrowers frequently stated in their contracts that they were compelled to borrow at usurious terms because of extreme necessity or unusual circumstances such as preparations for a crusade.[29]

The Chanter, Courson, and Chobham added one final justification which permitted a borrower to pay usury.[30] If someone swore an oath to pay usury to a lender, he must respect the oath, although he could seek redress in the ecclesiastical courts afterwards. This decision was derived from a decretal of Pope Alexander III which held that the paying of usury was preferred over the breaking of oaths.[31]

In Fraudem Usurarum

To the popes and canonists of the late twelfth century the definition of usury as any profit exacted from a *mutuum* did not sufficiently embrace the scope of prohibited activities. An opinion of Augustine, restated in the *Decretum*, suggested that one was a usurer who not only realized such gains but also expected them.[32] The factor of usurious intention was emphasized by Pope Urban III (1185-1187) when he clarified the position that in the confessional even the hope of usury made a merchant a usurer,[33] thus providing churchmen the right to search for hidden forms of usury and to investigate apparently licit commercial contracts for usurious intentions. These practices, which the canonists called *in fraudem usurarum*,[34] were the various guises and concealments to which Peter the Chanter referred in his *Verbum abbreviatum* and which he described as "interior usury" in his *Summa de sacramentis*.[35]

1. Lending Cheap, Returning Dear

A specific example of usurious fraud noted in the Chanter's *Verbum abbreviatum* was the practice of lending goods when they were cheap to be returned when they were valued more dearly.[36] Its simplest form was to lend so many measures of grain in time of plenty to be repaid in time of dearth. Even though the transaction did not involve money both Augustine and Ambrose maintained that usury could be committed in goods such as grain, wine, and merchandise as well.[37] Peter conceded that in this form the transaction was not overtly usurious, but advocated that restitution be made for the increased value, and his conclusion was followed by Robert of Courson and Stephen Langton.[38] Robert of Flamborough, however, maintained that the lender could not be held accountable for the change in value.[39] Thomas of Chobham further exonerated the transaction if it could be established that the gain compensated damages incurred for a delay in returning the goods.[40] If a rich man, however, lent grain to the poor in time of dearth to be returned in time of plenty, the Chanter, like the canonist Huguccio, judged the transaction not only legitimate but also meritorious as a form of poor relief.[41]

2. Credit Sales

In the Chanter's mind the practice of loaning cheap and returning dear was closely associated with credit sales, which the canonists interpreted as contracts combining sale and loan.[42] A common form consisted of buying goods to be paid for at a later date. Since the contract price was set higher than the present value because of deferred payment, was the increased price a profit on the loan and thereby a disguise for usury? Treating this problem in a decretal to the Archbishop of Genoa, Pope Alexander III declared that although the external features of the transaction were not usurious, he judged it sinful if the seller was certain to gain from the delay.[43] If, however, there was reasonable doubt as to the market value of the goods at the future time of payment, the increased price was justified. When the Parisian theologians discussed credit sale, they also envisaged an alternative practice in which a buyer paid for goods to be received at a future date. For the deferment of delivery he received a lower price than the current price, thus advancing credit to the seller. This latter form of credit sale was not included in canon law until the time of Pope Gregory IX (1234), when it was declared governed by the same principles established by Alexander III.[44] The theologians specified different commercial enterprises in which credit sale was commonly employed. According to the Chanter, a buyer short on cash agreed to a price higher than the current value in exchange for a delay of payment until the next fair,[45] a frequent practice in the cloth trade.[46] Courson maintained that a merchant could scarcely be found who did not, for example, sell an ell of cloth worth ten shillings for the price of twenty-five because of the delay of payment.[47] Such credit was also common in the sale of wool, flax, iron, leather, skins, as well as other merchandise. Robert complained that cellarers and provisioners of religious houses even employed these procedures at the fairs, and Peter accused the Cistercians of selling wool on such terms.[48] Referring to installment buying of houses, the Chanter outlined a case where a buyer might choose between two alternatives: either to pay the present cash value of thirty pounds or to pay forty pounds in future installments.[49] To Peter the customary procedure of installment buying was usurious because the higher price was clearly based on the delay of time. As indicated by the Chanter's solution, the theologians condemned credit sales of both kinds where the future gain was fixed and certain.[50] In the Councils of Paris (1213) and Rouen (1214) Robert of Courson proceeded beyond the principle of Alexander III by simply affixing the guilt and penalties of usury on those who sold dearer on time.[51]

Following Pope Alexander III, the Chanter and Courson maintained that the certainty of realizing profit was crucial in judging credit sales. If at the future date of deferred payment or delivery the course of the market was uncertain so that either the buyer or the seller could lose in the transaction, this risk cleared the credit sale from usury.[52] Since these arrangements were justified by reasonable doubt as to the future trend in prices, the canonists often labelled them *venditio sub dubio*. To apply these criteria to credit sales required a knowledge about the seasonal behavior and the patterns of commodity price fluctuations. Thomas of Chobham suggested that a "good man" experienced in the market be selected to judge whether reasonable doubt was present.[53] If after considering the times and circumstances this expert could not predict the future price, the requisite element of uncertainty cleared the transaction of usury. Only those credit sales for which an expert could reasonably foresee a certain profit were condemned as usury.[54]

3. Security—Mortgages

Not only contracts of sale but pledges, gages, or security could disguise usury.[55] During the twelfth century lenders often received pledges of income-producing property which were ostensibly held as security for the loan. When the borrower returned the principal, the lender restored the pledge, but obviously the latter had enjoyed the revenue of the pledge which remunerated the loan. Since the income of the gage did not reduce the principal of the loan, these arrangements were termed *mortgages* (literally, dead pledges) in French and English customary law. Until the end of the twelfth century, for example, *mortgages* based on land were widely employed by Flemish and Norman monasteries for extending credit,[56] and it will be recalled that the Chanter himself borrowed money from a canon of Gerberoy pledging his house as security. Although the terms of the contract are not entirely clear, it appears as if the canon profited from the house during the duration of the loan.* In a concerted effort to stamp out this covert form of usury, Pope Alexander III at the Council of Tours (1163) commanded clerics holding such gages to apply the fruits of the pledge to reduce the principal of the loan after the normal expenses of the gagee had been deducted.[57] In contrast to the *mortgage* this approved arrangement was entitled a *vifgage* (live pledge).

* See above, p. 3.

In subsequent decretals Alexander extended the command to the laity as well.[58] Since churchmen were commonly agreed over the illicit character of the *mortgage* by the end of the twelfth century, the Parisian theologians referred to the practice only in passing. Where they did discuss it, they insisted that the gagee be permitted to deduct his expenses although he was not allowed to retain the revenues without reducing the principal.[59]

Peter the Chanter paid closer attention to the expenses in collecting the income of the property, by posing the case of a gagee who held a vineyard in pledge and who sought from the gagor not only the expense of cultivating the vines but also the price of his labor.[60] The Chanter opposed on two principal grounds the gagee's contention that his labor should be remunerated for what it would have brought if he had expended it in another enterprise. If the gagee had worked on his own vineyard there is no certainty that he would have realized a profit to compensate his labor. By holding the vineyard in gage the gagee denied to the gagor the opportunity to work in his own vineyard and to be compensated for his labor.[61] The Chanter therefore concluded that the gagor was not normally required to remunerate the gagee for his labor.[62] If, however, the gagee substantially improved the vineyard, he could be compensated because the gagor benefited from the improvement. For example, when Peter pledged his own house, he promised to reimburse the gagee for all necessary improvements.[63]

To the ecclesiastical restrictions against *mortgages* the theologians considered one exception. If a layman pledged tithes to a churchman as security for a loan, could the churchman retain the revenues without applying them toward the principal? Since by the twelfth century canon law considered laymen as unlawful possessors of tithes,[64] Peter the Chanter, Stephen Langton, and Thomas of Chobham decided that clerics as rightful possessors could treat the tithes as *mortgages* without incurring censure for usury.[65] The theologians obviously based their opinion on the canon of Pope Alexander III at the Council of Tours (1163) which allowed clerics to employ these means for redeeming benefices unlawfully held by the laity.[66] Again the theologians' teaching closely corresponded to practice. For example, although the Flemish monasteries, in relation to which the problem has been studied, had ceased to accept lands as *mortgages* by the end of the twelfth century, they lent money on tithe *mortgages* with increasing frequency throughout the following century.[67] What if a layman offered to pay a churchman two measures *per annum* from tithes in exchange for a loan?[68] Since the churchman neither held the tithes directly as a pledge nor collected the revenues himself, Peter counselled against this practice. Although the explanation is not explicit, this arrangement resembled a straight payment of usury more than the temporary restoration of unlawfully alienated property. Finally, the

Chanter proceeded from the specific exception to its logical extension by inquiring whether one is justified in employing usurious contracts to recover all unjust losses.[69] In sum, can one recover usury with usury? While Peter did not absolutely forbid, he advised against it because of the appearance of scandal. According to Thomas of Chobham many people taught that if one was in danger of poverty, if no other means were available for recovering damages, and if it could be accomplished without scandal, usury could be exacted to restore unjust losses.[70]

Apparently the papal campaign against the concealment of usury in land pledges became increasingly effective, because a modification of the *mortgage* appeared towards the end of the twelfth century. Instead of receiving an income-producing property as simple security, the lender now bought the property for the amount of the loan with the stipulation to sell it back after a certain time, thereby profiting from the revenues while the property was in his possession.[71] This arrangement merely added sale to the former combination of loan and security. As one of the first ecclesiastics to treat this device, Peter the Chanter modified his attitude during the course of his discussion.[72] He cited three examples of contracts of sale and resale, and the conclusion for each differed slightly from the others.

In the first instance the Chanter envisaged someone driven by necessity to sell his vineyard.[73] If a buyer appeared who bought the vineyard in perpetuity and paid the just price out of pity, could he not resell the vineyard at a later date and retain the income of the intervening period? Peter judged that the case was not usurious for two chief reasons. Since the buyer owned the property in perpetuity he thereby bore the intervening risks of destruction by war, hail, or flood. (As will be seen, immunity from risk was a salient characteristic of a loan.) Since the choice and time of repurchase was entirely at the seller's option, such an arrangement of sale and resale was further free from usurious implications. In a second case Peter cited a similar situation, of one driven by necessity to sell his property who was approached by a buyer who declined to purchase the land in perpetuity at the price of a hundred pounds, but proposed to pay forty pounds for twenty years, so that the seller would not be permanently disinherited.[74] When the time expired the seller would buy back the land at the original price and the buyer would have enjoyed the intervening revenue. Even if the buyer agreed to the original just price and bore all of the intervening risks, the condition of resale, according to the Chanter, rendered the contract not a true sale but actually a pledge. In effect the buyer was not bearing the risks if the seller was obliged to buy back the property at the original price after the time had lapsed. Only if the first sale was in perpetuity and the seller was free to refrain from repurchasing could this arrangement be cleared of usury. In the third example, a man in danger of losing an inheritance unless he raises a certain sum of money, seeks a loan from me.[75] Since I cannot part with the money without personal loss because I need its income, I can arrange a sale and resale. This time, however, the Chanter concluded that even if the contract of sale contains the condition of a repurchase, the arrangement is not usurious because the condition will not necessarily hold. Were the land to be damaged by war or sterility, the seller could not be compelled to buy back the property, so that in the final analysis I would bear the entire risk. This function of carrying the risk would have justified my profits while I held the property.

Although one cannot be assured which of these three conclusions represented the Chanter's final position, it is of interest that the last opinion most closely approximates the papal position. Considering the device of sale and resale in three letters, Pope Innocent III attempted to discern whether the legitimate forms of sale had concealed pledges and thereby usurious fraud.[76] On examining these cases the Pope did in fact detect presumptions of fraudulent intentions, such as a derisive price,[77] as the Chanter had noted in his second case. Like the Chanter, however, Innocent explicitly excluded the presence of a conditional second sale in the original agreement as prima facie evidence of usury.[78] For both the Parisian master and the Pope, when a contract of sale and resale was formally licit, usury must be demonstrated by other presumptions.

4. Loans Recompensed by Services

Profit from a loan could be realized not only in money or goods but also in intangible services. If a man lent a sum for which the borrower contributed a certain service, could this be considered a guise for usury? The theologians cited pertinent examples from which they derived principles for handling these problems. Peter the Chanter noted the case of one who lent money to another who in turn donated alms to a monastery or supported the lender's nephew while he was in school.[79] More important was lending to a courtier who interceded with a prince to remit unjust exactions imposed upon the lender.[80] To these examples Robert of Courson added that of a client who lent to the lawyer who pleaded his case.[81] In these examples, the masters decided that if the lender owed the services which the borrower performed in his behalf, the transactions represented gain above the principal and were usurious. If, however, the lender had no obligation to pay alms, or if the taxes were originally unjust, or if the lawyer pleaded from mercy or for public justice, the arrangements were not judged usurious. Furthermore, if the services were of a spiritually beneficial nature, they should not obstruct the granting of loans.[82] When one lent to thieves and prostitutes to halt their evil deeds, or to priests in return for prayers, these benefits were not regarded as usury. Peter the Chanter examined another case which required special attention.[83] A prince endowed a monastery with a large sum to be used for providing loans to magnates on the condition that they return the principal plus a certain donation for the support of the poor. In this way the functions of both credit and charity were satisfied, and the arrangement did not appear usurious, because the prince was not obligated to pay alms. Although the Chanter felt that the device was formally licit, he advised against it because of possible misunderstandings. Finally Thomas of Chobham pointed to a practice which was relevant to the mercantile profession.[84] It was the custom in certain cities that fathers who apprenticed their sons to merchants often loaned money to the merchant which would be returned at the end of the apprenticeship. The merchant profited from both the additional capital and the boy's labor, for which the father received the maintenance and education of his son as services above the principal. Thomas concluded that the arrangement was usurious only if the value of the boy's maintenance and training exceeded the labor which he contributed to the merchant's enterprise.

RECOMPENSE FOR CREDIT AND INVESTMENT

1. Special Exceptions to the Usury Prohibitions

When Parisian theologians concurred with the canonists that any profit derived from a contract of *mutuum* was usurious and that the employment of other contracts to conceal usurious intentions was equally illicit, did these restrictions suppress all possibility of rewarding credit and investment? In scholastic fashion, Robert of Courson enumerated several arguments which constituted exceptions to the usury prohibition, one of which noted that the law of Justinian permitted the *centisma*, a rate of usury of one percent per month.[85] Robert neglected to reply to this point and the other theologians passed by the Roman law argument in silence.[86] Fully aware of the discrepancy between Roman and canon law, the canonists insisted that human law should conform to divine law.[87] Even the contemporary Romanists were prepared to concede the superiority of canon law in this matter, although they occasionally permitted usury because of practical exigencies.

Another exception to the usury prohibition arose in the *Decretum* where Gratian included a text from the Church Father Ambrose declaring that usury may be exacted from whomever one may rightfully injure in warfare.[88] This rule of *ubi ius belli ibi ius usure* was ultimately derived from the Old Testament commandment (Deut. 23 : 20) which forbade Jews to lend at usury to their brothers but allowed them to demand usury from strangers. Applying these principles in the age of the crusades, the twelfth-century canonists generally permitted Christians to take usury from Saracens and heretics.[89] In an involved treatment of the Old Testament commandment, one version of the Chanter's *Summa* similarly concluded that usury could be exacted from pagans if it could be performed without scandal, lest Christians be called usurers.[90] Yet, as the chronicler Rigord pointed out, the rule was embarrassing because it could also serve Jews who demanded usury from Christians.[91] Canonists like Huguccio restricted the scope of the Ambrosian formula. In one passage he suggested that while high rents and prices could be demanded of the enemy, usury could not. In another he forbade usurious exactions from enemies in a just war from avaricious motives, but allowed it from charitable impulses. Huguccio's hesitant attitude towards the exception was adopted by the theologians. Peter the Chanter complained that princes adopted the rule to their advantage and for the protection of Christian usurers whom they simply called "their Jews" because they collected usury from other Christians.[92] Robert of Courson's first reaction to Ambrose's argument was to deny the text's authenticity and to attribute it to *Ambrosius Aupertus*.[93] Likewise troubled by the passage, Thomas of Chobham reported that some claimed it to be spurious.[94] Following Huguccio he stated that others forbade such usury only if it was exacted for the sake of greed. If, however, it was performed to impoverish the pagan so that he could not harm the faithful, such action promoted the worship of God and could not be impugned.

Finally, by recounting a complicated case between a wife and a thriftless husband, Peter the Chanter raised a special exception to the usury prohibition which safeguarded the wife's rights to her dowry.[95] Since the husband in question was dependent on his spouse, the wife reserved a special fund, perhaps the dowry itself, to provide for herself and her husband. Her husband, however, wished to borrow the money at usury. Complying through a third party, the wife received not only the principal but also the usury, which she applied to the needs of her husband. Although this contract was patently usurious, Peter judged it blameless in content as long as the wife was not tempted to employ the usury to her own uses, nor to increase her dowry. By means of this dissemblance she kept the dowry intact. In 1206 Innocent III sent to Genoa a decretal which decided a similar case between an impoverished and spendthrift husband H. on one side, and his wife and a third party, Master R., to whom she had committed a dowry, on the other.[96] To protect the marriage portion which was already depleted, the Pope ordered the husband to furnish guarantees that he would keep it intact or to commit it to some merchants from whose honest profits the husband could support the marriage expenses. In both Peter's and Innocent's cases the wife's funds were safeguarded and placed in trust for the irresponsible husband, but while the Chanter allowed them to be placed at usury, the Pope permitted them to be invested in a partnership. In another decretal, however, Pope Innocent III sanctioned an arrangement to protect the dowry which constituted a clear exception to the usury restrictions.[97] A father who was unable to furnish a son-in-law an agreed dowry offered a property in its place as security. The Pope allowed the husband to enjoy the revenues of the pledge without deducting them from the marriage expenses. Peter the Chanter, therefore, was among the first to enunciate a principle later confirmed by Pope Innocent III and developed by the canonists. As a rule, wives and their dowries constituted a class of persons and property requiring protection so special that they were occasionally excepted from the usury restrictions.[98]

2. Gifts

One form of recompensing loans which the canonists never questioned was the gift.[99] Bernard of Pavia, for example, explained that if a debtor offered a gift to his creditor without compulsion or constraint, this voluntary remuneration was entirely licit.[100] Even if the creditor applied pressure on the debtor to reward him with a gift, the transaction was overtly licit, although the lender must admit in the penitential to guilt of usurious intentions. Roman law further suggested that a borrower naturally felt an obligation to reciprocate the lender's generosity out of gratitude if not out of justice.[101] It was this aspect of gratuitously rewarding loans to which the theologians paid particular attention. Since usury was defined not only as an exaction but also as hope of gain based on a loan, were not these transactions also to be condemned? Peter the Chanter envisaged one motivated by a philanthropic spirit who lent to another in need realizing that the favor might never be returned. Even if the lender harbored the hope that the borrower would some day repay the kindness, the transaction was not to be judged usurious according to the Old Testament example where Jonathan performed a favor for David, which afterwards David repaid to Jonathan's son, Mephiboseth (I Sam. 20 : 16 and II Sam. 9 : 6).[102]

In these cases Peter had two kinds of favors in mind: an outright gift, which was licit, and what might be called an accommodation loan, which required more careful investigation. Although one party might legitimately loan to another with the hope that the loan would be reciprocated at a later date, the return loan should be of commensurate size.[103] If, however, one lent ten pounds in hopes that the borrower would later reciprocate with forty, this accommodation loan was clearly usury because the original lender had use of the additional thirty pounds. Although Robert of Courson agreed with his master that this unwarranted (*indebita*) hope was illicit,[104] Thomas of Chobham did not share these lenient views.[105] Just as a knight cannot alienate his fief without his overlord's permission, he reasoned, so a Christian cannot pay usury even as a gift when his Divine Lord has forbidden all such increments. After considering the Chanter's arguments for accommodation loans, he nonetheless maintained that the lender received an additional benefit from the principal, which constituted usury.[106] Despite Thomas' dissent, Peter the Chanter and Robert of Courson approved of the contemporary practice of offering loans *pro amore* for which the recompense, if any, would take the form of gifts or reciprocal loans.[107]

3. Interest

While discussing gifts, Peter the Chanter imagined a situation where someone with a needy family encountered another in similar straits.[108] If he impoverished his own family by offering the other a loan, Peter queried, was he not worthy of remuneration? Implicit in the Chanter's question was the principle that damages incurred by the lender should be compensated. In ancient Roman law such damages were termed "interest" (*interesse*) and were distinguished from usury.[109] If usury consisted of payment beyond the principal to recompense a loan, interest (*quod interest*) represented the difference between the lender's position and that in which he would have been if he had not made the loan. In other words, interest compensated the damages of making a loan. Developed by the medieval Romanists, this concept was recognized by the canonists at the time of Huguccio and Bernard of Pavia.[110] Also familiar with the term, Peter the Chanter used it to discuss restitution of theft.[111] Elsewhere in his *Summa* he considered specific cases of damages incurred in loans, and there it is evident that he was thinking of interest, although he did not employ the term. The most obvious situation occurred when a debtor was unable to return a loan after a specified time.[112] Was the creditor permitted to borrow the principal from a usurer and compel the original debtor to pay the usury? The Chanter judged that if the creditor was in need—if, for example, he had counted on the money for medical expenses—he could expect the debtor to pay the usurer's demands not as usury but as compensation for damages suffered for non-payment of the original loan. If, however, the creditor was not in need, or, in other words, if he suffered no damages when the loan was not repaid, it was usurious to arrange the second transaction. This solution resembles two decretals of Pope Lucius III involving the responsibility of guarantors for the default of debtors.[113] When the guarantors were obliged to borrow money at usury to satisfy the creditors, the Pope ordered the debtors to pay the usury as damages incurred by the guarantors. The Chanter's and Pope Lucius' examples involved the special conditions of a defaulting debtor and the necessity to have recourse to a usurer. If, however, the borrower simply delayed returning the principal, could the lender receive compensation for damages incurred in the delay? Stephen Langton concluded that since such compensation was not considered usury but interest, it was licit.[114]

Closely related to interest was the legal device of penalty.[115] It was common procedure in the Middle Ages to attach penal clauses involving monetary fines to encourage the fulfillment of contractual agreements. These devices were considered licit in canon as well as secular law. It is obvious that the attachment of penalties to loan contracts could be converted with relative ease into a means of profiting from loans. Since a penalty for failing to repay a loan by a fixed date could be set with the hope or certain knowledge that the loan would not be paid at that time, the canonists were obliged to investigate these devices for usurious intentions. Huguccio presumed usury if the creditor who set the penalty was known to be a usurer. Bernard of Pavia agreed, if the penal clause had usurious characteristics, that is, if it was adjusted to the size of the principal or to the length of time.[116] Yet Huguccio and Bernard distinguished not only a coercive but also a compensatory function of penalties. Since the penalty could be legitimately employed to compensate damages incurred by the lender for delayed payment, the penal clause was justified as interest. Aroused by the fact that the pope often affixed his seal to loan contracts bearing penal clauses, Robert of Courson maintained that the pope was unaware of their nature.[117] In his opinion these penalties were licit only if they were truly punitive and encouraged the fulfillment of the contract. Since the penalties were not designed to profit the creditor, which would, of course, be usury, they should be donated to the poor. Perhaps referring to Courson's scruples, Thomas of Chobham declared that some people accused the pope of sanctioning usury by confirming such contracts.[118] In contrast to Robert, Thomas maintained that these penal clauses were not usurious either in substance or in form, but were justified as compensation. If a debtor, for example, did not repay his loan at the agreed time the creditor might not be able to meet his rent and thereby lose his pledge or house, a merchant might lack funds to make purchases at an approaching fair, or a father might fail to provide his daughter with a dowry. According to Thomas of Chobham, interest should be paid because the Lord has commanded satisfaction of injuries inflicted on others.

The above cases in which the creditor resorted to a second loan at usury or to a monetary penalty involved special faults of the debtor, such as delay. Could interest also legitimately indemnify a lender at the beginning of the loan for damages incurred through no special fault of the borrower? Although the contemporary canonists seem not to have raised this problem,[119] Peter the Chanter treated it in his *Summa*.[120] If for example, he queried, I owe a creditor money which he needs so badly that he suffers physically, should I provide for his needs until I am able to return the loan? Since this increment was not intended for greedy profit but for compensating losses, the Chanter dared not call it usury. If, on the other hand, the creditor has no need for the principal, he should receive no interest because he has incurred no losses. Since neither delay nor special fault of the borrower were involved, Peter envisaged a situation where interest was justified solely as compensating the lender's damages at the beginning of the loan. Elsewhere he simply stated that every lender should be indemnified to the extent of his losses.[121] Although his particular example was an extreme case, Peter the Chanter foreshadowed the extrinsic title of *damnum emergens* developed by the scholastic theologians of the thirteenth century.[122]

In addition to incurring losses, a creditor may also be denying himself a profit which he might have realized with the principal if he had put it to uses other than the loan. In ancient Roman law interest compensated not only actual damages but also loss of profit suffered by the lender.[123] Although in the second half of the thirteenth century the canonists and theologians designated this title to interest as *lucrum cessans,* or profit ceasing, to distinguish it from *damnum emergens,* the canonists at the turn of the twelfth century give no evidence of treating the matter.[124] Again, here was the problem first raised within the Chanter's circle. Peter approached *lucrum cessans* by considering restitution of theft, but he was unable to arrive at a conclusion.[125] If a thief stole a hundred shillings from a merchant, was he required to restore the interest as well as the sum? If he stole a fructifying object, of course he was held to return the natural yield along with the object, but what about the chance yield (*proventus casualis*) of a merchant's capital? On the one hand, it is not easy to determine in good conscience whether the merchant should receive both the hundred shillings and the gain he might have made, as is permitted in Roman law; on the other, it seems unusually harsh to deny him anything beyond the capital. While some allow him the profits after the necessary expenses for realizing them have been deducted, others maintain that it is sufficient to restore the original money. Although Peter half-heartedly concluded that the solution should be left to the judgment of a good man, he was not certain of the decision. Even if one granted that a merchant or a creditor cannot ask for casual interest (*interesse casuale*), this does not solve all problems. If a poor man is dependent on selling his grain at a higher price to support himself, should he not be allowed this contingent profit in restitution? But if the judgment of the good man awarded such interest, Peter the Chanter nonetheless decided that in the final analysis it would be better to forego *lucrum cessans* because of the danger of scandal.[126]

The Chanter's hesitations in this matter, however, were resolved by his students Thomas of Chobham and Robert of Courson. Posing cases parallel to his master's, Thomas cited a usurer who invested one hundred pounds of his gains in a vineyard from which he made an additional profit of a hundred pounds.[127] If he were compelled to do restitution to those whom he defrauded in usury, was it sufficient to return only the original hundred pounds? Chobham decided that he was obliged to restore the entire two hundred pounds, deducting only his just expenses and the just price of his labor in cultivating the vineyard, because a thief is required to return not only a fructifying object but also its natural fruit, as the Chanter had maintained. If, however, the usurer had placed the original hundred pounds of usury in a chest, could he who was defrauded seek not only the hundred pounds but also the gain he would have had if he had had the money? Would this not be equivalent to allowing the vineyard to lie fallow and himself to be deprived of the natural yield of his money? Like Peter, Thomas held that since the two examples were not similar, the usurer was not obligated to restore the *lucrum cessans* on the money in the chest, because unlike a vineyard money does not bear fruit.

Paralleling the examples of *damnum emergens*, the Chanter's and Chobham's cases of *lucrum cessans* involved special situations. One might say that the "borrowers" exacted "loans" by theft or usury, thereby depriving the "lenders" of their due profit. Since Peter and Thomas did not recognize interest justified by loss of commercial profit in these forced loans, it was less likely that they would have conceded compensation for *lucrum cessans* in a loan freely made by a creditor. Robert of Courson considered this possibility, and clearly rejected it, as might be expected. Enumerating the laity's arguments in defense of usury, he outlined the following situation:[128] If I were in prison at Rome and someone lent me money to set me free, would not the lender be worthy of remuneration? Since it can be shown that he could have gained one hundred [shillings] by investing the money in business, I am depriving him of profit if I return only the principal. Robert nonetheless concluded that the creditor could demand no remuneration because the Gospel commanded to lend freely hoping for nothing in return. If he had lent hoping for gain beyond the principal, he committed mental usury. Against this common rejection of the title of *lucrum cessans* by the Chanter, Chobham, and Courson was one voice of dissent. Stephen Langton raised the problem of whether one should receive compensation for work lost through making a loan.[129] Summarily and awkwardly phrased, the conclusion to Stephen's question was clear. Compensation of damages for work lost is not usury but interest.

By the end of the Middle Ages *damnum emergens* (loss arising) and *lucrum cessans* (profit ceasing) were the two major ecclesiastical justifications for receiving more than the principal from a loan.[130] Although not formulating general rules, the theologians at Paris considered specific cases of both titles at the turn of the twelfth and thirteenth centuries. In general they accepted *damnum emergens* as sufficient justification for demanding interest to compensate for the special fault of the borrower and for losses suffered by the lender from the beginning of the loan. Although they rejected *lucrum cessans* as a legitimate title to interest, they did consider arguments which eventually prevailed. More important, by recognizing *damnum emergens* they took the first step towards formulating the modern theory of interest.

4. Bearing of Risk

Not only did Peter the Chanter and his followers permit compensation for losses in lending, but they proposed that the bearing of risk in credit should also be remunerated. It has already been seen how they approved credit sales when the one who deferred payment or delivery was uncertain about the price of goods at a future date. Since the future price involved a risk as to whether the enterprise would be profitable, Robert of Courson interpreted this uncertainty as committing one's capital to the hazards of fortune.[131] Similarly, Peter the Chanter permitted a gagee to enjoy the income of property held as security for a loan as long as he truly owned the property and fully bore its risks.[132] Discussing Biblical examples of employing gifts to remunerate loans, Peter further explored the factor of risk.[133] If someone lent to a friend in need and was uncertain whether he would ever receive the principal or a profit, he was blameless of usury, even if he hoped for eventual gain. For example, if someone encountered King David in flight from his rebellious son Absalom (II Sam. 15 : 14), he might loan the king a thousand pounds to be repaid with increment if David was restored to his throne. The Chanter judged that such profit was not usurious because the lender bore the risk of the King's political success. Elsewhere Peter pointed out that greater risk justifies a higher rent for a house leased on monthly rather than annual terms.[134] If a landlord collects rent for a whole year his position is more secure than one who rents from month to month, thereby risking more frequent vacancies. On the other hand, any profit on a loan fully secured by pledges or other guarantees known in French as *craant* must be condemned as usury.[135]

The Chanter's treatment of risk involved Roman law distinctions between loans and other contracts.[136] The church lawyers discovered in Justinian two basic characteristics of a *mutuum* (loan).[137] Since it consists of fungibles (goods such as money, grain, and wine) which can be counted, measured, or weighed, one may lend a specified amount of goods and receive back their equivalent, but not the identical objects. A *mutuum*, moreover, involves the transfer of ownership from the lender to the borrower for the duration of the loan. According to a fabricated etymology of the ancient Roman jurists, a *mutuum* consists of what is mine (*meum*) becoming thine (*tuum*). In contrast to the *mutuum*, a loan designated as a *commodatum* involves a particular item, such as a horse or a tool, which is given to the borrower for his use. Since the borrower must return the exact same object, in a *commodatum* no ownership transfer takes place. Huguccio noted that the *mutuum* and *commodatum* are by definition gratuitous contracts.[138] Recompense for a *mutuum* produces usury which is illicit for reasons which will be seen. Recompense for *commodatum* transforms the contract into hire or *locatio*, which is the sale of the object's use, and is legitimate. In *locatio* the ownership of the goods loaned remains with the lender as in the case of a *commodatum*. The important distinction, therefore, between the *mutuum* on one hand and the *commodatum* and *locatio* on the other was that the former involved a transfer of ownership not found in the others.

Why is profit condemned in *mutuum* and permitted in *locatio*? In practical terms, why is one forbidden to sell the use of money but not that of a horse? The obvious answer is that since the horse can be worn out by use and money cannot, the lessor of the horse should be compensated, but the answer involved more than this. After the groundwork was laid by the canonists, the Chanter, Courson, Chobham, Langton, and Master Martin all agreed that the transfer of ownership was accompanied by the transfer of risk.[139] When a lessor leases his horse (except for culpable negligence of the lessee) he retains the risks and is thereby entitled to recompense. On the other hand, when a creditor lends money in a *mutuum* he retains neither the ownership nor its risk. Come what may, the borrower must return the loan. By demanding recompense for the capital and its risk which he no longer bears, the lender is unjustly selling something not his own. Since in Roman law terminology usury is profit from a *mutuum*, immunity from risk is the decisive characteristic of a *mutuum* which renders usury illicit.

To illustrate risk-bearing, Peter the Chanter investigated a specific agreement in which nine sheep were given in perpetuity for a fixed annual income of nine shillings, or one shilling per sheep per year.[140] The holder of the sheep retained their fruits in exchange for the fixed income. (This arrangement closely resembled the agricultural credit known in French as *bail à cheptel*.)[141] Observing that this arrangement rendered the sheep immortal, something which God Himself had not cared to do, the Chanter attacked it as usurious because of the assignment of risks. Since he who held the sheep (the borrower) assumed the risks, the agreement did not qualify as hire (*locatio*). Since he who received the fixed income (the lender) was guaranteed his money without risk, the transaction was unjust. Of particular importance to the English economy in the twelfth century, especially in the north where monasteries possessed extensive pastures, this example of sheep-raising attracted notice from the English members of the Chanter's circle.[142] Robert of Flamborough referred to it in passing,[143] but Thomas of Chobham probed it in greater detail.[144] Describing the arrangement as putting the sheep "to farm," Thomas resolved the problem by having recourse to the judgment of a good man. If the good man decided that the sheep were sickly or the pastures barren, Thomas judged the agreement usurious. With the Chanter, Chobham felt that the "farmer" or the borrower unjustly bore the risks. If, however, the good man felt that no unusual hazards were incurred by the "farmer," the arrangement was licit as long as the value of the lambs, wool, and cheese corresponded to the fixed income paid by the "farmer."

It is evident that this arrangement involving flocks approximated credit known as the *census* or rent contract, which consisted of a fixed return from a fruitful property.[145] As a matter of fact, Robert of Flamborough designated it as *census*. While the one who gives the fruitful property or the sheep is the creditor, the debtor is the "farmer" who returns a fixed payment derived from the sheep. Since the rent contract was often based on land, it played an important role in the extension of credit in agricultural areas in the twelfth century.[146] Peter the Chanter and Thomas of Chobham probably realized that a *census* derived from flocks entailed more risks for the borrower than the landed variety, and for this reason Peter viewed the contract adversely. When Thomas was convinced that the presumption of risk was not great, he was inclined to approve, and his major concern was that the rent correspond to the just price of the fruits of the property. The opinions of the Parisian theologian on this specific example represent an incipient discussion by churchmen of the *census* contract. By the middle of the thirteenth century, when it received attention from the canonists, the earlier doubts of the Chanter were overcome, and rent was generally accepted as a licit form of credit.[147]

PARTNERSHIPS

In the twelfth and thirteenth centuries trading was beset from all sides by shipwreck, piracy, embargoes, reprisals, hostility of foreign governments, lack of information, and instability of prices.[148] With little assurance of profiting in a particular enterprise, merchants often diversified their activities to absorb their losses. A major problem facing the medieval merchant, therefore, was the bearing of risk. This background renders intelligible the churchmen's resistance to profits based on loans which shared none or little of the typical commercial hazards. On the other hand, since ecclesiastics agreed that risk-bearing merited compensation, the obvious channel open to creditors and investors was the partnership which performed this function. The distinguishing features of the partnership (*societas*) originated in ancient Roman law where it was defined as two or more persons who combined their money and skills and shared the profits or losses according to proportions previously agreed upon.[149] Of greatest importance to medieval conditions was the rule that risks must be shared by all partners. By the twelfth century merchants employed a wide variety of partnerships under names such as *commenda, collegantia*, and *societas maris*.[150] Although terminology was never uniform, medieval partnerships can be divided into two large groups: the permanent associations, often formed within families, which continued beyond the individual ventures, and the terminal associations which dissolved with the completion of a specific venture. Within the latter group two additional forms may be discerned in medieval practice. In one form, which may be designated as unilateral, a partner stayed at home (*stans*) and contributed the money while the other travelled (*tractator*) and contributed his labor. Three-fourths of the profits were commonly assigned to the investor and one-fourth to the worker. While the investor risked his capital, the travelling partner bore the hazards of life and fruitless labor. In another form, which may be considered bilateral, the *stans* often invested two-thirds of the capital and the *tractator* supplied the other third and the labor. Under this arrangement the partners equally shared the profits and the losses.[151] The unilateral and bilateral partnerships were popular because they were well-suited to the conditions of medieval trade. In an age when capital was scarce, they provided opportunities for energetic but impecunious merchants to begin in business. Their simplicity and flexibility allowed investors numerous combinations and diversity for their ventures. Contributing the useful function of sharing risk, they provided outlets for investment which, as will be seen, were approved by churchmen.

No evidence has as yet appeared that the canonists discussed partnerships before the thirteenth century.[152] Perhaps finding no objection to the institution, they took it for granted. The principal evidence for its widespread use is furnished by the mass of notarial and commercial documents produced by the Italian merchants. In northwest Europe, however, at the turn of the twelfth and thirteenth centuries Peter the Chanter and his two disciples, Robert of Courson and Thomas of Chobham, appear to be the first churchmen to be familiar with the main features of the terminal partnership.[153] Although they do not clearly distinguish between the unilateral and bilateral types, they describe the partnership as combining two commercial agents: an investor who contributed capital and a travelling merchant who contributed labor. Since neither Peter nor Robert indicate that the working partner contributed funds, it is likely that they had the unilateral variety of partnership in mind. Thomas, on the other hand, may have been thinking of the bilateral partnership because he speaks of an equal division of profits.

All three theologians began by investigating a "safe" form of partnership of which they disapproved. The Chanter cited an example in which the investor possessing surplus cash confided to a merchant a sum with which to trade and share the gains with the investor. If, however, the venture was unsuccessful, the merchant was nonetheless obliged to restore the original investment. Because the investor shared none of the risks, Peter judged this transaction usurious. To this hypothetical case Robert of Courson added the historical example of William Cade, a financier who flourished during the reign of King Henry II.[154] Originating from Saint-Omer, Cade spun a web of financial, commercial, and lending operations which encompassed England, Normandy, and Flanders and included the English king himself. When the royal agents took over his accounts at his death, his clients owed him the impressive sum of £5,000. There are excellent presumptions and some direct evidence that he profited by outright usury or *mortgages*. Forty years after his death Robert of Courson attested that in addition to openly usurious practices Cade formed partnerships with lesser usurers in different parts of the world in which he shared the profits but always kept the capital safe. Courson condemned these activities because Cade neither contributed labor nor shared the risks. Similarly, Thomas of Chobham decried commercial associations where the investor was assured of his capital and half of the profits but bore none of the hazards.

By contrast, the Chanter declared, if one invests in a partnership and shares in the expenses and net losses as well as the gains, this arrangement is not usurious. After relating the example of William Cade, Courson considered the position of an old merchant who was able to contribute funds but not labor. He formed a partnership with an active merchant, but unlike Cade, he also shared the risks and expenses, just as the active merchant contributed labor personally or through his employees. Chobham likewise concluded that if both partners undertake the losses as well as the gains, they may divide the profits after the expenses have been deducted. Even in his sermons, Stephen Langton insisted that true partnerships must share losses as well as profits.[155] In 1206 Pope Innocent III confirmed these opinions when he ordered a dowry to be invested in a commercial partnership whose honest gains would sustain the marriage expenses.[156] If immunity from risk vitiated profits from a *mutuum*, in the opinion of the theologians, the sharing of the hazards of medieval commerce constituted for them a legitimate service deserving remuneration. By rejecting the "safe" forms of loans and approving risk-sharing partnerships they attempted to channel credit and investment into forms which performed this socially useful function.[157]

Credit, Investment, and Exchange

In the twelfth century currencies were as varied as the political rulers of western Europe. Since merchants who traded beyond the local markets dealt with different currencies, one of their fundamental needs was to exchange money of one locality for that of another.[158] Wherever interregional commerce extended, men were found who performed exchange. Originally designated as money-changers (*campsores*), in twelfth-century Genoa they were occasionally identified as bankers (*bancherii*), from their tables (*banca*) located in the commercial quarter. From early times their simplest activities consisted of manual exchange, that is, the immediate conversion of currencies. The Genoese notarial documents indicate that exchange functions were further developed during the second half of the twelfth century. In addition to manual conversion performed on the spot, exchange of currencies between distant localities could be accomplished by written instruments. For example, a certain merchant acknowledged in writing that he received a sum of Genoese money in Genoa and promised to pay a specified amount of Provins money when he arrived at the fairs of Champagne. Since a designated time separated the receipt and the repayment, this arrangement not only performed exchange but also extended credit. From these functions of exchange and credit Italian money-changers and merchants created the essential techniques of exchange banking during the thirteenth century. Although the canonists of the twelfth and early thirteenth centuries were silent about these early procedures,[159] the contemporary theologians at Paris took some notice of them. From the Genoese evidence it is known that the Italian merchants employed exchange techniques in the fairs of Champagne. Perhaps because of their proximity to Paris or perhaps with the appearance of Italians at Paris or at the nearby fair of Lendit at Saint-Denis, the Parisian masters became aware of these developments. Although their discussions were not nearly as refined as actual practice, the theologians clearly discerned the essentials of exchange banking.

From the end of the eleventh century the professional money changers at Paris were located chiefly on the Grand-Pont, the bridge connecting the Cité with the commercial quarter of the Right Bank.[160] During the first half of the twelfth century when the bridge was reconstructed in stone and adorned with houses and shops on both flanks, the money-changers occupied the buildings on the up-stream side so that it was later called the Pont-aux-Changeurs. Undoubtedly their principal service to the academic and mercantile community was manual exchange, for which they charged commissions. Inquiring whether a money-changer could give thirty-nine shillings Paris for a silver mark which was worth forty, Stephen Langton investigated the profits of manual exchange.[161] He noted the rules governing exchange commissions, and concluded that the money changer should charge the current price of the silver mark from which he could deduct a moderate profit. In a more condensed version of this *questio* Stephen simply stated that it was sinful to sell a mark of silver for more than it was worth according to the rules of the money-changers.[162]

Langton's brief account concerns only the most elementary exchange, but the procedure became more complicated when applied to the larger business of the fairs. The clearest picture of these operations is furnished by the great fairs of Champagne which dominated trade between Flanders and Italy at the turn of the century.[163] Following a prescribed schedule, a yearly cycle of six fairs was held successively at Lagny, Bar-sur-Aube, Provins (two fairs) and Troyes (two fairs). The course of each fair lasted at least six weeks and was divided into five phases: an entry period for setting up shop, periods designated for selling cloth, cordovan, and items sold by weight, and finally a time for settling accounts (*pagamentum*), which was important not only to merchants who sold wares but also to those who bought other goods during the fair. Because of the fixed schedule merchants were often compelled to buy before they could sell, and during the frenzy of trading little time was spared for payments and exchange of currencies. The settlement of accounts and conversion of monies necessarily awaited the last period after the confusion of trading had subsided. Since intervals of up to six weeks intervened between agreements, payments, and deliveries of goods, it was obvious that credit was unavoidably necessary. In all probability other fairs such as those at Saint-Denis followed techniques comparable to those at Champagne. Noting that traders in fairs customarily withheld payments until the final days (termed *paement* in French), Robert of Flamborough investigated the relations between exchange and credit which were of concern to churchmen.[164] If, for example, a merchant can obtain twenty-three pounds Angevin for twenty pounds Paris by the current manual exchange rate (*de manu ad manum*), can he demand the rate of twenty-six pounds Angevin at the final *paement*? In Robert's opinion the increment for the delay in settlement was not usurious because it did not constitute the sale of a determined amount of time. Whenever the merchant was approached by other creditors, his debtor could immediately satisfy him. The increased exchange rate was justified not by a fixed delay in time, but by a convenience which allowed creditors to settle their accounts at the end. To raise the exchange rates for a fixed deferment in payment, on the other hand, was another matter.[165] If back in Paris, where the current manual rate was forty shillings Paris for one mark of silver, the merchant demanded an additional five shillings for each week's delay, the arrangement was clearly usurious. Evidently Robert considered it a loan for which usury was concealed as exchange commission. Because of the involvement

of time and credit, the theologians were obliged to probe exchange transactions more carefully.

Manual exchange performed on the spot did not satisfy the demands of
expanding international trade. Italian merchants trading between distant
localities required not only exchange but also transfer of money. To this
end they created an instrument of exchange which permitted a merchant
to pay in the currency of one place and to receive in that of another.[166]
Since this exchange from place to place also involved a factor of time, it
provided credit which the merchants were quick to realize. To return to
the earlier example, a merchant could receive Genoese money in Genoa
and by means of an instrument of exchange promise to repay at the fairs
of Champagne in Provins money.[167] With the money received at Genoa he
could buy spices which he would sell in Champagne for the money of
Provins to pay off his obligation. At the turn of the century such transactions appear with greater frequency, indicating that instruments of
exchange satisfied the requirements of long-distance trade. Often designated as loans (*mutua*), these written instruments candidly acknowledged
their credit function. Since the service charges demanded for exchange
could also be extended to remunerate the loan, they constituted a guise for
usury in the eyes of churchmen. Robert of Courson indicates how instruments of exchange were converted into usurious loans.[168] For example,
bishops and abbots in need of money for their affairs at the Roman *curia*
could buy exchange contracts from Italian merchants. Selling in exchange
a thousand pounds of silver at the rate of forty shillings per pound,
when the current rate was sixty shillings, they agreed to buy back the sum
at the current rate at the fairs on a later date. Moreover, the merchants
were able to induce the pope to notarize these agreements with his seal.
Distracted by another problem, Robert neglected to solve the question of
exchange, but it is evident that he judged it usurious. By affixing his
seal the pope was unaware of what he was doing.

In Robert's example the Italian merchants demanded 33⅓ percent for
the exchange and the loan over an unspecified amount of time. Most of
this profit probably consisted of usury rather than an exchange charge. The
frequency of these high exactions by Roman money-lenders is further
indicated by Robert's countryman Gerald of Wales. On the last of his
journeys to Rome Gerald incurred legal expenses which obliged him to
borrow from Bolognese money-changers.[169] Since Gerald agreed to
satisfy his creditors with both the principal and usury (which almost
equalled the principal) on his arrival in Bologna, it is apparent that
this loan was made in the form of exchange. When the unfortunate
Gerald reached Bologna his finances had not improved and he was forced
to extend his loan until his arrival at Troyes, but one dares not imagine
upon what terms.

Chapter XIV

The final conversion of exchange into credit was produced by a technique known as exchange and re-exchange or "dry exchange." Towards the end of the twelfth century the Genoese notaries recorded contracts which stipulated that a merchant might not only receive money in Genoa to be repaid in Provins, but also had the option to pay back in Genoa at a specific rate if he did not pay in Provins.[170] In addition to exchange from place to place such agreements provided opportunity for exchange and re-exchange in the same place. Although this device could serve the *bona fides* needs of exchange, it could obviously also be employed as a straight loan which eliminated travelling to another place and in which the usury consisted of the exchange charge. Thomas of Chobham discussed an example of exchange relevant to this form of credit.[171] A money-changer sold a mark of silver at a contract price of fifty or sixty shillings in a foreign currency to be paid at a fixed date in the future. When the mark was delivered to the debtor it was currently worth only forty shillings in foreign currency. Receiving his money at a low rate, the debtor paid at a high rate. Although not many details are revealed, this transaction could have involved an exchange from place to place (as did Courson's example) or an exchange and re-exchange in the same place, since Thomas does not specify where the repayment was made. By a written instrument the debtor nonetheless contracted to pay the higher rate of sixty shillings, purposely overlooking the lower current rate at which he received the mark. As in Courson's example, this document was confirmed by the pope, who was ignorant of the facts. The written contract described by Chobham closely resembles the early exchange contracts found in the Genoese notarial documents. Whether dealing with exchange from place to place or with re-exchange, these instruments often neglected to specify how much money the debtor received but almost always indicated the amount to be repaid.[172] By stipulating in advance the final rate of exchange the lender eliminated risks in the fluctuations of the money market and assured his profit. By omitting the amount received, no written proof specified the money-changer's charges. Although for this reason Thomas of Chobham had to admit reluctantly that the contract was formally licit, he maintained that the contract's terminology did not alter its real character. Even though the agreement said "sell," it really meant "lend to a certain date." Since the money-changer was certain to profit from the delay in time, this exchange contract was judged usurious.

The theologians' descriptions of currency exchange lagged behind the contemporary practices revealed in the Genoese notarial documents. Although often unaware of the refinements of exchange techniques, the masters nonetheless understood the essential operations and were able to pass judgment consistent with their views on credit. On the whole approving of money-changers who performed immediate exchange, the theologians accorded them a moderate profit for their service. When the process of exchange extended over a period of time, thereby involving credit, they formulated their opinions with greater caution. They nonetheless allowed a rise in the exchange rates for delayed payments at fairs because these delays were mutually convenient to merchants and not calculated for the sole profit of creditors. When, however, the Italian merchants devised exchange instruments which demanded remuneration for credit, the Parisian theologians could not approve despite papal confirmation of these contracts. Although the merchants might argue that such profits were derived from the licit services of exchange (at least in exchange from place to place, if not from "dry exchange"), the theologians contended that such exchange also extended a loan for which the creditor was assured calculated compensation. By all criteria governing usury, the theologians were obliged to judge such contracts as *in fraudem usurarum*. Not until the end of the thirteenth century was a defender of the exchange instrument found among churchmen.[173]

❧ CHAPTER XV ❧

The Campaign Against Usury

LTHOUGH unjust prices, dishonest weights and measures, and other fraudulent practices were punished according to the normal operation of the confessional, the sin of usury received special attention.[1] Since churchmen declared usury a crime, it was primarily their responsibility to impose sanctions. The earliest pronouncements against usury were directed towards clerics. From the time of the Council of Nicea of the fourth century, those who took usury had been rejected from the ranks of the clergy.[2] By the end of the twelfth century the church councils, popes, and canonists had formulated penalties against usurious clerics varying from suspension from office to degradation. Not until the twelfth century, however, did churchmen direct their attention to lay usurers. The Lateran Council of 1139 deprived laymen who practiced usury of the ministrations of the church,[3] a sanction which was repeated by subsequent popes and councils. In the following Lateran Council (1179) the condemnation was extended to manifest usurers, who were forbidden communion at the altar, denied Christian burial if they died unrepentant, and whose offerings were refused.[4] In effect, churchmen considered usury an extraordinary crime calling for extraordinary sanctions. At the turn of the century the canonists and theologians discussed ways to eradicate the pest of usury.

The Campaigns of the Theologians

The theologians' participation in the anti-usury campaign was not limited to discussion—they also entered the lists. From 1195 to 1215 the Chanter's circle was responsible for two concerted drives against usury. It will be seen that Peter himself was reputed to have intervened directly in one case involving usurers at Paris,* but more important, during the years 1195 to about 1200 his disciple Foulques de Neuilly conducted a preaching campaign in northern France.[5] Using Paris as his base, he travelled widely in Champagne, Burgundy, Normandy, and particularly in the urban areas of Picardy, Flanders, and Brabant. After two relatively ineffectual years, his exhortations suddenly took force, accompanied by wonders and miracles. The chroniclers reported that Foulques leveled his preaching at two groups of sinners: prostitutes and usurers. Not only were

* See below, p. 309.

his sermons effective in recalling women from lives of shame, as has been seen, but public usurers, previously impervious to censure, renounced their profession to make amends. Although there is no way to determine the actual effect of these missions, it is nonetheless known that his efforts attracted notice from most of the contemporary French and English chroniclers.

There is some evidence that Robert of Courson was initiated to the battle against usury in one of Foulques' early missions.[6] In all events, while a master at Paris, Robert devoted the greater part of his discussions on usury to the problem of enforcement of sanctions. There is also reason to believe that during the spring or summer of 1213 he joined forces with Stephen Langton to preach against usurers in the populous regions of Arras, Saint-Omer, and Flanders in a campaign resembling that of Foulques.[7] From 1213 to 1215 as cardinal legate Courson travelled widely throughout France. The canons of his councils held at Paris (1213), Rouen (1214), and Montpellier (1214) attempted to put into practice his theories concerning the repression of usury. Although Robert's campaigns attracted notice not nearly comparable to Foulques', one convincing piece of evidence survives of his effectiveness. Sometime in 1214 after the councils of Paris and Rouen which contained Courson's most important anti-usury legislation, King Philip Augustus wrote to Pope Innocent III protesting the legate's severity against usurers and charging that his measures lacked specific papal authorization.[8] Although the Pope defended his legate by maintaining that curbing sin was legitimately connected with preaching the crusade, he promised the King that he would counsel Robert moderation lest the honest customs and reasonable usage of the general council be exceeded. Although Foulques de Neuilly's and Robert of Courson's endeavors emanated directly from the Chanter's circle, they were probably only part of a general ecclesiastical movement inspired by the Lateran Council of 1179. For example, in the distant and heresy-ridden region of Toulouse the orthodox bishop Foulques of Marseilles (1206-1231) sought to extirpate usury as well as heresy and his efforts were not without effect.[9]

THE PREVALENCE OF USURERS

In their writings the Chanter's circle exposed the blueprints for their actions. Employing the *questio* for probing the complexities of usury, Peter the Chanter often attempted in his *Summa* to accommodate his theories to practical realities, but in the *Verbum abbreviatum,* his popular manual on ethics, Peter replaced these subtleties with rhetorical protest. For this reason the *Verbum abbreviatum* is quite different in tone from the *Summa.* With colorful and vigorous expression, he attacked the usurers of his day. Pope Alexander III and the fathers of the Lateran

Council had complained in 1179 that so profitable were usurious practices that in almost every locality other—legitimate—business affairs were abandoned.[10] With moralistic fervor Peter rehabilitated this theme by declaring that whereas in ancient cities scarcely a single usurer could be found because of the shame of his profession, in present times usurers were everywhere and openly practicing their crimes.[11] Similarly Robert of Courson bewailed that so widespread was the pestilence that merchants, money-changers, burghers, or even prelates possessed neither "hide nor hair" (*pilus aut pellis*) immune from infection.[12] These statements may be regarded as moralistic exaggerations, yet when compared with papal correspondence, they do not seem excessive. Writing in 1208 to the Bishop of Arras, where Foulques de Neuilly and perhaps Robert of Courson concentrated their efforts, Pope Innocent III urged caution in applying the penalties of the Lateran Council against usurers. By selecting only a few notorious offenders for prosecution, the Bishop could more effectively dissuade others.[13] If he, however, attempted to condemn all the guilty, many of the churches would have to close. Under such circumstances it is difficult to believe the Pope was indulging in exaggeration.

The Chanter believed that the prevalence of usurers could be explained in part by support they received from contemporary princes and prelates.[14] Infamous usurers became the intimates of the rulers of state and church; their sons obtained positions through the intervention of ill-gotten gains. In Peter's judgment the toleration of lay usurers was related to the privileged position of Jewish money-lenders in contemporary society.[15] The terms "Jew" and "usurer" became synonymous around the end of the twelfth century. Not only had popes and councils kept silent on Jewish usury up until this time,[16] but in England Jews had enjoyed royal protection since the beginning of the twelfth century. Because the Jews belonged to the king alone, any offense against them was exclusively reserved to the crown. Across the Channel the Capetians limited their rights to the Jews of their domain, while elsewhere jurisdiction was assumed by local lords. For these special privileges the Jews dearly paid their protectors. Since all that they owned in England ultimately belonged to the crown, the king could cancel their debts, confiscate their property and tallage them at will. Although the Angevins were not inclined to abuse these powers until the first decade of the thirteenth century, they nonetheless found the Jews a substantial source of income. In France, where jurisdiction was equally arbitrary, the young Philip Augustus suddenly turned against the Jews in his royal domain. In a series of violent measures from 1180 to 1182 he successively arrested and exorbitantly ransomed them, released their debtors but collected a fifth of their debts for himself, and finally expelled them from the domain and confiscated their lands.

Although he undoubtedly profited enormously from these policies, in 1198 the king readmitted them to his domain. By and large the theologians of the Chanter's circle protested this royal mulcting of the Jews. While it was reported that the zealous Foulques de Neuilly advocated the repudiation of Jewish debts[17] (a former policy of Philip Augustus), Robert of Courson maintained that princes could not confiscate Jewish property because it consisted entirely of ill-gotten gains which should not be appropriated but restored to the victims.[18] Faithfully reflecting English conditions, Thomas of Chobham reported arguments justifying the royal policy.[19] Since the king defended the Jews from Christian subjects and all who would expel them from the country, he was entitled to their money and goods. Yet Thomas rebuked the church for acquiescing to this exploitation, since their goods were tainted with usury. Although the king was too powerful to be punished by the church, he was not excused before God.

Keeping these Jewish privileges in mind, Peter the Chanter claimed that princes assimilated all money-lenders, Christian as well as Jewish, under the Jew's status.[20] Since the prince declared usurers "as his Jews," they could not be prosecuted for their crimes. In a letter of 1207 to the Bishop of Auxerre, Pope Innocent III noted the numerous usurers in the diocese who openly plied their trade and complained that no one dared to bring them to justice because of fear of princes.[21] Like the Jews, the Chanter maintained, these money-lenders were the prince's leeches and coffers who sucked in usuries and disgorged them into their protectors' treasuries.[22] There is little evidence on the exploitation of usurers in France, but in England, where the picture is clearer, the king claimed the chattels of all deceased usurers throughout the realm.[23] Even though the usurer was theoretically safe from confiscation during his lifetime, the royal exchequer nonetheless exacted substantial fines from living usurers. In England, therefore, the usurer's liabilities vis-à-vis the king resembled the Jew's. Robert of Courson was undoubtedly thinking of his native England, if not of France, when he reported that as soon as a Christian was identified as a usurer, all his goods pertained to the prince.[24] As in the case of Jews, Robert contested the king's right to avail himself of ill-gotten gains. The Chanter's observation that usurers and Jews were the leeches of princes was further corroborated by Innocent III.[25] When writing a second letter to Auxerre, in 1208, this time addressed to the Count of Nevers, he complained of princes who exacted usury from their subjects through Jewish intermediaries. Although not supplying the details, the Pope apparently agreed with the Chanter that by protecting and profiting from Jews and usurers, princes siphoned money from their subjects.

Princely protection extended not only to Christian laymen who practiced usury but also to clerics. Peter the Chanter noted that since princes call such clergy "our clerical Jews and our clerical usurers," they have the right to confiscate their gains.[26] At their death the prince seized all of their goods, totally disregarding their clerical privileges, the jurisdiction of their bishops, or even their right to bequeath property. Here again it is possible that Peter had English practice in mind because the Angevin kings claimed the chattels of deceased clerical usurers as well as of laymen. In the *Dialogus de Scaccario* in the last quarter of the twelfth century Richard fitz Neal argued that all clergy practicing usury lost their clerical privileges and became liable to the same penalties as the laity.[27] Contesting this policy in 1190, the Norman clergy won from King Richard the concession to respect the ecclesiastical jurisdiction over deceased clerics, even if they were usurers.[28] In such cases the bishop was empowered to distribute the cleric's property in works of charity. It is unlikely that the agreement of 1190 extended beyond Normandy because Peter the Chanter, writing after the event, still protested the prince's traditional customs.

In the Chanter's opinion the usurer's current prosperity was due also to the complacency of prelates. As a concrete example of this attitude, Peter referred in his *Verbum abbreviatum* to the decree of the Lateran Council of 1179 against manifest usurers.[29] Writing at least a decade after the event, the Chanter offered an intriguing account of how this canon was formulated.[30] When Pope Alexander III made it known to the fathers of the Council that the plague of usury was to be extirpated by anathema, certain persons inquired who would be its object. To this question one prelate answered that only the notorious culprits were envisaged. When the questioning proceeded as to who were notorious, it was decided that the anathema applied only to those who publicly confessed or who displayed some well-known sign such as a purse suspended from a pole.[31] It is evident that the conciliar prelates were thinking of pawnbrokers, whose places of business were known and open to all. (Elsewhere in his *Summa* Peter compared the manifest usurer with the public prostitute whose establishment was similarly notorious and accessible.)[32] The Chanter contended that by designating only manifest usurers, the prelates of the Council restricted their anathema to pawnbrokers and thereby crippled the canon's effectiveness. Yet in the thirteenth century when the canonists attempted to define manifest usurers they accepted the Council's interpretation, reported by the Chanter.[33] Although not confining the condemnation explicitly to pawnbrokers, they declared that whoever conducted such places of business open to all were by notoriety of fact manifest usurers.

To notoriety of fact the canonists added notoriety of law. Since mere reputation was not sufficient, only accusation and conviction of the crime in an open law court rendered one a manifest usurer. The Chanter offered an example of how this second interpretation also hindered usury prosecution.[34] Some individuals publicly confessed before a certain priest and his parishioners that they were usurers. Although refusing to do penance, they nonetheless sought the Eucharist. Some people held that the priest could not rightfully deny them the host because he did not possess a court of law. Unless they were convicted of usury in a court, their confession did not carry legal force. On the contrary, Peter argued, since the priest is the penitential judge of his parish, especially in affairs dangerous to the soul, and since the usurers' confessions are valid in the confessional, the priest can rightfully refuse them at the altar. Robert of Courson also noted that some usurers, well-known by reputation, are yet defended by bishops, archdeacons, and rural deans who tolerate them because they have neither confessed nor been convicted in law.[35] In such situations the priests are powerless, and the simple cry out against the prelates' compliance. Both the Chanter and Courson concurred that by limiting prosecution to manifest usurers and by interpreting "manifest" in terms of notoriety of fact and law, churchmen hampered the campaign against usury. To these protests, however, Stephen Langton offered one afterthought of caution.[36] Posing the question of whether a secret usurer was required to confess his sins openly before a preacher who publicly decried the crime, he remembered the crowds of usurers who confessed their sins during the popular preaching of Foulques de Neuilly. Stephen decided that it was better if usurers refrained from public confession because of scandal, but undoubtedly he held that private confession to one's priest was the more appropriate remedy.

THE CHURCHMEN'S WEAPONS

Thomas of Chobham explained that in the churchman's view usurers are equated with thieves and brigands because they take from others what does not belong to them.[37] Although they are not hanged like other criminals according to secular law because they perform their deeds quietly, the church nonetheless prosecutes them because they earn their living from a profession which is in open contempt of God. Thomas' statement essentially agreed with contemporary French and English practice. Since the secular prince claimed the right to intervene only at the death of a money-lender, he relegated principal responsibility for repressing usury to the church. During their lifetime usurers were threatened with excommunication and its attendant consequences. As churchmen the theologians at Paris contributed to convincing the faithful of the wickedness and folly of practicing usury through preaching missions and the formulation of conciliar canons. The writings of Peter the Chanter and his followers provided numerous arguments to aid the preacher protest effectively against usury.[38]

But perhaps the masters' most valuable contribution to the preachers' effectiveness was their use of the *exemplum*, the brief story drawn from saints' lives and other tales, to portray most vividly the dire consequences to those who practiced usury. Peter the Chanter and Robert of Courson repeated examples concerning Tobias, Saint Furseus, and Saint Laudomarus of Blois, and their dealings with usurers,[39] stories which were multiplied in the sermons of Jacques de Vitry.[40] Much of Foulques de Neuilly's success as a popular preacher was most likely founded on his skill in recounting these graphic tales. Among the various themes embodied in the *exempla,* the most popular depicted the wretched death of usurers. The Lateran Council of 1179 forbade the burial of manifest usurers in consecrated ground to emphasize the sinner's loss of salvation. The Chanter dramatized this theme with narratives about usurers who were refused Christian sepulchre at Saint-Denis and elsewhere.[41] Robert of Courson, while he was a papal legate, is reported to have ordered the corpse of a recently entombed usurer to be removed from a churchyard.[42]

Refusal of Christian burial and sermons bristling with grim stories about usurers' deaths had only limited effectiveness against hardened sinners. One remembers Robert of Courson's lament against the helplessness of priests faced with usurers who had neither confessed nor been convicted in law and so remained under a prelate's protection.[43] For these desperate conditions Robert proposed a drastic remedy. He advised priests to encourage their parishioners to bring accusations by all possible means. If the faithful are reluctant, the priest should command them to do this in place of fasting, alms-giving, and other normal penance. In short, the accusation of usurers became a good work acceptable for salvation. Equating usury with heresy, Robert maintained that just as the faithful are bound to work for the heretics' conversion, so they should redeem usurers first by attempting to convert them and finally by public accusation if other means fail. When Robert convened the Council of Paris in 1213, he endowed this proposal with the force of church law.[44] As a fulfillment of penance, and if necessary, prodded by censure, the parishioners of Paris were ordered to report the names of all manifest and secret usurers to be inscribed on a list. If after threefold admonition these miscreants refused to desist and make amends, they were solemnly excommunicated with the penalties prescribed by the councils. Doubtless an extreme measure, this decree goes far to explain Robert's unpopularity with Philip Augustus and his barons.

RESTITUTION OF USURY

Recurrent among the *exempla* was the theme that usurers must restore their ill-gotten gains before receiving absolution. The chronicler Rigord was impressed with Foulques de Neuilly's success in persuading usurers to do restitution.[45] Augustine had declared, thus formulating a fundamental principle of canon law, that no forgiveness for theft could be pronounced without the restoration of stolen goods.[46] Huguccio clearly taught that usurers' profits were distinct from those of prostitutes and actors, in which ownership was legitimately transferred and restitution was not required.[47] Equating usury with fraud, theft, robbery, and simony in which ownership did not legitimately pass from the injured party to the dispossessor, the canonists maintained that all usurious gain must be restored to the rightful possessor, and the usurer cannot bestow profits in alms.[48] By and large the Parisian theologians concurred with the canonist doctrine.[49] Summarizing his colleagues' opinion, Robert of Courson prescribed a procedure for those desiring to make restitution.[50] The usurer should avail himself of the services of a prelate or another man of good repute (if he did not trust the prelate) for distributing the goods. If those despoiled were dead, the executor should first hasten to make restitution to the poor who can pray for their souls because, as Peter the Chanter had noted, the dead have the greatest need while they are in purgatory.[51] After their release into heaven restitution is of less benefit. In the second place, if the victims were still living, restitution should be made to them and their heirs. If they were alive but their whereabouts unknown, the executor could restore to their neighbors or to the poor. When the victims were dead or missing, these were the sole cases which justified giving alms from usury.[52] It will be seen that usurers' gifts to the church presented a particularly delicate problem to the Parisian theologians.

To enunciate the principle that all usurers must restore their gains was relatively simple; to apply it to the variety of practical circumstances was more difficult. The chief contribution of the Chanter and his followers to the problem of restitution was to attempt to apply principles to specific cases.[53] It was evident to all that the money-lenders' ill-gotten gains did not long remain in their possession but passed into commercial exchange, thus permeating the economy. The problem of how to restore usurious profits which were inextricably involved with legitimately circulating money resembled that of the restitution for other forms of theft. Peter wrestled with such cases in his *Summa* but found it difficult to arrive at firm solutions.[54] Stephen Langton and Thomas of Chobham, however, treated an example characteristic of this category of problems. What are the obligations of one who acquires a piece of land with money gained in usury? Although Pope Alexander III decreed that such possessions should be sold and the money restored to the victim,[55] Stephen and Thomas inquired further whether one should also return the revenues of the land gained while it was the usurer's.[56] In an involved *questio* Stephen distinguished two methods of acquiring the land.[57] If the usurer had not obtained outright ownership of the property, it was sufficient to restore the original amount without the additional revenues. If, however, he had acquired the ownership of the land, he was obligated to return not only the land or its equivalent but also his profits. Thomas' treatment of the problem was less complicated than Stephen's but arrived at the same conclusion.[58]

Other cases discussed by the Paris masters involved the usurer's inability to do full restitution. A usurer might wish to cease his practices and do penance, but find it impossible to restore his gains without impoverishing his family. By performing immediate and complete restitution he would force his sons into robbery, his daughters into prostitution, and his wife into desertion. In a series of *questiones* Stephen Langton investigated whether a usurer could delay payments of restitution to avoid bankruptcy.[59] After rehearsing conflicting arguments, Stephen concluded that it was preferable to refund everything at once, even at cost of injuring one's physical well-being, than to endanger one's spiritual destiny. If, however, the victims agreed, the time of restitution could be prolonged as long as neither fraud nor evasion were envisaged. If the victims could not be found, thereby necessitating restitution to the poor, the bishop had the authority to extend the time of restitution, provided again that it was done in good faith.

Peter the Chanter treated of usurers whose victims were known and apparently demanded immediate restitution.[60] In favor of immediate payment, Peter recalled not only the Augustinian principle, but also the Roman law dictum that he who owes a debt without a specified term is required to pay immediately because to return late is to return less.[61] To solve this problem Peter distinguished between usurers who possessed legitimate property in addition to their unlawful profits and those who had only usurious income. In the first instance the usurer should retain his legitimate income for maintaining his family and restore immediately whatever he had of usurious gain. The remainder of what he owed his victims could be returned in installments. Since he was not required to liquidate his lawful possessions, he could employ them for repaying his victims after he had retained enough for his necessities. If, however, he possessed nothing but the profits of usury, his case was more difficult. Although certain wise men advised a remedy similar to the first instance, where the usurer, reserving a certain amount from his usury to cover his necessities, restored the remainder in installments, Peter dared not approve this because it permitted one to live knowingly from plunder. Rather he advised the usurer to seek from his victims a reduction of what he owed. If, for example, he owed one hundred [pounds], he might ask to be released from twenty so that his family would not have to beg. This reduction must be granted by the victims without a shadow of constraint; otherwise, the usurer should be ready to restore everything and suffer impoverishment. Robert of Courson merely repeated his master's conclusions verbatim.[62] In the end Stephen Langton, Peter the Chanter, and Robert of Courson permitted either a delay or a reduction of restitution only as a gift freely bestowed by the victim. Thomas of Chobham sided with the other opinion reported by Peter.[63] Thomas declared that if this grace was refused, the usurer in dire necessity was justified to retain part of his usurious gains as long as he lived in extreme frugality and maintained a firm resolve to restore everything as soon as possible.

Implicit in the above solutions was a direct agreement between usurers and their victims. Stephen Langton pointed out that only when the victim was unavailable should ecclesiastical authority intervene. When Robert of Courson convened the Council of Paris in 1213, he attempted to generalize this role of churchmen as intermediary.[64] Claiming a special command from the pope, he decreed that both usurer and victim should commit their mutual affairs to the arbitration of a prelate, papal legate, or judge delegate, who would take into consideration the circumstances of the usurer, whether he had many children, whether he was infirm, whether he had taken the cross, as well as the position of the victims. This churchman would finally decide the terms binding on both parties. By relying on the services of the prelacy Robert of Courson hoped to implement the theories of his colleagues.

If usury constituted stolen goods, it followed that they could not be lawfully enjoyed by the heirs of usurers. Pope Alexander III established a canonical principle that the sons of usurers were required to restore the same amount of any ill-gotten gains as their parents would have had to during their lifetime.[65] Since there was little controversy over the general rule, the theologians directed their attention to specific circumstances. For example, Robert of Flamborough advised the heir of a usurer who had acquired property with usurious money to restore the price of the property to the victims if he wished to retain possession.[66] If the victims were not known, with the bishop's permission he should give alms to a monastery in installments until the entire sum was restored. If the father had made his living entirely from usury, the heir was obliged to restore all that he had received in his father's house from the time he was an adult. If, however, the father had some legitimate income, the heir was permitted to retain that part, while he did restitution for his unlawful inheritance. In effect Robert applied the Chanter's and Langton's procedures to usurers' heirs. In the Council of Paris of 1213 Robert of Courson simply denied all usurers testamentary power to bequeath their gains from usury.[67]

More complicated was the situation of the usurer's wife who, although she had vowed conjugal fidelity to her husband, was forbidden to partake of his ill-gotten gains. While teaching in Paris, Robert of Courson summarily maintained that wives of incorrigible usurers should live by their own labor and not from their husbands' robbery.[68] They were nonetheless required to fulfill their conjugal duties at specific times. Thomas of Chobham, however, reported two points of view.[69] Referring to an opinion similar to Robert's, he noted that some would have the wife live from her own labor or from friends' donations. If she had neither friends nor skill to support herself, she should nonetheless separate herself from her husband and refuse to serve his conjugal needs. Thomas, however, preferred another solution. Just as Christ associated with robbers and partook of ill-gotten goods at their tables in order to induce them to restore to their victims, so the usurer's wife should attempt to persuade her husband to amend his ways. If she sincerely pleaded in behalf of her husband's victims, she could licitly live from their stolen goods. It is possible that Robert of Courson also considered this second opinion, for when he turned to the problem in the Council of Paris he attempted to combine the two opinions.[70] A wife could live with her usurious husband as long as she attempted to convert him and to induce him to do restitution. In such a position she served as the victims' advocate. Whenever she became convinced that her husband was incorrigible, however, she was required to separate herself from his table and company, though not from his bed, thus relying on others for food and clothing. Yet if sickness or abandonment rendered her situation desperate, she was allowed to return to her husband, but with the intention of restoring whenever opportunity presented itself. These same obligations applied to the usurer's sons, daughters, and nephews as soon as they were old enough to assume responsibility.

Not only were wives and families accountable, but also all others who associated with usurers in business. From Psalm 49 : 18—"When thou watched a thief, then thou ran with him"—Peter the Chanter developed an elaborate theory of criminal complicity and the obligations of restitution,[71] which his students Robert of Courson and Thomas of Chobham applied directly to the associates of usurers. All who sold their services to Jews, usurers, and robbers were condemned as "running with thieves."[72] Servants, agents, witnesses, and particularly notaries were required to restore whatever they received from usurers.[73] In the Council of Paris Robert summarily declared that those who served excommunicated usurers incurred the same penalties as the usurers themselves.[74] Peter the Chanter, however, expressed his embarrassment when a certain notary asked advice about his duties at the fairs.[75] In the service of a merchant for many years, he had recorded usury obligations, exchange transactions, and other illicit as well as licit affairs, for which he had received ten pounds. Was he required to restore all his earnings? On the one hand, he had knowingly cooperated with a usurer; on the other, since the merchant was also involved in legitimate affairs, the notary could not distinguish from what sources his wages were drawn. As long as the situation was unclear, the Chanter counselled him against immediate and complete restitution. While the notary owed no restitution for recording licit contracts, he must, however, return all money knowingly received from usury. At the Council of Paris Robert of Courson overcame his master's hesitations when he condemned any cleric who served usurers by computing their loans or credit sales or by drawing up their contracts.[76] To the clerical notary he added the lawyer who pleaded the usurer's case in court. If after admonition they refused to desist, they were suspended from office and benefice and excommunicated. To these examples of complicity Thomas of Chobham could think of one exception.[77] Inquiring whether someone could labor in a usurer's vineyard or in some other capacity, knowing that his earnings stemmed from usury, Thomas decided that if other employment was available, he committed mortal sin. If, however, no other opportunity existed, he could out of necessity accept wages from the usurer.

The theologians searched for a variety of means by which the church could compel the usurer to do restitution. Not only did they threaten him with excommunication, but they attempted to apply spiritual pressure in a more effective manner. Extending the anathema to his business associates, they separated him from the companionship of his wife and family. They proposed that prelates serve as arbitrators between usurers and their accusers. When these means failed, one final recourse remained—the secular authority. Reminding the prince of his coronation oath to reward the righteous and punish evildoers, Robert of Courson suggested in his *Summa* that this obligation involved compelling usurers to do restitution.[78] Similarly, in the Council of Paris, Robert declared that after the prelate's mediating services failed, the sword should be used against the usurer.[79] In the *Summa* Robert was not clear how the prince was to cooperate. In contemporary England and probably in France, princes refrained from seizing goods of living usurers but generally despoiled them after their death. Probably with this practice in mind Robert enjoined the princes in the Council to seize usurers' goods on their death and to distribute them according to the direction of the church.[80] Rather than the prince appropriating the wealth for himself, however, Robert most likely intended him to enforce restitution according to the masters' principles.

ALMS FROM USURERS

A problem which vexed churchmen was whether alms could be accepted from usurers. When sinners were converted, they were expected to give alms for the salvation of their souls, and when bishops and abbots were zealously building churches and promoting pious causes, they were tempted to accept these donations. Such practices, however, were clearly forbidden in canon law.[81] Huguccio explained that usury was like theft in which ownership did not pass from the victim to the wrongdoer.[82] Not rightfully possessing his earnings, the usurer could not give them in alms. Since there was little controversy over the principle, the theologians at Paris accepted it as a matter of course.[83] To this rule Rufinus designated one important exception.[84] If the victims could not be found, the ill-gotten gains could be distributed in alms according to the judgment of the church. Robert of Courson, it has been noted, expanded this exception by outlining the procedure for doing restitution.[85] If the victims were defunct but without heirs, the usury should be given to the poor so they would pray for the souls of the despoiled. If the victims were alive but could not be found, the ill-gotten earnings could be given to the victims' neighbors or to the poor for the same purpose. Peter of Poitiers of Saint-Victor added that if the usurer could not locate his victims because of the minutely dispersed character of his dealings, he could do satisfaction by giving to churches where he believed his victims were parishioners.[86] In order to prevent abuse Robert emphasized that the alms must be distributed by a prelate or some other man of good repute and not by the usurer himself. If an abbot, for example, received alms directly from a usurer without the bishop's intervention, his action was unlawful and the donation void.

Two cases arose at Paris which well illustrate the problem of usurers' alms. One version of the Chanter's *Summa* reports that a certain lay converse by the name of Reginald had papal authority to preach publicly in the churches and streets of Paris.[87] His sermons were well received by the townsmen and prompted munificent contributions to the Hôtel-Dieu of Notre-Dame. Among the donors, however, were certain usurers, whose alms provoked objections from the clergy. Inquiring whether Reginald could receive usurers' contributions in certain knowledge, Peter the Chanter wrestled not only with the problem of the preacher turning this money to his own use but also with that of the propriety of using ill-gotten gains to support the poor. It could be argued that the poor would pray for the usurers' victims, that the church depended on such alms, that the guilty were too numerous to be refused, and that priests could not reject usurers' oblations on Easter day without causing scandal. On the other hand, the *Glossa ordinaria* explained that when the Apostle collected contributions for the poor in Jerusalem (1 Cor. 16 : 3), he would receive nothing from the Corinthians before their evil deeds were corrected. If the *Glossa* is true, Peter concluded, nothing should be received from usurers before they have been reformed.

Although the Chanter's conclusion in this case is ambiguous, Caesar of

Heisterbach narrates another story, in the *Dialogus miraculorum*, which clarifies the Chanter's position.[88] A certain fabulously rich usurer, Thibaut by name, was touched by divine repentance and wished to make amends for his misdeeds. When he sought advice on performing satisfaction, Maurice of Sully, Bishop of Paris, who was preoccupied with the construction of Notre-Dame, told him to donate his money to this worthy enterprise. Yet, dissatisfied with this counsel, Thibaut turned to Peter the Chanter for further confirmation. On the contrary, Peter maintained that the usurer should first restore to all whom he defrauded before he could safely contribute alms. In compliance with the Chanter's advice Thibaut sent a crier throughout Paris announcing that he was prepared to make restitution. When all just claims were satisfied, Thibaut still possessed considerable riches and from these he bestowed alms with a clear conscience. Some skepticism is permitted about a story which was recorded perhaps two decades after the death of Maurice and Peter,[89] yet Caesar of Heisterbach heard it from Daniel, at one time prior of Heisterbach and then abbot of Schönau, and the fundamental elements of the tale ring true. Among his contemporaries Maurice of Sully was reputed to be absorbed with the construction of his cathedral.[90] Failing to share his bishop's enthusiasm for magnificent buildings, Peter the Chanter charged in his *Verbum abbreviatum* that great churches were often founded on the offerings of usurers and robbers.[91] Although there is little chance of clearly identifying the Thibaut of the story with any historic personage, a certain Parisian bourgeois, known as Thibaut the Rich, played a prominent role in the royal administration of Paris about 1190 during the King's absence on the Crusade.[92] Most important, whether fact or tradition, the story agrees with the teaching of the canonists and theologians. In the light of the masters' discussions Maurice of Sully was wrong and Peter the Chanter was right.

Robert of Courson addressed himself directly to the problem raised by Thibaut the usurer by asking whether one should probe the sources of alms.[93] Against those who maintained that abbots need not investigate their donations, Robert marshalled authorities from the Old and New Testaments, Roman law, and saints' lives. His first conclusion declared that if the usurer is known to all, he cannot give alms until he has done public restitution before the neighborhood. In other words, Thibaut should indeed send his crier throughout Paris proclaiming his willingness to make satisfaction. In a similar manner Stephen Langton affirmed that abbots should diligently investigate the source of their alms in areas where usurers abounded.[94] In an effort to mitigate the severity of the first conclusion, Robert continued, some argued that although usurious money cannot be received in alms, things acquired with this money can be accepted.[95] According to Roman law stolen money does not change ownership, but since there is transfer of ownership of a piece of property bought with this money, the property itself may be bestowed in alms. While Robert acquiesced to this argument's validity in the public court, he would not concede to it in the confessional. The abbot should not under any circumstance accept from donors who possess only stolen goods. When, however, the donor possesses legitimate earnings, he may make a contribution if he also promises to restore to those whom he has defrauded. If, in fact, he does not pay to the defrauded, the abbot is not further liable. Elsewhere, Robert made still another concession to donors who possessed both illicit and licit income.[96] If the abbot diligently inquires whether the gift is not tainted, and the usurer himself swears that his donation does not come from usury, the alms may be accepted providing that they do not create a scandal. Ignoring these nuances in the Council of Paris, Robert of Courson simply affirmed that any priest, abbot, or other religious person who knowingly received alms from a usurer who was openly denounced in the churches and who had not made sufficient restitution, was excommunicated and suspended from both office and benefice.[97] Absolution from these penalties could only be obtained from the pope.

Although Courson's measures attempted to discourage churchmen from benefiting from usurers, what about the churches, dormitories, hermitages, Hôtels-Dieu and leprosaria which were already constructed from usury? Considering the responsibilities of the conscientious prelate towards these products of complacent churchmen, Robert's first solution provided counsel for perfection for the entire church.[98] He called for a general council of all bishops and princes under the presidency of the pope to decree that all men should work either physically or spiritually for their bread. By spiritual and temporal sanctions the devious, indolent, usurers, rebels, and brigands would be removed from the world. After the restoration of society to its pristine state, alms could be given and churches raised. Since Robert himself realized the utopian character of this proposal, he devised a second solution more adapted to real problems. If the churches were consecrated, the abbots and chapters should redeem them by paying the despoiled a sum equivalent to that illicitly received. If they did not possess means to make this redemption, they should attempt to arrive at a settlement with the despoiled either in the present or in the future. If the constructions were not consecrated, they should either be redeemed, destroyed, or sold for the profit of the victims. Robert in fact approved of dismantling several notable examples as dissuasion from building new ones. In the case of leprosaria and Hôtels-Dieu, which rendered valuable service to society, they should be redeemed at equivalent cost. All in all, Courson concluded, it was an indissoluble rule that no one can be in a state of salvation who knowingly and willingly lives from the fruits of usury.

Robert's opinions on usury and alms, expressed while he was yet a theological professor at Paris, reflect a mind scrupulous to the extreme. There is no way to measure what his proposals would have cost had they been seriously carried out, but the required surgery undoubtedly would have been drastic. When Robert was appointed papal legate for France by Innocent III, he showed little indication of modifying the harshness of his principles. The canons of the Council of Paris in 1213, for example, which implemented his former teaching, were the most severe anti-usury regulations of their time.[99] Accordingly they provoked protests from the French king and his barons.[100] Travelling about France, Robert continued to hold councils, but in May 1215, when he summoned a new council to be held at Bourges, the French prelates refused to respond.[101] Although the contemporary chroniclers are vague about the reasons underlying this rebuff, one writer points to the radical severity of the legate's actions.[102] Robert's agenda for the Council of Bourges is not known, but if he sought to put into effect his program for purging the church of usuriously financed property, the French prelates indeed had cause for alarm.

If the Chanter's circle occasionally mentioned the name of a renowned master, but cited historical examples of princes with greater reticence, they were practically mute about merchants. Eager to examine merchants' affairs in minute detail in order to judge their moral validity, they found no need to situate their cases in a historical setting. One exception may be found in the *questiones* attributed to Peter the Chanter. Referring to the Plantagenet-Capetian conflict, in which the merchants were captured and their wares confiscated, Peter cited the example of a bourgeois of Paris who was expert in disposing of confiscated merchandise for the profit of King Philip Augustus.[103] Peter's purpose was to inquire into the selling of illegally seized goods. Although having a specific case in mind, the Chanter revealed the name of the king but not that of the merchant. With the exception of William Cade, the notorious financier of the twelfth century, cited by Robert of Courson, the merchant remained anonymous in the writings of the Parisian theologians.[104]

PART

FIVE

REFORM

❧ CHAPTER XVI ❧

The Lateran Council of 1215

IN CHRISTIAN terms remedy must follow the debate and analysis of moral problems. As might be expected, Peter the Chanter's acute sensitivity to ethical issues was accompanied by a compelling desire to bring about improvement. Although disinclined to discuss reform on an abstract level,[1] Peter crammed his writings with concrete proposals for resolving existing evils. To him reform consisted of eliminating human traditions to return to the simple and purified commands of Scripture. In a long chapter of the *Verbum abbreviatum* entitled "Against the overwhelming multitude of human traditions,"[2] the Chanter distinguished three kinds of traditions: (1) those of diabolical origin which were directly contrary to the law of God, (2) those licit and useful which nonetheless placed obstacles to divine commandments, and (3) those honest traditions which also impeded the law of God because of their great number.[3] The first are unlawful, the second doubtful, and the last to be avoided if possible. Even more dangerous are new traditions which, although useful, should be omitted because their multitude obscures the Gospel precepts.[4] To illustrate this point Peter cited the eloquent plea of a certain Ivo of Chartres, delivered before the Lateran Council of 1179.[5] For God's sake, Ivo warned the conciliar fathers, neither renew the old decretals nor establish new ones lest the Council be convoked in vain. Providing occasion for disobedience, such decretals will only encourage wrangling among scholars in the schools and among lawyers in the courts. Even when they are useful, these new inventions should be set aside, lest we be overwhelmed by their number. Rather the council should command observance of the holy Gospel, which is honored today only in its breach. To this end papal legates should be dispatched throughout the world lest the Lord accuse us of rejecting God's commandment that we might keep our own traditions. This anecdote echoed a theme in the inaugural sermon of the Lateran Council pronounced by the canonist Rufinus, Bishop of Assisi.[6] Recalling the Biblical account of the rediscovery of the Book of the Law during the restoration of the Temple under King Josiah (II Chron. 34), Rufinus similarly envisaged the purpose of the assembled council to recover the Book of Law which was lost to the multitudes. The Chanter devoted the greater part of his chapter to citing examples of harmful traditions applicable to monastic customs, liturgical usage, ecclesiastical oaths, fasting, tithes, judicial procedure, marriage, and ordeals.

Yet the Scriptures could be rendered ineffective not only by the incrustation of tradition but also by the enervating of their strength. In a succeeding chapter entitled "Against those who undermine the fortress of sacred Scripture,"[7] Peter discussed how the force of God's law could be blunted by maintaining that certain Gospel precepts were ceremonial forms given to the Apostles but not to moderns, that others were only counsels for perfection or commands for terror, and that others could be modified according to time, place, and person.[8] Objecting to excessive allegorizing of the Bible, as has already been seen,* the Chanter maintained that the Scriptures were sufficient for Christian faith and morals. It is true that difficult cases arise in human affairs where Roman law, canon law, and even divine precepts present insufficient guidance. Although reason, custom, human interpretation, and the example of the wise should be followed, Peter nonetheless advocated final resort to the Scriptures, the abbreviated word of God, for guidance in faith and conduct.[9] A Biblical scholar himself, the Chanter conceived of reform as cutting away human traditions and debilitating interpretations to return to the pure Word of God.

Flourishing in the decades following the great Lateran Council of 1179, the Parisian theologians were inclined to view the general council as the principal means for producing reform. In a commentary to Psalm 118 : 126: "It is time for Thee, Lord, to work: for they have made void Thy law," Peter the Chanter proposed that the Pope convene a general council for dispatching preachers throughout the world to denounce evil and exhort good works.[10] Robert of Courson reported that his teacher was in favor of convoking a general council for returning the church to its primitive state in matters pertaining to clerical celibacy.[11] Courson not only seconded this summons, but it will be remembered that Robert himself advocated a general council under the presidency of the pope to encourage all men to work physically or spiritually for their bread in an effort to extirpate usury.† The theologians' call for a council merely echoed a general conciliar movement in progress throughout the twelfth century.[12] Deriving precedent from the Roman synods of the reform papacy of the preceding century, Popes Calixtus II, Innocent II, and Alexander III convoked three general councils at the Roman Lateran palace in 1123, 1139, and 1179. Since each council followed a serious schism in the papacy, they provided the victorious candidate opportunity not only to legislate but also to assert his authority. In 1179 the Pope succeeded in convoking almost three hundred bishops drawn from the breadth of Latin Christen-

* See above, p. 94.   † See above, p. 310.

dom. While the legislation of the first two Lateran Councils was rudimentary, Pope Alexander III and his assembled prelates produced twenty-seven statutes which were both comprehensive and coordinated. A canonist himself who had been trained in the schools of Bologna, Alexander founded his legislation on preceding conciliar canons and his own decretals.

When Innocent III mounted the papal throne in 1198, a general council had not been held for two decades, but it was not until the spring of 1213 that the Pope issued a summons for a new council, to meet in November 1215. From the beginning of his pontificate Innocent emphasized two preeminent goals, the launching of a new crusade to rescue the Holy Land and the reform of the universal church—aims which he repeated in his summons of 1213 and in the opening sermon before the assembled prelates in 1215. To prepare for the forthcoming council during the intervening period, the Pope dispatched legates throughout Christendom to investigate abuses to be corrected by conciliar legislation. In a similar manner the bishops were charged to inquire into their dioceses and to submit reports on needed reforms. Robert of Courson's legatine commission stemmed directly from the papal program and his councils held in France prepared for the Lateran Council.[13] As a bishop, Stephen Langton issued synodical statutes for the diocese of Canterbury between July 1213 and July 1214 which anticipated the legislation of the general council.[14] When the Lateran Council solemnly opened on 11 November 1215 the careful preparations were in large measure realized. Over four hundred bishops, eight hundred other prelates and numerous lay dignitaries constituted the largest convocation in the history of Christendom. When the council officially closed on 30 November some seventy-one statutes pertinent to church reform had been formulated by the Pope and the conciliar fathers.

What was the fate of the reform proposals of Peter the Chanter and his circle? Among the suggestions which flowed from the classrooms of the theologians, many never gained the attention of the authorities. A few, as has been seen, were repeated in the decretals of Innocent III. Specific matters such as marriage for prostitutes,[15] procurations for judge delegates,[16] partnerships,[17] the sale and resale of pledges,[18] and the employment of usury to preserve a wife's dowry,[19] received papal approval. While certain proposals, such as Courson's program for compulsory poor relief,[20] were eventually rejected, others were accepted by the Lateran Council of 1215. One need only recall the institution of diocesan preachers,[21] the regulation of displaying relics for gain,[22] the curtailing of monastic privileges which encroached on episcopal rights,[23] the permission accorded to learned men to hold more than one prebend,[24] and the assignment of chancery duties implicated with blood judgments to literate laymen.[25]

Courson's local councils contained other regulations governing the conduct of clergy which were directly adopted by the Lateran Council.[26] Undoubtedly the pronouncements of the Lateran fathers on transubstantiation and penance were conditioned by the discussions of the Parisian theologians.[27] For example, the doctrine of circumstances to be observed in administering penance had been carefully elaborated by the Chanter's circle.[28] The condemnation of the heretical views of Amaury of Bène, in which Robert of Courson had played a leading role at Paris, was given final confirmation at the Lateran Council.[29] To all of these measures the Parisian theologians contributed discussion, but there were four reforms relevant to their social theories in which Peter the Chanter and his colleagues took special interest. These concerned capital punishment, ordeals, marriage, and clerical celibacy. Although the masters pressed for action in all these areas, it will be seen that the Lateran Council accepted their proposals in two cases only, for ordeals and marriage.

CAPITAL PUNISHMENT

In twelfth-century France and England punishment of crime varied according to local custom, but by and large hanging was considered fit punishment for theft. So widespread was this practice that local lords displayed their gallows for hanging thieves in a prominent place to publicize their rights over justice.[30] Hanging was a simple, efficient solution to the problem which entailed little of the expense and inconvenience of imprisonment. Since the punishment of theft pertained to customary law beyond the jurisdiction of canon law, the contemporary canonists ignored the problem, but not Peter the Chanter. It will be recalled that Peter defended the right of theological scholars to dispute questions over the death penalty.[31] As a Biblical scholar who believed that reform consisted of eliminating human tradition to return to pure Scripture, the Chanter discovered a discrepancy between contemporary custom and Scriptural principle.[32] Why is it, he queried, that in the Old Testament adultery was punished with death but theft was not, while today we hang a thief but not an adulterer?[33] Neither Scripture nor Roman law sanctions hanging thieves; rather the law of God punished them with fines. Nor does the New Testament authorize alterations in these divine commands which were not ceremonial but moral and intended to be observed literally. Peter concluded that with the exceptions of self-defense, the capture of armed bandits, and the punishment of incorrigible criminals, no one had the right to kill for simple theft. In the course of his discussion he upbraided his fellow Biblical scholars for being more concerned with the allegorical interpretation of the numbers, positions, and descriptions of the tabernacle than with the moral questions raised in the sacred text. The frequency with which this issue appears in the Chanter's *questiones* confirms Robert of Courson's observation that his teacher was wont to treat the problem with feeling.

Elaborating the Chanter's discussion, Robert posed the question of whether a prelate sins mortally if he commands his official to execute justice according to the customs of the realm and thereby to hang someone who has stolen a mere twopence.[34] In greater detail Robert developed the contrast between the punishments for adultery and theft in the Old Testament and those of his own time. Arguing that crimes against human sanctity merited severer correction than those against personal property, he asked why one should be more concerned over the loss of an old cap than over abuse to his wife and children. Public thieves who steal because of hunger are more harshly treated than habitual corrupters of youths and virgins. Even arsonists of churches are punished more severely than those who pervert the body, the living temple of God. Robert concluded that a prelate should advise his *prévôt* to execute only those customary penalties which accorded with the Old and New Testaments.[35] It is true that the burden of the theologians' conclusion was to transfer the death penalty from theft to sex; their proposals were nonetheless designed to alleviate the customary execution of thieves. Turning next to incorrigible brigands, Courson objected to immediately hanging a robber caught in the third or fourth act who was impervious to previous correction. Although summary justice might discourage other malefactors, Robert proposed that the prelate exercising police powers substitute life imprisonment in its place. When Thomas of Chobham, however, wondered about customary punishments which contradicted the law of God, he concluded that they arose as deterrents to future crime in regions where theft and robbery were rampant.[36] Only for this reason did the church acquiesce to hanging thieves.

Thomas of Chobham also noted an example peculiar to England.[37] By contrast to other realms where authorized officials normally executed criminals, he reported the English practice of selecting someone at random from the highway and compelling him to perform the hanging, for which he received the criminal's clothes or a small fee from the royal treasury. Not finding this form of amateur justice very different from the more common practice of assigning execution to the plaintiff,[38] Thomas warned that in both cases if the impromptu executioner performed his services out of desire for gain, he was guilty in the confessional of homicide. If he was truly forced into the deed, such coercion mitigated his responsibility, although penance was nonetheless advisable.

While discussing the killing of thieves, Peter the Chanter raised a specific case.[39] If God gave the land, air, and water for the common enjoyment of mankind, how can princes prevent their subjects from hunting, fowling, and fishing? Does not a prince sin mortally who mutilates men for hunting beasts which are common to all? Obviously Peter was referring to the cruel forest laws of France. In contemporary England the forest laws were more notorious because of the vast extent of the royal forests and the increased effectiveness of forest administration.[40] Since Norman times those who poached in the king's woods were threatened by death, blinding, or emasculation. Since the second half of the twelfth century it is true that the Plantagenets preferred large fines to corporal penalties; nonetheless, the threat of cruel punishments encouraged payment of the fines. The English forest laws also offended the clergy because they ignored clerical immunities. Undoubtedly the clamor of outraged but articulate churchmen contributed to their notoriety.[41] Omitting these conditions peculiar to the clergy, Peter the Chanter criticized their patent barbarity and unfairness. In England the Chanter's protest was applied directly to local conditions by Thomas of Chobham.[42] Repeating his master's principle that the beasts and fowl of the forest belong to all by natural right, Thomas contended that royal officers who killed or mutilated in execution of the forest laws were guilty in the confessional of homicide. Contemporary to Chobham's writing, the barons who opposed King John included in their preliminary draft of liberties the abolition of forest penalties.[43] Although this provision was omitted in the final draft of Magna Carta, in the Forest Charter of 1217 the young King Henry III under tutelage of his barons promised that henceforth none should forfeit life or members for the sake of his venison.[44] It is of interest therefore that the protests of the Parisian theologians coincided with a baronial movement in England which did succeed in abolishing the barbaric sanctions of the forest laws.

The question of capital punishment was also relevant to an issue which concerned all of Latin Christendom. At the turn of the twelfth century the Parisian theologians were contemporaries to a mounting crisis of heresy. Challenged by the growing influence of the Paterini, the Waldensians, and especially the Cathars, the church adopted exceptional measures to stem the tide, among which was the death penalty. Sensitive to the abuses of capital punishment, Peter the Chanter could not help but take notice of this issue.

Since the church could not participate in blood judgments, the execution of heretics was linked with a procedure known as *traditio curie* by which the church consigned to the prince for temporal punishment those whom it judged hopelessly incorrigible to spiritual sanctions.[45] For example, the Lateran Councils of 1139 and 1179 enlisted aid from secular authorities for repressing heresy.[46] While the nature of punishment was rarely specified, precedent for punishing heretics by death went back to the time of the Christian Roman Emperors, and was revived by King Robert the Pious in France in the eleventh century.[47] Until the end of the twelfth century churchmen remained ambivalent about the legitimacy of this extreme remedy. Augustine, for example, had two minds on the subject and his hesitations were reflected in Gratian's collection of canon law.[48] Certain canonists such as Roland Bandinelli and Sicard of Cremona advocated it outright, others such as Rufinus and Huguccio were not as certain.[49] By the end of the twelfth century the increasing pressure from heresy ended hesitation. In the famous decretal *Ad abolendam* issued at Verona in 1189 Pope Lucius III prescribed specific procedures under which clerics and laymen judged incurably heretical by the church were handed over in the last resort to the prince to receive their due punishment (*animadversione debita*).[50] While the imperial statutes prescribing the penalties are no longer extant, the punishment left to the prince's discretion included death along with exile, fines, and confiscations. Naturally the Pope was not free to advocate the death penalty, if that was what he had in mind, but it was assuredly in his power to prohibit it if he wished. By leaving the nature of punishment open, the Pope allowed recourse to the death sanction, for which there was ample precedent. In France, for example, this was precisely the result of papal policy. The notorious heretic Evrard of Châteauneuf, convicted at the Council of Paris, was burned in 1201, and in 1210 the followers of Amaury of Bène prosecuted by Robert of Courson were condemned to death at Paris by the King.[51] In the south of France these policies culminated in the unconditional crusade against the Cathars which exterminated great numbers by inquisition and warfare.

As a sensitive observer, Peter the Chanter witnessed this shift in the church's official policy towards heretics. Unable to follow those who opened the way to killing heretics, he aligned himself with the older opinion. An incident which caught his attention was the particularly zealous efforts of William of White Hands, Archbishop of Reims, and Philip of Alsace, Count of Flanders, to exterminate the Paterini of Arras in 1182 by ordeals and the stake.[52] He noted that unscrupulous clergy and agents of the prince used their arbitrary powers to extort and blackmail.[53] For example, orthodox women who refused the solicitations of lecherous priests were threatened with enrollment on the lists of condemned persons so that many innocent perished along with the heretics. These abuses reported by the Chanter are quite remarkably confirmed by an independent account. The chronicler Ralph of Coggeshall tells of the English author, Master Gervase of Tillbury, who was a cleric in the service of Archbishop William at the time of the persecutions.[54] According to the story Gervase was involved in the seduction of a young lady, when he discovered that she belonged to the heretics, because she protested that if she lost her chastity she would irrevocably lose her salvation. (The close identification of sexuality with evil was a characteristic doctrine of the Paterini.) To make a long story short, when neither Gervase's arguments nor those of the archbishop's clerics could convince her of her error, she was led away to the stake. Although the girl was evidently a heretic, the ugly abuses against which the Chanter protested can be discerned in the background.

To oppose those who would kill heretics Peter the Chanter marshalled familiar passages from the Scriptures and the Church Fathers.[55] For example, the Apostle Paul (Titus 3 : 10) advised Titus to avoid those heretics who had been twice warned, but not to kill them or hand them over for punishment. The account of 1 Samuel (16 : 22 and 20 : 3) in which David refrained from killing the concubines whom his rebellious son Absalon had defiled, but rather kept them isolated for life, applied to present-day heretics defiled by the devil.[56] Peter's remedy was not capital punishment but life imprisonment to prevent the plague from contaminating others. In support of his proposal he cited the Council of Reims in 1148 under Pope Eugenius III which did not execute the convicted Breton heretic Eon (Eudo ?) *de Stella*, but consigned him for life to the prison of Sanson, Archbishop of Reims.[57] Only if the heretic physically fought against the church, could one find cause for condemning him to death.[58] About two decades after the Chanter, Thomas of Chobham made similar protests against the practice.[59] Thomas conceded, however, that many respected men advocated that if heretics rebelled against Christians and opposed the faith in public debate and preaching, they could be killed without their executioners falling into sin. If they remained quiet and submissive, however, they should not be harmed.

Although brief, the Chanter's protests against killing heretics were nonetheless audible, but by the beginning of the thirteenth century, the noise of battle against heretics on the continent drowned him out. Robert of Courson, who faithfully defended so many of his teacher's ideas, renounced this point of the Chanter's program. As he composed his *Summa*, Innocent III's call for a crusade against the Albigensians was still ringing in his ears.[60] In contrast to Peter's, Robert's was the age of *Ad abolendam*, which he often cited. By discussing the case of Evrard of Châteauneuf at Paris in 1201, Courson formulated a reply to the Chanter's solution of life imprisonment.[61] In the negotiations between the prince and the clergy over Evrard's punishment, the prince was prepared either to kill the condemned by hanging or burning or to set him free, but he would not agree to a lengthy incarceration for the reason that his prisons were not sufficient to hold the three or four thousand malefactors involved. The prince's reply was a practical answer not only to the Chanter but to Courson himself, for incarceration was his favorite solution to other cases. Here was expression of the major deficiency of the medieval system of incarceration. Prisons were too small and costly to be of widespread service. As always death was more practical and economical.

Hard pressed by the growing Cathar menace in southern France, Pope Innocent III continued in the path of *Ad abolendam*. When he coordinated his program for repressing heresy in the Lateran Council of 1215, he included consignment of heretics to the secular authority for due punishment.[62] It is true that in his famous decretal *Vergentis* (1199) the penalty was specified as confiscation[63] and in other letters infamy and exile were also proposed.[64] Nowhere, to be sure, did he advocate death (which was unlawful for him to mention), but, of equal significance, nowhere did he forbid it—as was argued by the Chanter. By leaving the penalty to the prince's discretion, the Lateran Council of 1215 set the pattern for the thirteenth century, in which the *autodafé* became a standard fixture. The protests of Peter on the punishment of heretics were relegated to oblivion for the remainder of the Middle Ages.

ORDEALS

To Peter the Chanter capital punishment was closely related to the issue of ordeals.[65] Originating during the early Middle Ages under the influence of Germanic tribes and popular religion, these customary proofs may be divided into two classes: the unilateral, represented by the hot and cold water and the hot iron trials, and the bilateral, represented by the judicial duel. They were often designated as judgments of God because they required direct divine intervention into the judicial process, and were particularly useful when normal means of proof were unavailable or inconclusive. To the judge of the early Middle Ages the ordeal was the philosopher's stone which, as if by miracle, could decide the vexatious uncertainties of the legal process. Since ordeals were non-Roman in origin, the Roman lawyers of the twelfth and thirteenth centuries ignored them when considering judicial proof.[66] To the Romanist legal proof consisted of written instruments and witnesses. Only when these means were lacking could the court resort to semi-complete proofs such as presumption, notoriety, and an oath designated as *purgatio*. By and large the contemporary canonists adopted the Romanist system and paid particular attention to the *purgatio*, which they utilized in clerical cases.[67] Unlike the Romanists, however, the canonists recognized the existence of ordeals, which they classified as purgations, that is, semi-complete proof to be used when normal means were deficient. By the middle of the twelfth century ordeals were designated as common purgations (*purgationes vulgares*), originating from popular practice, to be distinguished from oaths or canonical purgations (*purgationes canonice*), which arose from ecclesiastical tradition. Sometimes they were identified as *judicia peregrina* or judgments foreign to church law.

323

At the end of the twelfth century the attitude of churchmen towards these customary proofs was ambivalent. As early as the ninth century the papacy published statements against the practices and these were renewed by councils through the twelfth century.[68] On the other hand, from the eighth century certain councils under pressure of popular practice published canons which permitted various types of ordeals and were preserved in the collections of church law.[69] While succeeding popes and councils were usually unfavorable to these devices, on occasion they admitted exceptions to the general prohibition. As late as the eleventh and twelfth centuries Popes Gregory VII, Eugenius III, and Alexander III permitted ordeals in special instances, and even Innocent III, prior to the Lateran Council of 1215, was ambivalent.[70] This disagreement among authorities was accurately reflected in Gratian's *Decretum*. While he assembled the major decretals such as *Monomachiam* (867) of Pope Nicholas I which prohibited judicial duels as tempting God, the Biblical example of David and Goliath notwithstanding,[71] *Consuluisti* (886-889) of Pope Stephen V, which condemned the hot iron and water trials as superstitious inventions,[72] and an excerpt from a decretal of Pope Alexander II (1063) which prohibited hot and cold water and hot iron proofs as devoid of canonical sanction,[73] he nonetheless collected three authorities which favored special kinds of ordeals.[74] Later editors of the *Decretum* inserted *paleae* which supported Gratian's favorable inclinations.[75] But Gratian's hesitancy was not merely a matter of assembling contradictory authorities. After listing the decretal *Consuluisti* which condemned hot iron and water proofs, he asked whether this prohibition included all ordeals or merely the two specified and inserted a Scriptural quotation from Numbers (5 : 12-28) which described a proof designed for jealous husbands to test the fidelity of their wives by means of bitter waters administered by priests.[76] Containing features reminiscent of ordeals, this Biblical example cast doubt on the universal character of the papal prohibitions. Although Gratian's final judgment was to suppress the Scriptural example in favor of the papal decree, the question of customary proofs was nonetheless kept open.[77]

Gratian's conflicting texts and the ambivalence of popes and councils engendered hesitancy among the canonists.[78] Although opposed to these proofs in principle, many canonists were prepared to make exceptions. For example, the French author of the *Rhetorica ecclesiastica* excused them as customary practices.[79] Stephen of Tournai explained that they were useful for deterring heinous crimes.[80] For this reason Rufinus and Bernard of Pavia proposed that the unilateral kind was to be limited to servile classes.[81] If Augustine's principle was accepted that no one should tempt God while rational means were at his disposal, it could be assumed that when rational means were unavailable, one might be justified in recurring to ordeals.[82] Simon of Bisignano declared that one tempted God in judicial duels only when rational deliberation was available[83] and the Parisian author of the *Tractaturus magister* suggested that ordeals were superstitious if the verdict of the case was certain, but necessary if the verdict was inconclusive.[84] Undoubtedly the pressure of customary legal practices made it difficult for the canonists to be unequivocally against ordeals. The nature of these pressures is well illustrated by the canonist Stephen of Tournai. In his *Summa decretorum* Stephen made a neutral reference to duels,[85] but in 1179 a dispute arose between himself as Abbot of Sainte-Geneviève and his tenants at Rosny-sous-Vincennes, which confronted him with an actual example.[86] When the case was brought before the royal court, King Louis VII ordered a judicial duel "according to the custom of the Franks" because of the absence of authentic charters. After the champions of the men of Rosny, frightened by those of Sainte-Geneviève, retired from the field, the King confirmed the servitude of the losers. The event was witnessed by an imposing array of Parisian church dignitaries, including the Abbots of Saint-Germain-des-Prés and Saint-Denis and the Dean and Archdeacon of Notre-Dame, and the decision was confirmed by Popes Lucius III and Clement III. Such affairs were not exceptional in Paris in the twelfth and thirteenth centuries. While the canonists generally forbade trial by battle in canonical courts for ecclesiastical cases, they occasionally permitted it in secular justice[87] or to prelates exercising temporal rights.[88]

While the leading canon lawyers of Bologna and Paris were prepared to allow ordeals in exceptional cases, one canonist abandoned his hesitations over the traditional prohibitions. In his *Summa decretorum* the Bolognese master Huguccio treated ordeals with full discussion and resolute opposition.[89] Not only did he consider invalid those canons which permitted ordeals, but he answered at length the more important exceptions offered by previous canonists. To Gratian's question as to whether canons which prohibited specific ordeals should be applied generally, Huguccio replied with the dictum that all is prohibited which is not explicitly commanded or permitted. He denied validity to the *Summa Tractaturus'* contention that customary proofs, although superstitious, may be necessary. Against those who justified judicial duels from the Biblical example of David and Goliath, Huguccio maintained that their duel was permitted by special divine inspiration and like many Old Testament personages or more recent saints, their example should not set a precedent. Firmly convinced of the moral guilt of a plaintiff who volunteered battle, Huguccio also turned to the thorny question of the defendant who faced it. Despite the price of automatic loss of one's cause, Huguccio urged the defendant not to submit to battle. Under no circumstance of customary or frequent practice could judicial duels be justified, any more than could fornication or usury. Why then, one may ask, does the pope know about and yet not disapprove of such trials? He may tolerate judicial duels in practice, concluded Huguccio, just as he tolerates prostitutes and usurers in Rome, but this does not justify them in law. In answer to these practical questions Huguccio represents the first important canonist to take an uncompromising line against ordeals.

At the same time as Huguccio, Peter the Chanter launched a blistering attack upon ordeals from his school at Paris. Perhaps he was provoked by the French canonists, such as Stephen of Tournai, the *Tractaturus magister,* or the *Rhetorica ecclesiastica,* who failed to achieve a rigorous stand.[90] Repeatedly in his lectures,[91] his disputations, and especially in his *Verbum abbreviatum,*[92] Peter raised the issue of ordeals. Even an anonymous *florilegium* which excerpted opinions from contemporary theologians reported a statement typical of the Chanter.[93] In terms of length and intensity he offers the most important discussion of ordeals to be found in the twelfth century.[94] Peter's campaign was not limited to teaching or writing alone, but extended to personal intervention. His *questiones* indicate that he wrote one letter to a bishop on the subject,[95] and it will be seen that he argued his case before the cardinals.* Characteristic of Peter's attempts to put theory into action was his part in a case at Paris which involved a man accused of murder against whom were strong presumptions.[96] Offered the chance of clearing himself by cold water trial, he sought the counsel of the Chanter. Peter advised him to refuse the test and the man was rewarded for following this advice with the gibbet. In the Chanter's view the fight against ordeals was a cause worthy of martyrdom.

Peter the Chanter considered the use of ordeals to be a diabolical tradition patently unlawful by the authority of both the Old and New Testaments: "Thou shalt not tempt the Lord thy God" (Deut. 6 : 16 and Matt. 4 : 7).[97] By requiring miraculous intervention into the regular operation of the court, ordeals constituted a flagrant tempting of God. As an exegete Peter demonstrated how Biblical examples lent no justification to these customary proofs.[98] More important, he explained how the instances of divine intervention in the Old Testament provided no justifying precedent. For example, the Mosaic test of bitter waters for adultery, which caused Gratian so much trouble, was interpreted by Peter as a specific concession to the malice of Jews, just as God had conceded the right of divorce.[99] The well-known miraculous stories of the Bible represent the privileges of the few and not general law.[100] Although miracles are possible in our day, they are not always necessary, and therefore ordeals are wrong because they constantly demand miracles to function.[101] When God intervenes in an ordeal, He does so by His own volition and not by

* See below, p. 343.

reason of the priestly incantation.[102] God's promises of intervention apply only to the righteous, and our present sins hinder modern miracles.[103] In general the New Testament has abrogated the ordeals of the Old.[104]

Although Peter the Chanter condemned ordeals as immoral in theory, it was from the realm of experience that he drew the greater part of his arguments. According to the Scripture (Deut. 18 : 20, 21), if a man claiming to be God's prophet prophesies a certain event which does not come to pass, that man is to be killed as a deceiver.[105] Applying this empirical test, the Chanter found ordeals wanting. To him it was a fact that customary trials often produced false judgments. In opposition to the vast store of popular lore and saints' lives which illustrated the effectiveness of miraculous ordeals, Peter collected accounts showing how these devices did not work.[106] Frequently in his writings he delights in anecdotes of the failure of ordeals. For example, Pope Alexander III once lost a precious vessel and forced a certain suspect to undergo the proof of the hot iron.[107] The man was unfortunate, lost the judgment, and was compelled to make restitution, but more unfortunate was the pope when the stolen vessel was later found on the true thief. A similar case happened in Orléans, but this time the falsely convicted victim was hanged before the true thief was discovered.[108] Perhaps the most striking case was that of two English pilgrims who were returning from Jerusalem. The one diverted his path to the shrine of Saint James of Compostella; the other, on arriving home first, found himself accused by his companion's kinsmen of having murdered him. Put to the water test, he failed, and was promptly hanged, when, to the amazement of all, the "murdered" companion returned home shortly thereafter.[109]

Another argument from experience was based on the manner in which ordeals were administered. In trial by battle the participants invariably chose their champions according to their skill in arms. Why did they not choose decrepit men, asked Peter, to demonstrate clearly the miracle?[110] It is no marvel either that of three men accused of the same crime and compelled to carry the same hot iron, the last man has the best chance to prove his innocence. Innocence is too closely connected with calluses.[111] Perhaps the cold water probe, however, was most susceptible to manipulation. Controversy prevailed as to the standard of judging innocence. Must the victim sink to the bottom or merely be submerged? Some contended that his hair need not be submerged because this was not of the substance of the body. A participant could be taught to blow the air from his mouth and nose and thus sink. Finally, Peter considered the case of the father compelled to defend his inheritance through one of his sons. He privately confided to the Chanter that he had tested all his sons and found

one that was certain to win[112] and Peter concluded that it was only reasonable to respect the natural properties of heat and water and not to expect
them to produce the miraculous.[113]

If miraculous proofs were effective, queried the Chanter, why were
they not used by the church in important affairs? Despite Biblical precedents, prelates and popes, on whom depends the salvation of their charges,
are not chosen through lots but through the rational procedure of election.[114] Through a single trial of the hot iron would not the church be
able to prove the truth of its faith and convert the unbeliever? Peter cited
the incident of a severe drought that afflicted the city of Reims.[115] In
solemn procession the faithful of both sexes and all ranks carried the
sacred relics around the city to gain relief. When after three days not the
slightest cloud had appeared, the leader of the synagogue proposed that
the Jewish Torah be paraded in a similar manner. If rain did not fall
after three days, the Jewish community would embrace Christianity. A
number of the faithful were ready to accept the challenge, but Master
Albericus put a stop to the whole matter. Even the seductive prospect of
converting the Jewish community, he contended, did not justify jeopardizing the faith through presumptuous means. For similar reasons Peter
concluded that the church cannot entrust its position to the uncertainties
of the hot iron. To be consistent the Chanter had to oppose ordeals in
the trial of heretics. How can the heart, where matters of faith lie, be
examined by such proofs? He deplored the practice of the princes and
prelates who took no notice of the orthodox confession of an accused
heretic but demanded the hot iron trial. Such a case happened at Paris
in the presence of the king, princes, and prelates of France.[116] The accused consented to bear the hot iron to confirm his orthodoxy only if the
assembled churchmen could assure him that it would not tempt God.
Despite the protests of a certain Cistercian monk, Gerardus, the prelates
kept their silence, and the man was speedily assigned to the flames.

Peter the Chanter underscored the essential relationship between ordeals
and the church. Not only did churchmen sanction the practice by their
presence, but churches lent relics and books for consecrating the elements.[117] Since it was obvious that without the participation of the priesthood ordeals would be impossible,[118] the Chanter's line of attack was to
prohibit the clergy from involvement in these affairs. To this end Peter
could point to the canonical tradition which forbade clerics to become
involved in affairs resulting in the shedding of blood. Clearly priests were
forbidden to extend their blessing to judicial duels where the shedding of
blood was inevitable.[119] Peter complained specifically about the custom of
permitting champions to attend mass, although not to communicate, before the conflict.[120] How could this practice be justified when each participant has the intention to kill his opponent? No exception should be

made even for the defendant. Particularly vexing to the Chanter was the custom of holding judicial duels in the very courtyard of the archdeacon of Paris.[121] The Chanter's reply to this practice would surely be unequivocal, had it not been for Pope Eugenius III, who permitted such duels on the basis of custom. Canonical tradition not only prohibited direct clerical participation in blood judgments, but also participation in any affair which might eventually result in the shedding of blood. Peter referred to the example of Archbishop Sanson of Reims, who, although permitting the sole practice of the water ordeal, forbade clerical participation unless the temporal authorities furnished guarantees that the affair would not result in shedding of blood.[122] The Chanter constantly emphasized the close connection between ordeals and blood.[123] In practice priests could hardly remain neutral throughout the procedure, but tended to become implicated in the decision and the condemnation.[124] For example, it will be remembered that when Master Robert *de Camera* defended a client against the charge of counterfeiting, the defendant elected to clear himself by battle.* When the client won his decision, the accuser was hanged for false accusation. Although Robert had successfully defended his client, he felt obliged to perform penance for homicide because he had become implicated in both an ordeal and an execution. Just as one sins by furnishing the occasion to fornicate, so priests are guilty who bless the customary proofs which lead to bloodshed. Neither can the frequency of the practice remove the blame here any more than it can from adultery.[125]

Approving of Archbishop Sanson's example, Peter the Chanter himself went further by declaring that priests were forbidden to participate in ordeals even when there was no chance of shedding blood.[126] One version of his *questiones* quotes him as stating that it is preferable for a cleric to be implicated in a blood judgment than for him to bless an ordeal which was utterly devoid of legality.[127] By unequivocally dissociating the priesthood from them, Peter hoped to deal a mortal blow to ordeals. Despite the contrary examples of populace, priests, and popes, the Chanter's stand was clear: "Even if the universal church under penalty of anathema commanded me as a priest to bewitch the iron or bless the water, I would quicker undergo the perpetual penalty than perform such a thing."[128]

Raoul Ardent disseminated Peter's opinions by incorporating his more colorful anecdotes into his *Speculum universale.*[129] In England Thomas of Chobham applied his master's principles to local conditions. Composing his *Summa confessorum* about 1215, Thomas was apparently aware of the decree of the Lateran Council against ordeals.[130] He agreed with the Chanter in opposing unilateral ordeals to detect heresy,[131] but his attention was mainly directed towards the judicial duels which were commonly practiced in England. In one section of the *Summa* he considers profes-

* See above, pp. 154 and 197.

sional champions who hire their services to litigants.[132] Although such practices were condemned by the church, he notes that secular princes nonetheless protected them. While Thomas would not advise an accuser to resort to battle, he—unlike Huguccio and the Chanter—permitted it to a defendant whose position was similar to that of one resisting a robber.[133] In another passage Thomas refers to the English practice of approver.[134] According to the *Dialogus de scaccario* of Richard fitz Nigel it was possible for a notorious criminal to confess his crime and accuse his associates before the royal courts.[135] If he was able to prove his accusations by battle, he escaped his own penalty. Encouraging this method of purging the realm of crime, royal justice supported approvers with a daily wage. Thomas of Chobham inquired into the morality of such men who have royal authority to scour the land and secure the peace. Some would argue that if such men perform their duties out of zeal for justice and not merely through avarice or the desire to save their necks, they can rightfully accuse criminals. But Thomas did not concur because the judicial duel was forbidden by canon law and because divine law prevented confessed criminals from accusing others.

Not all of the Chanter's circle shared his unequivocal attitude towards ordeals. Although Robert of Courson faithfully rehearsed his teacher's ideals on many issues, he could not follow him here, just as he had hesitated over condemning the death penalty for heretics. Robert's *Summa* contains four perplexing cases, in three of which Robert acceded to customary practices. The first was an unhappy case, similar to one with which the Chanter dealt, of a man accused of murder who suffered martyrdom for the cause of resisting ordeals.[136] The second likewise involved the dilemma of a priest faced on one hand with pressure from his prince, bishop, and the custom to bless the ordeals, and on the other, with the knowledge of their immoral nature.[137] Robert's solution was to yield to the force of custom sanctioned by the decretal *Ad abolendam*. In a third case he discusses a perplexing situation faced by a bishop who held spiritual and temporal justice and before whom was brought a man of importance accused by public notoriety of a gross crime, such as heresy.[138] Since no one would personally testify against the man because of his influence, the bishop could not convict the accused through normal legal procedures. On the other hand, the bishop could not dismiss the case because of the presumptions involved and because of appearing to submit to bribery. The recourse to canonical purgations or the swearing of seven compurgators was held of no popular repute and common purgation through ordeals was forbidden by the canons. Robert offered two solutions. On the basis of public defamation the bishop could imprison the accused on bread and water until enough evidence had been secured to produce a conviction, thus satisfying popular opinion. Or the bishop could offer purgation through an ordeal on the grounds that when no legitimate proof was available, these means did not tempt God. In support of the second alternative Robert again cited the decretal *Ad abolendam*.

In discussing the fourth of the above cases Courson elaborated reasons for his hesitation in the matter of ordeals.[139] If the Old Testament bill of divorce has now been abolished by the church, Robert queried, why not also ordeals, which are comparably evil and contrary to God's law? Citing Augustine's argument, he maintained that when a judge has sufficient evidence, he tempts God by recurring to the ordeal. If, however, as in the above cases, rational solutions are not available, customary proofs can then be tolerated. As in the two cases cited, Robert's final justification was Pope Lucius III's decree *Ad abolendam*, of 1184.[140] Dealing with the detection and punishment of heretics, the Pope did not rigorously define the procedures of accusation but expressly allowed the accused to clear himself by locally approved customs, which included ordeals.[141] If public notoriety accused someone of heresy, Robert explained, he was turned over to secular judgment, when he could not be convicted in a church court. Because the secular courts were beyond the church's jurisdiction, the pope and bishops were helpless to prevent ordeals, particularly when no other remedies were available. Although Courson acknowledged the Chanter's position forbidding clergy any participation in ordeals even in secular trials,[142] he also cited the opinion of others who tolerated these proofs by dissimulation. When other means were unavailable and when demanded by the custom of the realm and the clamor of the people, ordeals could be employed as a last resort. These four cases present not the determined opposition of Peter the Chanter, but rather perplexities reminiscent of the twelfth-century canonists. At the Councils of Paris and Rouen, Robert did not come out fully against ordeals, but merely banished them from cemeteries and other sacred places.[143]

Perhaps the hesitant attitude of Pope Innocent III during the early years of his pontificate reflects the debate over ordeals in the faculties of canon law and theology at Bologna and Paris.[144] Prior to 1215, however, Innocent made up his mind against these practices and in the Lateran Council he declared his opposition. Canon 18 forbade the clergy from consecrating the hot and cold water or the hot iron of the unilateral ordeals and renewed the censures of former councils against judicial duels.[145] Like Peter the Chanter, Innocent clearly connected ordeals with clerical involvement in affairs resulting in the shedding of blood. Also like the Chanter he energetically prohibited further participation to the clergy. Although ordeals antedated the Christian era, in medieval practice the blessing of the elements was essential to their operation. Withdrawal of the clergy obviously placed serious obstacles in the way of their popular effectiveness. The Lateran legislation had immediate effect on legal practice in England, Normandy, and Denmark where unilateral ordeals were removed from the common law.[146] Elsewhere they died a slower death. Trial by battle persisted more tenaciously, particularly because it was the customary proof in cases concerning serfdom.[147] Beginning with King Louis VII the Capetians began to restrict judicial combats, a policy which culminated in King Louis IX's famous ordinance abolishing judicial duels in the French domain.[148] Likewise, the Emperor Frederick II forbade both unilateral and bilateral ordeals in Sicily.[149] To be sure, ordeals did not disappear altogether from judicial practice. The use of the water proof persisted in witchcraft trials as late as the seventeenth century. Nor was the Lateran Council solely responsible for their decline in practice, which must be viewed as within a larger movement towards rational legal procedure, as exemplified by the inquest in ecclesiastical and French law, the jury trial in English law, and merchant law throughout Europe. Nonetheless, the Lateran Council of 1215 may be considered as the turning point in the banishing of ordeals from European society. Looking back over the first half of the thirteenth century, the English chronicler Matthew Paris included the prohibition of water and iron proofs among the significant events of his times.[150]

MARRIAGE

It will be remembered that when Peter the Chanter upbraided ecclesiastical *officiales*, he accused them not only of employing water ordeals for a profit but also of manipulating marriage regulations to procure divorces at a price.[151]* Marriage, particularly the rules of consanguinity and affinity, attracted his attention as badly in need of reform.[152] Peter treated the subject of marriage in a chapter of the *Verbum abbreviatum* entitled "That positive justice has no stability." He maintained that positive law, both ecclesiastical and secular, lacks permanence because it can be easily changed and is subject to arbitrary interpretations of the judge.[153] In particular canon law resides in the heart of the pope who as the supreme judge may establish, interpret, and abrogate it at will. The Chanter quoted the advice of John of Bellesmains, Archbishop of Lyon (1182-1193), to some Parisian clerics who were travelling to Rome to settle a disputed election to a deanship: "Do not confide in your decretals for whether the pope decides for or against you it will be said that he has decided justly."[154] For similar reasons the peasants have the proverb: Wherever the king, there the law."[155] Because of this exasperating fluctuation of ecclesiastical law, the Chanter reported that Master Ivo of Chartres in the presence of his students dramatically hurled his book of decretals to the ground and abandoned teaching.[156] To illustrate this theme Peter cited examples from

* See above, p. 176.

rules governing witnesses, fasting and benefices, but it is obvious that the problem which provoked his particular criticism was marriage. Here contemporary canonists would probably have conceded his point for nowhere was canon law so open to confusion as in marriage. The Chanter was not so much concerned with the question of how a marriage was contracted—which sharply divided the canonists of Bologna and Paris[157] —but rather he focused attention on the problem of consanguinity and affinity, which demonstrated the exasperating impermanence of canon law.

The outlines of the ecclesiastical doctrine of consanguinity and affinity were established by the time of Gratian's *Decretum*.[158] A legitimate marriage in canon law could be prevented by the factors of consanguinity (relationship by blood), affinity (relationship by marriage), and spiritual affinity (relationship through the sacraments). Generally speaking, consanguinity in the transverse line was computed to the seventh degree. In other words partners could not marry if they possessed a common ancestor within seven generations. Affinity was divided into three kinds, for which subsequent canonists proposed varying scales. (For example, the first kind was limited to the seventh degree, the second to the third degree and the third to the second degree.)[159] The practical effect of these marriage impediments was to spin a far-reaching web around most individuals. In the Middle Ages, when the noble classes used marriage alliances for political advantage, and when the vast majority of the population was immobile, it was extremely difficult to contract a marriage outside of the prohibited scope. Since the traditional restrictions against consanguinity and affinity placed most medieval men and women in an impossible legal position, it was evident that the law of the church would either be ignored or be open to gross abuse.

The canonists who commented on Gratian until the Lateran Council of 1215 remained faithful to this authority in the matter of marriage impediments.[160] Except for a suggestion that the limits of affinity of the first kind be reduced to the fourth degree,[161] they adhered to the framework of the *Decretum*.[162] Some debate arose over the method of computing the degrees, which may be seen as an attempt to soften the severity of the regulations. For example, one method was proposed which reduced the degrees by half, but this legal computation, as it was designated, was rejected by most canonists in favor of the more rigorous canonical computation.[163] According to strict law, therefore, the canonists worked fully within the traditional system of consanguinity and affinity.

To accommodate the inevitable infractions of these rules the canonists employed dispensations.[164] In practice Pope Alexander III relegated the authority to dispense marriage impediments to local churches,[165] but by the time of Rufinus the canonists reserved this power exclusively to the papacy.[166] Following their advice, Innocent III, for example, exercised dispensations extensively.[167] In general the canonists taught that marriages beyond the second, third, or fourth degrees of consanguinity could remain uncontested by special papal permission if they were contracted unwittingly, endured a long time, and produced offspring. Closely related but not exactly equivalent to a dispensation was the alternative of dissimulation, by which a pope could recognize an irregular affair impossible of remedy and by simulating ignorance refuse to take action against it. Following the example of Alexander III the popes refused to dissolve marriages which were consanguineous beyond the third degree.[168] Through dissimulation the papacy, in effect, practiced a tacit dispensation. For example, Stephen Langton reported that when the king of England wished to arrange a marriage alliance between barons who were related within the prohibited degrees, he was able to obtain a dispensation from the papal *curia*.[169] At the end of the twelfth and the beginning of the thirteenth century, therefore, the canonists were in theory inclined to permit slightly consanguineous marriages through papal dispensation, and in practice the popes were reluctant to attack any marriage unless it was grossly consanguineous. Although these exceptional procedures mitigated the worst rigors of the traditional system, before the Lateran Council of 1215 neither canonists nor popes indicated any disposition to change the existing framework.

As a theologian by profession Peter the Chanter was not required to work within the canonical framework, but was free to go straight to the heart of the matter. Believing that examples were of greater effect than ratiocinations, he illustrated the legal confusion of consanguinity by a personal reminiscence. Two of his relatives married and related in the fifth and sixth degrees came to him for advice, knowing that their marriage was within the prohibited limits.[170] The Chanter sent them to the pope for a decision, but he referred them to the archbishop of Sens, who in turn passed them on to Maurice of Sully, Bishop of Paris, who finally confirmed the marriage. (Whoever the pope was, he apparently followed the practice of Alexander III in referring such cases to the local bishops.) Since the marriage regulations were nearly impossible to enforce, they placed inordinate responsibility on the judge or pope to exercise dispensation and dissimulation and thereby they contributed to the judge's excessively arbitrary powers.[171] Especially was this true in cases of spiritual affinity. Paraphrasing a certain canon or decretal, the Chanter quoted a judge as saying that he neither praised nor blamed, neither prohibited nor commanded, but neither would he break up a marriage impeded by affinity.[172] The Chanter saw that this reliance on the judge encouraged the frequency of such marriage cases, which in turn provided lucrative business for the legal profession.[173] It also encouraged fraudulent prac-

tices in marriage litigation.[174] In a casual remark Robert of Courson noted
—what must have been common knowledge—that false witnesses were
hired in divorce proceedings throughout the French church.[175]

Peter's chief objection to the traditional system of consanguinity and
affinity was that it encouraged divorce. Since most marriages contained
impediments, separations were possible. The canonical regulations
thwarted the church's fundamental principle of the inviolability of marriage. The Chanter noted that since the application of affinity allowed
couples to marry and separate at will,[176] the holy sacrament of marriage
was held in derision by the laity.[177] Repeatedly in his *questiones* Peter
wrestled with perplexing cases of separations based on consanguinity, to
some of which he was unable to find solutions.[178] Unlike the canonists, however, the Chanter was willing to go behind the law to examine
its effects. The type of situation which he described was well known. A
knight said to him in taking a wife: "She has a large dowry and is related
to me in the third kind of affinity. If she doesn't please me, I can procure
a separation."[179] What was possible throughout the nobility was particularly notorious among royalty. The Chanter's circle were contemporaries
to the famous divorce between King Philip Augustus and his queen,
Ingeborg, in which the fraudulent character of the alleged consanguinity was evident to all. Peter himself was appointed a judge in the
case by Pope Celestine III and Robert of Courson was involved in the
affair at various stages.[180] During the wearisome negotiations Philip Augustus complained that the papacy applied the impediment regulations
to his marriage with greater severity than to the Emperor Frederick
Barbarossa in repudiating Adela von Vohburg, King John of England
in repudiating Isabel of Gloucester, or even his father King Louis VII
in repudiating Eleanor of Aquitaine.[181] Although the theologians were
silent over these recent cases, they discussed the most remote *cause célèbre*
of Louis VII, Eleanor of Aquitaine, and Henry II. Robert of Courson
raised this affair as an example of papal dispensations.[182] He was not so
much concerned with the consanguineous marriage and the separation
between Louis and Eleanor, as with the second marriage between Eleanor
and Henry. This union, which was also within the prohibited degrees, resulted in warfare destructive to the lands of the kings of France
and England and to the church. By permitting this marriage the pope
violated the principles justifying the dispensing power, which were necessity, utility, or reason of just cause. Because his action was purely arbitrary
the pope's dispensation was unlawful, and he must share responsibility
for the consequences.[183] Although he did not express it directly, Robert
could not help but see that the dissolving of the first marriage because of
mild consanguinity also contributed to the misfortunate results of the
second alliance.

To the larger problem of the impermanence of positive justice Peter the Chanter offered general advice.[184] By counseling the judge to base his decisions on expressed laws or canons as much as possible, he hoped to avoid frivolous and arbitrary judgments. Since, however, even the expressed law depended on the will of the highest judge, the ultimate basis for judgment should be divine law interpreted by equity and reason. As a Biblical reformer, the Chanter's final solution to the confusion and arbitrariness of positive law was again to assert the fundamental authority of the Scriptures and the need for rational justification for all decisions. But Peter the Chanter also applied the reform principle to the specific problem of consanguinity and affinity. Having expressed doubts about the current system in his *questiones*,[185] he proposed reform in his *Verbum abbreviatum*: "The Lord has given," Peter declared, "certain and inviolable laws of matrimony which excluded twelve persons from marriage (Lev. 18 : 6-18 and 20 : 11-21), to which we have added as exceptions the fifth, sixth, and seventh degrees [of consanguinity]. . . . [Furthermore] to these we have joined the second and third kinds of affinity."[186] On Scriptural authority, therefore, the impediments of consanguinity should be limited to the fourth degree and those of affinity to the first kind, and the rest of the traditional system discarded. The Chanter's program was reechoed by his disciples. Raoul Ardent gave it wider publicity by recopying the pertinent passages.[187] Although Thomas of Chobham devoted space to explaining the traditional calculations, he reported the new scheme as the one currently practiced by the church.[188] Similarly, Robert of Flamborough in his *Penitentiale* reproduced the older system, but complained that the last two kinds of affinity hardly benefited the church because of their complications.[189]

Throughout his pontificate Innocent III was particularly concerned with the canon law of marriage and its application to specific cases.[190] According to one version of the Chanter's *Summa*, even before his elevation to the papacy, Master Lothario had personally posed a question concerning marriage for the Chanter to solve.[191] As might be anticipated Innocent included important matrimonial legislation in the canons of the Lateran Council of 1215. Prohibitions against secret marriages were elaborated.[192] Regulations were drawn up for the presentation of evidence in matrimonial cases, to suppress fraudulent testimony.[193] In particular, hearsay testimony was no longer admissible in cases involving impediments of consanguinity and affinity. Clerics were forbidden to profit from litigation over fictitious matrimonial impediments.[194] While these regulations attempted to correct abuses in the canonical system, Pope Innocent reformed the system itself. Repeating the Chanter's observation that human law varies with time, Innocent adopted the Chanter's specific proposal.[195] By action of the Council the impediments of consanguinity were reduced from seven to four degrees and those of affinity were limited to the first kind.[196] Not only did Innocent follow the suggestions of the Parisian theologians, but he also made church law conform in fact more closely to the practice of dispensations and dissimulations. To be sure, the Lateran Council did not eliminate all problems involving marriage impediments and divorce, but it did take a step in the right direction.

CLERICAL CELIBACY

Marriage presented problems not only to the laity but also to the clergy.[197] In the Chanter's day celibacy was normal in the Latin church for all clergy in holy orders. Only those clerics in minor orders beneath the rank of subdeacon were allowed to marry. While maintaining clerical continence presented difficulties to ecclesiastical authorities under any circumstances, these problems were amplified at Paris, where the schools attracted large numbers of clergy. Although not all of these clerics were actually in the major orders requiring celibacy, many hoped for future advancement into these ranks. It was evident to all that clerical celibacy tended to foster the well-known ills of prostitution, concubinage, and sodomy.

Clerical celibacy was not the normal regime in the early church, but was gradually introduced into the Latin church over many centuries.[198] Although the subject was debated in the early period, authoritative precedents favoring celibacy were established by the fifth century. In the fourth century Pope Siricius universally prohibited priests and deacons to live with their wives, and in the following century Pope Leo I extended these restrictions to subdeacons, which was later reconfirmed by Pope Gregory I. Marriage was nonetheless permitted below the rank of subdeacon. Although these canonical precedents were available, they did not find wide acceptance in the West during the following period. It was not until the second half of the eleventh century that the Gregorian reformers were able to secure acknowledgement throughout the Latin church of strict continence for the rank of subdeacon and above as an ideal. This Gregorian achievement was faithfully reflected in the *Decretum* of Gratian. While his collection included some opposing material for the sake of argument, he preserved the major authorities which defended clerical celibacy.[199] Under Gratian's influence, the succeeding canonists of the twelfth and early thirteenth century remained within the bounds of the *Decretum*.[200] Interpreting the requirement of celibacy as a historical development, they explained its discrepancies as resulting from canonical precedents valid for different times and places.[201] In particular they concentrated their attention on the subdeacon, who represented the dividing line between holy orders (priest, deacons, and subdeacons) to whom celibacy was obligatory and minor orders (acolytes, porters, readers, etc.) to whom marriage was permitted. Although they occasionally distinguished between marriages contracted before promotion to holy orders and those contracted while in holy orders, the canonists agreed that in their day the subdeacon assumed the obligation of continence.[202] Accommodations to this principle, however, were permitted in practice. While as a master Rolandus Bandinelli had advocated celibacy for subdeacons, as Pope Alexander III he granted dispensations or dissimulations for their marriage in extreme cases.[203] Although these exceptions were recognized by the canonists,[204] by the time of Pope Celestine III (1191-1198) Alexander's practice was discontinued.[205] Moreover, other interpretations encouraged the practice of clerical celibacy in the twelfth century. For example, although clerics in minor orders were permitted to marry, they were consequently required to resign their prebends.[206]

Celibacy for the clergy in holy orders was not won without a struggle. Under pressure from adversaries the Gregorians were forced to admit that clerical continence was not practiced by the early church. This alleged innovation was fiercely resisted in the eleventh century,[207] and even after the Gregorian position had gained acceptance traces of discontent remained throughout the Middle Ages.[208] A faint protest to this part of the Gregorian program may be heard among the theologians of Paris at the turn of the twelfth century. Advocating a return to the Scriptures and the early church, they were not altogether satisfied with the changes of the last century. To be sure, as moralists they decried the prevalence of concubinage and immorality among the French and English clergy of their day.[209] Instead of supporting stricter enforcement of the existing celibacy legislation, however, these writers intimated in one way or another that the legislation itself should be relaxed. Although their testimony is not always clear and unequivocal, their opinions nonetheless constitute a movement to reduce the requirements of clerical celibacy.

A favorite argument for those opposing clerical celibacy was drawn from an historical account concerning the Council of Nicea of 325.[210] According to this account, when a group of western prelates wished to impose continence on all the clergy they were opposed by a certain Paphnutius, Bishop of a city in upper Thebes. Although renowned for his own continence and austerity, he maintained that an externally imposed restriction would bring more harm than benefit to the clergy at large. His eloquence apparently carried the day, because the Council refused to enact the proposals of the western party. In the eleventh century the story played a prominent role in the controversy between the Gregorians and their adversaries, and Pope Gregory VII even felt constrained to deny its authenticity at the Synod of Rome in 1079.[211] When the account of

Paphnutius reappears in the writings of Raoul Ardent at the turn of the twelfth century one may suspect that the debate had already been renewed.[212] Although Raoul errs in some of his facts,[213] he arrives at a similar conclusion to that of Paphnutius, that the church is better served by openly married ministers than by clerics sorely tempted to fornication, adultery, and sodomy.

The issues underlying clerical celibacy are discussed more extensively in the *Summa* of Robert of Courson, where three *questiones* are devoted to the problem. One treats at length whether the subdiaconate was a part of sacred orders.[214] In scholastic fashion Robert assembled canonical texts to demonstrate that subdeacons were not included in holy orders until the time of Pope Gregory I.[215] After presenting an opposing authority,[216] he formulates two solutions to his *questio*. The first concludes that for the period between the primitive church and Gregory I, subdeacons were not in holy orders and could legitimately marry, just as acolytes can today. After Gregory had in a general council instituted subdeacons as a holy order they assumed an obligation to celibacy which could not be secretly dispensed by the pope but could only be revoked by equivalent action of a general council. As was often his custom, Robert proposed a second solution which to him seemed more satisfactory. Here he claimed that the subdiaconate had been a sacred order since the Apostles, but that it was simply first enunciated by Pope Gregory I.[217]

Approaching clerical celibacy directly in a second *questio*, Robert applied the solution of the general council.[218] He noted the case of a young deacon troubled by fears that he could not persevere continently and who therefore petitioned the pope for a dispensation to marry. In Courson's opinion this young cleric had more merit than many older clergy who were far beyond fleshly temptation, but who actually enjoyed wives. As a matter of fact, Robert observed, many deacons and subdeacons in the French church and in remote regions claimed papal dispensations to marry, such as Pope Alexander III had issued in the past. Following the assumptions of the previous *questio*, Robert argued that as a rule permission to marry could only be authorized by a general council inspired by the Holy Spirit, instituted by the holy fathers, and confirmed by the pope. Although he rejected Alexander III's practice of dispensing celibacy, Robert nonetheless approved of the general purpose of such dispensations. In a third *questio* he directly advocated reducing the requirements of continence for the clergy.[219] What was a benefit to one era could become a damnation to another. Although the serpent of bronze was a source of salvation to the children of Israel in the wilderness, it later became the occasion for idolatry. In a similar manner, while the vow of continence served a useful purpose for the clergy in holy orders, it was now a source of immorality and sodomy. It even produced nepotism because, as the saying went, "the Lord has taken away our sons and has given us so many nephews."[220] As a solution Robert of Courson urged the convocation of a general council to restore the clergy to their original status in the primitive church. Although he did not specify how far within the sacred orders reform should penetrate, Robert hoped to reduce the celibacy requirements.

The call for a general council was also picked up by Gerald of Wales.[221] Apparently approving of dispensations for subdeacons who desired to marry, he felt that these means were not sufficient for priests. To institute such a reform required the authority of a council under the pope and cardinals. As a matter of fact, Gerald had heard that Pope Alexander III would have decreed such measures had it not been for the opposition of the austere abbot and papal chancellor, Albert of Moras, who later became Pope Gregory VIII. This episode represented a reversal of the older Paphnutius story. Although Gerald is not always reliable in recounting anecdotes,[222] there is no doubt where his own opinions lay. Since clerical marriage was not forbidden in the Scriptures, the present restrictions only impeded the piety of the clergy. Considering the current practice of forbidding prebends to married clerics in minor orders, he reported that some men of repute declared that such clergy were better married than living in concubinage, and Gerald counselled them to seek papal dispensations.[223] One of these men of repute was Thomas of Chobham. In his *Summa confessorum* Thomas pointed to the discrepancy between the current custom and the ancient canon which permitted benefices to minor clerics who could not remain continent.[224] When an acolyte, therefore, came to a priest to confess his incontinence Thomas conceded that the confessor would not be grossly sinning to advise the acolyte to marry secretly and thus deceive his bishop. He was convinced that it was less sinful to retain one's benefice and to be married secretly without scandal than to commit fornication which was directly against the divine commandments. Even if the prelate later forced the cleric to advance to holy orders, he would sin less by remaining with his wife than by fornicating with another. In the course of his discussion Thomas enumerated the traditional arguments for reducing clerical celibacy. For example he noted that in ancient times, subdeacons were not a sacred order,[225] that among the Greeks even bishops have wives, and that the fathers of the Nicene Council had no right to institute clerical celibacy which opposed the sacrament of marriage constituted by God and the Apostles.[226] Since Thomas wrote about 1215 when, as will be seen, the Gregorian program had recently been reconfirmed by the Lateran Council, he therefore concluded that it was frivolous to dispute these issues further because the authority of the Roman church should be obeyed.

In 1208 the papal legate Cardinal Gallo held a council at Paris in which he formulated a statute of unusual severity against clerical incontinence. All priests and all other clerics who had any relations in their homes or anywhere else with women of dubious reputation were declared solemnly excommunicated.[227] Clerics in minor orders were allowed to be married legally but could not retain their benefices. Gallo's terminology, which affected all clergy without distinction, was apparently considered extreme, because in 1212 Pope Innocent III felt it necessary to write a special directive to the French episcopacy allowing them to absolve clerics who had fallen under the legate's ban if urgent necessity and special utility required.[228] Some years later Gallo's decree provoked another protest, from Gilles de Corbeil.[229] Writing as a medical professor, Gilles' treatment of clerical celibacy has a clinical air to it. In his opinion Gallo's measure which unequivocally cut off all clergy from feminine contact would never be obeyed in practice and would only revive ancient enormities. Although he did not treat the problem at length, Gilles de Corbeil is on record as in favor of reducing, not strengthening, clerical celibacy.

Since Raoul Ardent, Robert of Courson, Gerald of Wales, Thomas of Chobham, and Gilles de Corbeil all moved within the Chanter's circle, one may ask if they also reflect their master's opinions on clerical celibacy. Gerald of Wales testified that he heard Master Peter Comestor advocate the reduction of clerical celibacy in the presence of his entire school at Paris.[230] Since the Comestor, who died about 1179, was of an earlier generation, might not Peter the Chanter also have championed this cause in later years? Nowhere has explicit discussion of this issue been found in the Chanter's writings,[231] but Robert of Courson, who was closest to his master, declared that Peter the Chanter was accustomed to assert that a general council should be convened to restore the church to its primitive state and to revoke the vows of continence for sacred orders.[232] If Robert's testimony is not sufficient, four other members of the Chanter's circle give corroborating support that Peter was very probably the source of inspiration for this reform. When the general council anticipated by Peter the Chanter and Robert of Courson did convene in 1215, it refused, however, to adopt their reforms on clerical celibacy. Prior to it Pope Innocent III removed all ambiguity about subdeacons by officially declaring them members of holy orders subject to continence.[233] Rather than reducing the Gregorian program, the Lateran Council of 1215 renewed it with strengthened sanctions.[234] On this issue as on the abolition of the death penalty for heretics Peter the Chanter and his colleagues lost their battle, and celibacy has been mandatory for priests, deacons, and subdeacons until recent years.

While it is relatively simple to enumerate the theologians' reform proposals and the corresponding legislation of the Lateran Council of 1215, it is more difficult to establish a causal connection between the two lists and thereby assess the influence of the Chanter's circle on the Council. Undoubtedly their concern over the reform of Christian society was shared by other groups such as the canonists of Bologna and Paris. Many of the theologians' proposals, such as the curtailing of monastic privileges or the exemption of learned men from the prohibitions of pluralism, were in all likelihood argued also by canonists who would have been equally influential in the deliberations of the conciliar fathers. Certain reforms of the Council, however, appear not to have attracted the notice of the canon lawyers. For example, they leave no evidence of having discussed how chanceries staffed with clerics were to deal with affairs involving bloodshed. Over the question of ordeals the canonists of Bologna and Paris were ambivalent except for the notable opinions of Huguccio. As far as can be determined, they never challenged the traditional system of marriage impediments prior to 1215. Not only did the Parisian theologians press for these reforms, but the very language of the conciliar legislation reflects the arguments of Peter the Chanter. Both the Council and the theologian condemned ordeals on the basis of blood judgments and forbade further clerical participation. Both, moreover, commented on the variability of human law when they proposed changes in the rules for marriage impediments. To be sure, the Council rejected several of the theologians' reforms, but with the correlation between the masters' proposals and the conciliar legislation and the absence of alternative influence, is it too much to see Peter the Chanter and his circle as a moving spirit behind the reforms concerned with ordeals and marriage in the Lateran Council of 1215?

There is also circumstantial evidence to support the Chanter's influence on the Lateran Council. While the eyewitness accounts of the Council of 1215 describe at some length the liturgical solemnities and the ecclesiastical and political disputes, unfortunately virtually nothing was recorded about the drafting of the seventy-one canons of legislation.[235] Among the close members of the Chanter's circle, only two are known to have been in attendance at the Council and both arrived in disgrace. When the French prelates refused to attend the Council of Bourges announced by Robert of Courson in May 1215, the papal legate withdrew from France under a barrage of criticism.[236] According to the chronicler of Auxerre, upon arriving at Rome Robert found that a number of his acts had been rescinded by Pope Innocent at the insistence of the French episcopacy. Similarly, on the eve of the Council Stephen Langton became embroiled with the Pope over the excommunication of King John's enemies.[237] When Langton refused to publish the sentences, he was suspended from office, and this judgment was confirmed on his arrival in Rome to attend the Council. But this inauspicious appearance of the Parisian theologians should not have adversely affected the Chanter's important reform proposals. Although Courson's legislation on the clergy's conduct was influential in the Lateran Council, he was ambivalent on ordeals and said little about marriage impediments. Langton's opinions on the significant reforms of the Council are not known.

Although the participation of the Chanter's followers in the Council may have been reduced, his own personal influence may have been more persuasive than the obvious facts might suggest. According to the long version of the *Verbum abbreviatum* Peter the Chanter argued before the cardinals that since ordeals were mortal sin, the church erred grievously by not prohibiting them.[238] If this statement is true, Peter must have appeared before the cardinals long before the Council of 1215, for he was dead by 1197. It is known, however, that Peter was in Rome during the pontificate of Pope Celestine III (1191-1197).[239] If his plea was made then, it undoubtedly was heard by Cardinal Lothario di Segni, who became Pope Innocent III in 1198.[240] Although Innocent's biography prior to his elevation is obscure, it is known that as a young man Lothario studied at Rome, Paris, and Bologna.[241] At Bologna between 1187 and 1189 he studied law with Bernard of Pavia and Huguccio, whom he rewarded with the bishopric of Ferrara.[242] Huguccio's teaching on ordeals obviously could have impressed the future pope as much as his teaching on other subjects. Before Bologna, however, Lothario had prepared himself in philosophy and theology at Paris, where, as he later averred, he had received the gift of knowledge.[243] His one acknowledged master of theology at Paris was Peter of Corbeil, whom Innocent later promoted to the archdeaconry of York, the bishopric of Cambrai, and the archbishopric of Sens.[244] Peter was renowned for his Scriptural studies, but since his academic writings have not been identified, his opinions on reform are not known. But Lothario was in Paris (a few years before 1187) when Peter the Chanter was a flourishing theological master, having exercised the dignity of Chanter of Notre-Dame since 1183. Since the Chanter died before Innocent's election to the papacy, the Pope could not reward him as he had his other teachers, but he did favor Stephen Langton and Robert of Courson, other members of the Chanter's circle. Among Peter's *questiones* is a problem on marriage posed to the Chanter by *Magister Lotharius Cardinalis*, who could only be the future pope.[245] Because of the close agreement between the pope and the theologian over ordeals, marriages, and other questions, because of Innocent's studies at Paris, and the Chanter's trip to Rome, is it too much to include Pope Innocent III within the Parisian circle of Peter the Chanter?